T0258420

CATO
SUPREME COURT
REVIEW

2023—2024

CATO
SUPREME COURT
REVIEW

2023 — 2024

BRENT SKORUP
Associate Editor

ROGER PILON
Founder

THOMAS A. BERRY
Editor in Chief

ROBERT A. LEVY
Associate Editor

WALTER OLSON
Associate Editor

CLARK NEILY
Associate Editor

Board of Advisors

Jonathan H. Adler
Case Western Reserve University

Gregory Dolin
University of Baltimore

Saikrishna B. Prakash
University of Virginia

Lynn A. Baker
University of Texas

James W. Ely Jr.
Vanderbilt University

Adam C. Pritchard
University of Michigan

Randy E. Barnett
Georgetown University

Richard A. Epstein
New York University

Glenn Harlan Reynolds
University of Tennessee

William Baude
University of Chicago

Elizabeth Price Foley
Florida International University

Nicholas Quinn Rosenkranz
Georgetown University

David E. Bernstein
George Mason University

Nicole Stelle Garnett
University of Notre Dame

Bradley A. Smith
Capital University

Lillian R. BeVier
University of Virginia

James Huffman
Lewis & Clark College

Ilya Somin
George Mason University

Josh Blackman
South Texas College of Law Houston

Gary Lawson
Boston University

Alexander Volokh
Emory University

Steven G. Calabresi
Northwestern University

Luke Milligan
University of Louisville

Eugene Volokh
UCLA

G. Marcus Cole
University of Notre Dame

Mark K. Moller
DePaul University

Todd Zywicki
George Mason University

David G. Post
Temple University

ROBERT A. LEVY
CENTER FOR CONSTITUTIONAL STUDIES

INSTITUTE
Washington, D.C.

THE CATO SUPREME COURT REVIEW (ISBN 978-1-952223-96-9) is published annually at the close of each Supreme Court term by the Cato Institute, 1000 Massachusetts Ave., N.W.,Washington, D.C. 20001-5403.

CORRESPONDENCE. Correspondence regarding subscriptions, changes of address, procurement of back issues, advertising and marketing matters, and so forth, should be addressed to:

Publications Department
The Cato Institute
1000 Massachusetts Ave., N.W.
Washington, D.C. 20001

All other correspondence, including requests to quote or reproduce material, should be addressed to the editor.

CITATIONS: Citation to this volume of the Review should conform to the following style: 2023-2024 Cato Sup. Ct. Rev. (2024).

DISCLAIMER. The views expressed by the authors of the articles are their own and are not attributable to the editor, the editorial board, or the Cato Institute.

INTERNET ADDRESS. Articles from past editions are available to the general public, free of charge, at www.cato.org/pubs/scr.

978-1-952223-96-9 (print)
978-1-952223-97-6 (digital)

Printed in the United States of America.

Cato Institute
1000 Massachusetts Ave., N.W.
Washington, D.C. 20001
www.cato.org

Contents

An Optimist's Appreciation of the Term's Highlights

*Thomas A. Berry**

The Cato Institute's Robert A. Levy Center for Constitutional Studies is pleased to publish this 23rd volume of the *Cato Supreme Court Review,* an annual critique of the Court's most important decisions from the Term just ended plus a look at the Term ahead. We are the first such journal to be released, and the only one that approaches its task from a classical liberal, Madisonian perspective. We release this volume each year at Cato's annual Constitution Day symposium.

Like every Supreme Court Term, this past Term featured some decisions that were cause for celebration and some that were cause for concern. But I'm an optimist at heart. So for this Foreword, I'd like to highlight three cases from this Term that I believe classical liberals should be excited about. Taken together, they represent important victories for the separation of powers, individual rights, and freedom of speech.

Loper Bright Enterprises v. Raimondo

Herring fishing is hard work on a crowded boat, but the federal government wanted to make it even harder. Every inch of space on a small fishing boat is valuable room for supplies, fishers, and the catch. Space becomes even tighter when the government forces fishers to carry a monitor to track compliance with federal regulations. And profits become even narrower when the fishers are forced to *themselves* pay that monitor's salary.

* Legal fellow, Robert A. Levy Center for Constitutional Studies, Cato Institute, and editor in chief, *Cato Supreme Court Review.*

A federal statute lays out three specific circumstances in which the government may force fishers to pay a monitor's salary. Outside of those three cases, the statute is silent. Yet the government nonetheless took that silence as permission, issuing a rule that forced herring fishers in New England waters to pay for their own monitors. The regulation would have cost those herring fishers around $700 per day and reduced their profits by about 20 percent.

Several fishers sued to challenge this rule, including Loper Bright Enterprises, a family-owned fishing company that operates in New England waters. Because they did not fall within any of the three categories mentioned in the statute, they argued that the government did not have the authority to force them to pay their monitors' salaries. Their challenge reached the D.C. Circuit, which held that the statute was ambiguous on this question of monitor salary. But under a precedent called *Chevron v. NRDC*, that ambiguity meant the government won.

Chevron set out a two-step process that courts had to follow when reviewing an agency's interpretation of a statute. First, the court had to apply the traditional tools of statutory interpretation and determine if the statute had a clear meaning. If the statute was clear, then the court had to apply that clear meaning. If, however, the statute was "ambiguous," the court then had to move to the next step and defer to the agency's interpretation so long as it was "reasonable." The court was required to defer to an agency's reasonable interpretation even if the court believed that the agency's interpretation was not the *best* interpretation.

Chevron thus gave judicial power—the power to interpret the meaning of the law—to the executive branch. The Constitution, however, grants all judicial power to the *judicial* branch. And *Chevron* deference applied even when the agency demanding deference was also a party to the case. *Chevron* thus biased the courts toward government agencies, stripping the judiciary of impartiality and denying litigants basic due process.

In addition to these fundamental problems, *Chevron* was also ahistorical and unworkable. *Chevron* was ahistorical because courts did not reflexively defer to the executive at the time of the Constitution's framing or for a hundred years after. The nineteenth-century precedents that some have cited to support *Chevron* were all fundamentally different, such as when courts gave interpretive weight to long-held or contemporaneous executive interpretations. It was not until the New Deal era that the Supreme Court began to defer to the executive solely *because* it was the executive. And it was not until *Chevron* that deference to the executive became a binding rule for all federal courts.

Further, *Chevron* was unworkable because courts failed to ever find a consistent definition of "ambiguous." The Supreme Court itself went back and forth, sometimes applying all the tools of statutory construction rigorously at the first *Chevron* step and other times quickly deferring with little statutory analysis. Even when the Supreme Court declined to defer for seven years, lower appellate courts continued to find statutes ambiguous more than half the time. The failure to reach a consensus on the meaning of "ambiguous" itself demonstrated that *Chevron* was arbitrary and unworkable.

When the *Loper Bright* case reached the Supreme Court, the Court could have ruled for the fishers on narrower grounds, attempting to pare back *Chevron* without ending it. But instead the Court went big and overruled *Chevron* once and for all. That's an outcome that would have been unthinkable even a decade ago. And it's not one that should be taken for granted.

SEC v. Jarkesy

The Securities and Exchange Commission (SEC) has become increasingly reliant on in-house adjudications, which replace juries with in-house administrative law judges (ALJs) who work for the same team as the prosecutors. The Commissioners are the ultimate adjudicators of SEC cases, since they hear appeals of the judges' decisions. But that's cold comfort to the defendants, since the Commissioners have a close working relationship to the prosecutors, are allowed to pre-judge the evidence at an early stage, and give the green light about whether to proceed with investigations in the first place. Not surprisingly, the SEC is able to amass a higher win rate when it litigates in house, and Commissioners rarely overturn ALJ decisions.

George Jarkesy had managed several investment funds geared toward sophisticated parties who wanted high-risk, high-reward investments. After the funds suffered losses during the 2008 market collapse, the SEC launched an investigation into Jarkesy's management of the funds. In 2013, the SEC alleged that he had violated federal securities law and elected to prosecute its case through the agency's in-house court system.

Before the 2010 Dodd-Frank Act, Jarkesy would've gotten his day in court before a jury of his peers. Instead, he was subjected to an administrative adjudication that lasted more than seven years. Predictably, the SEC ruled against Jarkesy and imposed a lifetime ban on employment in the securities industry in addition to a $350,000 fine.

Jarkesy challenged the SEC's ruling, arguing that its in-house proceedings violated his due process guarantees and his Seventh Amendment right to a trial by jury. He won in the Fifth Circuit, and then the Supreme Court took up his case.

Once again, the Supreme Court could have gone small, but instead it went big. The Court held that Jarkesy was entitled to a jury under the Seventh Amendment. And in the process, the Court took a major step toward restoring the protections of that amendment against the administrative state.

Moody v. NetChoice

Three years ago, Texas passed a law declaring that large social media services are "common carriers" subject to onerous regulations dictating what speech they must disseminate. The law prohibits services from removing, demonetizing, or blocking a user or a piece of content based on the viewpoint expressed. Services found to violate this requirement face liability for each piece of content they remove.

The law was soon challenged by NetChoice and CCIA, two internet trade associations whose members operate a variety of websites covered by the law. Although a federal district court held that the law violated the First Amendment, a panel of the Court of Appeals for the Fifth Circuit reversed that decision by a 2–1 vote. The panel held that the law does not inflict a First Amendment injury because the websites "are free to say whatever they want to distance themselves from the speech they host" and thus would not be falsely identified as endorsing the speech they are forced to disseminate.

Meanwhile, Florida passed a similar law around the same time as Texas's, which was also challenged by NetChoice and CCIA. In that case, the Court of Appeals for the Eleventh Circuit struck down key portions of the law as violating the First Amendment rights of the websites.

The Supreme Court granted review of both cases and issued a single decision in both. Although the court did not resolve the cases—due to the need for more factfinding on the full scope of the laws—the high court completely rejected the Fifth Circuit's misguided holding that social media platforms have no First Amendment right to control the content of their feeds. As the Court put it, "the editorial judgments influencing the content of those feeds are, contrary to the Fifth Circuit's view, protected expressive activity."

As Justice Elena Kagan explained, writing for a majority of the court, social media platforms have the same First Amendment rights as newspapers, magazines, and others who compile and present speech. Social media platforms "include and exclude, organize and prioritize—and in making millions of those decisions each day, produce their own distinctive compilations of expression. And while much about social media is new, the essence of that project is something this Court has seen before." As the court summed up, the principle that the First Amendment protects editorial freedom "does not change because the curated compilation has gone from the physical to the virtual world."

Two points are particularly important in the Supreme Court's opinion. First, the court rejected the theory proffered by Florida and Texas (and accepted by the Fifth Circuit) that the government has an interest in regulating the balance of speech on a private platform. The Court explained that it "has many times held, in many contexts, that it is no job for government to decide what counts as the right balance of private expression—to 'un-bias' what it thinks biased, rather than to leave such judgments to speakers and their audiences. That principle works for social media platforms as it does for others."

As the Court explained, this principle holds true no matter how biased a speech marketplace may be, because the "cure" of governmental regulation will be worse than the disease. "However imperfect the private marketplace of ideas, here was a worse proposal—the government itself deciding when speech was imbalanced, and then coercing speakers to provide more of some views or less of others," wrote Kagan. Put simply, "a State may not interfere with private actors' speech to advance its own vision of ideological balance."

Second, the Court held that "the major social-media platforms do not lose their First Amendment protection just because no one will wrongly attribute to them the views in an individual post."

The court explained that its decisions have "never hinged a compiler's First Amendment protection on the risk of misattribution." Instead, the Court clarified that the relevant question is whether the "host of the third-party speech was . . . itself engaged in expression." This holding will go a long way toward ending lower courts' expansion of the so-called *PruneYard* doctrine, which the Fifth Circuit and other courts have wrongly relied on when forcing private entities to host speech.

The cases have now gone back to the Fifth and Eleventh Circuits for further factfinding because the laws were challenged "facially." As the Court explained, the lower courts will have to determine what effect these laws have on other websites besides classic social media feeds. The courts will then have to weigh the legitimate applications of the laws (if there are any) against the unconstitutional applications to decide if they should be struck down in full.

But despite this uncertainty, the principle the Court reaffirmed was far from a sure thing, and its holding is a great relief for anyone who publishes the speech of others online.

* * *

In all three of *Loper Bright*, *Jarkesy*, and *NetChoice*, the Supreme Court took just about the most libertarian position it could have. The result is less concentrated power, more procedural safeguards for the accused, and more rights for those in the business of publishing others' speech. While there is plenty to make libertarians pessimistic in the world, this Term showed once again that the Supreme Court is often (though certainly not always) a major bright spot. The articles in this volume of the *Review* will give a fuller picture of the Term, both the good and the bad. But it never hurts to start with a healthy dose of optimism. We hope you enjoy the 23rd volume of the *Cato Supreme Court Review*.

Introduction

Thomas A. Berry*

This is the 23rd volume of the *Cato Supreme Court Review*, the nation's first in-depth critique of the most recent Supreme Court Term, plus a look at the Term ahead. This is also my second year as editor in chief of the *Review*. It's an honor to continue to lead a publication I've long admired, and I feel a responsibility to keep the *Review* at the same high level of quality our readers expect.

While the personnel behind the *Review* may change, its core purpose and unique speed remain the same. We release the *Review* every year in conjunction with our annual Constitution Day symposium, less than three months after the previous Term ends and two weeks before the next Term begins. It would be almost impossible to publish a journal any faster, and credit for that goes first and foremost to our authors, who year after year meet our unreasonable but necessary demands and deadlines.

This isn't a typical law review. We want you to read this, even if you're not a lawyer. We don't want to scare you off with lots of weird Latin phrases, page-long footnotes, or legalistic jargon. And we don't want to publish articles that are on niche topics, of interest only to the three other academics who write on the same topic. Instead, we publish digestible articles that help Americans understand the decisions of their highest court and why they matter, in plain English.

And as my predecessors were wont to note in the introductions to previous volumes, we freely confess our biases. We start from the first principles: We have a federal government of limited powers, those powers are divided among the several branches, and individuals have rights that act as shields against those powers. We take seriously those liberty-protective parts of the Constitution that have been too often neglected, including the affirmation of unenumerated

---

* Legal fellow, Robert A. Levy Center for Constitutional Studies, Cato Institute, and editor in chief, *Cato Supreme Court Review*.

rights in the Ninth Amendment and the reservation of legislative power to only the *legislature* (not the President) in Article I.

We also reject the tired dichotomy of judicial "restraint" vs. "activism." We urge judges to engage with and follow the law, which includes most importantly the Constitution. If that means invalidating a statute or regulation, it is the judiciary's duty to do so, without putting a "deferential" thumb on the scale in favor of the elected branches. At the same time, judges should not be outcome oriented. Some decisions may lead to a bad *policy* outcome, but that's not an argument that the decision was *legally* wrong. Indeed, any honest legal philosophy must sometimes lead to policy outcomes a judge doesn't prefer, or else it is not really a *legal* methodology.

And there is another core value of the *Review*: We acknowledge that many cases are hard and that people of good faith can disagree on both outcomes and reasoning. We don't want the *Review* to simply echo every Cato position on every case. Rather, we gather a stellar group of authors we respect and give them the freedom to write what they believe. We don't want the *Review* to be an echo chamber.

We fully acknowledge the fact that lawyers applying originalism, textualism, and a presumption of liberty can reach differing conclusions on the same questions. We believe that the differing views of authors who broadly share our judicial philosophies are evidence of the strengths and nuances of these theories, not of their weakness or under-determinacy.

*   *   *

This Term, there were eleven cases in which the Court split 6–3 along ideological lines, an increase from five such cases last Term. Some of the biggest cases of the Term were among those 6–3 splits, including cases on *Chevron* deference, the right to a jury in agency adjudications, and the legal status of "bump stocks." But many other cases produced ideological coalitions in the majority, including cases on the First Amendment rights of social media platforms and the constitutionality of an indefinite appropriation. So while the ideologically split cases may get the most attention, the Court is not a legislature and the Justices don't just vote along party lines.

Within these pages, you'll read about many cases with all sorts of unexpected lineups, cases that prove litigants and advocates can't take anything for granted with this Court.

*   *   *

Turning to this year's *Review*, we begin as always with last year's annual B. Kenneth Simon Lecture. The lecture was delivered by the Honorable Bridget Mary McCormack, president and CEO of the American Arbitration Association–International Centre for Dispute Resolution and former Chief Justice of the Michigan Supreme Court. McCormack's topic is access to justice and public confidence in courts. She begins by setting out with startling clarity "the massive market failure of the civil justice system and its role in undermining the rule of law." But she also brings solutions. She sets out how both regulatory reform and impact litigation have begun to loosen the stranglehold that lawyers currently possess on providing anything resembling legal advice. The rule of law may be wobbly, but "lawyers and judges are uniquely positioned to shore it up."

Next, Jack Beermann of Boston University School of Law writes on *Loper Bright v. Raimondo*. Although most have treated the end of the *Chevron* doctrine as a momentous occasion, Beermann writes that "the demise of *Chevron* deference standing alone may turn out to be much less important for the future of administrative law and agency regulation than many believe." That is because the Supreme Court "explicitly approved of deference under the *Skidmore* factors, which instruct reviewing courts to 'resort for guidance, even on legal questions' to 'the interpretations and opinions of the relevant agency, made in pursuance of official duty and based upon specialized experience.'" Beermann concludes that whether *Chevron* was good or bad, it "was doomed from the start because the opinion was internally inconsistent and hopelessly unclear."

Will Yeatman of the Pacific Legal Foundation then covers *SEC v. Jarkesy*, which held that the subjects of SEC enforcement actions have the right to request a jury. Yeatman predicts that *Jarkesy* "will alter agency enforcement from the course it has run for nearly a half century." Yeatman points out that to see the decision's full effects, scholars will need to look past jury decisions and evaluate how *settlements* change. Given that "more than 90 percent of money penalty actions end in settlement," a defendant's improved bargaining position against the government may end up being more consequential than the actual decisions reached by juries.

Next, Chad Squitieri of The Catholic University of America Columbus School of Law writes on *Consumer Financial Protection Bureau v. Community Financial Services Association of America*. The Supreme Court upheld a unique, indefinite funding arrangement (called Section 5497) against a challenge that it violated the Constitution's Appropriations Clause. Squitieri writes that "the Supreme Court got it right in *Community Financial*. But here's the kicker: That does *not* mean that Section 5497 is constitutional." Squitieri explains that the "appropriate" challenge would have looked to other provisions and asked whether the indefinite appropriation is a "'necessary and proper' means of carrying Congress's Commerce Clause power 'into execution.'"

Sean McElroy of Fenwick & West then writes on *Moore v. United States*, which rejected a challenge to the unusual one-time "mandatory repatriation tax." McElroy explains that although the tax at issue may have seemed technical, the case actually addressed a more fundamental question: "What, precisely, are the limits of Congress's taxing power? Specifically, how do those limits fit into the design of the U.S. international tax system?" Unfortunately, "although the Court ruled in *Moore* that the MRT was constitutional, the answer to this question remains unclear." As McElroy explains, the majority opinion seems motivated in large part not by first principles, but rather by consequentialism: "Specifically, the Court gave significant weight to the fear that constitutional limitations on the MRT would be too expensive to uphold."

Next, Eric Goldman of Santa Clara University School of Law writes on *Moody v. NetChoice*, which evaluated two state laws regulating social-media content moderation. Goldman explains that "although the Court's remand was anti-climactic, Justice Elena Kagan's majority opinion was a rousing celebration of the First Amendment online. Critically, the majority said that the First Amendment protects social media platforms' content moderation efforts. This conclusion jeopardizes much of the Florida and Texas laws as well as many other laws being enacted around the country." As Goldman soberingly observes, "both Democrats and Republicans favor censorial restrictions of the internet," and "this leaves the Supreme Court as the last line of defense for internet freedoms of speech and press." The question now is "how long the Court's resolve will last."

The next article is by Derek Bambauer of the University of Florida Levin College of Law, writing on *NRA v. Vullo* and *Murthy v. Missouri*. These two "jawboning" cases reached different outcomes, with one a win for the challengers and one a win for the government. Although both cases appear to have been resolved on procedural issues rather than on the merits, Bambauer concludes that "upon closer inspection, there is far more bang than whimper in *Vullo* and *Murthy*." The cases show that "jawboning as a species of First Amendment violation is alive and well." But because none of the opinions of the Court provided the specifics of what is needed to win such a claim, Bambauer provides his own proposed "three-part test," which "would both guide courts in determining when jawboning occurs and focus attention on the most problematic instances of the phenomenon."

Anya Bidwell and Patrick Jaicomo of the Institute for Justice next write on *Gonzalez v. Trevino*, a case they themselves litigated up to the Supreme Court. The case concerned what evidence a people may use to prove that the police arrested them because of their protected speech. They explain that the Court's opinion "is an encouraging development for free speech and bad news for those looking to use the power of arrest to silence their critics" because the Court "clarified that the only evidence that must be excluded at the threshold stage is state-of-mind evidence." The Court also "rejected the defendants' request for a sweeping rule that would have rubberstamped all retaliatory arrests supported by warrants." The upshot is that "retaliatory arrest claims . . . now stand a chance."

Next up is an article by George Mocsary of the University of Wyoming College of Law on *United States v. Rahimi*, the Term's Second Amendment case. In *Rahimi*, the Court rejected a facial challenge to a law that disarms people subject to certain restraining orders. In Mocsary's view, the Court illustrated that "its Second Amendment jurisprudence is a straightforward application of the centuries-old practice of common-law reasoning that is taught to first-year law students." *Rahimi* followed closely on the heels of the Court's important *Bruen* decision, and "*Rahimi* shows that *Bruen* is easy to apply if one does it in good faith." On this view, *Rahimi* is a success story, because "both the majority's and the dissent's common-law analyses fit within *Bruen*'s boundaries. . . . *Rahimi*, in other words, is an example of the common law working as it should."

Turning from the Second to the Eighth Amendment, John Stinneford of the University of Florida Levin College of Law writes on *Grants Pass v. Johnson*. The Court held that a ban on sleeping in homeless encampments did not violate the "Cruel or Unusual Punishments" Clause. Stinneford addresses not just the decision, but also a much bigger question about the current Court: "Will it be a serious originalist court or merely a conservative political one? If the former, its decisions may endure. If the latter, they will be written in sand. . . . The *Grants Pass* opinion gives us some reasons to be hopeful, but also significant reasons to worry." Stinneford concludes that *"Grants Pass* is an easy case under the original meaning of the Cruel and Unusual Punishments Clause," but it's not clear that the Court is ready to apply a fully originalist methodology to the Eighth Amendment.

Up next is an article written by three law professors, Ann Woolhandler, Julia Mahoney, and Michael Collins, all of the University of Virginia School of Law. They write on a case concerning the Fifth Amendment's "Takings Clause," *DeVillier v. Texas*. As they explain, *"DeVillier* had the makings of a major property rights decision, because the question of whether the Takings Clause is 'self-executing' has long remained unresolved." But the Court "declined the opportunity to overhaul constitutional doctrine, opting instead to take a 'wait and see' approach toward modifying the existing and highly complicated system of just compensation remedies."

Cato's own Clark Neily authors the next article, on *FBI v. Fikre*. The case raised the question of whether a lawsuit challenging a placement on the "No Fly" list became moot when the government, without explanation, took the plaintiff off the list. Neily notes that it is "one of several cases this Term in which government officials employed various stratagems designed to forestall judicial review of their alleged misconduct." In this case, the stratagem did not work. *"Fikre* was neither a close call nor a difficult case to get right," because the government had not guaranteed that it would refrain from putting the plaintiff back on the list for an improper reason. Neily notes that "the Justices should be commended for sending a clear and unanimous message that when government actors seek to moot judicial review of their plausibly unlawful policies by suspending those policies after the commencement of litigation, the judiciary will not presume the purity of their motives where no such presumption is remotely warranted."

Our final two articles on cases from this past Term both address the unique status of the President in our system of separated powers. First, Keith Whittington of Yale Law School writes on *Trump v. United States*, the presidential immunity case. Whittington finds the majority opinion lacking, writing that it "bears all the hallmarks of an uneasy negotiation and compromise among the Justices in the majority." Because its opinion did not resolve key issues, "the Court has thrown the hot potato back into the hands of the lower courts, perhaps hoping that the case will not return to the Court too soon or that the circumstances will look rather different when it does." Among all the opinions in the case, Whittington argues that Justice Amy Coney Barrett's is the most persuasive.

Last but not least among our articles on the Term's cases, Ilya Somin of Antonin Scalia Law School tackles *Trump v. Anderson*, the disqualification for insurrection case. The Court held that the Fourteenth Amendment alone cannot disqualify someone from holding *federal* office unless Congress has passed a statute providing a mechanism for disqualification. All nine Justices agreed that the Colorado Supreme Court had improperly removed Trump from the ballot. But Somin writes that "the Court achieved unanimity by making a grave error. In so doing, they went against the text and original meaning of the Fourteenth Amendment and undermined a potentially vital constitutional safeguard of liberal democracy." Somin concludes that the Court's opinion contains "highly dubious reasoning at odds with text and original meaning," and "is also defective on consequentialist grounds."

Finally, Jeremy Broggi of Wiley Rein authors our annual "Looking Ahead" article. Broggi identifies several major cases to watch next Term, on topics ranging from sex-transition treatments for minors to laws requiring "adult" websites to verify the age of their visitors to homemade "ghost guns." The Court will also potentially consider cases on mandatory disclosures of donor identity and state-based climate-change lawsuits against oil companies. With the overruling of *Chevron* this Term, Broggi notes that "the October Term 2024 should provide an early glimpse at the Court's revised approach to the proper interpretation of statutes that are administered by federal agencies."

* * *

As mentioned at the outset, this is my second year as editor in chief of the *Review* after two years as its managing editor. Cato has been a huge part of my professional life since I first interned here in my second year of law school nine years ago. Reading through the introductions of past volumes of the *Review* offers snapshots of my own professional milestones, from intern, to legal associate, onto contributor, and then to managing editor. Now, as I author my own introduction as editor in chief for the first time, I'm filled with immense gratitude to both Ilya Shapiro and Trevor Burrus, who were there on my first day as an intern and who have both been invaluable mentors in getting me to this point. I'm grateful to both for showing me the ropes and teaching me best editorial practices by example. And by the transitive property of mentorship, I also owe Roger Pilon a great deal for creating Cato's Robert A. Levy Center for Constitutional Studies and for bringing Ilya and Trevor aboard so that they could in turn bring me on.

This year, as always, I have had help from many other people. Most important, of course, are the authors themselves, without whose work there would be no *Review*. Our authors this year produced excellent, polished articles under tremendous time pressure and for that I thank them all sincerely. Thanks also go to my Cato Institute colleagues Clark Neily, Walter Olson, and Brent Skorup for help in editing the articles and for taking on a heavier load of other Cato work in August when I was buried in editing. Legal associates Christine Marsden, Charles Brandt, Ethan Yang, Christopher Barnewolt, Nathaniel Lawson, Alexander Khoury, and Caitlyn Kinard performed the difficult (believe me, I remember) and vital task of cite checking and proofreading. Legal intern Finn McCarthy also provided essential research assistance. And special thanks to Laura Bondank, who handled all the nuts and bolts of publishing the *Review* (along with pitching in on edits as well). Laura learned a complex process on the fly two years ago and I now rely on her completely to remind me what needs to get done and when; this volume couldn't have happened without her.

We hope that you enjoy this 23rd volume of the *Cato Supreme Court Review*.

Access to Justice and Public Confidence in Courts: Whose Law Is It Anyway?

*Bridget Mary McCormack**

Thanks very much to the team at Cato for the invitation to join you today. It is an honor to be part of your Constitution Day celebration. I was the lucky beneficiary of your excellent work while serving on the Michigan bench; thank you for what you do.

Introduction and Road Map

My topic today is the massive market failure of the civil justice system and its role in undermining the rule of law. I'll start with a description of the current state of civil justice in America. I want us all to be on the same page before I turn to diagnosing some of the causes of the brokenness. After that diagnosis, I will describe some ripples of change I see on the horizon and what's at stake if we don't get it right.

Here is my thesis: We can't go on like this. But first, a word about what I am *not* talking about and what you should not infer from my remarks. Please don't take my focus on the *civil* justice system to mean that the criminal justice system is ably serving the rule of law. In most jurisdictions, you can be punished for conduct that a jury has said you did not commit. That's not great for the rule of law. And what happens if you are represented by ineffective counsel when the state seeks to terminate your parental rights and you lose your kids as a result of that inadequate representation? In almost every jurisdiction, there is no process for addressing that wrong. It's a too-bad-so-sad rule.

OK, back to the topic I came to discuss.

* President and CEO, American Arbitration Association, and former Chief Justice, Michigan Supreme Court. I am grateful to Cato for the opportunity and to Ishika Toor and Clare Clement for research assistance.

I. The Civil Justice Gap

Justice system data are hard to come by, but *some* data about the civil justice system capture its failures. The Legal Services Corporation's 2022 *Justice Gap* report found that 92 percent of the civil legal problems of low-income people get either no or inadequate help.[1] That is a six-percentage-point increase over the prior study from 2017.[2] And it isn't a COVID-19 pandemic blip. During that same period, total revenue to legal aid programs *increased* by 31 percent.[3]

And there is this: The National Center for State Courts estimates that both parties have lawyers in only 24 percent of civil cases in state courts, which is where about 95 percent of civil litigation occurs.[4] In other words, in more than three-quarters of civil cases, at least one party struggles to navigate a legal system where rules are written in a language that the person doesn't speak or understand.

And this: Every year, the World Justice Project ranks the world's countries on their compliance with various measures of the rule of law. One of those measures is the accessibility and affordability of civil justice. The most recent Rule of Law Index, released in late 2023, ranks the United States 115th out of 140 countries on the accessibility and affordability of civil justice.[5] Among the 46 wealthiest countries in the world, the United States ranks . . . 46th.[6]

Many countries do justice better than we do. In a popular idea of our justice system—the one we see on TV and teach in our law

[1] *See* MARY C. SLOSAR, LEGAL SERVS. CORP., THE JUSTICE GAP: MEASURING THE UNMET CIVIL LEGAL NEEDS OF LOW-INCOME AMERICANS 7 (Apr. 2022), https://lsc-live.app.box.com/s/xl2v2uraiotbbzrhuwtjlgi0emp3myz1.

[2] *Cf.* NORC AT THE UNIV. OF CHICAGO, LEGAL SERVS. CORP., THE JUSTICE GAP: MEASURING THE UNMET CIVIL LEGAL NEEDS OF LOW-INCOME AMERICANS 6 (June 2017), https://lsc-live.app.box.com/s/6x4wbh5d2gqxwy0v094os1x2k6a39q74.

[3] *See* Jim Sandman, "Where Is the Outrage?," Keynote Speech (excerpts) at the *Stanford Law Review*'s Symposium "Access to Justice" (Mar. 21, 2023), *in* PENN CAREY L., NEWS & EVENTS, https://www.law.upenn.edu/live/news/15655-where-is-the-outrage.

[4] PAULA HANNAFORD-AGOR, DIRECTOR, NCSC CENTER FOR JURY STUDIES, NAT'L CTR. FOR ST. CTS., CIVIL JUSTICE INITIATIVE: THE LANDSCAPE OF CIVIL LITIGATION IN STATE COURTS 31 (2015), https://www.ncsc.org/__data/assets/pdf_file/0020/13376/civiljusticereport-2015.pdf.

[5] *See* WORLD JUSTICE PROJECT, WJP RULE OF LAW INDEX: CIVIL JUSTICE FOR UNITED STATES (2023), https://worldjusticeproject.org/rule-of-law-index/country/2023/United%20States/Civil%20Justice.

[6] *See id.* This is referenced as the "income rank" of the United States for subfactor 7.1, accessibility and affordability of civil justice.

schools—both parties are represented by lawyers who present evidence and make legal arguments for their clients, and the best legal argument wins. That popular idea is a fiction in the vast majority of civil cases in the United States today.

The high rate of litigants without a lawyer is particularly troubling because of the kinds of cases they manage on their own: high-stakes cases. They are high stakes not because billions of dollars are on the line but because they often involve something more fundamental—shelter, personal safety, family, or financial stability.

This state of affairs is relatively new. As recently as the start of the last quarter of the 20th century, lawyerless litigants were the exception. The rate steadily rose until, by the early 2000s, we were seeing the numbers we have today. In 1977, two Yale Law students did a study of 2,500 divorce cases in two trial courts in Connecticut and published their results as an unsigned "project" in the *Yale Law Journal*.[7] The students were Deborah Rhode and her husband-to-be, Ralph Cavanagh. They found that 2.7 percent of the divorce cases that they studied involved an unrepresented litigant.[8] They also cited a then-recent study in San Mateo County, California, showing that 20 percent of divorce petitioners were proceeding without lawyers. They characterized this as "an unprecedented surge" in self-representation.[9]

Of course, there are many government services that people navigate without experts. What are the consequences of lacking an expert to help you navigate our justice system? I now turn to what the lack of a lawyer means in practice.

A. Equal Justice under Law without Lawyers?

The lawyers in the room know the fundamental legal fiction that we are all charged with knowing the law. For those of you who are not lawyers, ignorance of the law is never a defense to any claim or charge.[10]

---

[7] *See generally* Deborah L. Rhode & Ralph C. Cavanagh, *The Unauthorized Practice of Law and Pro Se Divorce: An Empirical Analysis*, 86 YALE L.J. 104 (1976).

[8] *See id.* at 149–50.

[9] *See id.* at 110 n.25.

[10] *See generally* Paul Matthews, *Ignorance of the Law Is No Excuse?*, 3 LEGAL STUD. 2, at 174–92 (July 1983), https://www.cambridge.org/core/journals/legal-studies/article/abs/ignorance-of-the-law-is-no-excuse/31F800ED44C5CF1FAFA1562889D8ED0D.

There is a lot of law to know! Take crimes, for example. "According to best estimates—and estimates are all we have—there are about 4,500 federal crimes in the United States Code, and more than 300,000 federal crimes dispersed throughout federal regulations."[11] And each state has a similar offering.

Fortune-telling is still a crime in most jurisdictions.[12] And in North Carolina, it is a crime if your bingo game lasts more than five hours,[13] or if you play bingo while intoxicated.[14] In Vermont, it's still a crime for a woman to get false teeth without getting permission from her husband.[15]

There isn't one place to find out what the law is. No resource explains in plain language what exactly the law requires of you or provides for you. Do you know what happens to your stuff if you die without a will? I asked Google and got this answer: If you die without a will, you are "intestate," and a probate court will apply the intestacy laws of the state where you reside to determine how to distribute your property among your next of kin. Naturally, I next asked what the intestacy laws of Michigan are.

Things went downhill from there. One result seemed to be a link to a Michigan statute, but the link didn't work. The rest were lawyers' websites, one scarier than the next. Here is one example: "Dying without a Will may become a less-than-ideal situation. For example, the Court could find that a distant relative that you never intended to give your money or property to could be entitled to your Estate, leaving the people you love with nothing. To avoid this scenario, at a minimum, you should have a Last Will and Testament drafted that outlines who should receive your money and property." Yikes.

Many people have some familiarity with some parts of the U.S. Constitution. But even when we know the particular words in a

---

[11] GianCarlo Canaparo & Zack Smith, *Count the Crimes on the Federal Law Books. Then Cut Them.*, THE HERITAGE FOUND. (June 24, 2020), https://www.heritage.org/crime-and-justice/commentary/count-the-crimes-the-federal-law-books-then-cut-them.

[12] *See* David L. Hudson, Jr., *Fortune Telling*, FREE SPEECH CTR. (July 2, 2024), https://firstamendment.mtsu.edu/article/fortune-telling/.

[13] *See* N.C. GEN. STAT. § 14-309.8.

[14] *See id.* § 18B-308.

[15] *See* Anna Fridman, *The Law That Won't Be Missed*, 18 THE CATALYST 2, AT 7 (May 2013), https://www.isba.org/committees/women/newsletter/2013/05/thelawthatwontbemissed.

constitutional provision, we don't generally know what they mean in practice. The words have been interpreted by judges for 200 some years, and it's those interpretations that are in fact the rule of law. The *latest* interpretations, I should say.

And judicial interpretations of the Constitution aren't always very intuitive. Most of us know that we have a constitutional right to be tried by a jury of our peers if we are accused of a crime. But in most cases, exercising that right will mean exposing yourself to significantly longer punishment if convicted. And judges have found that consequence to be perfectly constitutional.[16] We have a right to a jury trial-ish.

As for statutes, you might find your way to reading them online. But after spending 10 years trying to make sense of many statutes with six other people trained and paid to do just that who disagreed regularly—well, best of luck. Then there are other legal principles that are also judge-made but are more freewheeling and can overlay constitutional or statutory law. These "rules of decision" are generally not tied directly to any language in a constitution or statute. Google "mootness," "ripeness," "standing," or "qualified immunity." To have access to a comprehensive collection of these judicial pronouncements about the law, also known as . . . *the law*, you need a subscription to the most user-unfriendly search engine you'll ever interact with.

There's more still. There are also sets of rules that govern how you can use the law in courts. And a particular rule of law will often be different from state to state, sometimes even from courthouse to courthouse. Within a single courthouse, the rules for how to interact with a court can differ from courtroom to courtroom. That's right: In addition to sorting out the legal rules and principles and court rules that govern your dispute, you better check Judge Whatshername's website for any special rules that you have to follow. That is, if she has a website. If she doesn't, you can try to call her office and see whether they can fax you her standing order.

I wish we could take a short field trip right now to an eviction docket or a debt collection docket. I think it would shock all of

---

[16] *See* Nat'l Ass'n of Criminal Defense Lawyers, The Trial Penalty: The Sixth Amendment Right to Trial on the Verge of Extinction and How to Save It 40–42 (2018), https://www.nacdl.org/Document/TrialPenaltySixthAmendmentRighttoTrialNearExtinct.

us. In some places, you can see some dockets online—a pandemic bonus. I watched some eviction cases recently before a thoughtful judge in Michigan. I'm going to read you one short eviction hearing transcript:[17]

> JUDGE. We'll come to order. The record may reflect we're next concerned with a summary proceedings matter involving Courtyard Apartment versus Joshua Salinas . . . and all other occupants. . . . Counsel . . . is appearing on behalf of the plaintiff Courtyard. The defendant has failed to appear as I understand it. Not in the hallway either.

> COUNSEL. He's not.

> JUDGE. Alright. [Counsel,] anything for the record? Good afternoon.

> COUNSEL. Good afternoon, Your Honor. For the record, if it pleases the Court, . . . I'm with the law firm of Swistak Levine and I represent Courtyards. This particular matter is set for a second hearing after a magistrate call a week ago. Mr. Salinas failed to appear at that time as well, so this is a second consecutive failure to appear. This matter is a health hazard matter. We're seeking immediate turnover of the property. So . . . we would ask that a judgment for possession be entered at this time and that we be allowed to submit a writ immediately and that an order for eviction be issued as soon as the fees and the form is received by the Court.

> JUDGE. Alright. Do you have someone available for brief testimony in support of the default judgement today?

> COUNSEL. I don't. Miss Soto, she has been with us before, is the property manager. . . . She is ill at the moment, and this was a summary proceeding and I thought that we could possibly do that.

> . . .

> JUDGE. So on this the notice to quit was served August 4. I would note that the notice to quit indicated in bold face type "**landlord will seek immediate issuance of writ of restitution.**"

---

[17] For a recording of the proceedings, see *Brent Weigle's Personal Meeting Room*, ZOOM starting at 11:10 (Sept. 8, 2023), https://tinyurl.com/3dnu76vp.

The options given to the tenant were to remove the health hazards, repair and allow inspection by the landlord within seven days, or move out. Again, that was served—and proof of service shows August 4—on the defendant. Complaint was then filed in this particular matter for termination of tenancy based upon health hazard or damage to the property. And paragraph nine, it's the standard scale DC form 102b, has checked in boldface: "**The plaintiff requests**," and then in regular type, "an immediate order of eviction." That was filed with the Court properly, and the lawsuit was mailed. A certificate of mailing was perfected for a mailing done on August 17. And the lawsuit is posted; proof of service . . . indicat[es] it was posted attached to the premises on August 26. Under MCR 4.201, that is sufficient notice in the Court's view for a default judgment for possession only. . . . The defendant's dog unattended in the apartment, not cleaned up after. The apartment is in terrible condition, horrible condition, no personal service goes to the next hearing. Plaintiff will likely ask for the immediate order. Under the totality of the circumstances and based on the content—I should also indicate as required by court rule the lease was attached to the complaint and it's signed by our defendant. On the totality of circumstances, a default judgment may enter for possession, and plaintiff may submit contemporaneously with that a request for an eviction order. I will sign both the possession judgment and the writ of restitution, as well if they're provided to the Court.

COUNSEL. Thank you and we will also get the fee for the writs to you as quickly as possible so that it may be effectively served.

* * *

How much of that would Mr. Salinas have understood if he were there? Why did the judge ask for a witness and then not require one? Is there a rule that requires testimony? Is it a court rule? A statute? How would you figure that out if you were not a lawyer? Did the tenant have any defenses? How would you figure that out? When you say it all out loud it starts to sound . . . not very fair. It is not justice to compel people who can't afford a lawyer to play by the rules of a system designed only for those who can. It is wrong.

II. How Did We Get Here?

How did we get here? The American legal system was built by lawyers for lawyers at a time when everyone had a lawyer. Four industrial revolutions passed, and the complexity of our economy and society changed dramatically. Yet almost no updates have been made to our legal processes. A surgeon dropped from 1890 into a modern surgical suite would be confused and lost. But a lawyer who practiced in the Iron County, Michigan, Courthouse in 1890 would feel entirely at home in that courthouse today.

A. Change Management in Legal Profession

Why hasn't change come for the legal profession the way it's come for so many other industries? Where is the civil justice Netflix? Why are lawyers terrible at solving problems that require innovation and collaboration and also excellent at boxing out others who might be better at it?

Part of it is cultural: Our training and culture are risk-averse and backward-looking. We are trained to believe that incremental change leads to lasting solutions with less conflict. And lawyers are committed to the way we have always done things. One of our most essential decisionmaking norms is *stare decisis*: What was decided before governs what we decide today. And a strong cultural norm favors the status quo: "We all did it this way, so you should too."

Part of it is practical: We lawyers (and judges) attend to emergencies first, and we always have emergencies. We focus on lots of critical immediate problems, which keep us from focusing on the structural problems. I've been meaning to write a law review article for 30 years for which I have a great title: "Let's Do Emergencies Last." This is true for individual lawyers and judges, as well as institutions. Each stakeholder group may work in good faith to address the immediate problems squarely in its wheelhouse, but none have time to step back and explore upstream solutions.

Part of it is lack of resources: Except for those lawyers in Big Law (a small minority of those in the profession), lawyers' priorities are structured around financing their practices and paying their employees. Courts struggle to keep the lights on, keep judges trained, and pay court staff a living wage. There is minimal funding for technology, data collection, evidence-based study, and reform. And the competing priorities of dispensing daily justice are formidable.

Bar examiners are competing for resources with underfunded court systems. They must try to stretch their dollars to ensure that a new version of the old exam is error-free, ready to be administered on the appointed day, and graded promptly and fairly.

Finally, part of it is bar federalism: Bar examiners in each state work separately, often duplicating work, and often missing the others' insights.

B. Stakeholder Silos

Legal system stakeholders react to one another but rarely collaborate. Law schools have primarily built their curricula to accommodate a complex web of state licensing requirements, educational accreditation requirements, and university policies, further structured by a ranking system built on criteria that lock in an anachronistic vision of the profession.

Although law schools and courts operate independently, they are, in fact, interlocking systems. Each is dependent on and reactive to the other. And each is bound by funding models, traditions, and cultures. These entrenched qualities of law schools and courts have, over time, magnified the gap between those who become lawyers and those who need the justice system to protect their rights and ensure that their problems are resolved fairly. Neither courts nor law schools have direct control over the other. Both serve many other stakeholders, from state legislatures to alumni to bar associations to university presidents. In most jurisdictions, state supreme courts and law schools interact very rarely. In a system characterized by self-regulation and licensure federalism, there is no obvious first mover for systemwide reform.

C. And Lawyers Are Often Resistant to Allowing Others to Help

Let me turn to the supply side of the legal services market. According to American Bar Association (ABA) data, in 2018, around 84 percent of law school graduates were employed in positions requiring bar passage or where a JD provides an advantage.[18] But the ABA data

---

[18] *See ABA legal education section releases employment data for graduating law class of 2018*, Am. Bar Ass'n (Apr. 29, 2019), https://www.americanbar.org/news/abanews/aba-news-archives/2019/04/aba-legal-education-section-releases-employment-data-for-graduat/.

have been criticized for overstating employment rates by including short-term and nonprofessional jobs. The organization Law School Transparency has suggested that full legal employment is likely 10–20 percent lower.[19]

America's lawyers devote three years and hundreds of thousands of dollars to "learn the law." Some graduate with crippling debt, and a significant number of them are underemployed. But I don't mean to suggest that this market mismatch is a solution waiting to happen. We're not going to lawyer our way out of the civil justice problem. If the paying work available now is not enough to keep our current roster of lawyers fully employed, the 92 percent of our neighbors who can't afford to pay lawyers to help with their justice problems will not close that gap in our current model.

D. UPL

But those who can't afford lawyers can't get help from anyone else, either. In most states, anyone who is not a lawyer risks criminal punishment for the unlicensed practice of law. The definitions of "the practice of law" and "the unauthorized practice of law" (UPL) are not uniform and not easily understandable. But most restrictions on UPL prohibit people from giving out-of-court legal advice or helping prepare legal documents.[20]

This wasn't always the case in the United States. At the Founding, while only lawyers could advocate in most courts, you could get help from your family and friends with legal problems outside of court. That started to change in the early part of the 20th century when courts prohibited legal help by people who were not lawyers outside of courthouses, too. This prohibition first applied when legal help was given for a fee, and then eventually when it was given at all.[21] Now, lawyers' monopolies across the country

---

[19] *See Limits of Our Reports*, LAW SCHOOL TRANSPARENCY (Oct. 2018), https://www.lawschooltransparency.com/help/Limits-of-the-LST-Reports.

[20] *See generally* Derek A. Denckla, *Nonlawyers and the Unauthorized Practice of Law: An Overview of the Legal and Ethical Parameters*, 67 FORDHAM L. REV. 2581 (1999).

[21] Alan Houseman & Linda E. Perle, *Securing Equal Justice for All: A Brief History of Civil Legal Assistance in the United States*, CTR. FOR LAW AND SOCIAL POL'Y (May 2018), https://www.clasp.org/sites/default/files/publications/2018/05/2018_securingequaljustice.pdf.

restrict anyone who is not a lawyer from helping another person with a legal problem.

It isn't like that in other professions where resources are critical to basic human needs. You don't go to a surgeon or doctor every time you have a medical problem. Sometimes, a physician assistant or a nurse practitioner is the right fit for your health care needs. Eighty-two percent of all health care workers have a bachelor's, associate's, or vocational degree, and only 9.3 percent have an MD (Doctor of Medicine) or DO (Doctor of Osteopathic Medicine) degree. In contrast, 80 percent of legal service workers have a law degree.[22] We could have legal nurse practitioners, if lawyers wanted to.

* * *

This might sound like a requiem for the modern U.S. legal system, but I see hopeful ripples.

III. How Does the Jenga Tower Fall?

The current systemic barriers to improving access to justice seem to me like a Jenga tower; if the right pieces are pulled out, all of them could fall quickly. And a number of pieces are being pulled out, which I'll organize for today in three buckets: regulatory reform, litigation, and other stuff.

A. Regulatory Reform

Start with regulatory reform. You likely know this story. Two state supreme courts have attempted to be first movers to address the civil justice crisis.

1. Utah

In 2020, the Utah Supreme Court established a Licensed Paralegal Practitioner (LPP) program that allows qualified nonlawyers to provide limited legal services in debt collection, landlord–tenant

---

[22] *See* Bill Henderson, *Mindshare Matrix for Legal Professionals (349)*, Legal Evolution (Jan. 15, 2023), https://www.legalevolution.org/2023/01/mindshare-matrix-for-legal-professionals-349/.

disputes, and family law matters. Critics (lawyers) initially argued that LPPs might increase consumer confusion and harm.[23]

To become an LPP in Utah, individuals must possess an associate's or bachelor's degree and then complete an approved LPP education program, exams, and apprenticeship. LPPs must adhere to professional conduct rules and complete 12 hours of continuing education annually.[24] The Utah LPP program aims to address substantial unmet legal needs while maintaining consumer protections through licensing requirements, especially among low- and moderate-income populations.[25] In the first two years following the launch, more than 75 individuals had been approved as LPPs and began providing services across Utah.[26]

2. Arizona

In 2021, the Arizona Supreme Court adopted rules to create a new licensing program allowing qualified nonlawyers to provide specific legal services.[27]

Arizona licenses legal paraprofessionals (LPs) who meet specific education and training requirements set by the Arizona Supreme Court. To qualify, individuals must possess an associate's degree or higher and complete an LP education program approved by the court. LPs must adhere to rules of professional conduct and complete annual continuing education.[28]

---

[23] *See, e.g., Supreme Court Regulatory Reform Proposal-Comment Period Closes July 23, 2020*, UTAH STATE CTS. (Apr. 24, 2020), https://legacy.utcourts.gov/utc/rules-comment/2020/04/24/supreme-court-regulatory-reform-proposal-comment-period-closes-july-23-2020/ (listing comments criticizing the proposed rule, including one saying that "it seems like a disaster waiting to happen").

[24] *See Licensed Paralegal Practitioner (LPP) Program: Overview and Information*, UTAH STATE BAR (Jan. 2024), https://www.utahbar.org/wp-content/uploads/2024/02/LPP-Qualifications-Website-J24.pdf.

[25] *See Licensed Paralegal Practitioner (LPP): Program Overview*, UTAH STATE CTS., https://www.utcourts.gov/en/about/miscellaneous/legal-community/lpp.html.

[26] *See id.* ("In a recent survey conducted by the Utah Supreme Court's LPP Steering Committee, more than 200 paralegals expressed an interest in getting licensed as an LPP. The majority were interested in establishing an LPP practice within a law firm, while about a third were interested in starting an independent LPP firm.").

[27] *See Legal Services Reforms: Alternative Business Structures (ABS) Frequently Asked Questions*, ARIZ. JUD. BRANCH, https://www.azcourts.gov/accesstolegalservices/Questions-and-Answers/abs.

[28] *See* Ariz. Code Judicial Admin. §§ 7-210(I)-(J), https://www.azcourts.gov/Portals/0/admcode/pdfcurrentcode/7-210%20Legal%20Paraprofessional%20Amended%2008-2024.pdf?ver=EzUU2uMO8k59V70-Jy2sWA%3d%3d.

LPs can provide specific legal services in family law, landlord–tenant disputes, debt collection defense, and administrative appeals. They can prepare legal documents, advise clients on procedural issues, and represent clients in certain administrative hearings. But they can't appear in court or negotiate on a client's behalf.

Arizona's LP program launched in January 2022. From January 1 to December 31, 2022, 25 legal paraprofessionals were approved.[29] As of January 2023, 10 more applications had been processed and were recommended for licensure.[30]

In addition to creating the Legal Paraprofessional Program, the Arizona Supreme Court amended Rule 5.4 of the Rules of Professional Conduct. Rule 5.4 prohibits lawyers from sharing legal fees or forming partnerships with nonlawyers for law practice. The rationale for the rule is to prevent outside influence over lawyers' independent professional judgment.[31]

Arizona's revised Rule 5.4 allows for alternative business structures and nonlawyer ownership of law firms in Arizona, provided that specific requirements are met. For example, lawyers must still retain majority control of the firm and be responsible for ethical and professional conduct. And firms must not allow nonlawyer involvement in matters of legal judgment.[32]

---

[29] *See Board of Nonlawyer Legal Service Providers' Annual Report on the Status of the Legal Paraprofessional Program* 5, Sup. Ct. of Ariz. (Apr. 2023), https://www.azcourts.gov/Portals/26/Final%202022%20NLSP%20Board%20Report%20to%20Supreme%20Court%202023-05-09.pdf?ver=8vuBVt_Zj5sf9lwHXuk-NQ%3d%3d.

[30] *See id.*

[31] *See* ABA Model Rule 5.4: Professional Independence of a Lawyer – Comment, *Law Firms and Associations*, https://www.americanbar.org/groups/professional_responsibility/publications/model_rules_of_professional_conduct/rule_5_4_professional_independence_of_a_lawyer/comment_on_rule_5_4/.

[32] "Nonlawyers may partner with lawyers. Nonlawyers may own, have an economic interest in, manage, or make decisions in, an Alternative Business Structure that provides legal services. Lawyers will be permitted to split fees." *Legal Services Reforms: Alternative Business Structures (ABS) Frequently Asked Questions*, Ariz. Judicial Branch, https://www.azcourts.gov/accesstolegalservices/Questions-and-Answers/abs. However, "only lawyers and other individuals licensed or certified by the Arizona Supreme Court are permitted to provide legal services," and "[a]t least one lawyer licensed to practice law in Arizona must be appointed by the ABS to serve as its compliance lawyer." *Id.* For further discussion of the reforms in Arizona and some of their implications, see Kenneth R. Cunningham et al., *Arizona Non-Lawyer Ownership in Law Firms & Implications for Accounting Firms*, Bloomberg Law (Nov. 2020), https://www.bloomberglaw.com/external/document/XA9M2V18000000/corporate-compliance-professional-perspective-arizona-non-lawyer.

Arizona's rule change aligns with similar rules in England, Australia, and parts of Canada. It reflects the view that opening the door to new capital and business structures can increase access to legal services without undermining lawyers' duties to clients. More flexible rules facilitate financial investment in innovations like technology solutions for cost-effective legal services.[33]

3. Early evaluation of the Arizona and Utah programs: The sky hasn't fallen

Early evaluation of both programs has been encouraging. A team at Stanford conducted in-depth interviews with and analyses of authorized entities in Utah and Arizona up to June 30, 2022.[34] They found that innovations have emerged in five primary forms:

- *Traditional law firms* have adapted their business structures, service models, or capital structures, and make up 35 percent of the authorized entities. The motivation for their adaptation includes incorporating nonlawyer staff members or attracting external investments for technology or marketing purposes.[35]
- *Law companies* like Rocket Lawyer and LegalZoom represent 38 percent of authorized entities. These companies have chosen to become regulated to employ lawyers.
- *Nonlaw companies*, which are newcomers to the legal sector, comprise 18 percent of entities. These companies often set up holistic service models combining law with other services, such as accountants.
- *Small-sector intermediary platforms* connect lawyers to potential clients.

---

[33] *See* David Freeman Engstrom et al., *Legal Innovation After Reform: Evidence from Regulatory Change*, Deborah L. Rhode Ctr. on the Legal Pro. 4 (Sept. 2022), https://law.stanford.edu/wp-content/uploads/2022/09/SLS-CLP-Regulatory-Reform-REPORTExecSum-9.26.pdf (listing five types of innovation resulting from regulatory reform in the legal services market).

[34] *See id.* at 36–46.

[35] *See id.* at 4–7 (executive summary); *id.* at 24, 32, 44 (discussing marketing).

And finally,

- *Entities using nonlawyers to practice law* use the waivers for unauthorized practice of law that are available in Utah. One example, Rasa, uses artificial intelligence (AI) and nonlawyer experts to help Utah residents with criminal record expungements.[36]

The Stanford team drew some thematic conclusions from their interviews. They found that lawyers are pivotal in the innovations of these new entities. Lawyers are developing new concepts and are actively involved in various roles, such as owners, investors, and compliance officers. The Stanford team also found that a significant proportion of these entities are selling primarily to individual consumers and small businesses, the PeopleLaw market. Most importantly, the team found that according to the data, these reforms haven't resulted in significant consumer harm. Both Utah and Arizona have reported relatively low complaints about the new entities.[37]

But the regulatory reform story is one of two steps forward, 1.5 steps back. The year 2022 witnessed setbacks. California's initiative to introduce regulatory reforms met with significant resistance from the bar and the legislature, culminating in a legislative ban on specific reforms.[38] And the ABA issued a nonbinding resolution against states considering nonlawyer ownership changes.[39] But Oregon and Alaska both recently introduced legal paraprofessional programs. And other states are considering it.

---

[36] *See id.* at 6.

[37] *See* Shoshana Weissmann et al., *The World Needs More Lawyers*, REGUL. TRANSPARENCY PROJECT, FEDERALIST SOC'Y 9 (Sept. 28, 2023), https://rtp.fedsoc.org/wp-content/uploads/The-World-Needs-More-Lawyers.pdf.

[38] *See* Karen Sloan, *California lawmakers pull plug on legal industry reforms*, REUTERS (Aug. 29, 2022), https://www.reuters.com/legal/legalindustry/california-lawmakers-pull-plug-legal-industry-reforms-2022-08-26/.

[39] *See* Sam Skolnik, *ABA Sides Against Opening Law Firms Up to New Competition*, BLOOMBERG LAW (Aug. 9, 2022), https://news.bloomberglaw.com/business-and-practice/aba-sides-against-opening-law-firms-up-to-new-competition.

B. Litigation

Regulatory reform isn't the only Jenga piece that's been pulled out. Litigation is also having an impact.

1. Upsolve

In April 2019, the nonprofit organization Upsolve challenged New York's UPL statute as it applied to its program.[40] Upsolve provides a free web-based platform that helps low-income individuals file for Chapter 7 bankruptcy without an attorney. (Upsolve's CEO Rohan Pavuluri is not a lawyer.) Upsolve also wants to be able to help its users in debt collection actions. It would do so by having trained workers, who are not lawyers, "provide free legal advice on whether and how to respond to a debt collection lawsuit."[41]

Upsolve's planned conduct would trigger New York's UPL statute.[42] Upsolve argued that New York's ban on the unlicensed practice of law violated the First Amendment by restricting free speech.[43] The federal district court ruled in favor of Upsolve, finding that New York's ban on the unlicensed practice of law was unconstitutional because it violated the First Amendment by being overbroad and infringing on Upsolve's free speech rights.[44] New York's attorney general has appealed to the Second Circuit.

2. South Carolina case

The South Carolina NAACP has filed a federal lawsuit challenging that state's UPL statute.[45] The NAACP wants its members to be able to provide limited but critical guidance to low-income tenants facing eviction, like explaining the eviction process, possible defenses, and the importance of requesting a hearing before losing their homes by default. Like Upsolve, the NAACP believes that citizens have a First

[40] *See* Upsolve, Inc. v. James, 604 F. Supp. 3d 97 (S.D.N.Y. 2022).

[41] Jonathan Petts, *How Do You Answer a Summons for Debt Without an Attorney?*, UPSOLVE (Aug. 21, 2024), https://upsolve.org/learn/should-answer-summons/#.

[42] *See* N.Y. JUD. LAW. § 476-a.

[43] *See Upsolve*, 604 F. Supp. at 109–10.

[44] *See id.* at 120.

[45] *See* S.C. State Conference of the NAACP v. Kohn, No. 3:22-01007-MGL, 2023 U.S. Dist. LEXIS 4977 (D.S.C. Jan. 10, 2023) (denying motion to dismiss).

Amendment right to speak and associate by offering such guidance. Incidentally, you don't have to be a lawyer to be a magistrate who presides over eviction cases in South Carolina.[46]

The judge paused the case for the plaintiffs to petition the state supreme court to determine whether the intended conduct would violate South Carolina's prohibition on the unauthorized practice of law because the state supreme court has exclusive jurisdiction over interpreting what constitutes the practice of law in South Carolina.[47]

3. DOJ letter

The Antitrust Division of the U.S. Department of Justice (DOJ) has also weighed in on this issue. Recently, the DOJ submitted a letter in support of proposals to expand access to legal services in North Carolina.[48]

In the letter, the DOJ argued that consumers benefit from competition between lawyers and nonlawyers. It pointed out that with many legal services priced out of reach, lower-cost options are sorely needed. The DOJ noted that unlike at the federal level where antitrust is statutory, the North Carolina Constitution (adopted in December 1776) says that "monopolies are contrary to the genius of a free state and shall not be allowed."[49]

And the DOJ invoked the North Carolina Supreme Court, which has held that professional licensing restrictions cannot constitute "the creation of a monopoly or special privileges" and must instead be "an exercise of the [state's] police power for the protection of the public against incompetents and impostors." Thus, justifications for restraints on the delivery of legal services must be rooted in the protection of the public and not in the protection of lawyers from competition.

---

[46] *See* S.C. Code Ann. §§ 22-1-10(B)–(C).

[47] The ACLU has since settled the suit "in exchange for historical eviction records and timely access to all new eviction filings." *See NAACP v. Kohn*, ACLU S.C. (Aug. 2023), https://www.aclusc.org/en/cases/naacp-v-kohn.

[48] *See* Letter from Maggie Goodlander, Deputy Assistant Att'y Gen., Antitrust Div., U.S. Dep't of Just., to N.C. Gen. Assembly (Feb. 14, 2023), https://www.justice.gov/d9/pages/attachments/2023/06/14/414424.pdf.

[49] *See id.* at 2 (quoting N.C. Const. art. 1, § XXIII).

Federal agencies have long allowed nonlawyers to appear in proceedings, from Patent and Trademark tribunals to immigration courts.[50]

C. The Other Stuff

Then there is the other stuff. The state chief justices have become fed up. A new committee of the Conference of Chief Justices will be targeting the barriers to providing better service to people with civil justice problems. They worry that the civil justice crisis undermines all of their work.[51]

Frontline Justice is a newly launched bipartisan national effort to reform civil justice work and workers.

And the public can play a tremendous role. When the Arizona Supreme Court was working on its regulatory reform package, it held public meetings and sought public feedback by survey. Lawyers surveyed about the reforms were overwhelmingly against them. But the public surveys produced the opposite results, and that input played a significant role in the success of reform.[52]

And finally, the disrupter of all disrupters is generative AI, which I think could knock the tower over. Large language models (LLMs) are already transforming the business and practice of law, and legal education isn't far off. LLMs are automating many of the repetitive tasks that lawyers do, including analyzing data sets and writing code. GPT-4, an LLM released in March 2023, scored in the top 10 percent of takers of the Unified Bar Exam, and it did so in six minutes. This technology will democratize legal information. It can even a lot of playing fields.

---

[50] *See, e.g., Immigration Court Practice Manual*, ch. 2, §§ 1, 4, 5, 8, 9, https://www.justice.gov/eoir/reference-materials/ic/chapter-2/1 (section 1(a) citing and linking to the remaining relevant sections).

[51] *See Perspectives on Transforming Civil Justice in the United States*, NORC 1, 47 (Jan. 2020), https://www.norc.org/content/dam/norc-org/pdfs/NORC1924%20Civil%20Justice%20Report%20final%2030January.2020%20V3.pdf.

[52] "An overwhelming 80.3% of the public supported the proposal that was adopted as Legal Paraprofessionals." *Legal Services Reforms, Legal Paraprofessionals (LP): Questions and Answers*, ARIZ. JUDICIAL BRANCH, https://www.azcourts.gov/accesstolegalservices/Questions-and-Answers/lp (click "Does the public support the concept of Legal Paraprofessionals?") (last visited Aug. 24, 2024).

Of course, there will be problems to solve along the way. If AI learns from biased data (which are a lot of data), it learns biases. But humans who make decisions in courts right now also have biases. And there is no code to run to fix those. And there are many unanswered legal questions. Would TikToking the prompts you used in GPT-4 to respond to your eviction notice constitute the unlicensed practice of law? What about the technologists who built the models that can train on legal information and then answer legal questions?[53] Many of these questions remain untested and uncertain.

Conclusion: Constitution Day

Why am I talking about this on Constitution Day?

Some meat-and-potatoes constitutional questions are wrapped up in the unlicensed practice of law challenges. These restrictions can infringe on First Amendment freedoms of speech, press, assembly, and petitioning the government. But I have something more fundamental in mind.

The rule of law is an idea built on a foundation of public confidence. What if the public loses confidence? Today, about 1,400 eviction cases were heard in the City of Detroit district court. Most of them were heard without lawyers. Many defendants didn't show up. Some had legal defenses. Others didn't but might have been able to work out a resolution that would have made a difference. Tomorrow, there will be another 1,400.[54]

* * *

During the COVID-19 pandemic, courts across the country pivoted to remote proceedings to continue to administer justice and keep the public safe. It was easier in some places than in others. And we learned a lot. We were running an experiment, whether or not we were interested in the results. We learned that default rates in cases

---

[53] *See, e.g.,* Pa. Bar Ass'n Comm. on Legal Ethics & Prof'l Resp. & Philadelphia Bar Ass'n Prof'l Guidance Comm., Joint Formal Op. 2024-200 Ethical Issues Regarding the Use of Artificial Intelligence 13 (May 22, 2024), https://www.pabar.org/Members/catalogs/Ethics%20Opinions/Formal/Joint%20Formal%20Opinion%202024-200.pdf.

[54] This information comes from a conversation I had with the chief judge of that court, the Hon. William C. McConico, in preparation for this address.

where people must navigate courts without lawyers dropped significantly when people had remote options for appearing.[55]

In retrospect, this seems obvious. Yes, technology can be a barrier for some people. But other barriers can be more substantial: transportation, childcare, a job with no time off, a disability. A car is more expensive than a smartphone.

Legal aid lawyers estimated that their ability to provide representation increased sevenfold when they could eliminate transportation and parking. More people showed up for jury duty than ever.

When it was safe to go back into courts, we had choices. We could go back to doing things the way we always had. Or we could take account of these new data, which showed that giving people a remote option made it far more likely they could resolve their disputes, more likely they would be represented, and more likely they could serve as jurors. Courts make the rules about *how* they administer justice. With some exceptions, they returned to doing things the way they always had.

In Michigan, we published a proposed rule change and took public input on whether to continue some hearings remotely. The public hearing on the rule change was the most attended public hearing in my 10 years on the bench. The court adopted the rule change, but with dissents.[56] I responded to my dissenting colleagues in a concurrence to the order, which ended with this: "The judiciary should not and cannot be the only institution that does not benefit from the lessons learned from the COVID-19 pandemic and the accelerated innovation it brought. More importantly, the public who have traditionally been excluded from full participation in many of our courts should not lose a valuable new tool for accessing justice. Ours is a government instituted for the people, after all."[57]

---

[55] *See* Bridget Mary McCormack, *Why Do Lawyers and Judges Hate Evidence?*, ABA LITIG. J. (Aug. 13, 2023), https://www.americanbar.org/groups/litigation/resources/litigation-journal/2023-summer/remote-proceedings-why-lawyers-judges-hate-evidence/.

[56] *See* Order, ADM File No. 2020-08 (Mich. Aug. 10, 2022) (McCormack, C.J., concurring), https://www.courts.michigan.gov/4a42b2/siteassets/rules-instructions-administrative-orders/proposed-and-recently-adopted-orders-on-admin-matters/adopted-orders/2020-08_2022-08-10_formor_pandemicamdts.pdf, at 22. For the dissenting opinions, see *id.* at 22–24 (Zahra, J.); *id.* at 24–39 (Viviano, J.).

[57] *Id.* at 22.

Public confidence in courts is declining. It is declining in federal courts more than state courts, but in state courts too.[58] The rule of law is just a set of ideas that is only as strong as the public's confidence in those ideas. When the rules are hostile to you, you might stop caring about the rules. We all have a tremendous amount at stake when the rule of law is wobbly. Lawyers and judges are uniquely positioned to shore it up. If we want to. I hope we do.

Happy Constitution Day.

---

[58] *See The State of State Courts: A 2022 NCSC Public Opinion Survey*, Nat'l Ctrs. for State Cts. 4–6 (2022), https://www.ncsc.org/__data/assets/pdf_file/0019/85204/ SSC_2022_Presentation.pdf.

Chevron Deference Is Dead, Long Live Deference

Jack M. Beermann*

Finally!

Fourteen years ago,[1] I urged the Supreme Court to overrule its *Chevron*[2] decision. I argued that the Court should revert to applying the factors enunciated in the Court's pre–Administrative Procedure Act (APA) *Skidmore* decision, which set out the appropriate level of deference to executive branch legal interpretations.[3] In *Loper Bright Enterprises v. Raimondo*[4] and a companion case,[5] the Supreme Court did exactly that. In this article, I will explain and analyze both the Court's decision to abandon the *Chevron* rule of deference and what the demise of *Chevron* deference might mean for the future of judicial review of federal agency regulation. In doing so, I feel a bit like Brutus eulogizing Julius Caesar. *Chevron* was an important doctrine in administrative law, and it may have seemed like a good idea when it was decided. But over the years it proved to be at best a distraction from the regulatory issues at stake, and at worst a fundamental mistake.

---

* Philip S. Beck Professor of Law, Boston University School of Law. Apologies to Michael Herz for the similarity of the title to the title of his excellent essay Chevron *Is Dead, Long Live* Chevron, 115 Colum. L. Rev. 1867 (2015). Thanks to Brad Baranowski and Ron Cass for comments and suggestions on this article and to Barry Hartman and Minu Nagashunmugam of K&L Gates for alerting me to timing issues discussed in this article. Thanks also to Niamh Lang, Boston University School of Law Class of 2026, for excellent research assistance.

[1] *See* Jack M. Beermann, *End the Failed* Chevron *Experiment Now: How* Chevron *Has Failed and Why It Can and Should Be Overruled*, 42 Conn. L. Rev. 779 (2010).

[2] *See* Chevron U.S.A., Inc. v. Nat. Res. Def. Council, 467 U.S. 837 (1984).

[3] *See* Skidmore v. Swift & Co., 323 U.S. 134, 140 (1944).

[4] Loper Bright Enters. v. Raimondo, 144 S. Ct. 2244 (2024).

[5] Relentless, Inc. v. Dep't of Com., 144 S. Ct. 2244 (2024) (decided together with *Loper Bright*).

The *Chevron* rule, in brief, instructed reviewing courts to defer to reasonable agency constructions of ambiguous or incomplete regulatory statutes. The *Loper Bright* Court relied primarily on the language of the APA to hold that *Chevron* deference is unlawful. But in my view, *Chevron* deference was fatally flawed for a multitude of reasons besides its inconsistency with the language of the APA. These reasons include *Chevron's* lack of clarity on key issues and the numerous qualifications, side-issues, and exceptions that *Chevron* spawned. But the *Loper Bright* Court overstated its case against *Chevron* deference when it claimed that deference to agencies on questions of law was inconsistent with "the settled pre-APA understanding that deciding such questions was exclusively a judicial function."[6] In fact, as the *Loper Bright* opinion itself makes clear, the Supreme Court had approved a measure of deference to agency statutory interpretations well before both *Chevron* and the enactment of the APA. That pre-APA level of deference is consistent with the language of the APA, and the *Loper Bright* Court itself explicitly endorsed continuing deference under pre-*Chevron* standards.[7]

The demise of *Chevron* deference standing alone may turn out to be much less important for the future of administrative law and agency regulation than many believe. The Court explicitly approved of deference under the *Skidmore* factors, which instruct reviewing courts to "resort for guidance, even on legal questions" to "the interpretations and opinions of the relevant agency, made in pursuance of official duty and based upon specialized experience."[8] Further, the Court had already created numerous limitations to the reach of *Chevron* deference and, as the Court noted, it had not deferred under *Chevron* in nearly a decade. *Chevron* deference was already a rather weak doctrine, even in some lower federal courts. More fundamentally, many of the cases in which the government could have argued for *Chevron* deference pre–*Loper Bright* will now be decided under the relatively deferential APA standards of review such as arbitrary, capricious, and substantial evidence. Thus, agency action will continue to receive deference on judicial review. In any event, whether *Chevron* was the deciding factor in many or even any important cases is doubtful. In numerous

---

[6] *Loper Bright*, 144 S. Ct. at 2261 (internal quotation marks and citation omitted).

[7] *Id.* at 2262 (citing *Skidmore*, 323 U.S. 134).

[8] *Id.* at 2259 (internal quotation marks, citations, and ellipsis omitted).

instances, the Supreme Court and other courts overturned agency statutory constructions even while *Chevron* was good law.

While the demise of *Chevron* itself may have little material effect on federal regulatory power, those who believe that robust federal regulation is important for advancing and preserving social welfare may still have cause for concern. *Loper Bright* sends out anti-regulatory signals, and its effects may interact with other recent anti-regulatory Court decisions. The ascension of the major questions doctrine,[9] the Court's narrow reading of agency authority over "waters of the United States,"[10] its allowance of challenges to administrative rules even decades after they were finalized,[11] and its recognition of a right to a trial by jury in some agency civil enforcement actions[12] could all significantly reduce the scope of agency power.[13] For those skeptical of the social value of federal regulation, *Loper Bright* is cause for optimism. That is especially true if Justice Neil Gorsuch's concurring opinion—aimed at weakening the role of precedent in judicial decisionmaking—signals that the Court is willing to revisit additional fundamental pro-regulatory administrative law doctrines.

I. Past as Prologue

To put *Loper Bright* into perspective, it is first necessary to review (briefly) when and how *Chevron* deference arose and what happened to it between its appearance and its demise. In 1980, the Supreme Court seemed to be on the verge of reducing the degree to which Congress may delegate discretionary authority to administrative agencies. At the time, the Court had not invalidated a federal statute for excessive delegation since 1935.[14] But a plurality of four Justices

---

[9] *See* Mila Sohoni, *The Major Questions Quartet*, 136 HARV. L. REV. 262, 263–64 (2022).

[10] *See* Sackett v. EPA, 143 S. Ct. 1322, 1336 (2023) (limiting the statutory jurisdiction of the Environmental Protection Agency (EPA) over "waters of the United States" to include only "streams, oceans, rivers, and lakes") (internal quotation marks omitted); Craig B. Brinkerhoff et al., *Ephemeral Stream Water Contributions to United States Drainage Networks*, 384 SCIENCE 1476 (2024) (concluding that the *Sackett* decision leaves many waterways unprotected from damaging pollution).

[11] *See* Corner Post, Inc. v. Bd. of Governors of the Fed. Rsrv. Sys., 144 S. Ct. 2440 (2024).

[12] SEC v. Jarkesy, 144 S. Ct. 2117 (2024).

[13] For a more general view of the Court's recent suppression of agency regulatory power, see Jack M. Beermann, *The Anti-Innovation Supreme Court: Major Questions, Delegation,* Chevron, *and More*, 65 WM. & MARY L. REV. 1265 (2024).

[14] *See* Cass R. Sunstein, *Nondelegation Canons*, 67 U. CHI. L. REV. 315, 318 n.19 (2000).

invoked the possibility as support for a narrow reading of agency authority in a case concerning the Occupational Safety and Health Administration (OSHA). An opinion authored by Justice John Paul Stevens rejected OSHA's understanding of the scope of its own authority to regulate workplace exposure to suspected carcinogens, proclaiming that "[i]f the Government were correct . . . the statute would make such a 'sweeping delegation of legislative power' that it might be unconstitutional[.]"[15] A fifth Justice, William Rehnquist, would have invalidated the statute as an unconstitutional delegation of legislative power to the agency.[16] Then-Justice Rehnquist's primary normative justification for his view was that "Congress [is] the governmental body best suited and most obligated to make the choice confronting us in this litigation."[17] Delegation of regulatory authority to agencies seemed to be under attack by a majority of the Court.

However, the Court did not act on its skeptical view of delegations of regulatory authority. Just a few years later, in an opinion again written by Justice Stevens, the Court embraced judicial deference to agency interpretations of the statutes they administer.[18] In his opinion for the Court, Justice Stevens announced what would become an iconic two-step process for judicial review of agency construction of statutes it administers:

> First, always, is the question whether Congress has directly spoken to the precise question at issue. If the intent of Congress is clear, that is the end of the matter; for the court, as well as the agency, must give effect to the unambiguously expressed intent of Congress. If, however, the court determines Congress has not directly addressed the precise question at issue, the court does not simply impose its own construction on the statute, as would be necessary in the absence of an administrative interpretation.

[15] Indus. Union Dep't v. Am. Petroleum Inst., 448 U.S. 607, 646 (1980) (plurality opinion) (quoting A.L.A. Schechter Poultry Corp. v. United States, 295 U.S. 495, 539 (1935)).

[16] *Id.* at 675 (Rehnquist, J., concurring in the judgment).

[17] *Id.* at 672. The following year, Justice Rehnquist (this time joined by Chief Justice Warren Burger) argued that the Occupational Safety and Health Act unconstitutionally delegated legislative authority to the Department of Labor. Am. Textile Mfrs. Inst., Inc. v. Donovan, 452 U.S. 490, 543 (1981) (Rehnquist, J., dissenting).

[18] *See Chevron*, 467 U.S. at 865–66.

> Rather, if the statute is silent or ambiguous with respect to the specific issue, the question for the court is whether the agency's answer is based on a permissible construction of the statute.[19]

Rather than rein in agency discretion, the *Chevron* opinion embraced it. Indeed, the opinion even celebrated agency discretion as a way to keep unelected judges from intervening in what ought to be agency decisions. The opinion described judges as "not experts in the field," contrasting them with agencies that make decisions in light of both policy and political considerations.[20] The obvious tension between the Court's then-recently expressed delegation concerns and its new *Chevron* doctrine did not go unnoticed.[21] Although Justice Rehnquist did not participate in *Chevron*, Chief Justice Warren Burger did, and neither Chief Justice Burger nor Justice (later Chief Justice) Rehnquist expressed disagreement with the *Chevron* doctrine when the doctrine appeared in later cases.[22]

What changed after 1980 that led conservatives on the Court who might otherwise be concerned about delegation of power to agencies to accept judicial deference to agencies' legal interpretations of their own authority? Cynics supposed that it was the election of Ronald Reagan and his administration's efforts to ease federal regulatory burdens.[23] Judicial deference to Reagan's agencies allowed

---

[19] *Id.* at 842–43.

[20] *Id.* at 865.

[21] *See* Richard J. Pierce, Jr., *The Role of Constitutional and Political Theory in Administrative Law*, 64 Tex L. Rev. 469, 506 (1985).

[22] Justice Rehnquist never expressed disagreement with the *Chevron* doctrine. He also applied it at least once, cited it as governing law, and joined opinions applying it. *See* Rust v. Sullivan, 500 U.S. 173, 184 (1991) (Rehnquist, C.J.) (upholding agency's "plausible construction of the plain language of the statute" and noting that the construction "does not otherwise conflict with Congress' expressed intent"); Reno v. Koray, 515 U.S. 50, 61 (1995) (Rehnquist, C.J.) (citing *Chevron* for rule granting deference to an agency's "permissible construction of the statute."); Yellow Transp., Inc. v. Michigan, 537 U.S. 36, 46–48 (2002) (O'Connor, J., joined by, inter alia, Rehnquist, C.J.) (applying *Chevron* and upholding agency statutory construction).

[23] *See* Gregory A. Elinson & Jonathan S. Gould, *The Politics of Deference*, 77 Vand. L. Rev. 475, 508–15 (2022) (describing how conservatives embraced *Chevron* deference while liberals opposed it).

them to interpret and even reinterpret regulatory statutes to accommodate deregulation. Similarly, in *Chevron*'s early days, Republican-appointed judges seemed to embrace *Chevron* while Democratic appointees, as *Chevron* scholar Tom Merrill put it, "were having second thoughts."[24] Commentary also seemed to run along liberal/conservative lines, with newly appointed Justice Antonin Scalia leading the conservative charge in favor of *Chevron* deference.[25]

The tide of political and legal opinion on *Chevron* deference began to noticeably turn during Barack Obama's administration, when liberals on and off the bench embraced *Chevron* as supporting that administration's regulatory efforts. Conservatives, by contrast, realized that they had created a monster with the potential to overcome judicial resistance to innovative and expansive regulation.[26] Over the years, Republican opposition to *Chevron* deference became strong enough to lead the House of Representatives to repeatedly pass bills abolishing it, but none of those efforts passed in the Senate.[27] The House bills bore the title "The Separation of Powers Restoration Acts," reflecting the view that deference to agency statutory interpretation usurped judicial power in favor of excessive executive discretion.[28]

In the latter half of the 40 years during which *Chevron* deference was the law, the conservative Supreme Court displayed increasing discomfort with the doctrine. Opposition to the robust regulatory initiatives that *Chevron* deference seemed to facilitate led the Court to limit the doctrine's scope. During this era, the

[24] See Thomas W. Merrill, *The Story of* Chevron: *The Making of an Accidental Landmark*, 66 ADMIN. L. REV. 253, 280 (2014). More than second thoughts, Judge Harry Edwards of the D.C. Circuit opined that *Chevron* was inconsistent with separation of powers principles. *See* CSX Transp. v. United States, 867 F.2d 1439, 1445 (D.C. Cir. 1989) (Edwards, J., dissenting) (observing that the *Chevron* rule "appears to violate separation of powers principles" and usurp the role of the courts to conduct statutory interpretation).

[25] Antonin Scalia, *Judicial Deference to Administrative Interpretations of Law*, 1989 DUKE L.J. 511. The best example of an early attack on *Chevron* from a liberal perspective is Cynthia Farina, *Statutory Interpretation and the Balance of Power in the Administrative State*, 89 COLUM. L. REV. 452 (1989). By contrast, as early as 1985, liberal commentator Dick Pierce praised *Chevron* as a way to ensure that "policy choices [are] made by the most politically accountable branch of government, and . . . the judiciary is the least politically accountable branch." Pierce, *supra* note 21, at 506.

[26] *See* Elinson & Gould, *supra* note 23, at 523–30.

[27] *See* Beermann, *supra* note 13, at 1282 (describing legislation designed to overrule *Chevron* from 2016–2023).

[28] *See id.*

Court created exceptions, prerequisites, and competing doctrines, making it less and less likely that agency interpretations would receive *Chevron* deference.[29] These limitations included a rule known as "*Chevron* step zero," which limited *Chevron* deference to agency action pursuant to relatively formal procedures.[30] Other limitations included a rule that *Chevron* deference does not apply in extraordinary cases[31] and a requirement that reviewing courts must apply all of the "traditional tools of statutory construction" before moving to *Chevron* step two and deferring.[32]

More fundamentally, the Court's major questions doctrine means that on important matters, courts resolve doubts about agency authority against the agency without resorting to conventional judicial review of the agency's interpretation of its enabling statute.[33] Eventually, the Court itself simply stopped applying *Chevron* or even citing it in cases which seemingly implicated *Chevron* deference.[34]

By the time *Loper Bright* reached the Supreme Court, *Chevron* deference was virtually irrelevant in that Court. And it had lost much of its vitality in some lower federal courts, despite complaints that it was being applied uncritically by panels at the courts of appeals.[35] With several conservative Justices expressing doubts about the wisdom of *Chevron* deference, it seemed only a matter of time before the Supreme Court either overruled *Chevron* or further confined it, as it had with a related form of deference in 2019.[36]

---

[29] *See generally* Beermann, *supra* note 1, at 810–48.

[30] *See* United States v. Mead Corp., 533 U.S. 218 (2001) (limiting *Chevron* deference in most cases to agency rulemaking and agency formal adjudication).

[31] FDA v. Brown & Williamson Tobacco Corp., 529 U.S. 120, 159 (2000); King v. Burwell, 576 U.S. 473, 485 (2015).

[32] *See* Epic Sys. Corp. v. Lewis, 584 U.S. 497, 521 (2018).

[33] *See* West Virginia v. EPA, 597 U.S. 697, 723 (2022) (in cases involving major questions, agency must point to "clear congressional authorization" for the power it claims) (citation and internal quotation marks omitted).

[34] *See* Am. Hosp. Ass'n v. Becerra, 142 S. Ct. 1896 (2022); Beermann, *supra* note 13, at 1281 & n.65.

[35] *See* Solar Energy Indus. Ass'n v. FERC, 59 F.4th 1287, 1297–98 (D.C. Cir. 2023) (Walker, J., concurring in part and dissenting in part); *see also* Isaiah McKinney, *The* Chevron *Ball Ended at Midnight, but the Circuits Are Still Two-Stepping by Themselves*, YALE J. REGUL. NOTICE & COMMENT BLOG (Dec. 18, 2022), https://perma.cc/V4AD-B8KW.

[36] *See* Kisor v. Wilkie, 588 U.S. 558 (2019).

II. *Loper Bright*

In *Loper Bright* and a companion case,[37] the Supreme Court granted certiorari "limited to the question whether *Chevron* should be overruled or clarified."[38] Both cases involved a simple legal question: Did the National Marine Fisheries Service (NMFS) have statutory authority to require Atlantic Ocean herring fishing vessel operators to pay for onboard observers who monitor compliance with fishery management requirements? Because the relevant statutes explicitly required *other* vessels to pay for monitors, the operators had a strong, but not conclusive, statutory construction argument that the relevant statutes did *not* authorize a requirement for them to pay.[39] However, both the D.C. and First Circuits upheld the NMFS's payment requirement under *Chevron*.[40] That the Supreme Court limited its review to *Chevron* and did not grant certiorari to review the two decisions on the statutory merits heightened the expectation that the Court was finally going to address the future of *Chevron* deference.

On June 28, 2024, the Court issued its decision. In an opinion by Chief Justice John Roberts, the Court left no doubt that *Chevron* deference is dead, proclaiming that "*Chevron* is overruled."[41] A statement to this effect was required to prevent lower courts from continuing to apply *Chevron*. According to black letter law, unless and until the Supreme Court announces that a decision is overruled, lower federal courts and state courts are required to apply that decision—even if it seems that the Court itself no longer would.[42]

---

[37] *Loper Bright*, 144 S. Ct. at 2257. The Court appears to have taken both cases—*Loper Bright* and *Relentless, Inc.*—so that Justice Ketanji Brown Jackson, who recused herself in *Loper Bright*, could participate in considering whether *Chevron* should be overruled.

[38] *Loper Bright*, 144 S. Ct. at 2257.

[39] The fact that the statute itself required some vessels to pay for monitors is not logically inconsistent with an implicit power in the NMFS to require other vessels to pay, but it suggests that Congress may have intended that a payment requirement was limited to those mentioned in the statute.

[40] *See* Loper Bright Enters. v. Raimondo, 45 F.4th 359, 368–69 (D.C. Cir. 2022); Relentless, Inc. v. U.S. Dep't of Com., 62 F.4th 621, 633–34 (1st Cir. 2023). The First Circuit did not specify whether it was applying *Chevron* step one or step two, concluding that either way, the agency had the authority to require payment. *Relentless*, 62 F.4th at 633–34.

[41] *Loper Bright*, 144 S. Ct. at 2273.

[42] Agostini v. Felton, 521 U.S. 203, 238 (1997); *see also* Jack M. Beermann, Loper Bright *and the Future of* Chevron *Deference*, 65 WM. & MARY L. REV. ONLINE 1, 9–10 (2024).

The original justification for *Chevron* was that statutory silence or ambiguity indicates Congress's intent to delegate interpretive authority to the administering agency. But the *Loper Bright* Court batted away that justification as a "fiction."[43] Now, the federal courts know that when they are reviewing an agency's interpretation of a statute, *Chevron* deference is no longer an acceptable mode of analysis. To put the final nail in *Chevron*'s coffin, just a few days after issuing its decision, the Court remanded nine lower-court decisions applying *Chevron* for reconsideration in light of *Loper Bright*.[44]

The primary basis for the Court's decision to overrule *Chevron* was the language of the APA, which instructs courts conducting judicial review to "decide all relevant questions of law [and] interpret . . . statutory provisions."[45] The Court read this section of the APA to require *non*deferential judicial review of legal questions. And the Court found further support for this reading by comparing this section to other APA provisions specifying deferential standards of review only for "agency policymaking and factfinding."[46] Thus, although the Court also mentioned *Chevron*'s indeterminacy and unworkability,[47] *Loper Bright* was not a case in which the Court overruled a precedent primarily because it proved, over time, to be unworkable or out of step with other legal developments. Rather, *Loper Bright* found, akin to the *Dobbs* decision overruling *Roe v. Wade*, that *Chevron* was "wrong from the start."[48]

---

[43] *Loper Bright*, 144 S. Ct. at 2268.

[44] *See* Supreme Court Order List (July 2, 2024), https://www.supremecourt.gov/orders/courtorders/070224zor_2co3.pdf.

[45] 5 U.S.C. § 706; *see Loper Bright*, 144 S. Ct. at 2261.

[46] *Loper Bright*, 144 S. Ct. at 2261 (citing 5 U.S.C. §§ 706(2)(A), (2)(E)).

[47] *Id.* at 2270–71.

[48] Dobbs v. Jackson Women's Health Org., 597 U.S. 215, 231 (2022). In addition to the plain language of the APA, the Court relied on the APA's legislative history. The Court cited House and Senate Committee Reports and floor statements by one of the APA's leading proponents, all to the effect that Congress expected courts to use their independent judgment on questions of statutory interpretation arising in judicial review cases. *See Loper Bright*, 144 S. Ct. at 2262 (referring to House and Senate Reports and floor statements in Congress on the APA). It remains to be seen whether resort to legislative history will become routine now that Justice Scalia is no longer around. Justice Scalia would often remind the Court that legislative reports lack the status of enacted law and that references to legislative history, and especially to floor statements, are akin to looking into a crowd and finding your friends. *See, e.g.,* Conroy v. Aniskoff, 507 U.S. 511, 519 (1993) (Scalia, J., concurring in the judgment) (attributing the "friends" comment to Circuit Judge Harold Leventhal).

The Court characterized the APA as incorporating a "settled pre-APA understanding that deciding such questions [of statutory meaning] was 'exclusively a judicial function.'"[49] It is a common tool of statutory construction that when a statute is enacted, it presumptively incorporates well-established preexisting legal principles unless the statute explicitly says otherwise.[50] The problem with this line of reasoning in *Loper Bright* is that when the APA was enacted in 1946, it was far from clear that courts would presumptively exercise independent judgment over statutory construction issues in cases involving agency action.

Two well-known decisions issued in 1944, *Hearst Publications*[51] and *Skidmore*,[52] held that reviewing courts owed some deference to an agency's legal conclusions. In *Hearst*, the Court granted strong deference to the National Labor Relations Board (NLRB) in reviewing that agency's application of the law to facts.[53] And in *Skidmore*, the Court determined that an agency's legal views are entitled to "respect" when an agency with jurisdiction has opined on a statutory matter arising in litigation between two private parties. In that situation, *Skidmore* held that the court adjudicating the case may resort

---

[49] *Loper Bright*, 144 S. Ct. at 2258 (quoting United States v. Am. Trucking Ass'ns, 310 U.S. 534, 544 (1940)).

[50] This tool of construction is, for example, the basis for the Court's recognition of official immunities in cases against government officials arising under 42 U.S.C. § 1983. Even though the language of that statute imposes liability on "every person" who injures another person while violating their constitutional rights, the Court has held that Congress intended to preserve well-established common-law immunities. This means that judges, legislators, and prosecutors are absolutely immune from damages and that all other officials enjoy a qualified immunity. *See* Jack M. Beermann, *A Critical Approach to Section 1983 with Special Attention to Sources of Law*, 42 STAN. L. REV. 51, 66 (1989).

[51] NLRB v. Hearst Publ'ns, 322 U.S. 111 (1944).

[52] Skidmore v. Swift & Co., 323 U.S. 134 (1944).

[53] *Hearst*, 322 U.S. at 131 (holding that a state-law definition of "employee" did not govern NLRB's determination of employee status, and that "where the question is one of specific application of a broad statutory term in a proceeding in which the agency administering the statute must determine it initially, the reviewing court's function is limited. . . . [T]he Board's determination . . . is to be accepted if it has 'warrant in the record' and a reasonable basis in law").

to the agency's legal views "for guidance."[54] Further, a pre-APA report by the Attorney General's Committee on Administrative Procedures, formed in 1939 by President Franklin Roosevelt and chaired by renowned administrative law Professor Walter Gellhorn, opined, "Even on questions of law [independent judicial] judgment seems not to be compelled."[55] Whatever these relatively vague characterizations mean, they do not establish a settled practice of judicial independence that should be presumed to have been incorporated by the Congress that enacted the APA. The Court would have done better to stick to the statutory language and stress the doctrinal mess that *Chevron* had created in its 40-year life.

The Chief Justice's opinion in *Loper Bright* has several additional notable aspects. Its discussion of the merits of *Chevron* deference begins with references to Article III of the Constitution, *The Federalist Papers*, *Marbury v. Madison*, and other early cases. All these sources indicate that the Framers and early jurists expected that "the final 'interpretation of the laws' would be 'the proper and peculiar province of the courts.'"[56] The opinion is a wishy-washy discussion of constitutional principles: The Court does not say flat out that *Chevron* was unconstitutional, which some have contended over the years.[57] In my view, the notion that *Chevron* was unconstitutional cannot be based on an originalist understanding of the separation of powers. Discretionary executive branch action is now subject to judicial review as codified

[54] *Skidmore*, 323 U.S. at 140 ("We consider that the rulings, interpretations and opinions of the Administrator under this Act, while not controlling upon the courts by reason of their authority, do constitute a body of experience and informed judgment to which courts and litigants may properly resort for guidance. The weight of such a judgment in a particular case will depend upon the thoroughness evident in its consideration, the validity of its reasoning, its consistency with earlier and later pronouncements, and all those factors which give it power to persuade, if lacking power to control.").

[55] Scalia, *supra* note 25, at 513 (quoting S. Doc. No. 8, 77th Cong., 1st Sess. 90–91 (1941)).

[56] *Loper Bright*, 144 S. Ct. at 2257 (quoting Federalist No. 78, at 525 (Alexander Hamilton) (Jacob Cooke ed., 1961) (citing, inter alia, Marbury v. Madison, 5 U.S. (1 Cranch) 137, 177 (1803) (Marshall, C.J.) and United States v. Dickson, 40 U.S. (15 Pet.) 141 (1841) (Story, J.)).

[57] *See* Clark Byse, *Judicial Review of Administrative Interpretation of Statutes: An Analysis of* Chevron's *Step Two*, 2 Admin. L.J. 255, 261 (1988); Philip Hamburger, Chevron *Bias*, 84 Geo. Wash. L. Rev. 1187 (2016); H. Rep. No. 114-622, at 4 (2016) (report on the Separation of Powers Restoration Act which would have overruled *Chevron*).

in the APA, but such action had been immune from judicial review from the time of the Founding until relatively recently.[58] Such review is necessary to control executive excess, but it is not supported by any plausible originalist constitutional understanding. Further, it does not appear that the *Loper Bright* Court intended to cast doubt on the constitutionality of statutes in which Congress has expressly granted agencies the power to define statutory terms. Although it may have been irresistible to the Court's conservative supermajority, the Court should have left Article III and the separation of powers out of the discussion unless it was willing to base its decision on constitutional law and rewrite the history of the law of the United States in the name of originalism.

In its *Loper Bright* opinion, the Court noted that the dissent's primary argument for preserving *Chevron* turns on "*Kisor*izing"[59] it. A reference to the Supreme Court's earlier *Kisor* decision, this would have meant retaining *Chevron* but emphasizing that courts should defer only when they are unable to discern Congress's meaning after exhausting all of the tools of statutory construction.[60] Had the lower courts followed the Supreme Court's lead over the last decade and rigorously applied all of the traditional tools of statutory interpretation, the scope of *Chevron* deference might have been narrow enough that the attacks on it would have subsided. However, in the Court's view, the risk was too great that lower courts would continue to find circumstances in which Congress has left "policy space" for agencies in the form of statutory silence and ambiguity.[61] In fact, the majority simply denied that a reviewing court would ever be unable to arrive at a judgment concerning a statute's "best meaning."[62] This understanding is completely inconsistent with the basis of *Chevron* deference, that when courts are unable to determine

---

[58] *See Marbury*, 5 U.S. (1 Cranch) at 170 ("Questions, in their nature political, or which are, by the constitution and laws, submitted to the Executive, can never be made in this court.").

[59] *See* Kisor v. Wilkie, 588 U.S. 558 (2019) (requiring that a reviewing court exhaust the traditional tools of statutory construction before deferring to an agency construction of its own regulation).

[60] *See Loper Bright*, 144 S. Ct. at 2271.

[61] *See* Peter L. Strauss, *"Deference" Is Too Confusing — Let's Call Them "Chevron Space" and "Skidmore Weight,"* 112 COLUM. L. REV. 1143 (2012).

[62] *Id.*

a statute's meaning due to silence or ambiguity, they should defer to the agency's views on the meaning of the statute. *Chevron* and the *Loper Bright* majority's view of reality cannot exist in the same legal universe.

The Court next addressed whether the 40-year-old *Chevron* precedent should be preserved under principles of *stare decisis*. The Court held that *Chevron* was so plainly inconsistent with the language of the APA that the Court's obligation to obey Congress's instructions outweighed the strength of precedent. And the Court found additional flaws in *Chevron*'s workability. These included, most importantly, the lack of a clear understanding of when a statute is ambiguous. The Court also found that its own constant tinkering with the *Chevron* doctrine had made reliance on that doctrine impossible.[63] But even in the discussion of *stare decisis*, the Court's primary basis for overruling *Chevron* remained its conclusion that *Chevron* was simply inconsistent with a governing statute.

Justice Gorsuch detailed his own views on *stare decisis* in his concurring opinion in *Loper Bright*. These views are worth extended treatment in their own right, which is not possible in this article. In brief, he argued for relatively weak adherence to *stare decisis* based on the classical view of judicial decisionmaking in which the judge searches for a correct answer to a legal question in a preexisting universe of legal rules and principles.[64] To Justice Gorsuch, the judge's job is not to blindly follow precedents but rather to assess their validity, including their congruence with the overall fabric of the law and whether they are the product of the particular facts and arguments that led to them. In this sense, he adopted Karl Llewellyn's "grand style" of judging in which judges openly assess the persuasive value of precedent,[65] while at the same time characterizing law as composed of preexisting rules and principles with no judicial creativity in the mix.

---

[63] *Loper Bright*, 144 S. Ct. at 2272.

[64] *Id.* at 2276 (Gorsuch, J., concurring); *cf.* Roscoe Pound, *The Theory of Judicial Decision*, 36 HARV. L. REV. 641, 660 (1923) (describing an archaic view of the law as "something given absolutely by logic on a basis of authority [or] revealed absolutely and definitely by history [or] deducible infallibly from an absolute, fundamental metaphysically-given datum").

[65] KARL LLEWELLYN, THE COMMON LAW TRADITION 5 (1960).

Justice Gorsuch linked the willingness to reexamine precedents with judicial humility, reasoning that judges should not prioritize their previous decisions, or those of their predecessors, over the work of the legislature or the Framers of the Constitution.[66] The irony of this aspect of Justice Gorsuch's theory is self-evident; he is using modesty to justify increasing the power of judges to ignore, limit, or overrule precedents. This view undeniably increases the power of current judges, unless, I suppose, you believe that judges override precedents only to correct their predecessors' (or their own) errors by following preexisting legal rules that they have discovered through better reasoning. Justice Gorsuch's weaker version of *stare decisis* would reduce the ability of Congress to legislate in reliance on the Court's statutory precedents. In any event, Justice Gorsuch agreed with the majority's central conclusion that *Chevron* should be overruled because it was inconsistent with the APA. He added that the case for overruling *Chevron* is strengthened by the fact that "*Chevron* deference runs against mainstream currents in our law."[67]

Justice Gorsuch's concurrence espouses a premodern view of the importance of judicial independence to the rule of law. *Chevron*, by contrast, was based in part on a realistic and modern view of judicial behavior. For all its faults, one of *Chevron*'s central understandings was that politically insulated judges lacking technical expertise are likely to impose their own policy views when reviewing agency decisions on how to interpret ambiguous regulatory statutes or how to fill statutory gaps.[68] The *Chevron* Court characterized agency officials as being part of a "political branch of the Government," and agency decisionmaking as preferable to judicial decisionmaking. Justice Gorsuch's concurrence and the *Loper Bright* majority opinion ignore this central modern paradox: Federal judicial independence,

---

[66] *Loper Bright*, 144 S. Ct. at 2279 (Gorsuch, J., concurring).

[67] *Id.* at 2281.

[68] *Chevron*, 457 U.S. at 865 ("Courts must, in some cases, reconcile competing political interests, but not on the basis of the judges' personal policy preferences."); *see* Richard J. Pierce, Jr., Chevron *and Its Aftermath: Judicial Review of Agency Interpretations of Statutory Provisions*, 41 VAND. L. REV. 301, 313 (1988). Differences in ability or interpretive approaches cannot explain the oft-observed fact that liberal judges tend to interpret regulatory statutes more generously than conservative judges. But even under *Chevron*, deference to agency interpretations seemed to line up along those political lines. *See* Jack M. Beermann, Chevron *at the Roberts Court: Still Failing after All These Years*, 83 FORDHAM L. REV. 731, 733–38 (2014).

fundamental to the rule of law, allows unelected, unaccountable, and often highly partisan judges to impose their will[69] over the preferences of the government and the electorate. Pretending that judges are neutral arbiters of the law does not make it so.

Thus far, I have said little that did not enter into Justice Elena Kagan's dissenting opinion in *Loper Bright*. She complained, on behalf of the three-member liberal wing of the Court, that Congress would prefer agency resolution of issues implicating agency expertise.[70] She also argued that the Court had undervalued *stare decisis*. In her view, this consideration was especially strong because Congress, throughout *Chevron*'s 40-year reign, could have statutorily overruled *Chevron*. Congress presumably would have done so if it, as a body, had disagreed with the Court's assessment that Congress meant to delegate interpretive authority to agencies.[71] And she urged that, between courts and agencies, democratic accountability counsels in favor of agency power.[72] Finally, Justice Kagan argued that allowing agencies interpretive freedom is not inconsistent with the text of the APA, so long as that freedom is not exercised beyond the limits specified by Congress.[73]

Although I share the concern that overruling *Chevron* is part of a larger plan to prevent the federal government from engaging in what I consider important regulatory efforts, I remain unconvinced that *Chevron* was worth preserving. No matter how theoretically attractive agency primacy in regulatory decisionmaking may be, the *Chevron* doctrine as it developed was too unclear, manipulable, and ineffective to realize the potential it may have initially borne. In my view, *Skidmore* provides a simpler and at bottom clearer roadmap for reviewing courts to follow. However, there are causes for concern for the future of judicial review of both agency interpretive decisions and agency policy decisions. Let us turn to the possible future without *Chevron*.

---

[69] The mantra of the premodern view of judicial decisionmaking is that judges exercise judgment while the political branches impose their will. *See Loper Bright*, 144 S. Ct. at 2283 (Gorsuch, J., concurring); PHILIP HAMBURGER, IS ADMINISTRATIVE LAW UNLAWFUL 144 (2014).

[70] *Loper Bright*, 144 S. Ct. at 2294 (Kagan, J., dissenting).

[71] *Id.* at 2295.

[72] *Id.* at 2294.

[73] *Id.* at 2302. In my view, Justice Kagan understated the inconsistency between *Chevron* and the language of APA Section 706.

III. *Loper Bright* and the Future of Judicial Review of Agency Construction

What happens next? The best we can say at this point is "it depends." The fear from the pro-regulatory side is that the conservative Supreme Court, and conservative lower court judges, will use their power of independent review to read regulatory statutes narrowly and restrict agency power even more than they have already done in recent years.[74] Less conservative judges on the courts of appeals may be unable to prevent this, because even though relatively few cases reach the Supreme Court, challengers will continue to bring cases in sympathetic forums such as district courts in Texas and the Fifth Circuit. Further, as already noted, the Court remanded several cases to the courts of appeals for reconsideration in light of *Loper Bright*. Those cases may provide a good early test of *Loper Bright*'s effect. Whether agencies lose the remanded cases that they had won under *Chevron* will be more enlightening than the public speculation that has been rampant since *Loper Bright* was announced, including the views expressed here.

Another unanswered question is whether *Loper Bright* weakens the precedential status of the numerous cases decided over the last 40 years in which *Chevron* step two was applied to uphold an agency's statutory interpretation. Although that would seem to be a logical implication of overruling *Chevron*, in *Loper Bright* the Court insisted that cases decided under *Chevron* are still good law:

> [W]e do not call into question prior cases that relied on the *Chevron* framework. . . . Mere reliance on *Chevron* cannot constitute a "'special justification'" for overruling such a holding, because to say a precedent relied on *Chevron* is, at best, "just an argument that the precedent was wrongly decided[,]" . . . [which] is not enough to justify overruling a statutory precedent.[75]

---

[74] For an example of a very recent ruling that appears to limit agency regulatory authority, see *Ohio v. EPA*, 144 S. Ct. 2040 (2024) (granting stay of EPA Clean Air Act "good neighbor" rule due to agency's failure to address important public comments). This case was decided the day before *Loper Bright* and provoked a dissent from Justice Amy Coney Barrett, joined by Justices Sonia Sotomayor, Kagan, and Jackson. *See id.* at 2058 (Barrett, J., dissenting).

[75] *Loper Bright*, 144 S. Ct. at 2273.

It's not clear how this can be so, because in cases decided under *Chevron* step two, the reviewing court would not have determined the statute's best meaning. Further, *Loper Bright* concluded that *Chevron* "defie[d] the command of the APA" and "turn[ed] the statutory scheme for judicial review of agency action upside down."[76] This language indicates that *Chevron* was not just wrong but so fundamentally wrong that anything built on its foundation should also be questioned. When confronted with a renewed attack on an agency's action approved years or even decades before under *Chevron* step two, lower courts may feel empowered to ask whether, under *Loper Bright*, the earlier court wrongly ignored the statute's "best meaning" and deferred to an agency's second or third (or even fourth) best construction. It remains to be seen whether the courts, including the Supreme Court, will treat precedents based on *Chevron* step two as binding.

Another likely consequence of *Chevron*'s demise is that agencies will channel their decisions away from statutory issues and toward policy issues where the judicial review is governed by the relatively deferential "arbitrary or capricious" standard or the "substantial evidence" test. Further, the *Loper Bright* opinion leaves room for judicial deference to agency statutory construction under the pre-APA and pre-*Chevron* factors that were summarized best in the Supreme Court's *Skidmore* decision. And it remains to be seen whether *Loper Bright* signals the end of the agency flexibility that was built into the *Chevron* framework. The rest of this article explores these and other potential implications of the abandonment of *Chevron* deference.

A. Revival of Skidmore

Although it seems to be in tension with much of the opinion's reasoning, the *Loper Bright* Court acknowledged and appeared to approve of the pre-APA and pre-*Chevron* tradition of giving weight, even great weight, to agency interpretations of regulatory statutes.[77] Most important, the Court apparently revived what has been referred to as "*Skidmore* deference." As the *Loper Bright* Court put it, in *Skidmore* "the Court explained that the 'interpretations and opinions' of the relevant agency, 'made in pursuance of official duty' and 'based

---

[76] *Id.* at 2265.

[77] *See id.* at 2259.

upon . . . specialized experience,' 'constitute[d] a body of experience and informed judgment to which courts and litigants [could] properly resort for guidance,' even on legal questions."[78] *Skidmore* appears to have replaced *Chevron* as the governing deference standard.[79]

The *Loper Bright* Court's approval of deference to agency statutory construction seemed strongest when it addressed statutes that grant interpretative authority to agencies. The relevant passage is worth quoting:

> When the best reading of a statute is that it delegates discretionary authority to an agency, the role of the reviewing court under the APA is, as always, to independently interpret the statute and effectuate the will of Congress subject to constitutional limits. The court fulfills that role by recognizing constitutional delegations, "fix[ing] the boundaries of [the] delegated authority," . . . and ensuring the agency has engaged in "'reasoned decisionmaking'" within those boundaries, . . . By doing so, a court upholds the traditional conception of the judicial function that the APA adopts.[80]

This language characterizes deference to reasonable agency interpretations as consistent with the APA, at least when a regulatory statute leaves space for agency construction. According to *Loper Bright*, *Chevron*'s central error was that it viewed silence or ambiguity as the equivalent of a congressional delegation of interpretive authority to an administering agency. So perhaps the Court is not similarly hostile to agency construction pursuant to clearer delegation.

---

[78] *Id.* (quoting Skidmore v. Swift & Co., 323 U.S. 134, 139–40 (1944)) (alterations in original).

[79] In an earlier case in which the Court determined that *Chevron* did not apply, the Court similarly invoked *Skidmore* as the proper standard of review for agency constructions of ambiguous statutes. *See* United States v. Mead Corp., 533 U.S. 218, 234–35 (2001). In *Loper Bright*, the Court did not quote the entire *Skidmore* formulation of the factors relevant to deference to agency interpretations. But Justice Gorsuch did, lending credence to the view that the *Loper Bright* Court intended to revive *Skidmore. See Loper Bright*, 144 S. Ct. at 2284 (Gorsuch, J., concurring) (quoting *Skidmore*, 323 U.S. at 140) ("[C]ourts may extend respectful consideration to another branch's interpretation of the law, but the weight due those interpretations must always 'depend upon the[ir] thoroughness . . . , the validity of [their]reasoning, [their] consistency with earlier and later pronouncements, and all those factors which give [them] power to persuade.'").

[80] *Loper Bright*, 144 S. Ct. at 2263 (citations omitted).

What does this imply for litigation in the immediate future over agency decisions on the meaning of ambiguous statutes? In my view, the analysis will center on the factors outlined in *Skidmore*: (1) whether the contested issue implicates agency expertise, (2) whether the agency's interpretation is longstanding, (3) whether the interpretation was made after thorough consideration, (4) whether the interpretation is consistent with other agency pronouncements, and (5) whether the agency's reasoning is persuasive.[81] However, the *Loper Bright* Court also contrasted fact-bound determinations with "pure legal question[s]," which are for the courts to resolve. Giving agency views "appropriate weight" echoes the more transformative change in administrative law of *Hearst* and *Skidmore* in 1944.[82]

Many of the arguments under *Skidmore* will echo arguments that, pre–*Loper Bright*, would have been relevant in debating whether a statute's meaning was clear enough to resolve the case without resort to the highly deferential standard of *Chevron* step two. Importantly, under no circumstances will the agency's determination of statutory meaning be binding on the courts. Nonetheless, *Loper Bright* appears to allow for greater deference when a statute assigns to an agency the authority to apply the law to facts.[83] As this discussion illustrates, *Loper Bright* leaves open substantial questions surrounding the future of judicial review of agencies' interpretations of ambiguous statutes.

Assuming that *Loper Bright* does indeed revive *Skidmore*, a glance back at pre-*Chevron* post-APA cases that applied the *Skidmore* factors may be helpful to predicting the future course of administrative law. In one such case, the Court explained the meaning of deference under *Skidmore* in terms that bring *Chevron* deference to mind:

> [I]n determining whether the Commission's action was "contrary to law," the task for the Court of Appeals was not to interpret the statute as it thought best but rather the narrower inquiry into whether the Commission's construction was "sufficiently reasonable" to be accepted by a reviewing court. . . . To satisfy this standard it is not

---

[81] *Skidmore*, 323 U.S. at 139–40.

[82] *Loper Bright*, 144 S. Ct. at 2260 n.3.

[83] *See id.* at 2259. Here, the Court cited Gray v. Powell, 314 U.S. 402 (1941), and NLRB v. Hearst Publ'ns, Inc., 322 U.S. 111 (1944), as examples of deferential review of "fact-bound determinations."

necessary for a court to find that the agency's construction was the only reasonable one or even the reading the court would have reached if the question initially had arisen in a judicial proceeding.[84]

In another roughly contemporaneous case, the Court upheld the legality of an OSHA regulation that allowed employees to refuse to perform dangerous tasks. The Court cited *Skidmore* for the statement that its "inquiry is informed by an awareness that the regulation is entitled to deference unless it can be said not to be a reasoned and supportable interpretation of the [statute]."[85] In another case, the Court invalidated a regulation for failing *Skidmore*'s "power to persuade" factor, explaining that it did so because the agency had failed to identify the source of its statutory authority to promulgate the regulation.[86] Interestingly, in a decision approving an order issued by the Interstate Commerce Commission, the dissenters cited *Skidmore* in opposition to the agency, noting that the agency's "interpretation was adopted largely as a matter of expediency rather than as a reasoned interpretation."[87]

Before moving on, two points are worth noting. First, the Court's rejection of *Chevron* may lead it and the lower courts to similarly reject the more deferential formulations of *Skidmore* deference. If the Court believes that judges can and should always arrive at a statute's best meaning, it is difficult to imagine that it would approve of an interpretation other than "the reading the court would have reached." Second, as Justice Scalia complained in his dissent in *United States v. Mead Corp.*,[88] the *Skidmore* factors are uncertain and manipulable. Thus, it remains to be seen whether a revived *Skidmore* will provide any more clarity to the law of judicial review than did *Chevron*. Further, as always, judges' and Justices' attitudes toward the wisdom of regulation may be more important to the future of regulation than the language of *Skidmore* or *Loper Bright*.

---

[84] Fed. Election Comm'n v. Democratic Senatorial Campaign Comm., 454 U.S. 27, 39 (1981) (citations omitted).

[85] Whirlpool Corp. v. Marshall, 445 U.S. 1, 11 (1980).

[86] *See* Adamo Wrecking Co. v. United States, 434 U.S. 275, 287 n.5 (1978).

[87] Pan-Atl. S.S. Corp. v. Atl. Coast Line R. Co., 353 U.S. 436, 447 (1957) (Burton, J., dissenting).

[88] *See* United States v. Mead Corp., 533 U.S. 218, 240–41 (2001).

B. *The Shift to "Arbitrary or Capricious" Review*

Why a particular case would be evaluated under *Chevron* or one of the other standards of review was never particularly clear, except that the government had an incentive to invoke *Chevron* to receive what it viewed as maximum deference.[89] Now, the government is likely to do whatever it can to move cases into the more deferential "arbitrary or capricious" realm.

Under the APA, courts should "hold unlawful and set aside" an agency action if it is "arbitrary[or] capricious."[90] One of *Chevron*'s recurring problems was that the arbitrary or capricious standard for reviewing agency policy decisions seemed to vanish whenever the *Chevron* standard applied. This was frustrating because the question whether an agency has statutory authority to do something is separate from the question whether exercising that authority makes sense in light of the overall statutory scheme.[91] Early on, at least one court applied a third step in a *Chevron* case, asking whether the agency's application of its statutory authority was arbitrary or capricious.[92] The Supreme Court remained vague on the relationship between *Chevron* deference and arbitrary or capricious review. Sometimes, the Court seemed to equate *Chevron* step two with review under the arbitrary or capricious standard.[93] The Court once even stated that whether an agency decision was reviewed under "arbitrary or capricious" or *Chevron* did not matter. The Court stated that regardless, its "analysis would be the same, because under *Chevron* step two,

---

[89] *See, e.g.,* Judulang v. Holder, 565 U.S. 42, 52 & n.7 (2011) (applying the arbitrary or capricious standard despite the government's argument that *Chevron* was the applicable standard of review).

[90] 5 U.S.C. § 706(2)(A).

[91] For example, the question whether an agency has the statutory authority to regulate the emissions from an entire plant rather than each individual smokestack or vent is separate from the question whether doing so makes sense in light of the statutory scheme. This example is, of course, drawn from the *Chevron* decision itself.

[92] Int'l Bhd. of Elec. Workers v. Interstate Com. Comm'n, 862 F.2d 330, 338 (D.C. Cir. 1988). This opinion was written by Judge Harry Edwards, who had also expressed the view that *Chevron* step two violated the separation of powers. *See* CSX Transp. v. United States, 867 F.2d 1439, 1445 (D.C. Cir. 1989) (Edwards, J., dissenting).

[93] Mayo Found. for Med. Educ. & Rsch. v. United States, 562 U.S. 44, 53 (2011); Household Credit Servs., Inc. v. Pfennig, 541 U.S. 232, 242 (2004).

[the Court asks] whether an agency interpretation is 'arbitrary or capricious in substance.'"[94]

Of course, agency efforts to push cases into the arbitrary or capricious category will not always be successful. Inevitably, parties seeking judicial review will sometimes convince reviewing courts that a case presents an issue of statutory interpretation and that the agency's construction is not the statute's best reading. But lower courts more open to upholding regulatory action will in many cases be able to play up the prominence of policy questions and play down issues of statutory construction, shielding some cases from Supreme Court review. Thus, at the margin, the uncertain boundary between cases presenting legal questions and cases presenting policy issues is likely to reduce the importance of *Chevron*'s demise.

Further, this discussion assumes that the application of the arbitrary or capricious standard is and will remain deferential, or at least more deferential than the review of statutory construction questions under the revived *Skidmore* factors. The Court has, in recent years, given some indications that the era of highly deferential review of agency policy decisions may be ending or already over.[95] Or the level of deference may depend on the political and policy context. For example, the Court recently applied a fairly stringent standard of review when it stayed enforcement of an EPA rule under the Clean Air Act.[96] But it applied a highly deferential arbitrary or capricious standard of review to a rule that generally ran in a direction favored by free-market conservatives, upholding the Federal Communications Commission's decision to ease restrictions on media ownership.[97]

C. *Agency Flexibility without* Chevron

One of *Chevron*'s few virtues was that it facilitated agency innovation, reserving to agencies at least some power to revisit statutory questions. Under *Chevron*, if an agency interpretation was upheld

---

[94] *See Judulang*, 565 U.S. at 52 n.7 (quoting *Mayo Found.*, 562 U.S. at 53) (internal quotation marks and citation omitted); *see also* Verizon Commc'ns, Inc. v. FCC, 535 U.S. 467, 527 n.38 (2002); *Mayo Found.*, 562 U.S. at 53; Household Credit Servs., Inc. v. Pfennig, 541 U.S. 232, 242 (2004); Beermann, *supra* note 1, at 835; Beermann, *supra* note 68, at 746.

[95] *See* Beermann, *supra* note 13, at 1276, 1314–22.

[96] Ohio v. EPA, 144 S. Ct. 2040 (2024).

[97] FCC v. Prometheus Radio Project, 592 U.S. 414 (2021).

as permissible under step two, the agency remained free to change course and adopt a different permissible interpretation. This aspect of *Chevron*, which was explicitly approved in the Supreme Court's *Brand X* decision,[98] became extremely controversial in recent years. But this ability to change course was inherent in the original *Chevron* decision, since that case involved an agency's reversal of its previous construction of the governing statute.[99] Now, when a Court upholds an agency's interpretation under the *Skidmore* factors, the Court's decision will presumably have precedential effect. Going forward, the only way an agency can change its interpretation is to convince the reviewing court to overrule its prior decision.[100]

In my view, this is unfortunate: "[W]hen a court applies the *Skidmore* factors to uphold an initial agency statutory construction decision, it should allow the agency to disavow that interpretation in favor of what it now considers a better understanding of the statute."[101] Of course, when an agency changes its interpretation, the *Skidmore* factors of consistency and longevity will point against deference. But if an agency's revised understanding of its statute implicates the agency's expertise and the agency justifies the change in a thorough, well-reasoned analysis, *Skidmore* points in favor of judicial deference to the agency's decision. Otherwise, one of the consequences of overruling *Chevron* would be a power shift from agencies to the courts. Without the *Brand X* power to reconsider agency interpretations, only the federal courts or Congress would be able to alter those aspects of the rule that depend on the meaning of the governing statute.

---

[98] Nat'l Cable & Telecomms. Ass'n v. Brand X Internet Servs., 545 U.S. 967, 969 (2005).

[99] Under well-established Supreme Court precedent, agencies that act through adjudicatory orders remain free to reverse their views on the meaning or at least application of statutes. *See* FCC v. Fox Television Stations, Inc., 556 U.S. 502 (2009). In the *Fox Television* case, the Court approved of an agency reversal of policy related to statutory meaning that took the law in a more conservative direction, just as the *Chevron* Court moved the law to what was considered a more conservative position. Perhaps if agencies begin to use this flexibility to move the law in a more liberal direction, the Court will figure out a way to discard the principles underlying *Fox Television* as well.

[100] This was one of Justice Scalia's arguments against reviving *Skidmore* in the *Mead* case. *See Mead*, 533 U.S. at 247 (Scalia, J., dissenting). The importance of agency flexibility under *Brand X* depends, in part, on how often agencies actually used this authority, which is unknown.

[101] *See* Beermann, *supra* note 42, at 17.

This power shift to the judiciary may be aggravated by another decision late in the Court's recent Term, *Corner Post, Inc. v. Board of Governors of the Federal Reserve System*.[102] In that case, the Court held that parties newly subject to longstanding agency regulations have the full six years allowed under the federal statute of limitations to challenge them. That means some agency rules will be perpetually subject to challenge by, for example, new businesses or people born after the rule's promulgation. This consequence is not universal because many regulatory statutes require that challenges to agency rules be brought within a specified number of days (often 60) from the rule's promulgation or publication, in language that may be read as a statute of repose.[103] But there are exceptions and one important complication. The exceptions are that some statutes preserve the right to bring a challenge later based "on grounds arising after such sixtieth day."[104] The complication is that, consistent with the spirit of *Corner Post*, a court might entertain a challenge to the application of an old rule when a newly regulated party is ordered to comply with the rule or is otherwise made subject to it.[105] *Corner Post* thus potentially enhances the power of today's federal judges by allowing them to review decades-old rules that may have never been challenged, or that were challenged and upheld years or decades ago.

Those who view *Loper Bright* as a manifestation of the Court's anti-regulatory attitude fear that the Supreme Court and some lower federal courts will use their newfound power to review longstanding regulations and further suppress the ability of federal agencies

---

[102] Corner Post, Inc. v. Bd. of Governors of the Fed. Rsrv. Sys., 144 S. Ct. 2440 (2024).

[103] Examples include the Hobbs Act, which covers numerous agencies. *See, e.g.*, 28 U.S.C. § 2344; 42 U.S.C. § 7607(b)(1) (requiring that petitions for review of rules issued under the Clean Air Act be brought within 60 days "from the date notice of such promulgation, approval, or action appears in the Federal Register"); 29 U.S.C. § 655(f) (allowing challenges to standards promulgated under the Occupational Safety and Health Act to be brought "at any time prior to the sixtieth day after such standard is promulgated").

[104] 29 U.S.C. § 7607(b)(1).

[105] *See, e.g.*, United States v. Nova Scotia Foods Prods., Corp., 568 F.2d 240 (2d Cir. 1977) (allowing a party subject to an order based on a seven-year-old regulation to contest and avoid enforcement based on the regulation's alleged invalidity). However, more recently, the D.C. Circuit has twice rejected claims brought to challenge new applications of old rules. *See* Coal River Energy LLC v. Jewell, 751 F.3d 659, 663 (D.C. Cir. 2014); Sierra Club de Puerto Rico v. EPA, 815 F.3d 22, 26–29 (D.C. Cir. 2014).

to regulate in the interest of public health, safety, and welfare. The Supreme Court, in particular, seems hell-bent on depriving federal agencies of their authority to enforce the nation's environmental laws and financial regulations. Just how far this Court will go remains to be seen, perhaps when the next pandemic hits, the next financial crisis strikes, or the effects of climate change threaten to overwhelm vital infrastructure.

D. The Silver Lining?

Is there a regulatory silver lining to the demise of *Chevron* deference? Perhaps, but it depends on numerous unknowns and possible futures. If the federal courts, including the Supreme Court, somehow became dominated by judges and Justices who are less skeptical of the benefits of regulation, then less deferential judicial review could result in rulings that force conservative administrations to regulate more robustly than they might have otherwise. But that scenario is unlikely to occur in the near future. More immediately, less deferential judicial review could temper the ability of an extremist administration to move the law very far in either a pro- or anti-regulatory direction. Courts will no longer be able to hide behind *Chevron* deference when an agency mangles the meaning of a regulatory statute to pursue policies seriously at odds with those Congress expressed in the law.

Thus far, with few exceptions,[106] the current Court's nondeferential decisions have run in favor of business interests and against less powerful individuals who benefit from robust regulation, such as consumers, individual investors, people who suffer the ill effects of environmental degradation, workers in unsafe workplaces, and people whose health is at risk from communicable disease. But in some areas, less privileged litigants may benefit from more stringent judicial review. For example, immigration lawyers are hopeful that less deferential judicial review could benefit their clients, where courts have tended to be highly deferential to immigration

---

[106] One exception is *King v. Burwell*, 576 U.S. 473 (2015). The ruling denied *Chevron* deference to the IRS's broad reading of a provision of the Patient Protection and Affordable Care Act but then agreed with the IRS that persons who purchased health care insurance on a federally operated exchange were entitled to tax credits to subsidize the costs.

enforcement agencies.[107] The same could be said of government benefits determinations. Courts have reviewed benefits denials fairly deferentially, and more stringent judicial review might prevent agencies from twisting statutes to justify benefits denials when the best reading of the governing statute would support a favorable result for the applicant.

Of course, the effects of *Chevron*'s demise depend on how the courts, agencies, litigants, and Congress behave going forward.

Conclusion

The *Chevron* doctrine, in my view, was doomed from the start because the opinion was internally inconsistent and hopelessly unclear. It was further undermined when it spawned a complicated, virtually inscrutable set of limits, exceptions, and counter-doctrines. Had *Chevron* created a clear standard of review that facilitated certainty and uniformity across the circuits and validated agency action when expertise and experience were vital to effective regulation, I might mourn its passing. I believe the health, welfare, safety, and economic prospects of the American people depend to a great extent on agency regulatory power. But *Chevron* never met the ambitions that some had for it. Thus, I write not to praise or mourn *Chevron*, but to observe its burial, with a tinge of regret for those positive aspects of the doctrine that may have been worth preserving but that likely have met their demise along with their progenitor. On the bright side, at least none of us will have to write, or perhaps even read, another word criticizing *Chevron*.

---

[107] Brian Green et al., *Think Immigration:* Chevron *Is Dead! Thoughts on the Immigration Impact of* Loper Bright Enterprises, AM. IMMIGR. LAWS. ASS'N BLOG (July 2, 2024), https://www.aila.org/library/think-immigration-chevron-is-dead-thoughts-on-the-immigration-impact-of-loper-bright-enterprises; *see also Judulang*, 565 U.S. 42 (overruling an immigration agency's policy determination as arbitrary and capricious and rejecting *Chevron* as the proper standard of review).

SEC v Jarkesy: The Past, Present, and Future of Administrative Adjudication

*William Yeatman**

In any other Term, *SEC v. Jarkesy* would have been the big block-buster in administrative law.[1] During the 2023–24 Term, of course, a different decision involved the demise of *Chevron* deference, which ranks among the most important changes not just in "admin law," but in the entire history of American jurisprudence.[2]

Despite having been overshadowed in its own field within days of publication, *SEC v. Jarkesy* carries generational significance. The decision will alter agency enforcement from the course it has run for nearly a half century. This article explains the case, its historical context, and what's next.

A Very Brief History of Regulatory Penalties

SEC v. Jarkesy marks an inflection point in the history of American regulation. To properly describe the case, therefore, we must start at the beginning.

Agencies have operated in-house tribunals since the dawn of the administrative state. Through adjudication, agencies render regulatory policy much like courts find the common law: Individual actions engender rule-like orders, which in turn govern the behavior of regulated entities.[3]

The Federal Trade Commission (FTC), for example, was established in 1914 to regulate "unfair methods of competition."[4] In 1938, Congress

---

* Senior legal fellow, Pacific Legal Foundation.

[1] *See* SEC v. Jarkesy, 144 S. Ct. 2117 (2024).

[2] Loper Bright Enters. v. Raimondo, 144 S. Ct. 2244 (2024).

[3] For a nice explanation of how agencies render policy through adjudication, see Roger Nober, *Regulation by Adjudication*, REGUL. STUD. CTR. (Mar. 20, 2024), https://regulatorystudies.columbian.gwu.edu/regulation-adjudication.

[4] *See* Federal Trade Commission Act, Pub. L. No. 63-203, ch. 311, 38 Stat. 717 (1914).

57

added the regulation of "unfair or deceptive acts or practices" to the FTC's mandate.[5] To this day, the agency gives meaning to these nebulous phrases through case-by-case adjudicative proceedings. In finding that a particular business committed an "unfair method of competition," or an "unfair or deceptive act or practice," the agency telegraphs to everyone that these behaviors will not be tolerated. Thus, rules are made.

At first, in the late 19th century, federal courts reviewed agency orders without any bias. By the early 20th century, however, courts pivoted to the "judicial review" model of regulatory oversight, which is characterized by deference to agency decisionmaking and fact-finding.[6]

Today, every significant regulatory agency can access an in-house tribunal for regulatory enforcement. Those in-house tribunals are subject to deferential judicial oversight, as they were a century ago. While agencies have always operated adjudicative systems, the stakes changed dramatically in the decades preceding the Roberts Court. The key development was the onset of pocketbook punishments.

On June 26, 2024—the day before *Jarkesy* came down—the leading sanction in administrative enforcement was the civil money penalty. In 2022, federal regulatory agencies sought civil money penalties in 69 percent of enforcement actions, totaling $6,897,533,973 in exactions.[7] Despite its present-day prevalence, this punishment was a latecomer in the 150-year history of the administrative state.[8] For about a century, until the 1970s, domestic regulatory agencies were limited to two types of *non*monetary sanctions: (1) the suspension or revocation of a government-granted license or subsidy; and (2) injunctive-type relief, the most common being the cease-and-desist order.[9]

There were exceptions, to be sure, but they serve only to prove the general rule. Money penalties have been available since the

---

[5] *See* Pub. L. No. 75-447, ch. 49, § 3, 52 Stat. 111 (1938).

[6] *See generally* Thomas W. Merrill, *Article III, Agency Adjudication, and the Origins of the Appellate Review Model of Administrative Law*, 111 COLUM. L. REV. 939 (2011).

[7] *See* Will Yeatman & Keelyn Gallagher, *The Rise of Money Sanctions in Federal Agency Adjudication*, 76 ADMIN. L. REV. (forthcoming 2024).

[8] I'm taking the establishment of the Interstate Commerce Commission, in 1887, as the starting date of the administrative state.

[9] *See* Yeatman & Gallagher, *supra* note 7, at Part II.B.

19th century to agency tribunals operating within certain policy areas: immigration, taxation, and customs. Unlike other regulations, this special troika involves the administration of functions that are central to sovereignty, such as raising revenue or regulating the cross-border flows of goods and people.[10] As early as 1909, the Supreme Court noted its "settled judicial construction" that these three weighty subjects are "matters exclusively within [Congress's] control."[11] Accordingly, the political branches may "impose appropriate obligations and sanction their enforcement by reasonable money penalties . . . without the necessity of invoking the judicial power."[12] But outside of immigration, taxation, and customs, Congress could not avoid "invoking the judicial power" to resolve legal controversies. This is why Congress harbored "constitutional doubts" about the administrative imposition of money penalties at economic regulatory agencies, as noted by an influential 1941 report on administrative law.[13]

For most of the 20th century, these "constitutional doubts" kept Congress from empowering domestic regulatory agencies to pursue money penalties through adjudication. Eventually, however, these doubts would wane. Evolving legislative intentions provided the impetus for change. Initially, in the 19th century, federal regulation focused on the channels and instrumentalities of interstate commerce, such as waterways and railroads. Then, during the Progressive and New Deal eras, the federal government took to regulating entire industries. Next, starting in the 1960s, the administrative state subsumed social and behavioral matters, such as environmental quality and occupational health.[14] As Congress's regulatory ambition grew, lawmakers took on a greater willingness to test novel agency authorities.

---

[10] There were other important differences. For example, these early penalties (in immigration, taxation, and customs) were fixed and in rem, whereas today's penalties are variable and in personam). *See id.* at Part II.C.

[11] Oceanic Steam Nav. Co. v. Stranahan, 214 U.S. 320, 339 (1909).

[12] *Id.*

[13] Robert H. Jackson, Final Rep. of the Att'y Gen.'s Comm. on Admin. Proc., S. Doc. No. 8, at 147 (77th Cong., 1st Sess. 1941).

[14] This is the standard retelling of how federal regulation has evolved. Of course, it's a simplification.

Finally, in 1970, Congress for the first time passed an express authorization for the administrative imposition of civil money penalties through a domestic regulatory agency that was *not* involved in immigration, taxation, or customs. The Occupational Safety and Health Act of 1970 (OSHA) established an adjudicative system to impose money penalties for workplace safety violations.[15] After the Supreme Court upheld the OSHA penalties against a Seventh Amendment challenge (more on that consequential case later), the rise of administrative money sanctions really took off.[16] Congress interpreted the Court's decision as a green light. What followed was a sustained period of penalty creation. Over the next 33 years, Congress passed 172 authorizations for domestic regulatory agencies to pursue civil money penalties through their in-house proceedings, for a total of at least 188 in the U.S. Code (none of which existed before 1970).[17]

Congress further increased or expanded the scope of these penalties another 72 times through legislative amendments.[18] For example, the maximum penalty established by the Occupational Safety and Health Act was originally $10,000 (about $53,000 in today's dollars).[19] Currently, the statutory maximum is set at $70,000, but that's misleading.[20] Congress requires the Labor Department to increase its penalties to account for inflation, so the actual present-day maximum penalty is $161,323.[21]

The evolution of the Securities and Exchange Commission (SEC) provides another example, one that is germane to the discussion of *Jarkesy*. For the first four decades of its existence, the agency's tribunals were limited to *non*monetary sanctions—primarily the suspension or revocation of registrations to do business in the securities industry. This changed only in 1990, when Congress empowered the SEC to seek civil money penalties of up to $725,000 through

---

[15] *See* Pub. L. No. 91-596, 84 Stat. 1590 (1970); *see also* 29 U.S.C. § 659 (enforcement procedures); 29 U.S.C. § 666 (establishing penalties).

[16] Atlas Roofing Co. v. OSHRC, 430 US 442 (1977).

[17] *See* Yeatman & Gallagher, *Money Sanctions*, *supra* note 7, at Part III.A.

[18] *Id.*

[19] *See* Pub. L. No. 91–596, § 17, 84 Stat. 1606 (1970).

[20] *See* Federal Civil Penalties Inflation Adjustment Act Improvements Act, Pub. L. No. 114-74, tit. VII, § 701 (2015) (amending the Federal Civil Penalties Inflation Adjustment Act of 1990) (codified in a note to 28 U.S.C. § 2461).

[21] *See* 89 Fed. Reg. 1810, 1817 (Jan. 11, 2024).

agency adjudication.[22] Although the statutory maximum remains at $725,000 per violation, the real-world maximum is $1,152,314 when accounting for congressional directives on inflation.[23] At first, the SEC's administrative money penalties reached only registered entities. However, the 2010 Dodd-Frank Act expanded the jurisdiction of SEC adjudicators, such that the agency could proceed administratively with civil money penalties against "any person," including non-registered brokers and investment advisors.[24]

Enter George Jarkesy

Among the first wave of post–Dodd-Frank defendants at the SEC was George Jarkesy. Shortly after that statute's passage, the SEC's enforcement division began a two-year investigation of Jarkesy and his investing advisor businesses.[25] In March 2013, the SEC formally accused him of securities fraud and commenced enforcement proceedings.[26] Agency prosecutors sought the highest allowable tier of civil money penalty, among other sanctions.

Before the Dodd-Frank Act, the SEC's tribunal would have lacked jurisdiction to impose a penalty on an *un*registered investment adviser like Jarkesy. But after Dodd-Frank, the agency could pursue such penalties against *anyone* through its own in-house proceedings. Alternatively, the agency could bring the same action in federal court. Congress left it entirely up to the agency to decide in which forum it wished to file its enforcement actions involving money penalties.

---

[22] *See* Securities Enforcement Remedies and Penny Stock Reform Act of 1990, Pub. L. No. 101-429, tit. II, § 202, 104 Stat. 937 (2002) (amending Securities and Exchange Act of 1934 by inserting section 21B).

[23] *See* SEC, *Inflation Adjustments to the Civil Monetary Penalties Administered by the Securities and Exchange Commission (as of January 15, 2024)*, available at https://www.sec.gov/enforce/civil-penalties-inflation-adjustments (last accessed Mar. 27, 2024, at 6:12AM).

[24] *See* Dodd-Frank Act, Pub. L. No. 111–203, tit. VII, § 773, tit. IX, § 929P(a)(2), 124 Stat. 1802, 1863 (2010) (extending civil money penalty sanction to subjects of cease-and-desist orders, which had been made applicable to "any person" for violations of "any provision") (codified at 15 U.S.C. § 78u–2(a)(2)).

[25] *See* Admin. Proc. File No. 3-15255, Div.'s Response to Respondents' Objections, at 33 (SEC Enforcement Division, Dec. 14, 2018) (describing investigation).

[26] *See* Admin. Proc. File No. 3-15255, Ord. Instituting Proc. (SEC, Mar. 22, 2013).

By delegating to the SEC the choice of where to file its enforcement actions, the Dodd-Frank Act "effectively gave the [agency] the power to decide which defendants should receive *certain legal processes* (those accompanying Article III proceedings) and which should not."[27] If, for whatever reason, the SEC chooses to proceed with a civil penalty action in federal court, then the defendant has recourse to the safeguards provided by the Federal Rules of Evidence and the Federal Rules of Civil Procedure. In federal court, the defendant also has the right to demand that a jury determine the facts. Perhaps most importantly, "a life-tenured, salary-protected Article III judge presides."[28]

"Things look very different in agency proceedings," as Justice Neil Gorsuch observed in a *Jarkesy* concurrence.[29] Instead of uniform standards of procedure and evidence, the SEC's tribunals are governed by the agency's house rules.[30] Instead of an impartial judge and a jury of peers, the SEC's political leadership (or its employees) serve as both the judge and the jury in administrative proceedings. A 2015 *Wall Street Journal* report quoted a retired SEC administrative law judge as saying that the agency's judges were forced to operate from the perspective that the "burden [is] on the people . . . accused to show that they didn't do what the agency said they did" instead of being presumed innocent.[31]

At the SEC's home court, Jarkesy was given the full benefit of administrative "justice." To comply with its obligation to provide exculpatory evidence gathered during its investigation, the SEC inundated the defense with "between 15 and 25 million pages of information."[32] The proceeding lasted seven years. Jarkesy's initial judge, an agency employee, sided with the government in a recommended decision.[33] His ultimate judge was the five-member Commission—the same entity that approved the charges against him.[34] In a 2020 order, the SEC

[27] Jarkesy v. SEC, 34 F.4th 446, 462 (5th Cir. 2022).

[28] SEC v. Jarkesy, 144 S. Ct. 2117, 2125 (2024)

[29] *See id.* at 2141 (Gorsuch, J., concurring).

[30] The SEC's Rules of Practice are codified at 17 C.F.R. §§ 201.100–900.

[31] Jean Eaglesham, *SEC Wins with In-House Judges*, WALL ST. J. (May 6, 2015), https://tinyurl.com/y2h3a7pk.

[32] *Jarkesy*, 144 S. Ct. at 2141 (Gorsuch, J., concurring).

[33] Admin. Proc. File No. 3-15255, Initial Decision Release No. 693 (SEC, Oct. 17, 2014).

[34] Admin. Proc. File No. 3-15255, Release Nos. 10834, 89775, 5572, 34003 (SEC, Sept. 4, 2020).

found Jarkesy liable for securities fraud and imposed a civil penalty of $300,000, among other sanctions.[35]

Jarkesy petitioned for judicial review in the Fifth Circuit. A divided panel of that court granted the petition and vacated the final order. The panel's majority identified "three independent constitutional defects: (1) Petitioners were deprived of their constitutional right to a jury trial; (2) Congress unconstitutionally delegated legislative power to the SEC by failing to provide it with an intelligible principle by which to exercise the delegated power; and (3) statutory removal restrictions on SEC ALJs [administrative law judges] violate Article II."[36]

The SEC petitioned for *certiorari*, seeking review on all three of the Fifth Circuit's constitutional holdings. The Supreme Court granted the agency's petition. During oral argument, the Justices seemed to focus on the jury trial question, to the exclusion of the other two constitutional questions. In late June, the Court issued its decision. As presaged by the hearing, the six-Justice majority addressed only the Seventh Amendment question, affirming the court below.

Unpacking *Jarkesy*

Before unpacking *SEC v. Jarkesy*, we must establish the jurisprudential context. That legal backstory begins with the Court's crucial role in bringing about the rise of money sanctions at agency tribunals.

Again, Congress did not expressly authorize administrative money penalties until 1970, with the Occupational Safety and Health Act. It took seven years for the Supreme Court to hear a constitutional challenge to this novel regime. In that case, *Atlas Roofing v. Occupational Safety & Health Review Commission*, the Court sustained the statute. As previously discussed, *Atlas Roofing* galvanized Congress to legislate more of these sanctions into existence. Over the ensuing decades, civil money penalties became the leading sanction for administrative enforcement.

---

[35] The Commission also directed Jarkesy to cease and desist committing or causing violations of the antifraud provisions, ordered him to disgorge earnings from his business, and prohibited him from participating in the securities industry and in offerings of penny stocks.

[36] Jarkesy v. SEC, 34 F.4th 446, 451 (5th Cir. 2022).

Atlas Roofing involved a Seventh Amendment challenge to the administrative imposition of money penalties for workplace safety violations. The Seventh Amendment guarantees "the right of trial by jury" in "Suits at common law," and the petitioners argued they were denied this jury right.[37] In considering their claim, the Court cast aside its prevailing Seventh Amendment framework, which asked whether the underlying action is "analogous" to common-law causes of action ordinarily decided in English law courts in the late 18th century.[38] Rather than working through the existing doctrinal test, the Court in *Atlas Roofing* established an exception. For controversies involving "public rights," the jury right did not apply, "even if the Seventh Amendment would have required a jury where the adjudication of those rights is assigned to a federal court of law instead of an administrative agency."[39]

It was the breadth of this constitutional carveout that led to the rise of money sanctions in federal agency adjudication. According to *Atlas Roofing*, Congress creates "public rights" whenever it establishes "new statutory obligations" enforced by the government "in its sovereign capacity."[40] Repeatedly, the Court indicated that Congress has the discretion to decide whether the Seventh Amendment applies, simply by choosing which forum hears the case.[41] The obvious problem with this conception of public rights is that it is capacious enough to subsume agency enforcement for *any* regulatory regime. Naturally, that's how Congress construed the case.

From the start, the "public rights" exception to the Seventh Amendment created controversy. Scholars have been overwhelmingly, perhaps uniformly, critical of the constitutional jurisprudence set forth in *Atlas Roofing*.[42]

---

[37] U.S. CONST. amend. VII.

[38] Curtis v. Loether, 415 U.S. 189, 195 (1974).

[39] Atlas Roofing Co. v. OSHRC, 430 US 442, 455 (1977).

[40] *Id.* at 450; *see also id.* at 458.

[41] *See, e.g., id.* at 455 ("Congress is not required by the Seventh Amendment to choke the already crowded federal courts with new types of litigation . . ."); *id.* at 460 ("We cannot conclude that the Amendment rendered Congress powerless—when it concluded that remedies available in courts of law were inadequate to cope with a problem within Congress' power to regulate—to create new public rights and remedies by statute and commit their enforcement, if it chose, to a tribunal other than a court of law—such as an administrative agency—in which facts are not found by juries.").

[42] *See Jarkesy*, 144 S. Ct. at 2138 n.4 (citing to critical literature).

And the Supreme Court further complicated matters with its avowedly "confusing precedents."[43] Twelve years after *Atlas Roofing*, the Court seemed to contradict itself on the scope of the public rights exception. That case, *Granfinanciera, SA v. Nordberg*, pertained to (non–Article III) bankruptcy courts.[44] The controversy arose in a bankruptcy proceeding after the trustee sued a third party (the petitioner) to recover an allegedly fraudulent monetary transfer by the debtor.[45] The third party's request for a jury trial was denied by the bankruptcy court, the district court, and the Eleventh Circuit. On *certiorari*, the question presented was whether the Seventh Amendment permitted Congress to assign actions to recover a money judgement for fraudulent conveyance to a bankruptcy Court, where there is no jury right.

Ultimately, the *Granfinanciera* Court determined that the disputed action was a "matter[] of private rather than public right," such that the Seventh Amendment applied.[46] In reaching this conclusion, the Court apparently reinterpreted the public rights doctrine. I say "apparently" because the Court's message was unclear—at least it was until *SEC v. Jarkesy* came down last Term.

On public rights, the *Granfinanciera* Court majority struck a tone at odds with the Court's posture in *Atlas Roofing*. The tension with its precedent was so great that Justice Byron White dissented to object that *Granfinanciera* "can be read as overruling or severely limiting the relevant portions of" *Atlas Roofing* (which he had authored).[47]

The key difference was how the two decisions dealt with legislative intent. *Atlas Roofing* oozed deference for Congress; the Court was unwilling to accept "that the [Seventh] Amendment rendered Congress powerless."[48] In *Granfinanciera*, the Court replaced deference with skepticism. Throughout the controlling opinion, the majority evinced a suspicion that Congress might "conjure away" or "eviscerate" the Seventh Amendment "merely by relabeling the cause of

---

[43] Thomas v. Union Carbide Agric. Prods. Co., 473 U.S. 568, 583 (1985) (internal quotation marks omitted).

[44] Granfinanciera, SA v. Nordberg, 492 U.S. 33 (1989).

[45] *Id.* at 36 (explaining case history).

[46] *Id.* at 56.

[47] *Id.* at 71 n.1 (White, J., dissenting).

[48] Atlas Roofing Co. v. OSHRC, 430 US 442, 460 (1977).

action to which it attaches and placing exclusive jurisdiction in an administrative agency."[49] Justice White took note of this shift in his dissent, accusing the majority of "blithely ignoring the relevance of the forum Congress has designated to hear this action" and instead focusing only on the nature of the claim.[50]

The *Granfinanciera* Court approvingly quoted *Atlas Roofing* for the proposition that "public rights" arise when Congress "create[s] a new cause of action . . . unknown to the common law."[51] But after introducing this "decisive" criterion, the *Granfinancieria* majority proceeded to give this formulation an entirely different meaning. In *Atlas Roofing*, the Court had reasoned that a novel statutory suit is "unknown to the common law" simply because it is new.[52] In *Granfinanciera*, by contrast, the majority took "unknown to the common law" to mean that the underlying action is not "legal in nature."[53] Because actions for fraudulent conveyance are "quintessentially suits at common law," the Court in *Granfinanciera* determined that the Seventh Amendment right attached to the bankruptcy proceedings.

Atlas Roofing and *Granfinancieria* present competing interpretations of public rights. Under *Atlas Roofing*, a cause of action could be assigned to a jury-less agency tribunal, if that's what Congress wanted, period. *Granfinanciera* put forth a much narrower conception of the public rights exception. Under the reasoning of that case, the public rights exception applies only if the underlying suit is entirely "unknown to the common law," meaning that the substance of the claim has no analogous action at the common law in the late 18th century.

The problem was that *Granfinanciera* departed from *Atlas Roofing* without saying as much. Far from addressing the conspicuous

---

[49] *Granfinanciera*, 492 U.S. at 52.

[50] *Id.* at 81 (White, J., dissenting).

[51] *Id.* at 60 (majority opinion) (internal quotation marks omitted).

[52] *Atlas Roofing*, 430 U.S. at 450 ("Congress has often created new statutory obligations, provided for civil penalties for their violation, and committed exclusively to an administrative agency the function of deciding whether a violation has in fact occurred."); *see id.* at 455 ("In sum, the cases discussed above stand clearly for the proposition that when Congress creates new statutory 'public rights,' it may assign their adjudication to an administrative agency with which a jury trial would be incompatible[.]").

[53] *Granfinanciera*, 492 U.S. at 53.

conflict between the two cases, *Granfinanciera* expressly affirmed *Atlas Roofing*.[54] The *Granfinanciera* majority even expanded the *Atlas Roofing* holding by clarifying that the government does *not* have to be a party in a dispute for the public rights exception to apply.[55] Relatedly, the absence of the government as a party in *Granfinanciera* provided a way to distinguish it from *Atlas Roofing*, where the agency was in a prosecuting role.

The upshot is there was no way to tell how the two cases related to one another. As Richard Pierce explained in his administrative law treatise,

> After *Granfinanciera*, the Court could take any of several directions. It could extend the majority's reasoning to invalidate agency adjudication of numerous classes of disputes that agencies long have resolved without juries . . . Or it could return to the pragmatic test urged by the dissenting justices and adopted by a unanimous Court in *Atlas Roofing*[.][56]

For decades, the contradiction persisted, in large part because more than 90 percent of money penalty actions end in settlement.[57] Article III courts, therefore, rarely had an opportunity to scrutinize the constitutional propriety of these proceedings.

At last, in *SEC v. Jarkesy*, the Court resolved the matter: "*Granfinanciera* effectively decides this case."[58] The Court definitively clarified that, in identifying public rights, "what matters is the substance of the action, not where Congress has assigned it."[59] This is true, the Court said, "[e]ven when an action originate[s] in a newly fashioned regulatory scheme."[60]

After waxing eloquent about the jury right ("the glory of the English law"), the *Jarkesy* Court then minimized the public rights exception, which "is, after all, an *exception*."[61] The Court identified six

---

[54] *Id.* at 51 (stating that "[w]e adhere to that general teaching" of *Atlas Roofing*).

[55] *Id.* at 53–54.

[56] RICHARD PIERCE, ADMINISTRATIVE LAW TREATISE § 2.8 (4th ed. 2002).

[57] *See* Yeatman & Gallagher, *supra* note 7, at Part V.

[58] *Jarkesy*, 144 S. Ct. at 2135.

[59] *Id.*

[60] *Id.* (internal quotation marks omitted).

[61] *Id.* at 2134 (emphasis in original).

areas of sovereignty-heavy subjects—including immigration, taxation, and customs—that "historically could have been determined exclusively by [the executive and legislative] branches," with "[n]o involvement by an Article III court in the initial adjudication."[62] These were public rights. Beyond these "historic categories," the Court called for judicial scrutiny ("close attention") to ensure that the public rights exception does not "swallow the rule."[63] Even where the exception seemingly applied, "the presumption is in favor of Article III courts."[64]

The *Jarkesy* Court described *Atlas Roofing*'s take on public rights as "circular."[65] Moreover, the Court allowed for the possibility that its precedents might have "effectively overruled" *Atlas Roofing*.[66] In short, *Jarkesy* does everything short of putting a little red flag next to *Atlas Roofing* in Westlaw. Still, the Court didn't upset its precedent. Instead, the *Jarkesy* Court, as in *Granfinancieria*, implicitly eviscerated *Atlas Roofing* by interpreting the phrase "unknown to the common law" to mean only those actions that are dissimilar in "substance" and "nature" from common-law suits.[67] Again, *Atlas Roofing* had taken "unknown to the common law" to mean whatever actions Congress assigned to an administrative tribunal. Because fraud is known to the common law, *Atlas Roofing* "does not control."[68]

Doctrinally, *Jarkesy* blessed the Fifth Circuit's two-part test for discerning whether the Seventh Amendment extends to a non–Article III adjudicative proceeding. At step one, the courts should ask whether the action "implicates" the Seventh Amendment.[69] Here, the Court tells us that the remedy is the paramount consideration; presumably, all civil money penalties meet this test and "implicate" the jury right.[70]

---

[62] *Id.* at 2132; *see generally id.* at 2131–34 (discussing six categories of historical "public rights.").

[63] *Id.* at 2134.

[64] *Id.* (quotations and citations omitted).

[65] *Id.* at 2139.

[66] *Id.* at 2137 & n.3.

[67] *Id.* at 2135.

[68] *Id.* at 2137.

[69] *Id.* at 2127 ("The threshold issue is whether this action implicates the Seventh Amendment.").

[70] *Id.* at 2129 ("In this case, the remedy is all but dispositive.").

At step two, courts inquire whether the public rights exception applies. After *Jarkesy*, this test is to be applied narrowly. Outside of the six "historical categories" identified by the Court, public rights apparently are limited to actions that "bring no common law soil with them."[71]

What's Next?

So, how will *SEC v. Jarkesy* affect agency adjudication?

Most directly, the decision will preclude the SEC from employing its in-house proceedings to prosecute fraud-based claims for money penalties. It's unclear how this holding will affect the SEC's operations. The *Jarkesy* Court characterized the alleged fraud at issue in the case as knowing or reckless misstatements, but the SEC's conception of "securities fraud" is so broad that it includes some violations that do not include a false statement. This "could lead to a parsing of fraud allegations in SEC actions, depending on whether they are based on a misstatement or otherwise covered by the securities laws."[72]

Of course, the SEC is not the only agency that punishes fraud-based violations with the administrative imposition of money penalties. The Commodity Futures Trading Commission,[73] the Consumer Financial Protection Bureau,[74] and the Federal Energy Regulatory Commission (FERC)[75] all have the authority to pursue money penalties, in-house, for regulatory violations that are analogous to, if not "quintessentially," common-law fraud.

Apart from fraud-based actions, *SEC v. Jarkesy* casts a constitutional pall over *all* money penalty proceedings. As explained previously, *Atlas Roofing* ushered in tremendous change at the administrative state. Now that *Atlas Roofing* has been severely diminished, it stands to reason that there will be ramifications in how agencies adjudicate. Many open questions remain. For example, in parsing public

---

[71] *Id.* at 2137.

[72] *See* David. R. Fredrickson, *What Happens to the SEC's Proceedings after* Jarkesy?, BLOOMBERG L. (Apr. 2024), https://tinyurl.com/49mj3mtd.

[73] *See* 7 U.S.C. § 6b (any fraudulent or deceptive practices).

[74] *See* 12 U.S.C. § 5536(a)(1)(B) ("any unfair, deceptive, or abusive act or practice").

[75] *See* Energy Policy Act of 2005, Pub. L. No. 109-58, §§ 315, 1284, 119 Stat. 691, 979 (2005) (amending Natural Gas Act and Federal Power Act to empower FERC to police market manipulation).

rights, an essential factor is whether the "nature" or "substance" of the underlying claim is comparable to an action at common law or at equity at the founding. What happens when there is evidence on both sides? *Jarkesy* provided no express guidance, though the Court seemed to establish a presumption against finding new public rights outside of the six "historical categories." For now, these sorts of questions will percolate.

Beyond civil money penalties, the next frontier of Seventh Amendment scrutiny is likely to involve the administrative imposition of remedies derived from the law of restitution. A handful of agencies, including the SEC, have statutory authority to exact restitution or "disgorgement" from defendants. Jarkesy, for example, was subject to a $600,000 disgorgement order, in addition to the $300,000 civil money penalty. In 2022, agencies collected $3,546,558,822.18 in such sanctions.[76] Arguably, these penalties are punitive and, therefore, "implicate" the Seventh Amendment.[77] If so, then the next question (after *Jarkesy*) is whether actions underlying this restitutionary relief are in the "nature" of a common-law suit, or if they more closely resemble a suit at equity. That question will determine whether the public rights exception applies. Keep an eye on this space.

We should be clear about the practical consequences. Regardless of where civil money penalty suits are brought—agency tribunal or federal court—these actions settle more than 90 percent of the time.[78] For all intents and purposes, therefore, the practical effect of *Jarkesy* will be to influence settlement negotiations. This was also the case for *Atlas Roofing*, in the opposite direction. The important effect of potential penalties on settlement negotiations was recognized in an influential 1972 report by the Administrative Conference of the U.S. ("ACUS"), which advocated for greater use of agency tribunals

[76] *See* Yeatman & Gallagher, *supra* note 7, at Part III.B (discussing rise of administrative remedies supposedly modeled on the law of restitution); *see also id.* at Part V (presenting results of survey).

[77] *See* Kokesh v. SEC, 581 U.S. 455, 457 (2017) (finding that an SEC disgorgement order was a "penalty" under the Administrative Procedure Act's statute of limitations).

[78] In 1972, agencies had to bring virtually all their civil money penalty actions in federal court and settled "well over 90%" of these cases. *See* Harvey J. Goldschmid, *An Evaluation of the Present and Potential Use of Civil Money Penalties as a Sanction by Federal Administrative Agencies*, in 2 RECOMMENDATIONS AND REPS. OF THE ADMIN. CONF. OF THE U.S. 896, 919 (1972). A recent survey of administrative money penalties performed by this author found that 92 percent of such actions settle.

for money penalty proceedings. Back then, agencies generally had to prevail in an original action in an Article III Court before they could impose such penalties, and the parties settled "well over 90% of [these] cases."[79] ACUS objected not to the fact that almost all these suits settled; rather, ACUS bemoaned the "inferior" quality of these settlements.[80] According to the ACUS report, "regulatory needs are being sacrificed for what is collectable."[81] To increase the agency's hand at the bargaining table, ACUS recommended that Congress empower administrative tribunals to impose civil money penalties, subject to deferential judicial review.[82] In sum, the primary effect of *Atlas Roofing* was to enhance the government's negotiating leverage, while the primary effect of *Jarkesy* will be to give a greater hand to regulatory defendants at the settlement table.

Conclusion: Politics? Or History?

Predictably, the commentariat has presented *Jarkesy* through a political lens.[83] We're told that the Court's conservative majority acted like conservatives. Of course, it's a bit silly to purport that there is a partisan divide regarding the right to a jury, which seems as bipartisan as apple pie. More to the point, attributing *Jarkesy* to the Justices' politics is historically illiterate. Rather than animating "conservative" values, the *Jarkesy* decision is best viewed as a belated judicial check on increasing agency power. For decades preceding the Roberts Court, Congress pushed the envelope of the agencies' sanctioning authority. Finally, Congress pushed too far. Seen in this light, *SEC v. Jarkesy* is less about the Justices' politics, and more about our dynamic system of checks and balances.

---

[79] *Id.* at 919.

[80] *See id.* at 900, 921.

[81] *Id.* at 900, 921.

[82] *Id.* at 930.

[83] *See, e.g.*, Justin Jouvenal et al., *In Conservative Win, Supreme Court Limits Use of SEC In-House Tribunals*, WASH. POST (June 27, 2024), https://tinyurl.com/6efrw5jp. Noah Rosenblum, *The Case That Could Destroy the Government*, THE ATL. (Nov. 27, 2023), https://tinyurl.com/yeyvzh2j (presenting Jarkesy in political terms).

"Appropriate" Appropriations Challenges after *Community Financial*

*Chad Squitieri**

Introduction

The standard federal agency must come to Congress each year, hat in hand, and request another round of congressional funding. This annual appropriations process ensures that Congress maintains at least *some* influence over the vast array of rules and regulations that govern Americans' daily lives. Sure, Congress might have delegated broad authority to administrative agencies to develop national policy on Congress's behalf. But an agency reliant on annual appropriations is an agency with the financial incentive to exercise its delegated authority with an eye toward pleasing congressional appropriators. The annual appropriations process is therefore a sensible (even if insufficient) step toward ensuring democratic oversight of how taxpayer dollars are spent. But in Washington, sensibility does not often win the day. And so it is little surprise that, when it came to designing the Consumer Financial Protection Bureau (CFPB), Congress sought to do things a bit differently.

Unlike the standard administrative agency, the CFPB never has to sink so low as to *request* that Congress fund its agency operations. Instead, a federal statute—referred to as Section 5497—purports to empower the Director of the CFPB to *demand* that the Federal Reserve (which is itself insulated from the congressional appropriations process) provide the CFPB with the funding it needs.[1] And just how

* Assistant Professor of Law, Columbus School of Law, the Catholic University of America. Substantial portions of this article are based on an essay I published prior to oral argument in *CFPB v. Community Financial*. *See* Chad Squitieri, *The Appropriate Appropriations Inquiry*, 74 FLA. L. REV. F. 1 (2023). I thank Marc O. DeGirolami for helpful comments on a prior draft and McKenzie Mixon for her excellent research assistance.

[1] 12 U.S.C. § 5497.

much of the public's money can the CFPB demand? That decision is left to the discretion of the CFPB Director—at least up to a statutory limit set too high to be of any real relevance.[2] What's more, Section 5497 does not even require the Director to explain why the CFPB has demanded a certain amount of money. As one former CFPB Director put it: A funding demand could be accomplished by scribbling a handwritten note on a napkin, sending the demand over to the Federal Reserve, and waiting for the money to roll in.[3]

If you think that the manner in which the CFPB is funded sounds problematic, you are not alone. In 2018, an association of regulated entities filed a lawsuit alleging that Section 5497 ran afoul of the Constitution's Appropriations Clause. That Clause provides that "[n]o money shall be drawn from the treasury, but in consequence of appropriations made by law."[4] The idea behind the lawsuit was that Section 5497 did not amount to a congressional "appropriation." The association argued that Section 5497 was not an appropriation because it purported to give the CFPB the power to demand funds from an entity outside of Congress into perpetuity.

The challengers to Section 5497 had some initial success. To wit, the United States Court of Appeals for the Fifth Circuit described Section 5497 as a "self-actualizing, perpetual funding mechanism" that constituted an unconstitutional "abdicat[ion]" of Congress's "appropriations power."[5] But this early success would not prove to

---

[2] *Id.* § 5497(2)(a)(iii) (capping the transfer amount at 12 percent of the Federal Reserve System's total operating expenses). "At present, the CFPB's maximum annual draw is nearly $750 million," and "unlike most agencies, [the CFPB] does not have to return any unspent funds to the Treasury." Consumer Fin. Prot. Bureau v. Cmty. Fin. Servs. Ass'n of Am., 601 U.S. 416, 450 (2024) (Alito, J., dissenting).

[3] Former CFPB Director John Michael "Mick" Mulvaney, Remarks at Gray Lecture Panel 2: Congress's Power of the Purse in the Modern Administrative State, at 32:05 (Mar. 31, 2023), https://vimeo.com/815046082 ("I could go down . . . and literally on a napkin write 'Please give me 180 million dollars' and [the Federal Reserve] would have to do that. That is not an exaggeration."); *id.* at 35:09 ("The funding flow is, there's a piece of paper that leaves the office of the Director of the CFPB. It is taken down to the Fed[eral Reserve]. And they say please move money into this account and they move money into that account. That is the process.").

[4] U.S. CONST. art. I, § 9, cl. 7. Throughout this article, the capitalization of words in constitutional quotes has been normalized.

[5] Cmty. Fin. Servs. Ass'n of Am. v. Consumer Fin. Prot. Bureau, 51 F.4th 616, 623, 638 (5th Cir. 2022).

be long lasting. Just last Term, in *CFPB v. Community Financial*,[6] the Supreme Court overturned the Fifth Circuit, explaining that Section 5497 satisfied the rather lax requirements of the Appropriations Clause.

According to the Supreme Court, the Appropriations Clause requires only that "a law . . . authorize[] the disbursement of specified funds for identified purposes."[7] Section 5497 identified both a "source" of funding (i.e., a Federal Reserve fund) and a general "purpose" for the funding (i.e., to pay the expenses of the CFPB in carrying out its "duties and responsibilities"). For those reasons, the Court held that the statute satisfied the limited demands imposed by the Appropriations Clause.[8]

As this article will explain, the Supreme Court got it right in *Community Financial*. But here's the kicker: That does *not* mean that Section 5497 is constitutional. As I've argued before and as the Supreme Court now agrees,[9] it is not the Appropriations Clause that vests Congress with the authority to appropriate funds. It is *other* constitutional text that vests Congress with the authority to enact appropriations laws. Thus, future "appropriate" appropriations challenges (as I have termed them) should focus on the limitations imposed by that *other* constitutional text—and not the Appropriations Clause itself. Understanding as much provides crucial context concerning the Court's careful effort in *Community Financial* to explain that its "narrow" holding was limited to the requirements of the Appropriations Clause alone. The Court explicitly declined to address "other constitutional checks on Congress' authority to create and fund an administrative agency."[10]

---

[6] 601 U.S. 416 (2024).

[7] *Id.* at 438.

[8] *Id.* at 422–23, 435, 441 (citing 12 U.S.C. § 5497(c)(1)).

[9] Chad Squitieri, *The Appropriate Appropriations Inquiry*, 74 FLA. L. REV. F. 1, 8 (2023) ("[T]he Appropriations Clause simply offers a limitation: *if* an appropriation is to occur (pursuant to some other power vested elsewhere), *then* that appropriation must be 'made by law.'") (citing Kate Stith, *Congress' Power of the Purse*, 97 YALE L.J. 1343, 1348–49 (1988), and GARY LAWSON & GUY SEIDMAN, THE CONSTITUTION OF EMPIRE: TERRITORIAL EXPANSION AND AMERICAN LEGAL HISTORY 27 (2004)) (citations omitted); *Cmty. Fin. Servs. Ass'n of Am.*, 601 U.S. at 438 ("To be sure, the Appropriations Clause presupposes Congress' powers over the purse. But, its phrasing and location in the Constitution make clear that it is not itself the source of those powers.").

[10] *Cmty. Fin. Servs. Ass'n of Am.*, 601 U.S. at 441.

Part I of this article will begin with a brief overview of the Supreme Court's narrow Appropriations Clause holding in *Community Financial*—a holding that should be of only limited relevance to "appropriate" appropriations challenges going forward. Parts II and III will then use Section 5497 to demonstrate what should be the focus of "appropriate" appropriations challenges in the future.

In particular, Part II will elucidate the question that the Court was careful to *not* decide in *Community Financial*: whether Section 5497 ran afoul of the constitutional text that actually vests appropriations authority in Congress. As I will argue, the constitutional provisions that give Congress its best shot at lawfully enacting Section 5497 are the Necessary and Proper Clause and the Commerce Clause. Thus the "appropriate" appropriations question, for purposes of the CFPB's funding mechanism, asks whether Section 5497 is a "necessary and proper" means of carrying Congress's Commerce Clause power "into execution."

Part III will then answer that "appropriate" appropriations question and conclude that Section 5497 is unconstitutional. I will explain how Section 5497 can be distinguished from the various historical funding examples that served as a central (but fundamentally confused) focus in *Community Financial*. The upshot is that although Congress may be able to appropriate funds to some entities outside of the annual appropriations process (such as the Post Office, National Mint, or Customs Service and Revenue Officers), Congress cannot appropriate funds to the CFPB in the manner codified in Section 5497. That is partly because each of those previous, valid appropriations constituted exercises of *different* congressional powers.

I. Case Overview

Community Financial began as a challenge to the CFPB's Payday Lending Rule, which limits how loan payments may be collected.[11] A group of entities regulated by the Payday Lending Rule, referred to here collectively as "Community Financial," sued the CFPB on multiple grounds.[12] The most notable of these arguments was that

---

[11] *Id.* at 423 (citing 12 C.F.R. § 1041 (2018)).

[12] Cmty. Fin. Servs. Ass'n of Am. v. Consumer Fin. Prot. Bureau, 558 F. Supp. 3d 350, 356 n.1 (W.D. Tex. 2021).

the Payday Lending Rule was promulgated using funds that had been appropriated in violation of the Appropriations Clause.[13]

A. Appropriations Clause Arguments

The Appropriations Clause provides that "[n]o money shall be drawn from the treasury, but in consequence of appropriations made by law."[14] The statutory provision addressing the funding of the CFPB, Section 5497, provides that

> [e]ach year ... the Board of Governors [of the Federal Reserve] shall transfer to the [CFPB] from the combined earnings of the Federal Reserve System, the amount determined by the Director to be reasonably necessary to carry out the authorities of the [CFPB] under Federal consumer financial law, taking into account such other sums made available to the Bureau from the preceding year (or quarter of such year).[15]

Other portions of Section 5497 indicate that Congress made a conscious effort to insulate the CFPB from the congressional appropriations process. Those portions include a statement that "[f]unds obtained by or transferred to the [Federal Reserve fund set aside for the CFPB] shall not be construed to be Government funds or appropriated monies,"[16] and a statement that the CFPB's funds will not be "subject to review by the Committees on Appropriations."[17] The gist of Community Financial's Appropriations Clause argument was that the Payday Lending Rule could not be enforced because Section 5497 purported to fund the CFPB through means that did not conform to the requirements of the Appropriations Clause.

Given the way in which Community Financial structured its challenge, the parties' arguments naturally coalesced around different theories as to why Section 5497 either did or did not run afoul of the Appropriations Clause.[18] After considering those arguments, the U.S. Court of Appeals for the Fifth Circuit ruled in favor of

---

[13] *Id.* at 364.

[14] U.S. CONST. art. I, § 9, cl. 7.

[15] 12 U.S.C. § 5497(a)(1).

[16] *Id.* § 5497(c)(2).

[17] *Id.* § 5497(a)(2)(C).

[18] *Cmty. Fin. Servs. Ass'n of Am.*, 558 F. Supp. 3d at 367 (describing the parties' arguments).

Community Financial.[19] Having lost at the Fifth Circuit, the government then sought review from the Supreme Court. The Supreme Court agreed to review the case to determine "[w]hether . . . the statute providing funding to the . . . CFPB . . . violates the Appropriations Clause . . . ."[20]

As could be expected, the parties' Supreme Court briefing continued to offer different arguments concerning the Appropriations Clause. The government, for example, argued that the Appropriations Clause "does not . . . limit the manner in which Congress itself may exercise its authority to make 'Appropriations' 'by law.'"[21] In contrast, Community Financial argued "that [Section 5497] is not a 'Law' making an 'Appropriation[],' but rather the repudiation of one" given that Section 5497 "cede[s] virtually unfettered discretion to an agency to determine the size of its own purse in perpetuity."[22]

B. The Majority Opinion

Having been asked to decide whether Section 5497 violates the Appropriations Clause, the Supreme Court dutifully limited itself to answering only that narrow question. Indeed, in the seven-Justice majority opinion authored by Justice Clarence Thomas, the Court stressed on two occasions that it was only tasked with answering a "narrow" question concerning Section 5497's compliance with the Appropriations Clause.[23]

Left unaddressed by the Court were "other constitutional checks on Congress' authority to create and fund an administrative agency."[24] The Court's willingness to refer to those "other constitutional checks"

---

[19] *Cmty. Fin. Servs. Ass'n of Am.*, 51 F.4th at 642.

[20] Petition for a Writ of Certiorari at I, Consumer Fin. Prot. Bureau v. Cmty. Fin. Servs. Ass'n of Am., 601 U.S. 416 (2024) (No. 22-448). The question presented also asked whether "the court of appeals erred . . . in vacating a regulation promulgated at a time when the CFPB was receiving such funding." *Id.*

[21] *Id.* at 12.

[22] Brief in Opposition at 18, Consumer Fin. Prot. Bureau v. Cmty. Fin. Servs. Ass'n of Am., 601 U.S. 416 (2024) (No. 22-448).

[23] *Cmty. Fin. Servs. Ass'n of Am.*, 601 U.S. at 421 ("In this case, we must decide the narrow question whether this funding mechanism complies with the Appropriations Clause."); *id.* at 424 ("We granted certiorari to address the narrow question whether the statute that provides funding to the Bureau violates the Appropriations Clause.").

[24] *Id.* at 441.

suggests that the Court was well aware of the fact that the Appropriations Clause is just one of many constitutional provisions that speak to Congress's power of the purse. Indeed, the majority explicitly stated that Consumer Financial had "err[ed] by reducing the power of the purse to only the principle expressed in the Appropriations Clause."[25]

Having limited its analysis to the requirements of the Appropriations Clause, the majority analyzed historical appropriations made in early England and the American colonies, as well as appropriations made by early Congresses.[26] After reviewing such history, the majority concluded that all the Appropriations Clause required is "a law that authorizes the disbursement of specified funds for identified purposes."[27] And because Section 5497 identified both a "source" of funding (i.e., a Federal Reserve fund), and a general "purpose" for the funding (i.e., to pay the expenses of the CFPB in carrying out its "duties and responsibilities"), Section 5497 satisfied the Appropriations Clause's limited demands.[28]

C. The Dissenting Opinion

Justice Samuel Alito authored a dissenting opinion, which was joined by Justice Neil Gorsuch. Like the majority, the dissent analyzed English and colonial history as well as the practices of early Congresses.[29] But unlike the majority, which maintained a narrow focus on the Appropriations Clause, the dissent drifted into discussions of the "power of the purse" more generally. For example, the dissent invoked Montesquieu to argue that "a legislature will lose its power of the purse if it passes an appropriation that lasts 'forever.'"[30] The dissent also explained how "the power of the purse played a central role in disputes between the Crown and Parliament,"[31] and that the Supreme Court's decision in *Seila Law v. CFPB*[32] "made the

[25] *Id.* at 438.

[26] *Id.* at 427–33.

[27] *Id.* at 438.

[28] *Id.* at 422–23, 435, 441 (citing 12 U.S.C. § 5497(c)(1)).

[29] *Id.* at 453–63 (Alito, J., dissenting).

[30] *Id.* at 448.

[31] *Id.* at 455.

[32] In *Seila Law*, the Court held that "the CFPB's leadership by a single individual removable only for inefficiency, neglect, or malfeasance violates the separation of powers." Seila L. LLC v. Consumer Fin. Prot. Bureau, 591 U.S. 197, 213 (2020).

CFPB accountable to the President, but . . . did nothing to protect Congress's power of the purse."[33]

To be sure, the dissent did focus parts of its analysis on the Appropriations Clause specifically (rather than Congress's power of the purse more generally). For example, the dissent explained that Congress's power of the purse was "protect[ed]" by the Appropriations Clause.[34] And the dissent explained that the Appropriations Clause "specifically addresses the question at hand."[35] But in the end, the majority was unconvinced by the dissent's efforts to funnel its broad, power-of-the-purse arguments into the specific text of the Appropriations Clause. As the majority explained, although the dissent "wind[s] its way through English, Colonial, and early American history about the struggle for popular control of the purse," the dissent "never connects its summary of history back to the word 'Appropriations.'"[36]

D. The Concurring Opinions

Two Justices authored concurring opinions. Justice Elena Kagan authored the lead concurrence, which was joined by Justices Sonia Sotomayor, Brett Kavanaugh, and Amy Coney Barrett.[37] Justice Kagan's concurrence, which was less than five pages long, offered a relatively breezy analysis.[38] What it added to the majority opinion (which all the concurring Justices joined) was a reference to 19th-, 20th-, and 21st-century congressional practice. Justice Kagan felt that this more modern practice underscored the ratification-era evidence highlighted in the majority opinion. As she explained, "[t]he founding-era practice" outlined by the majority opinion "became the 19th-century practice, which became the 20th-century practice, which became today's."[39]

---

[33] *Cmty. Fin. Servs. Ass'n of Am.*, 601 U.S. at 467 (Alito, J., dissenting).

[34] *Id.* at 447.

[35] *Id.* at 471 n.20. This comment was in part a response to the majority's reference to other constitutional principles, located outside of the Appropriations Clause, which speak to Congress's power of the purse.

[36] *Id.* at 438–39 (majority opinion).

[37] *Id.* at 441 (Kagan, J., concurring). All four of these concurring Justices also joined the majority opinion.

[38] This may have been because the Justices who joined the lead concurrence also joined the majority opinion (although the 22-page majority opinion was itself fairly short). *See Divided Argument, p(doom)*, at 42:01 (May 24, 2024), https://dividedargument.com/episodes/pdoom-6mmWoT6t?t=42m01s (Professor Daniel Epps noting that the majority opinion was "not as long as it could be for a big case involving constitutional law").

[39] *Cmty. Fin. Servs. Ass'n of Am.*, 601 U.S. at 442 (Kagan, J., concurring).

Justice Kagan wished to "therefore add one more point to the Court's opinion."[40] Namely, that in addition to "the Appropriations Clause's text and founding-era history," the "continuing tradition" of congressional appropriations practice in the 19th, 20th, and 21st centuries offered another reason to uphold the constitutionality of Section 5497.[41]

Justice Ketanji Brown Jackson authored her own solo concurrence.[42] In it, she stated that "nothing more" than "the plain meaning of the text of the Appropriations Clause" was "needed to decide th[e] case."[43] She also expressed her view concerning the proper judicial role. As she explained, "When the Constitution's text does not provide a limit to a coordinate branch's power, we should not lightly assume that Article III implicitly directs the Judiciary to find one."[44] Because she concluded that Consumer Financial's argument would require the Court to "find unstated limits in the . . . text" of the Appropriations Clause, she thought that the Court was right in its decision not to "undercut the considered judgments" of Congress.[45]

II. Elucidating the "Appropriate" Appropriations Question

To be blunt, the Supreme Court was asked to answer the wrong question. As noted above, the question presented in *Community Financial* asked the Court to determine whether Section 5497 violates the Appropriations Clause.[46] But that question does not get at the core of the issue, which concerns whether Congress has the underlying authority to enact Section 5497.[47]

---

[40] *Id.* at 445.

[41] *Id.*

[42] *Id.* (Jackson, J., concurring).

[43] *Id.*

[44] *Id.* at 446.

[45] *Id.* at 447.

[46] Petition for a Writ of Certiorari, *supra* note 20, at I.

[47] The limitations inherent in how the parties framed the case are the reasons why I previously argued that the Court should either dismiss the writ of certiorari as improvidently granted, or at least request supplemental briefing so that further argument could develop concerning the constitutional source (and thus constitutional limitations) of Congress's authority to enact appropriation statutes. *See, e.g.*, Chad Squitieri, *Which Appropriations Power?: Getting Back to Basics in the Supreme Court's Upcoming CFPB Funding Case*, YALE J. ON REGUL., NOTICE & COMMENT BLOG (July 5, 2023), https://www.yalejreg.com/nc/which-appropriations-power-getting-back-to-basics-in-the-supreme-courts-upcoming-cfpb-funding-case-by-chad-squitieri/.

To determine whether Congress has the authority to enact a particular appropriations statute, a court must first identify the constitutional text that arguably vests Congress with the authority to enact appropriations statutes. A court must then determine whether the appropriations statute at issue runs afoul of that text. Part II will therefore apply the first step of that two-step framework to Section 5497 and conclude that the Necessary and Proper Clause and the Commerce Clause offer Section 5497 its best bet at constitutionality. Part III will then turn to the second step of that two-step framework and conclude that Section 5497 runs afoul of the power vested in Congress by the Necessary and Proper Clause and Commerce Clause.

A. Constitutional Allusions

Where, precisely, is Congress vested with the authority to enact appropriations statutes? Two natural places to look are the Constitution's two references to appropriations. The first reference is the Appropriations Clause of Article I, Section 9, Clause 7, which provides that "[n]o money shall be drawn from the treasury, but in consequence of appropriations made by law."[48] The second reference is offered in Article I, Section 8, Clause 12, which provides that Congress shall have the power "[t]o raise and support armies, but no appropriation of money to that use shall be for a longer term than two years."[49]

Those two constitutional provisions certainly *allude* to Congress having appropriations authority. But a close reading of the clauses reveals that neither clause actually vests Congress with the authority to appropriate funds unrelated to the military.[50] As the Supreme Court explained in *Community Financial*, although "the Appropriations Clause presupposes Congress' powers over the purse," the "phrasing and location [of the Appropriations Clause] in the Constitution make clear that [the Appropriations Clause] is not itself the source of those powers."[51] Instead, the Appropriations Clause (like

---

[48] U.S. CONST. art. I, § 9, cl. 7.

[49] *Id.* § 8, cl. 12.

[50] Article I, Section 8, Clause 12 could be interpreted as vesting in Congress the authority to appropriate military funds to the extent that doing so inheres in "rais[ing] and support[ing] armies." *Id.*

[51] *Cmty. Fin. Servs. Ass'n of Am.*, 601 U.S. at 438.

other limitations outlined in Article I, Section 9) constitutes a "limitation" on congressional power, not a grant of power.[52]

Another sensible place to look for Congress's appropriations authority is the Taxing Clause of Article I, Section 8.[53] The Taxing Clause states that "Congress shall have power to lay and collect taxes, duties, imposts and excises, to pay the debts and provide for the common defense and general welfare of the United States."[54] The Taxing Clause is sometimes referred to as the Spending Clause. That misleading name is a reference to the latter portion of the clause, which refers to "pay[ing] the debts and provid[ing] for the common defense and general [w]elfare."[55] But for reasons that others have explained in detail, it cannot be the case that the Taxing Clause gives Congress a free-floating power to spend money.[56] To the contrary, the best reading of the Taxing Clause recognizes that the phrase "to pay the debts and provide for the common defense and general welfare" constitutes a *limitation* on Congress's authority to "lay and collect taxes, duties, imposts and excises."[57] As Justice Thomas has explained elsewhere, "the only authority vested by [the Taxing Clause] is a power to 'lay and collect Taxes, Duties, Imposts and Excises,'" which is a power that is further "qualified by the Debts and General Welfare Clauses, which limit the objects for which Congress can exercise that power."[58]

---

[52] *Id.*

[53] Squitieri, *supra* note 9, at 2–3.

[54] U.S. Const. art. I, § 8, cl. 1.

[55] *Id.*

[56] Lawson & Seidman, *supra* note 9, at 24–25.

[57] U.S. Const. art. I, § 8, cl. 1; Squitieri, *supra* note 9, at 3.

[58] Health & Hosp. Corp. of Marion Cnty. v. Talevski, 599 U.S. 166, 206 (2023) (Thomas, J., dissenting). At least one scholar has argued that Congress's spending authority is connected to the Article IV Property Clause. *See* David E. Engdahl, *The Basis of the Spending Power*, 18 Seattle U. L. Rev. 215, 216 (1995). That clause empowers Congress "to dispose of and make all needful Rules and Regulations respecting the Territory or other Property belonging to the United States." U.S. Const. art. IV, § 3, cl. 2. "According to Professor Engdahl, the phrase 'Territory or other Property' includes not only real property, but federal funds, and thus Congress's power to 'dispose of' such property includes a power to dispose of (*i.e.*, appropriate) federal funds." Squitieri, *supra* note 9, at 14 n.64 (quoting Engdahl, *supra*, at 250). For reasons I have explained in earlier work, I "agree with Professors [Gary] Lawson and [Guy] Seidman that 'the Property Clause can[not] bear th[e] . . . weight' that Professor Engdahl places upon it." *Id.* (quoting Lawson & Seidman, *supra* note 9, at 28).

B. *The Necessary and Proper Clause*

So where, then, is Congress vested with the authority to enact appropriations statutes? I argue that Congress's appropriations authority is vested by the interplay between two categories of constitutional provisions.[59] The first category contains those provisions vesting Congress (and other federal actors) with various substantive powers. Those substantive powers include Congress's powers to regulate various forms of commerce,[60] constitute tribunals,[61] punish piracies,[62] and so on. The second category concerns the powers vested in Congress by the Necessary and Proper Clause, which provides Congress with the authority to "make all laws which shall be necessary and proper for carrying into execution the foregoing powers, and all other powers vested by this Constitution in the government of the United States, or in any department or officer."[63]

The Necessary and Proper Clause is particularly important because it is the portion of the Constitution that actually vests Congress with its familiar authority to "make . . . laws."[64] And as will prove crucial, the Necessary and Proper Clause makes clear that Congress's authority to "make . . . laws" is *limited* by the requirement that any such laws "*shall* be necessary and proper" means of "carrying into execution" some other power vested elsewhere in the Constitution.[65] So if Congress relies on its Necessary and Proper Clause authority to make laws (including appropriations laws), then such

---

[59] *See* Squitieri, *supra* note 9, at 3.

[60] U.S. Const. art. I, § 8, cl. 3 (vesting Congress with the power "[t]o regulate Commerce with foreign Nations, and among the several States, and with the Indian Tribes").

[61] *Id.* cl. 9 (vesting Congress with the power "[t]o constitute Tribunals inferior to the supreme Court").

[62] *Id.* cl. 10 (vesting Congress with the power "[t]o define and punish Piracies and Felonies committed on the high Seas, and Offences against the Law of Nations").

[63] *Id.* cl. 18.

[64] *Id.*

[65] *Id.* (emphasis added).

laws "shall" be a "necessary and proper" means of carrying some other power into execution.[66]

In sum, it is the interplay between Congress's substantive powers and Congress's Necessary and Proper Clause authority that vests Congress with the authority to enact a limited category of appropriations laws—namely, appropriations laws which are a "necessary and proper" means of carrying some other power "into execution."[67] To offer one example, "a necessary and proper method for Congress to carry its power to 'punish piracies' into execution might be for Congress to enact a statute appropriating funds to pay for efforts to intercept pirates on the high seas."[68] Similarly, a "necessary and proper" component of Congress carrying its power to "constitute Tribunals inferior to the supreme Court" into execution might be to enact an appropriations statute funding the construction of a federal courthouse.[69]

C. The Commerce Clause

What substantive power might Congress have sought to carry "into execution" by enacting Section 5497? An analysis of Section 5497 reveals that its best shot at constitutionality rests on the argument that the statute is a "necessary and proper" means of carrying Congress's *Commerce Clause* power "into execution." To better see why, let's break that conclusion down into its integral parts.

---

[66] Congress may be able to rely on other authority to enact legal mandates, although in instances unrelated to the CFPB. For example, Article I, Section 8, Clause 17 empowers Congress "[t]o exercise exclusive Legislation in all Cases whatsoever, over" Washington, D.C. And Article IV, Section 3, Clause 2 empowers Congress to "make all needful Rules and Regulations respecting the Territory or other Property belonging to the United States." One might argue that such text empowers Congress to enact *un*necessary and *im*proper "Legislation" (including appropriations legislation) concerning Washington, D.C., and *un*necessary and *im*proper "Rules and Regulations" (including appropriations rules and regulations) concerning U.S. territories. The merits of such arguments fall outside the scope of this article.

[67] Squitieri, *supra* note 9, at 4.

[68] *Id.* (citing U.S. CONST. art. I, § 8, cl. 10).

[69] *See* U.S. CONST. art. I, § 8, cl. 9.

Section 5497 purports to empower the CFPB to demand funds from the Federal Reserve to pay for the CFPB's "duties and responsibilities."[70] That vague reference to the CFPB's "duties and responsibilities" is precisely what allowed the Supreme Court to conclude in *Community Financial* that Section 5497 offered a "purpose" sufficient to satisfy the Appropriations Clause's "source" and "purpose" requirements.[71]

So what are the CFPB's "duties and responsibilities"? A related statutory provision informs us that the CFPB has the statutory mandate to "regulate the offering and provision of consumer financial products or services under the Federal consumer financial laws."[72] Another statutory provision indicates that the CFPB is empowered to "ensur[e] that," among other things, "consumers are provided with timely and understandable information to make responsible decisions about financial transactions," "consumers are protected from unfair, deceptive, or abusive acts and practices," and "markets for consumer financial products and services operate transparently and efficiently to facilitate access and innovation."[73]

Together, these statutory provisions indicate that the CFPB's responsibilities and duties relate to consumers and economic markets. It is thus the Commerce Clause—which empowers Congress to "regulate Commerce with foreign Nations, and among the several States, and with the Indian Tribes"—that offers Section 5497 its best bet at constitutionality.[74]

To view the question from the inverse perspective: What other power, besides the Commerce Clause, could Congress have possibly relied on to fund an agency tasked with regulating consumer and economic matters on Congress's behalf? When faced with an "appropriate" appropriations challenge, the government should, of course, be free to defend the constitutionality of an appropriations statute by demonstrating that the statute was enacted pursuant to some other,

---

[70] 12 U.S.C. § 5497(c)(1).

[71] *Cmty. Fin. Servs. Ass'n of Am.*, 601 U.S. at 435 (citing 12 U.S.C. § 5497(c)(1)).

[72] 12 U.S.C. § 5491(a).

[73] 12 U.S.C § 5511(b); *see also id.* § 5511(c) (the CFPB's "primary functions" include "conducting financial education programs" and "collecting, investigating, and responding to consumer complaints").

[74] U.S. CONST. art. I, § 8, cl. 3.

less obvious source of power.[75] But a reviewing court should not be required to think up fanciful arguments on the government's behalf.

To be sure, it is not clear that an original understanding of the Commerce Clause would permit Congress to regulate (either directly, or by delegating regulatory authority to an agency) or fund the various matters that fall within the CFPB's broad remit.[76] And I do not claim that the CFPB's regulatory authority is consistent with an original understanding of the Commerce Clause. Instead, I merely posit that, if *any* of Congress's powers enable Congress to create and fund the CFPB as it exists in current form, then it has got to be Congress's Commerce Clause power. This is what I mean when I say that the Necessary and Proper Clause and the Commerce Clause give Section 5497 its "best bet" at constitutionality.

Having identified the precise constitutional text that Congress presumably sought to rely on to enact Section 5497, the dispositive question for determining the constitutionality of Section 5497 becomes clear. To wit, the dispositive question (i.e., the "appropriate" question) asks whether Section 5497 is a "necessary and proper" means of carrying Congress's Commerce Clause power "into execution."[77]

III. Answering the "Appropriate" Appropriations Question

The narrow Appropriations Clause holding in *Community Financial* should be of only limited relevance to future courts tasked with answering the "appropriate" appropriations question identified above. That is because the holding in *Community Financial* does not speak to the constitutional text that vests Congress with appropriations authority. How, then, should courts go about interpreting the limitations imposed by the constitutional text that vests Congress with appropriations authority? Part III will offer an answer.

In particular, Part III.A will outline what might be two different methodologies offered by the Justices in *Community Financial*, arguing that both methodologies should determine the constitutionality

---

[75] *See* Squitieri, supra note 9, at 19 (proposing questions that the Justices could ask the government concerning other potential sources of congressional authority).

[76] *See, e.g.,* Randy E. Barnett, *Why Congress and the Courts Should Obey the Original Meaning of the Commerce Clause,* NAT'L CONST. CTR., https://constitutioncenter.org/the-constitution/articles/article-i/clauses/752 (discussing "the original meaning of the Commerce Clause") (last visited July 26, 2024).

[77] U.S. CONST. art. I, § 8, cl. 17; *see also* Squitieri, *supra* note 9, at 17–18.

of appropriations statutes by conducting a power-specific analysis. Part III.B will focus primarily on the methodology that is currently dominant at the Court (originalism) and use that methodology to conduct a power-specific analysis of Section 5497. Under this analysis, Section 5497 runs afoul of the power vested in Congress by the Necessary and Proper Clause and Commerce Clause. Finally, Part III.C will conclude by explaining that, although the Justices telegraphed a lack of interest in hearing appropriations challenges in the future, that preference may not be satisfied given that lower courts do not enjoy the same luxury in shaping their dockets.

A. Two Methodologies

Justice Thomas's majority opinion employed an interpretative methodology that is currently dominant at the Court: originalism. Originalism is defined by two core tenets: first, that the meaning of the Constitution became fixed at the time it was ratified, and second, that this fixed meaning constrains government action today.[78] Today, the most prominent form of originalism focuses on elucidating a text's "original public meaning," which "roughly" refers to "the meaning that the text had for competent speakers of American English at the time each provision of the text was framed and ratified."[79] Justice Thomas's majority opinion analyzed the Appropriation Clause's "text, the history against which that text was enacted, and congressional practice immediately following ratification."[80] The opinion thus falls comfortably within the confines of original public meaning originalism.

Justice Kagan's concurring opinion showcased what is arguably a second methodology: traditionalism.[81] The precise contours of traditionalism (including the extent to which it overlaps with, or is encompassed by, originalism) are still being worked out.[82] But I will

[78] Lawrence B. Solum, *The Fixation Thesis: The Role of Historical Fact in Original Meaning*, 91 NOTRE DAME L. REV. 1, 1 (2015) (referring to the Fixation Thesis and the Constraint Principle).

[79] Lawrence B. Solum, *The Public Meaning Thesis: An Originalist Theory of Constitutional Meaning*, 101 B.U. L. REV. 1953, 1957 (2021).

[80] *Cmty. Fin. Servs. Ass'n of Am.*, 601 U.S. at 426.

[81] *See* Josh Blackman, *CFPB v. CFSAA: Originalists v. Traditionalists*, VOLOKH CONSPIRACY (May 17, 2024, 3:29PM), https://reason.com/volokh/2024/05/17/cfpb-v-cfsaa-originalists-v-traditionalists/.

[82] *See, e.g.*, United States v. Rahimi, 144 S. Ct. 1889, 1916 n.4 (2024) (Kavanaugh, J., concurring) (flagging open questions and collecting scholarship).

presume for the moment that traditionalism offers a distinct methodology that may appeal to some Justices. It is therefore useful to briefly define traditionalism.

On one account, traditionalism is "defined by two key elements."[83] The first is that "concrete practices, rather than principles, ideas, judicial precedents, and so on, [are] the determinants of constitutional meaning and law."[84] The second element considers "the endurance of those practices as a composite of their age, longevity, and density, evidence for which includes the practice's use before, during, and after enactment of a constitutional provision."[85] Justice Kagan's attempt to connect Section 5497 to "more than two centuries [of] unbroken congressional practice" can therefore be characterized as traditionalist.[86]

The distinction between originalism and traditionalism can seem slight, in part because many originalists (like traditionalists) also examine concrete practice. Justice Thomas's majority opinion, for example, examined "[t]he practice of the First Congress."[87] Moreover, aspects of Justice Kagan's concurrence could be characterized as employing a form of "liquidated originalism," which is distinct from traditionalism because it gives special attention to practice in order to "settle practically underdeterminate new law by adopting one permissible interpretation rather than another."[88]

---

[83] Marc O. DeGirolami, *Traditionalism Rising*, 24 J. OF CONTEMP. LEGAL ISSUES 9, 14 (2022).

[84] *Id.*

[85] *Id.*

[86] *Cmty. Fin. Servs. Ass'n of Am.*, 601 U.S. at 445 (Kagan, J., concurring).

[87] *Id.* at 432 (majority opinion).

[88] Jeffrey A. Pojanowski & Kevin C. Walsh, *Enduring Originalism*, 105 GEO. L.J. 97, 142 (2016); *see also* Elias Neibart, *Methodological Convergence in* Community Financial Services, HARV. L. REV. BLOG (May 26, 2024), https://harvardlawreview.org/blog/2024/05/methodological-convergence-in-community-financial-services/ (arguing that the opinions in "*Community Financial Services* suggest[] that we are all (still) originalists," in part because "Justice Kagan agreed with the majority that the fixed original meaning should control."). The best reading of Justice Kagan's concurrence is that it was written in consciously broad terms so that different Justices (with different interpretive theories) could speak as a single cohort. *See* Divided Argument, *p(doom)*, at 1:00:54, https://dividedargument.com/episodes/pdoom-6mmWoT6t?t=1h0m54s (Professor William Baude stating that "the whole [concurrence] is phrased in a sufficiently broad way that . . . [the concurring Justices] can all join [the concurrence] comfortably").

But the two methodologies consider historical practice for different reasons.

For originalists, historical practice offers a means of elucidating the Constitution's *original* meaning. Traditionalists, by contrast, are more comfortable focusing on the Constitution's *present* meaning (so long as that meaning is a faithful development of its initial source). Thus, some "originalists will assign much more weight to practices at enactment (or immediately post-enactment) than to pre-enactment or later post-enactment practices, while this is not so for traditionalists."[89] This distinction might explain why Justice Kagan was more comfortable than Justice Thomas with concluding that Section 5497 would "fit right in" with congressional practice from the 20th and 21st centuries.[90] Indeed, one of the few historical funding statutes that Justice Kagan cited was a national defense funding statute from 1989—a statute enacted more than two centuries after the Constitution's ratification.[91]

Future litigants would be wise to acknowledge that a methodological split may be growing at the Court—although several Justices have suggested that they consider tradition only within the confines of an originalist framework.[92] For now, I wish to highlight something common to both methodologies. When it comes to answering the "appropriate" appropriations question, both originalists and traditionalists should pay special attention to the *precise* power that Congress must rely on to enact a particular appropriations statute.

Originalism focuses on elucidating the original meaning of *specific* constitutional text vesting *specific* congressional powers. And traditionalism, properly applied, should also employ a power-specific analysis. Traditionalists should avoid relying on a "tradition" set at

---

[89] DeGirolami, *supra* note 83, at 27.

[90] *Cmty. Fin. Servs. Ass'n of Am.*, 601 U.S. at 442 (Kagan, J., concurring).

[91] *Id.* at 443 (citing Act of Nov. 29, 1989, § 1605(a), 103 Stat. 1598).

[92] *See, e.g.*, Vidal v. Elster, 602 U.S. 286, 323 (2024) (Barrett, J., concurring in part) (citing Justice Kagan's *Community Financial* concurrence as an example of "longstanding practice of the political branches" serving to "reinforce our understanding of the Constitution's original meaning," but cautioning that "tradition is not an end in itself"); Michael Ramsey, *Originalism-fest in* Rahimi v. United States, ORIGINALISM BLOG (June 22, 2024), https://originalismblog.typepad.com/the-originalism-blog/2024/06/originalism-fest-in-rahimi-v-united-statesmichael-ramsey.html (noting that each of Justices Gorsuch's, Kavanaugh's, and Barrett's concurring opinions in *United States v. Rahimi* "reaffirms a commitment to originalism").

such a high level of generality that it conflicts with the Constitution's fundamental structure. That structure imposes higher-order limitations on Congress's ability to develop or embrace new governmental practices.[93] A congressional "tradition" that allows Congress to vest itself with new power (by, say, claiming new appropriations authority from sources located outside of the enumerated list of powers vested by the Constitution) would permit Congress to transform itself into something it is not. And while other forms of government may permit a legislature to redefine its own *type*, ours does not. Instead, our government locates the sovereignty to change its form not in the legislature, but in "We the People"—whose Constitution established a Congress of carefully enumerated powers.[94]

B. Conducting a Power-Specific Analyses

Given originalism's dominance at the Court, I present here a power-specific analysis on primarily originalist terms. The analysis begins with a consideration of historical practice, which reveals an unmistakable conclusion: Annual appropriations have been a dominant way to fund governmental operations for quite some time.

In particular, the English Parliament, American colonial legislatures, and early Congresses all used the annual appropriations process in the normal course.[95] Given this history, annual

---

[93] *See* A.C. Pritchard & Todd J. Zywicki, *Constitutions and Spontaneous Orders: A Response to Professor McGinnis*, 77 N.C. L. Rᴇᴠ. 537, 538–39 (1999) (arguing that, "[w]hen operating as the Framers intended, federalism and the separation of powers pit government actors in a zero-sum game," and that government actors locked in a "zero-sum game inevitably will try to change the rules to make it a positive-sum game for themselves"); *see also* DeGirolami, *supra* note 83, at 35 (discussing the level-of-generality objection to traditionalism and explaining that "[d]rawing [a tradition] too broadly will dilute the tradition to the point where [traditionalism] begins to resemble something else altogether—often something like principle-driven adjudication").

[94] This would limit traditionalism's ability to "base[] its application of a text" on past interpretations of "some *other* text." Sherif Girgis, *Living Traditionalism*, 98 N.Y.U. L. Rᴇᴠ. 1477, 1491 n.65 (2023). This limit would apply at least in cases concerning the *source* of governmental power, rather than the scope of a *right*. *Cf. Rahimi*, 144 S. Ct. at 1940 n.6 (Thomas, J., dissenting) (concluding that, although the challenged statute fell outside of the nation's tradition of firearm regulation (and thus constituted a violation of the challenger's Second Amendment *right*), it was "doubt[ful]" that the challenged statute was "a proper exercise of Congress's *power* under the Commerce Clause") (emphasis added).

[95] Squitieri, *supra* note 9, at 21–22.

appropriations offer "something of a constitutional safe harbor (*i.e.,* a manner of funding the government that was so familiar to the objective reader [at the time of ratification] that its necessity and properness can rarely if ever be called into question)."[96]

Of course, even if the annual appropriations process offers a constitutional safe harbor, that does not mean Congress may *never* stray from that safe harbor. Congress can choose an alternative funding mechanism when doing so is a "necessary and proper" means of carrying some power "into execution." But absent a historical example of Congress using one of its enumerated powers to deviate from the annual appropriations process, "judicial suspicions should be heightened."[97] And this brings us to the fundamentally confused way in which various historical funding statutes were analyzed in *Community Financial.*

In *Community Financial,* the government defended the constitutionality of Section 5497 by comparing it to historical statutes funding other agencies (such as the Post Office and National Mint) through fees collected outside of the annual appropriations process.[98] The government argued that since those other agencies could be funded by fees earned outside of the annual appropriations process, the CFPB could also be funded outside of the annual appropriations process. Community Financial responded with a conduct-based argument. That conduct-based argument contended that agencies such as the Post Office and National Mint were "inherently constrained" because "the public can . . . refuse to buy the agencies' services to influence [the agencies'] conduct," whereas the public's refusal to buy the CFPB's services could not influence the CFPB's funding.[99] In the end, the Court dismissed Community Financial's conduct-based argument on the grounds that it made "no attempt to explain

---

[96] *Id.* at 23.

[97] *Id.* To say that judicial suspicions should be heightened is not to say that a court should adopt a "'use it or lose it' view of legislative authority." *Rahimi,* 144 S. Ct. at 1925 (Barrett, J., concurring). The failure to exercise power in a particular way is not dipositive proof that such an exercise is unlawful; it simply gives courts reason to carefully consider whether the exercise is lawful. *Cf.* Chad Squitieri, *"Recommend . . . Measures": A Textualist Reformulation of the Major Questions Doctrine,* 75 BAYLOR L. REV. 706, 761 (2023) ("When the President purports to find a particularly new power in a particularly old statute . . . there is increased reason to" be "suspect.").

[98] *E.g.,* Petition for a Writ of Certiorari, *supra* note 20, at 14.

[99] Brief in Opposition, *supra* note 22, at 22.

why the possibility that the public's choices could restrain fee-based agencies' revenue is relevant to the question whether a law complies with the constitutional imperative that there be an appropriation."[100]

The Court correctly concluded that Community Financial's conduct-based argument was immaterial to the question of what the *Appropriations Clause* requires. But the immateriality of the distinctions for purposes of the Appropriations Clause does not mean that the distinctions between Section 5497 and the historical funding examples are not important *at all*. To the contrary, the distinctions reveal quite a bit. The historical funding examples all speak to what past Congresses thought to be "necessary and proper" exercises of non-*Commerce Clause* powers. They thus offer little to no historical support for the argument that Section 5497 constitutes a "necessary and proper" means of carrying Congress's *Commerce Clause* power into execution.

Start with the government's argument that "[i]n 1792, Congress established a national Post Office, to be funded through its collection of postage rates."[101] That funding statute offers an example of what an early Congress thought to be a "necessary and proper" means of carrying into execution Congress's power to "[t]o establish post offices and post roads."[102] As I've argued before, the history of postal funding demonstrates that funding postal systems through postal fees was a constitutional (i.e, necessary and proper) departure from the annual appropriations safe harbor. "[P]rior to the Constitution, the Articles of Confederation had ensured that 'postage' could be 'exact[ed] . . . on the papers passing thro' [one state to another] as may be requisite to defray . . . expenses,'" and "postal systems in both the American colonies and England had been funded historically through the collection of postage fees."[103] The upshot of this history is that "maintaining a postal funding scheme similar to the ones that had existed in England, the colonies, and early America would have no doubt been understood by the objective reader in 1788 to be a 'necessary and proper' means of carrying Congress's postal powers 'into execution.'"[104] But an exercise of Congress's *postal*

---

[100] *Cmty. Fin. Servs. Ass'n of Am.*, 601 U.S. at 437.

[101] Petition for a Writ of Certiorari, *supra* note 20, at 14.

[102] U.S. CONST. art. I, § 8, cl. 7.

[103] Squitieri, *supra* note 9, at 25.

[104] *Id.*

powers is of little to no relevance to elucidating Congress's ability to exercise its *Commerce Clause* authority.

Consider also the government's argument that, in 1792, Congress "created a national mint, to be funded in part through its collection of fees."[105] That statute could offer an example of what an early Congress thought to be a "necessary and proper" means of carrying into execution Congress's power to "coin money."[106] And as I have demonstrated elsewhere, state governments operating under the Articles of Confederation funded the coining of their state currencies outside of the annual appropriations process.[107] This history suggests that the ordinary reader in 1788 "would have thought that maintaining a funding scheme for federal coin that was similar to how coining operations were funded prior to the Constitution was a 'necessary and proper' means of carrying Congress's *coining* power into execution."[108] But again, a 1792 exercise of Congress's *coining* power does not speak to the original meaning of Congress's *commerce* power.

In *Community Financial*, the government also cited the First Bank of the United States (which was funded through the sale of stock) as an example of Congress funding an entity outside of the annual appropriations process.[109] But "even assuming that the First Bank was established pursuant to a *constitutional* exercise of Congress's *Commerce Clause* authority (as compared to an (un)constitutional exercise of that or some other power),"[110] the First Bank does not lend sufficient support for the idea that Section 5497 is a constitutional exercise of Congress's Commerce Clause authority. "That is because funding central banks through the sale of stock has a historical pedigree," which indicates that a stock-funding regime constitutes a constitutional "departure from the standard method of funding government through annual appropriations."[111] This historical pedi-

---

[105] Petition for a Writ of Certiorari., *supra* note 20, at 14.

[106] U.S. CONST. art I, § 8, cl. 5.

[107] Squitieri, *supra* note 9, at 25–26.

[108] *Id.* at 26 (emphasis added).

[109] Brief for the Petitioners at 22, Consumer Fin. Prot. Bureau v. Cmty. Fin. Servs. Ass'n of Am., 601 U.S. 416 (2024) (No. 22-448) (citation omitted).

[110] Squitieri, *supra* note 9, at 27.

[111] *Id.* (referring to the Bank of England (1694), Bank of North America (1781), and the Bank of New York (1784)).

gree "demonstrate[s] that . . . it would not be out of the norm to fund that bank through private funds."[112] But "a long history of funding banks through private investments," which "might lend constitutional legitimacy to funding the First Bank through similar means, . . . does not offer support for the argument that the federal government could fund the enforcement of its consumer protection laws via a statute like Section 5497."[113]

As a final historical example, consider the government's 11th-hour argument that the "First Congress funded the Customs Service and Revenue Officers in part through the officers' collection of 'penalties, fines and forfeitures.'"[114] At oral argument, the government conceded that the Customs Service offered the government its "best example historically."[115] The concession was notable, given that the government did not mention this "best" example until its final reply brief.[116] But even this "best" example is readily distinguishable from Section 5497.

To start, the First Congress's funding of the Customs Service need not be understood as an exercise of Congress's Commerce Clause authority. Instead, the funding of the Customs Service, which Congress established to enforce "import and tonnage duties,"[117] is perhaps best understood as an exercise of Congress's Taxing Clause authority "[t]o lay and collect Taxes, Duties, Imposts and Excises."[118] This point is even more obvious when it comes to deducing the power that the First Congress relied on to fund Revenue Officers, who were tasked with "enforc[ing] the nation's first internal *tax*."[119] Recognizing the customs and revenue examples as exercises of Congress's

---

[112] *Id.* at 28.

[113] *Id.*

[114] Reply of Petitioners at 17, Consumer Fin. Prot. Bureau v. Cmty. Fin. Servs. Ass'n of Am., 601 U.S. 416 (2024) (No. 22-448).

[115] Transcript of Oral Argument at 31, Consumer Fin. Prot. Bureau v. Cmty. Fin. Servs. Ass'n of Am., 601 U.S. 416 (2024) (No. 22-448).

[116] This timing suggests the value of a well-written amicus brief, as the Customs Service was highlighted in an amicus brief filed before the government's reply. *See* Brief of Professors of History and Constitutional Law as Amici Curiae in Support of Petitioners at 3, 22–24, Consumer Fin. Prot. Bureau v. Cmty. Fin. Servs. Ass'n of Am., 601 U.S. 416 (2024) (No. 22-448) [hereinafter Amicus Brief].

[117] *Id.* at 22 (citations omitted).

[118] U.S. CONST. art. I, § 8, cl. 1.

[119] Amicus Brief, *supra* note 116, at 3 (emphasis added).

Taxing Clause authority would indicate that even the government's "best" example is (like most of the government's other examples)[120] an example of Congress invoking something *other than* Congress's Commerce Clause authority.

With that said, an originalist might conclude that the customs and revenue examples lend *some* support to the idea that Section 5497 is a "necessary and proper" means of carrying Congress's Commerce Clause power into execution. After all, the First Congress might have thought itself to be exercising its Commerce Clause power. And more fundamentally, in early America, "the word 'duties'" (which at least in England may have been partially interchangeable with the word "customs") was understood to "include[] levies on imports and exports, whether imposed for revenue or to *regulate commerce*."[121] Given as much, even the First Congress's exercise of its power to impose customs and duties might offer some insight into the contours of Congress's related power to regulate *commerce*.

But even if historical evidence speaking to Congress's Taxing Clause power helps inform the original meaning of Congress's Commerce Clause power, the customs and revenue examples are distinguishable from Section 5497. On this point the full relevance of the dissenting arguments in *Community Financial* comes into focus.

Justice Alito's dissent took aim at the government's reliance on the Customs Service. Unlike the Customs Service, he explained, "[t]he CFPB . . . is an entirely different creature," with uniquely "broad and vast" powers and "discretionary authority."[122] Further unlike the Customs Service, the CFPB "does not collect fees from persons and entities to which it provides services or persons and entities that are subject to its authority," and the CFPB "is permitted to keep and invest surplus funds."[123] What's more, Justice Alito high-

---

[120] The government also relied on statutes enacted long after the Constitution's ratification. Squitieri, *supra* note 9, at 29 n.141 (collecting citations). I do not analyze those statutes here because, "even if" they were "exercises of Congress's . . . Commerce Clause authority," they are "less probative to an originalist inquiry." *Id.*

[121] Robert G. Natelson, *What the Constitution Means by "Duties, Imposts, and Excises" — and "Taxes" (Direct or Otherwise)*, 66 CASE W. RSRV. L. REV. 297, 321 (2015) (emphases added).

[122] *Cmty. Fin. Servs. Ass'n of Am.*, 601 U.S. at 466 (Alito, J., dissenting).

[123] *Id.*

lighted how the text of Section 5497 (quoted earlier)[124] demonstrated a conscious effort to limit Congress's control over appropriations.[125] After considering these unique features of Section 5497, Justice Alito concluded that the statute "blatantly attempts to circumvent the Constitution."[126]

Justice Alito's argument was, at its core, an argument concerning the *necessity and properness* of Section 5497. That argument had a clear *structural* dimension: It focused on the ways in which Section 5497's unique characteristics permitted Congress to undermine the constitutional decision to place the power of the purse in the hands of an accountable Congress rather than the Executive Branch.[127] The argument also had a clear *historical* dimension: It explored the historical disputes that resulted in a need for legislative control of the purse strings.[128] The problem with the argument, however, was that it focused on the wrong constitutional *text*. Given the way in which the parties had litigated the case, the dissent's argument was judged by the majority for its ability to inform the language of the Appropriations Clause.[129] But the argument's persuasiveness is only fully understood when it is considered in terms of the Necessary and Proper Clause.

And so yes, the majority might have been correct to conclude that the dissent's "attempt to distinguish the Customs Service . . . from the [CFPB]" was not "convincing" because "it is unclear why these differences matter" for purposes of the *Appropriations Clause*.[130] But that narrow focus on the *Appropriations Clause* was precisely the problem. When the dissent's arguments are freed from the artificial constraints imposed by an unduly narrow focus on the Appropriations Clause, the import of the distinctions highlighted by the dissent becomes clearer.

However, the question that seems to lie—in unelucidated form—at the core of the dissent's analysis will be left to a future court to bring

---

[124] *Supra* Part I.A. (quoting 12 U.S.C. §§ 5497(a)(2)(C), (c)(2)).

[125] *Cmty. Fin. Servs. Ass'n of Am.*, 601 U.S. at 451 (Alito, J., dissenting) (citations omitted).

[126] *Id.* at 471.

[127] *See id.* at 467–68.

[128] *See id.* at 448–49, 453–58.

[129] *Id.* at 438 (majority opinion).

[130] *Id.* at 441.

to the forefront. Section 5497 consciously seeks to undermine the Constitution's historically informed structure. It permits Congress to severely limit its own ability to control the funding of an agency tasked with regulating commerce on Congress's behalf. The question therefore remains: Is such a statute a "necessary and proper" means of carrying Congress's Commerce Clause power "into execution"? When viewed in those more appropriate terms, the question would seem to answer itself.

C. Telegraphing a Lack of Interest

This article would be missing something important if it did not conclude by mentioning a point that the majority and lead concurrence seemed to telegraph, even if those opinions did not make the point explicit. Put more directly: The majority and lead concurrence signaled a lack of interest in entertaining future appropriations challenges.

This point is perhaps most palpable in the lead concurrence by Justice Kagan, which four Justices joined despite their all joining a majority opinion that offered a sufficient basis to resolve the case. Recall that the lead concurrence explained that modern congressional practice offered an additional reason (beyond ratification-era evidence) to conclude that Section 5497 satisfied the Appropriations Clause. With the obvious caveat that one should be careful before placing too much weight on judicial tea-leaf-reading, the concurrence's focus on modern practice seemed to express a desire to let sleeping dogs lie and not to unravel the various ways that modern Congresses have sought to fund the federal government.

To a lesser extent, the majority can also be read as signaling a lack of interest in upsetting the apple cart. It would have been relatively simple for the majority to briefly expand on its point that there may be "other constitutional checks on Congress' authority to create and fund an administrative agency."[131] Indeed, Justice Thomas has elsewhere explained in a dissenting opinion that "there are serious problems" with the "Court's modern doctrine" concerning Congress's authority to spend funds.[132] And in making that point, Justice Thomas explained that "the Necessary and Proper Clause is a natural candidate for the spending power because spending funds may be 'necessary and proper for carrying into Execution' the Federal Government's

---

[131] *Id.*

[132] *Talevski*, 599 U.S at 206 (Thomas, J., dissenting).

enumerated powers."[133] The fact that Justice Thomas did not take the time to offer similar guidance regarding the textual hook for Congress's appropriations authority in *Community Financial* seems important. But of course, the distinction between Justice Thomas's two opinions could be chalked up to the difference between a single-Justice dissent and a seven-Justice majority. The latter leaves the authoring Justice less freedom to expand on nondispositive topics (particularly when a four-Justice concurrence stands ready at the door).

Regardless of whether the majority and lead concurrence should be read as suggesting a lack of interest in considering future appropriations challenges, the Court might have little choice in the matter. Typically, lower federal courts must entertain cases as they are presented. Therefore, a lower court presented with an appropriations challenge based on the sort of power-specific analysis proposed in this article would have to consider the relevant analysis head on. And were the lower court to hold an appropriations statute unconstitutional, the Supreme Court would no doubt seek to review the constitutionality of the statute itself. Were it to do so, the Court would not be able to resolve the case by citing to its Appropriations Clause holding in *Community Financial*. Nor would originalist Justices be able to convincingly rely on congressional practice relating only to unrelated congressional powers. Instead, an originalist Court seeking to resolve the issue convincingly should consider the limitations imposed by the actual text that Congress presumably relied on to enact the appropriations statute at issue.

Conclusion

In *Community Financial*, the Court offered a narrow holding that spoke to the requirements imposed by the Appropriations Clause. But that holding should be of only limited relevance to "appropriate" appropriations challenges—that is, future challenges based on the constitutional text that actually vests Congress with authority to enact appropriations statutes. With regard to Section 5497, the "appropriate" appropriations question asks whether Section 5497 constitutes a "necessary and proper" means of carrying Congress's Commerce Clause authority "into execution." For the reasons sketched out above, the answer to that question is "no."

---

[133] *Id.* at 209.

Moore and the Limits of the Taxing Power

Sean P. McElroy*

Tax cases are not the bread and butter of the U.S. Supreme Court. The Court's "sporadic omnipotence in a field beset by invisible boomerangs"[1] in the tax law has become, indeed, sporadic. The labyrinth of the U.S. tax code is usually the territory of a handful of tax specialists and presidential campaigns—not the Supreme Court. So it is quite rare that a tax case receives the significant public attention that *Moore v. United States*[2] commanded. *The Wall Street Journal* ran two separate editorials on the case.[3] *The New York Times* said the case "could rewrite the Tax Code."[4] Editorials and commentary abounded.

On its face, *Moore* involves a highly technical provision of international tax law—what the parties refer to as the Mandatory Repatriation Tax (MRT). The MRT was passed in 2017 as part of the

---

* Sean P. McElroy is an attorney at Fenwick & West LLP in Seattle, Washington. He thanks Matthew Dimon, David Forst, and Larissa Neumann for their helpful comments. All views expressed are his own.

[1] Arrowsmith v. Comm'r, 344 U.S. 6, 12 (1952) (Jackson, J., dissenting).

[2] 144 S. Ct. 1680 (2024).

[3] Editorial, *The Supreme Court and a Wealth Tax*, WALL ST. J. (Dec. 5, 2023, 6:46 PM), https://www.wsj.com/articles/moore-v-u-s-supreme-court-wealth-tax-elizabeth-prelogar-34f7814f; Editorial, *A Supreme Court Mistake on Wealth Taxes*, WALL ST. J. (June 20, 2024, 5:39 PM), https://www.wsj.com/articles/moore-v-u-s-supreme-court-mandatory-repatriation-tax-brett-kavanaugh-amy-coney-barrett-23d99510.

[4] Andrew Ross Sorkin et al., *The Supreme Court Battle That Could Rewrite the Tax Code*, N.Y. TIMES (Dec. 5, 2023), https://www.nytimes.com/2023/12/05/business/dealbook/supreme-court-income-tax-code.html.

bill known as the Tax Cuts and Jobs Act (TCJA).[5] Specifically, *Moore* considered the application of the MRT to Charles and Kathleen Moore, U.S. citizens who were individual shareholders of an Indian corporation. As a result of the MRT, the Moores owed $14,729 in federal tax (based on a calculation of $132,512 in income). They paid the tax and then sued for a refund.

But the MRT had a much larger impact than the Moores' approximately $15,000 in federal tax. Despite its being a one-time tax, U.S. corporations (along with some individuals) paid a *lot* of tax under the MRT. Per one study, the MRT resulted in the payment of approximately $45 to $50 *billion* in U.S. tax from 2017 to 2020.[6] Finding the MRT unconstitutional could have led to refunds of unprecedented proportions to individuals and to U.S. multinationals.

But perhaps even more important, what the Court said about taxes in the context of the MRT could have had enormous ramifications for tax law yet to be enacted, including taxes on wealth and unrealized capital gains. And some argued that finding the MRT unconstitutional would have had ramifications for other taxes already on the books. They warned of a parade of horribles whereby *Moore* would give rise to challenges to broad swaths of the tax code currently in effect. As this article will discuss, the concern that *Moore* could have led to this parade of horribles was fundamentally misguided.

The nuances and technical details of the MRT are important to *Moore*. But more important, through *Moore* the Court revisited a crucial question: What, precisely, are the limits of Congress's taxing power? Specifically, how do those limits fit into the design of the U.S.

---

[5] The TCJA was passed through the budget reconciliation process (to avoid a potential filibuster in the Senate), not through the normal legislative process. The bill's full name is "An Act to provide for reconciliation pursuant to titles II and V of the concurrent resolution on the budget for fiscal year 2018." In a truly arcane ruling on Senate procedure, the Senate Parliamentarian ruled that because a short title for a bill has no impact on the budget, a budget reconciliation bill is not allowed to have a short title. *See* Naiomi Jagoda, *Senate Parliamentarian Rules against GOP Tax Bill's Name*, THE HILL (Dec. 19, 2017), https://thehill.com/policy/finance/365691-senate-parliamentarian-rules-against-gop-tax-bills-name/. This article will, nevertheless, refer to the bill as the Tax Cuts and Jobs Act or TCJA.

[6] Alex Arnon & Mariko Paulson, *Did Tax Cuts and Jobs Act of 2017 Increase Revenue on US Corporations' Foreign Income?*, BUDGET MODEL – PENN WHARTON (Oct. 12, 2023), https://budgetmodel.wharton.upenn.edu/issues/2023/10/12/did-tcja-increase-revenue-on-us-corporation-foreign-income.

international tax system? And although the Court ruled in *Moore* that the MRT was constitutional, the limits to Congress's taxing power remain unclear. Each of the four opinions in the case answered the question in different ways. And the majority opinion's analysis—even where misguided—raises key questions that any future drafters of tax legislation or litigants challenging a tax must consider.

The first part of this article provides a very high-level overview of the U.S. international tax system and how the MRT fits into that global system. The second part briefly provides background on the constitutional issues raised by the MRT. And the third part provides a critical discussion of the *Moore* decision itself.

I. U.S. International Tax Law and the MRT

In general, the United States taxes the international activities of U.S. persons in two ways. As used in this article, the term "U.S. persons" is a term of art in the tax code that includes U.S. citizens, residents, and domestic corporations.[7]

U.S. persons are generally taxed on *their* worldwide income (albeit with a large array of credits and deductions). Accordingly, if a U.S. citizen earns income in a foreign country, the U.S. citizen is subject to U.S. tax on that income. Likewise, if a domestic corporation earns income by operating in a foreign country, that domestic corporation is still subject to U.S. tax on that income. To prevent double taxation, the tax code provides foreign tax credits, and these credits may lower the U.S. tax owed to zero in certain cases when combined with other deductions. But even with these credits, the United States still fundamentally imposes tax on the individual or the corporation. And while the TCJA made various changes to the rules for crediting taxes, it did not change the United States' fundamental worldwide structure of taxation, which was in place both before and after the TCJA became law (albeit with various significant changes).[8]

But what happens when a U.S. person (either an individual or a corporation) owns a foreign corporation that itself earns foreign income? Here, the foreign corporation *itself* is not subject to U.S. tax

---

[7] Partnerships, although usually included in this term, are a special case—one addressed in more detail within.

[8] Unlike the United States, most countries have a territorial system—where the country only taxes income earned in their country.

on its foreign income (because it is not a U.S. person).[9] Instead, Congress has imposed taxes at the *shareholder* level on the U.S. persons that own the stock. It was these shareholder-level taxes that were significantly modified through the TCJA and at issue in *Moore*.

Before the TCJA, there were generally two ways a U.S. shareholder could be subject to tax on the income of a foreign corporation that the shareholder owned. The first was when the foreign corporation paid a dividend to the U.S. person, in which case that dividend was includable as income. The second was through an anti-deferral regime known as Subpart F, which had been in place since 1962. Subpart F imposed a shareholder-level tax on U.S. persons who were deemed to have a substantial degree of control over a foreign corporation, as determined through an ownership test. A corporation that passed this ownership test was considered a controlled foreign corporation (CFC).[10] Substantial U.S. owners were persons who owned, directly or indirectly, 10 percent or more of a CFC. These substantial owners were, in turn, required to include certain forms of income (very generally, passive income) in their tax returns in the same year that the CFC earned the income.

The policy rationale behind Subpart F taxation is straightforward: Passive income could be moved offshore relatively easily, and the United States wanted to remove the incentives for multinationals to source certain types of passive income in offshore entities. Thus, Subpart F taxes U.S. shareholders on the foreign companies' passive income *in the year such income is earned*. This accords with the structure of the U.S. income tax more generally. Taxpayers are taxed on the income earned each year. When the tax laws change, they generally do so prospectively (as in, during the next taxable year after the law is enacted). In some limited cases (discussed within), courts have allowed tax provisions to be applied retroactively for a period of less than a year. But such allowances have generally been for small, technical changes to the law.[11]

The TCJA added a new tax on global intangible low-taxed income (GILTI) to the Subpart F regime. Under the GILTI provision, virtually all of a CFC's residual income that is not subject to Subpart F is

---

[9] The United States, like many countries, has a regime for taxing foreign corporations that earn income through a U.S. office or fixed place of business. Those rules are not relevant here.

[10] *See* I.R.C. § 957 (defining "controlled foreign corporation").

[11] *See* United States v. Carlton, 512 U.S. 26 (1994).

taxed to the U.S. shareholder in the same year that the CFC earns the income. U.S. corporations that are required to include GILTI income pay tax on such inclusions at half the regular corporate rate of 21 percent. In other words, GILTI income is currently taxed at a rate of 10.5 percent.

After the TCJA, a U.S. shareholder is subject to tax on its pro rata share of all of its CFC's earnings in the year earned. Because of this, the TCJA correspondingly eliminated the tax on dividends paid by the CFC to a U.S. shareholder. But this created a policy question. Many CFCs had accumulated profits (before the TCJA) that had never been paid as a dividend to their shareholders. Under the new regime, cash held by these foreign corporations could be repatriated (that is, brought back into the United States through a dividend) tax free. Such amounts would effectively escape the scope of the U.S. international tax regime.[12]

Congress instituted the MRT to tax the untaxed accumulated profits of those CFCs at this transitional moment. It imposed a one-time tax (at rates varying from 8 to 15.5 percent) on significant U.S. shareholders of CFCs on the accumulated profits of CFCs that had never been repatriated, calculated as of late 2017.[13] The tax is payable over eight years. It is imposed on the significant U.S. shareholders whether or not the CFC at issue ever decides to repatriate any cash or profits to the U.S. shareholder.

Interestingly, this was not the first time that Congress attempted to tax the accumulated earnings of foreign corporations. An old version of Section 965 of the tax code was part of the American Jobs Creation Act of 2004.[14] The old Section 965 allowed CFCs, *at their election*, to pay a dividend of accumulated foreign profits at a U.S. tax rate of 5.25 percent to the domestic corporate owners, rather than the then-standard 35 percent U.S. corporate tax rate.

The old version of Section 965 was markedly different than the MRT. The old version did not impose tax unless U.S. shareholders realized income (through a dividend paid at the election of the CFC).

[12] Even absent a tax on the dividend to the U.S. corporation, such amounts could still be subject to U.S. taxation if the U.S. shareholder were a domestic corporation (say, the parent of a large multinational) and if it paid those amounts out as a dividend to *its* U.S. shareholders.

[13] *See* I.R.C. § 965. For simplicity, I will omit certain technical details and explain a simplified version of the tax.

[14] AMERICAN JOBS CREATION ACT, Pub. L. 108–357, 118 Stat. 1418–1660 (2004).

The very structure of the old Section 965 highlighted the need for an actual realization event (the payment of a dividend by the CFC) to trigger the tax liability. This point ties into a concept called "realization" which I will return to later. For now, the core point is this: Previous attempts to tax the accumulated earnings of foreign corporations avoided the unprecedented constitutional issues that the MRT raised.

II. Constitutional Questions in the MRT

The Moores were married individuals who sued for a refund of the $14,729 in federal tax that they owed as a result of the imposition of the MRT on their ownership of an Indian corporation, KisanKraft. The Moores were U.S. citizens who owned approximately 13 percent of the corporation during 2017. KisanKraft had never distributed any income to its U.S. shareholders, including the Moores. Thus, until the MRT, neither KisanKraft nor the Moores had paid any U.S. tax on KisanKraft's income.

In their original complaint and in the Ninth Circuit below, the Moores argued that the tax was unconstitutional for two separate reasons. First, they argued that the MRT violated the Direct Tax Clause of the Constitution. Second, they argued that the MRT violated the Due Process Clause of the Fifth Amendment. Although the Supreme Court in *Moore* considered only the first question, the framing of both constitutional challenges to the MRT are worth discussing.

A. The Direct Tax Clause

Article I, Section 8 of the Constitution grants Congress the power to "lay and collect Taxes." Under the Constitution, taxes are classified in two classes: direct taxes and indirect taxes. Article I, Section 9 of the Constitution prohibits Congress from levying "direct" taxes without apportioning such taxes among the states based on the states' respective populations. The meaning of "direct" taxes is subject to considerable debate among scholars (and has been since the late 18th century), but the general definition used by the Supreme Court in *Moore* is "taxes imposed on persons or property."[15] Thus, a federal property tax on the value of a house would need to be

---

[15] *Moore*, 144 S. Ct. at 1687 (citing Nat'l Fed'n of Indep. Bus. v. Sebelius, 567 U.S. 529, 570–71 (2012)).

apportioned among the states. For such a hypothetical tax to be constitutional, the citizens of, say, Washington State would have to pay a collective share of the tax equal to Washington's proportional share of the total U.S. population—irrespective of the value of the property being taxed in Washington. On the other hand, indirect taxes are "the familiar federal taxes imposed on activities or transactions."[16] These taxes can be levied without apportionment among the states.

Income taxes are indirect taxes. But the 1895 case *Pollock v. Farmers' Loan & Trust Co.* held that a tax on certain income derived from property equated to a tax on the property itself and was thus a direct tax.[17] A controversial decision (to put it mildly), *Pollock*'s holding directly led to the passage of the Sixteenth Amendment. The Sixteenth Amendment provides that "Congress shall have the power to lay and collect taxes on incomes from whatever source derived, without apportionment among the several States, and without regard to any census or enumeration." Thus, despite *Pollock*'s strange reasoning, the Sixteenth Amendment makes clear that income taxes are indirect taxes and not subject to apportionment.[18]

The question that the Court took up in *Moore* is whether the MRT is an income tax. The question could be framed this way: What is the distinguishing feature of a tax on income as opposed to a tax on property? That question turns on the definition of "income." *Merriam-Webster* defines "income" as "a coming in" and as "a gain or recurrent benefit usually measured in money that derives from capital or labor; also: the amount of such gain received in a period of time."[19] And in the landmark case *Commissioner v. Glenshaw Glass*, the Supreme Court crafted a three-part conjunctive test for income. The *Glenshaw Glass* test asks whether the taxpayers have received "undeniable accessions to wealth, clearly realized, and over which the taxpayers have complete dominion."[20]

---

[16] *Id.*

[17] 158 U.S. 601 (1895).

[18] In *Moore*, the Court appeared to reject the underlying reasoning of *Pollock*, stating expressly that "income taxes are indirect taxes" under the "exhaustive" grant of Congress's taxing power and that they are thus permitted without apportionment. *Moore*, 144 S. Ct. at 1688.

[19] *Income*, Merriam-Webster Online Dictionary, https://www.merriam-webster.com/thesaurus/income (last visited Aug. 8, 2024).

[20] Comm'r v. Glenshaw Glass, 348 U.S. 426, 431 (1955).

Although the *Glenshaw Glass* definition is not universal, it has nevertheless been employed by the government in a wide variety of contexts to determine if there has been taxable income.[21] The *Glenshaw Glass* definition includes a requirement that income be realized, and much of the debate as to what constitutes income turns on whether realization is a necessary component of income from a constitutional perspective. The Supreme Court has consistently interpreted "income," as used in the Sixteenth Amendment, to require a realization event—that is, an event in which something of value is received by the taxpayer. For example, in *Eisner v. Macomber*,[22] the Supreme Court held that a transaction similar to a stock split did not result in "income" to stockholders. A corporation issued a pro-rated "stock dividend" to its shareholders, issuing each shareholder a number of newly created shares proportional to its shareholdings. Thus, each shareholder's total percentage ownership in the corporation did not change.

Not every possible definition of "income" requires realization. One definition of income is the Haig-Simons definition, favored by some economists. As the Joint Committee on Taxation has explained, "Haig-Simons income is defined as consumption plus changes in net worth."[23] This definition thus looks not to whether income is realized, but instead to whether an individual's overall wealth has increased, taking into account their consumption.

Thus, under the Haig-Simons definition, there is no "event" fixing an income, merely an accession to wealth that results in income. But this theoretical definition, however useful in making economic determinations, has never been embraced by courts and has never been a tax base under the tax code. Neither the Constitution, the tax code, nor courts interpreting either source of tax law have ever conceptualized income in such a way. Treating income this way would run amok over any concept of gains and losses embedded within the code. And this definition cannot be squared with the language of the Constitution, which says income *must* be derived

---

[21] These include, for example, IRS guidance on the taxation of digital assets and cryptocurrencies. *See, e.g.*, I.R.S. Rev. Rul. 2023-14 (citing *Glenshaw Glass*, 348 U.S. 426).

[22] 252 U.S. 189 (1920).

[23] STAFF OF THE JOINT COMM. ON TAX'N, 112TH CONG., OVERVIEW OF THE DEFINITION OF INCOME USED BY THE STAFF OF THE JOINT COMMITTEE ON TAXATION IN DISTRIBUTIONAL ANALYSES 3 (2012).

from a source. This concept is intrinsic to the text of the Sixteenth Amendment, which states, "The Congress shall have power to lay and collect taxes on incomes, *from whatever source derived*."[24] Simply put, the Haig-Simons definition of "income" is not the definition that the Constitution uses, and it is not the meaning of "income" that has been understood to be part of any income tax.

Crucially, the *Macomber* Court instead looked to the plain meaning of the word "income" and concluded that a mere increase in the value of any particular asset is not income because such mere increase has not been realized. The argument for requiring a realization event is thus that without a realization event, nothing has "come in" to a taxpayer, no money has been derived from capital, and nothing has been received. Anyone who has bought a share of stock (or any asset), refrained from selling it when its price climbed, and then watched its company go bankrupt understands this fundamental concept. The Supreme Court has upheld this principle in numerous cases, each of which has looked fundamentally to a fixed event that resulted in a "coming in" to the taxpayer in order to constitute income.[25]

However, the Ninth Circuit, in deciding the *Moore* case below, squarely rejected this requirement, holding that whether "the taxpayer has realized income does not determine whether a tax is constitutional."[26] This ruling set the stage for the dispute that would eventually reach the Supreme Court. The Moores asserted that the MRT was *not* an income tax and rather a direct tax on property. The government asserted that the MRT *was* an income tax and thus an indirect tax. And given the reasoning of the Ninth Circuit, much of the parties' arguments turned on whether realization was a necessary component of income.

B. The Due Process Challenge

The MRT taxes, in large part, amounts that were income in *prior* years. A second potential constitutional issue with the MRT is thus whether the fundamentally "backward-looking" MRT (as the *Moore* majority opinion describes it) is permissible under the Due Process

---

[24] U.S. Const. amend. XVI (emphasis added).

[25] *See, e.g.*, Helvering v. Horst, 311 U.S. 112 (1940).

[26] Moore v. United States, 36 F.4th 930, 935 (9th Cir. 2022).

Clause of the Fifth Amendment. This argument concedes the question of whether the MRT is an income (or other indirect) tax. It instead argues that even if the MRT is characterized as an income tax, it is best characterized as an income tax on *prior* years' income.[27] Under this line of reasoning, the MRT can thus be distinguished from other taxes including Subpart F and GILTI, which tax amounts that were income only during the *current* year. And under this argument, those differences are constitutionally relevant to the permissibility of the tax.

The Fifth Amendment, which provides that no person shall be "deprived of life, liberty or property without due process of law" has been applied in previous cases that addressed Congress's ability to levy a retroactive tax. The most recent Supreme Court case to address this issue was *United States v. Carlton*.[28] *Carlton* considered a provision of the federal estate tax, specifically an amendment to a new rule allowing for a deduction. Congress had provided that the new provision would apply retroactively, taking effect one year *before* it was enacted into law. Thus, the Court considered whether the retroactive application of the amendment to the estate tax violated the Due Process Clause of the Fifth Amendment.

The Court concluded that the retroactive amendment did meet the requirements of due process and was thus constitutional. The Court applied the standard that is applicable to any retroactive economic legislation, asking whether the retroactivity provided a "legitimate legislative purpose furthered by rational means."[29] The Court noted that the law was adopted as a curative measure and that Congress did not contemplate the breadth of the new deduction when originally implementing it (absent the amendment). The amendment was, in effect, a technical correction that brought the text of the law in line with congressional intent. The Court also observed that "Congress acted promptly and established only a modest period of retroactivity"[30]—less than a year. Noting all of these factors,

---

[27] *See* Sean P. McElroy, *The Mandatory Repatriation Tax Is Unconstitutional*, 37 YALE J. REG. BULL. 69 (2018).

[28] 512 U.S. 26 (1994).

[29] *Id.* at 30–31 (quoting Pension Benefit Guarantee Corp. v. R.A. Gray & Co., 467 U.S. 717, 733 (1984)).

[30] *Id.* at 31.

the *Carlton* Court held that the amendment permissibly afforded due process.

But the Supreme Court has never applied *Carlton* to the question whether a retroactive tax on income extending much longer than a year would be constitutional. Because the MRT extends much farther back than the amendment in *Carlton*, the Moores argued in their initial complaint and in the Ninth Circuit that the MRT was unconstitutional on these grounds.[31]

However, the Moores did not raise the due process argument at the Supreme Court. They sought certiorari on only the question of whether the MRT was authorized under the Sixteenth Amendment, and the Court, accordingly, did not consider the due process argument.[32] That said, for reasons discussed shortly, due process was likely the stronger of the two arguments against the constitutionality of the MRT. And the Court's analysis strongly implies that it may have found retroactivity to be an important way of distinguishing the MRT from other (constitutional) exercises of Congress's taxing power, had the Moores raised the argument.

III. The Court's Ruling

The majority opinion was written by Justice Brett Kavanaugh and joined by Chief Justice John Roberts as well as Justices Elena Kagan, Sonia Sotomayor, and Ketanji Brown Jackson. As the majority put it, the Court was tasked with deciding whether the MRT "exceeds Congress's constitutional authority."[33] Ultimately, seven Justices concluded that the MRT did *not* exceed Congress's authority. That is, seven Justices agreed that the MRT was an indirect tax not subject to apportionment under the Constitution. But much can be gleaned from the Court's analysis, however "narrow" the majority insisted it was.[34]

A. Comparing the MRT to Three (Constitutional) Taxes

The majority's analysis spent considerable time comparing the MRT to three existing (and, to the majority, presumptively constitutional)

[31] Moore v. United States, No. C19-1539-JCC, 2020 U.S. Dist. LEXIS 216771 (W.D. Wash. Nov. 19, 2020); Moore v. United States, 36 F.4th 930 (9th Cir. 2022).

[32] *Moore*, 144 S. Ct. at 1697 n.6.

[33] *Id.* at 1687.

[34] *Id.* at 1696.

income taxes: taxes on partnerships, S corporations, and Subpart F income. The Court's majority's analysis can perhaps be summarized by the following logical steps:

(1) Taxes on partnerships, S corporations, and Subpart F income are constitutional income taxes. [Premise].

(2) There is no meaningful constitutional distinction between the MRT and taxes on partnerships, S corporations, and Subpart F Income [Premise].

(3) The MRT is a constitutional income tax [Follows from 1 and 2].

This argument begs the question.[35] It assumes that the MRT is an income tax and then says that there are no meaningful distinctions between different types of income taxes. But as will be discussed in more detail, the partnership and S corporation regimes are elective; taxpayers can decide whether to structure their businesses to fall within these regimes. The MRT, by contrast, is not elective; it is a *mandatory* tax on all U.S. shareholders of CFCs. In any event, the constitutionality of the MRT should be determined not by looking to whether it is somehow distinct from existing (presumably constitutional) laws, but to its own merits. Specifically, the constitutionality of the tax ought to be determined by asking whether the MRT is some type of indirect tax, such as an income tax. The Court's reasoning in this passage thus misses the point entirely:

> Critically, however, the MRT *does* tax realized income—namely, income realized by the corporation, KisanKraft. The MRT attributes the income of the corporation to the shareholders, and then taxes the shareholders (including the Moores) on their share of that undistributed corporate income.[36]

The MRT was levied in 2017 on amounts that a CFC may have accumulated as far back as 1987, and not the year the income was generated. Yet the Court apparently assumed that once an amount

---

[35] To "beg the question," in philosophical terms, is for an argument to be circular and to presuppose the very thing in question. For a discussion on the misuse of this term, see SCOTT R. SEHON, SOCIALISM: A LOGICAL INTRODUCTION 16–17 (2024).

[36] *Moore*, 144 S. Ct. at 1688.

was income realized by an entity, that entity can be subject to tax on such income *at any time.*

Consider the following hypothetical tax: Congress decides in 2025 that foreign corporations controlled by U.S. shareholders (CFCs) should pay a higher tax rate on their income from 2017–2020. Thus, Congress mandates that U.S. shareholders of that corporation should pay tax on that past income immediately in 2025 because they hold stock on that corporation in 2025. Such a tax would be the epitome of a tax on property (stock ownership) rather than a tax on the transaction itself.

That is effectively what the MRT does. The significant retroactivity and due process concerns aside, there is a significant disjoint between a controlling ownership of a foreign corporation today and income that the corporation earned in the past. All of the other attribution cases discussed in this article dealt with taxes on income *in the year it is generated.*

In any event, the Moores explicitly conceded Premise (1).[37] Thus, the majority opinion spends considerable time addressing whether there is a meaningful distinction between the MRT and these three types of taxation. The majority opinion characterizes the Moores' arguments as "an array of ad hoc distinctions to try to explain why those longstanding taxes are constitutional" but the MRT is not. The Court's tax-by-tax comparative analysis thus misses the key point, which provides the answer to Premise (2). Each of the three taxes are, unequivocally, income taxes (and thus constitutional). But the MRT cannot be accurately characterized as an "income" tax— at least not without running into serious retroactivity concerns.

1. Partnerships

The majority opinion rejects the distinction that the Moores offered between the MRT and partnership taxation: that partnerships were not seen as separate entities from their partners at the time of the Sixteenth Amendment's passage. To the majority, Congress has the right to choose whether to tax the owners of a partnership or the partnership itself, just as it does with any other business entity.

---

[37] *Id.* at 1693 ("The Moores explicitly concede that partnership taxes, S-corporation taxes, and subpart F taxes are income taxes that are constitutional and need not be apportioned.").

But analogies to partnerships are tricky, because partnerships occupy a special place in the tax code.[38] Congress explicitly decided to enact a separate taxing regime for partnerships, and the majority's discussion of partnerships in *Moore* gives short shrift to U.S. law's treatment of partnerships for tax purposes. Subchapter K (the part of the tax code that governs partnerships) does not simply wave a wand to tax all the owners of partnerships on their partnerships' income. Rather, Subchapter K represents a delicate balance between the competing treatment of partnerships as entities on the one hand and simple aggregations of partners on the other.[39]

A word on the concept of "pass-throughs" is warranted here. A pass-through is an entity whose income is taxed at the shareholder level rather than at the entity level. The choice of whether taxation is levied at the entity level or at the shareholder level for a domestic business entity is in many ways elective, and it has been for the entire modern history of tax law. Taxpayers have always been free to set up their business operations in whichever manner they decided was most appropriate, provided that they were willing to accept the tax consequences of their choices.[40] Nowadays, taxpayers can frequently make the choice outright.

Consider, for example, an extraordinarily common form of business entity: a limited liability company (LLC). An LLC defaults to tax as a partnership. But an LLC can elect to be taxable as a corporation by filing a very simple election with the government.[41] And going back even prior to the implementation of the check-the-box rule, taxpayers have been free to choose whatever type of business entity they wish to be. Foreign corporations (with some limited exceptions) may also elect to be taxed as pass-throughs or as separate entities.

This choice does not affect whether the income is subject to tax at all; it is merely an election as to who will pay the tax. Nobody seriously contests that partnerships have income, and nobody denies that Congress, within the limits of due process, has the right to tax income at either the shareholder or the entity level. The question

[38] *See* Subchapter K, I.R.C. §§ 701–77.

[39] *See* WILLIAM S. MCKEE, WILLIAM F. NELSON & ROBERT L. WHITMIRE, FEDERAL TAXATION OF PARTNERSHIPS AND PARTNERS, § 1.02 (4th ed. 2007).

[40] *See* Moline Properties v. Comm'r, 319 U.S. 436 (1943).

[41] *See* 26 C.F.R. § 301.7701-1. This type of election is known to tax professionals as a "check-the-box election," since it's literally as simple as checking a box on a form.

with the MRT is whether there is *income* that may be constitutionally subject to tax. And that is the question assumed away by the Court.

2. S corporation taxes

An S corporation (also known as a small business corporation) is a domestic corporation that elects to pass corporate income, losses, deductions, and credits through to its shareholders for federal tax purposes. There are various limitations on which corporations can make this election. Among other limitations, there can be no more than 100 shareholders, and the shareholders must all be individuals, trusts, or estates.

The government argued that if the MRT were found unconstitutional, then it would also be unconstitutional to tax S corporation shareholders on their income. The Moores argued that S corporations are distinguishable because their shareholders *consented* to the tax, rendering it constitutional. The *Moore* majority rejected the Moores' reasoning.

In fact, the question of consent was a red herring. Taxing the shareholders of an S corporation is constitutional for the same reason that the partnership tax is constitutional: It is fundamentally a tax on current-year income.

The S corporation election is not about *whether* the tax can be levied; everyone agrees that the S corporation has realized income that can be taxed. Instead, the election is about *who* will be responsible for paying the tax. In the normal case, the corporation pays tax on the income and then individuals pay tax on the dividends of profits. The S corporation election allows shareholders to instead pay the tax directly on the income. As with partnerships, there is no doubt that there is income, in that year, that can be constitutionally taxed by the federal government.

3. Subpart F

Third, the majority compared the MRT to the now six-decade-old tax on Subpart F income. As already noted, Subpart F imposes a shareholder-level tax on U.S. persons who are deemed to have a substantial degree of control over a foreign corporation through an ownership test. That tax applies to passive income, but the GILTI tax enacted by the TCJA expands this same form of tax to all income (albeit at a lower rate for the "active" income covered by GILTI).

How can Subpart F be distinguished from the MRT? The Moores gave two answers, neither of which the Court found persuasive. Once again, both of the Moores' arguments missed the fundamental distinction between two questions: whether there *is* income and who pays tax on that income. The Moores' first argument to distinguish Subpart F hinged on a concept called "constructive realization." This is a new concept—one that has not appeared before in the tax code or in Supreme Court precedent. The doctrine of constructive realization "treats as taxable income" that "which is unqualifiedly subject to the demand of a taxpayer . . ., whether or not such income has actually been received in cash."[42] That is, the income received must be subject to the control of the taxpayer. The Moores argued that Subpart F taxes constructively realized income but the MRT does not. However, the Court's majority squarely rejected this idea, reasoning that the standard of control is the same under Subpart F as it is under the MRT (which is accurate).

The Moores' second attempted distinction was that the taxation of "movable income" renders the MRT constitutionally distinct.[43] Once again, this seems to be constitutionally irrelevant to the question of whether the MRT is an income tax. Movable income is, to put it simply, still income.

But the policy point that the majority made in rejecting this reasoning is illustrative of the point that the majority missed. Justice Kavanaugh wrote that "like subpart F, the MRT responds to concerns that owners of American-controlled foreign corporations keep money offshore to defer taxation."[44] But the difference is that the MRT is about past earnings, while Subpart F is a tax on current-year income. To illustrate, Subpart F can only reach income in the taxable year upon which it is imposed. Thus, for 2017, the Subpart F tax looks to the income of CFCs in that year, and it taxes shareholders on that income. But the MRT looks to past income (say, earnings from 2011 which had never been paid as a dividend) and subjects that past income to a tax in 2017.

---

[42] Brief for Petitioners at 48, Moore v. United States, 144 S. Ct. 1680 (2024) (No. 22-800) (quoting Ross v. Comm'r, 169 F.2d 483, 490 (1st Cir. 1948)).

[43] This argument, however, would not work for the go-forward taxation of GILTI, something which is not substantially addressed anywhere in the majority's opinion.

[44] *Moore*, 144 S. Ct. at 1695.

As a side note, the Court did not consider the GILTI tax in its reasoning, except in listing the parade of horribles of taxes that might fall with the MRT. This despite GILTI being the most broadly applicable shareholder-level tax on foreign income. A constitutional analysis of the GILTI tax would have been the clearest illustration of the difference between the MRT and other constitutional taxes.

The majority treated *Moore* as a case about whether the MRT's attribution of a CFC's income to its shareholders was permissible. If there is a constitutional limit on such attribution, the MRT did not exceed that limit. Perhaps there is such a constitutional limit on attribution. And perhaps that would prevent the attribution of income to shareholders in extremely attenuated ways. Should an owner of a single share of Google stock be subject to (a presumptively small amount of) tax on Google's earnings? Justice Amy Coney Barrett's concurrence in the judgment spent much ink addressing this concern. And although Justice Barrett agreed with the majority that there is no meaningful constitutional distinction between Subpart F and the MRT,[45] she retained concern that the majority was "too quick to bless the attribution of corporate income to shareholders. . . ."[46]

But this all misses the point. The far more interesting and impactful question that both the majority and Justice Barrett failed to consider is whether the MRT is an *income* tax. Justice Clarence Thomas raised this point in dissent. His dissent correctly points out that the constitutional question turns on the novel nature of how the MRT operates: as a tax on the shares of the corporation, not as a tax on the income of that corporation.[47] He got this point absolutely right. The MRT does not tax income; it taxes the ownership of stock based on past income that the corporation earned and that was not previously subject to tax. During the year at issue, there was neither income nor a realization event that caused there to be income *in that year* (in marked contrast to the payment of a dividend under the old Section 965). And as to attribution, Justice Thomas argued that "Subpart F includes some minimal requirements to ensure that taxable 'income' belongs to the shareholder in some way; the MRT abandons that effort entirely."[48]

---

[45] *Id.* at 1709 (Barrett, J., concurring in the judgment).

[46] *Id.* at 1708.

[47] *Id.* at 1726 (Thomas, J., dissenting).

[48] *Id.*

A critic of this position could correctly point out that there *was* income—at some point in the past. In other words, there was income in some past year (however many years ago), and Congress could have taxed that income in that year. And, this argument would go, there is nothing wrong with Congress finally taxing that income now. But this reasoning leads inextricably to the question of whether that is functionally and fundamentally a retroactive income tax. Thus, perhaps the question of whether the MRT is an income tax misses the point. Especially given Justice Kavanaugh's assumption that the MRT taxes income, this case would have been best framed and thought of as a retroactivity issue all along. The retroactivity question raises none of the Court's parade of horribles concerns, and it better suits the strange function of the MRT.

It is a shame the Court did not consider the due process concerns raised by the MRT.

B. The Majority Opinion's Tax Consequentialism

One final note on the majority opinion bears discussion. After concluding that the MRT is no different from other (constitutional) taxes, Justice Kavanaugh then wrote that the "upshot is that the Moores' argument, taken to its logical conclusion, could render vast swaths of the Internal Revenue Code unconstitutional."[49] Justice Kavanaugh then cited several areas of taxes, without further analysis. The majority opinion continues:

> And those tax provisions, if suddenly eliminated, would deprive the U. S. government and the American people of trillions in lost tax revenue. The logical implications of the Moores' theory would therefore require Congress to either drastically cut critical national programs or significantly increase taxes on the remaining sources available to it—including, of course, on ordinary Americans. The Constitution does not require that fiscal calamity.[50]

This passage is remarkable. It focuses on the (alleged) practical consequences of striking down the MRT and other taxes, without making a case for why this should be relevant to the legal question

[49] *Id.* at 1696 (majority opinion).
[50] *Id.*

118

at issue. The implications of keeping or eliminating a tax should generally be removed from any question as to its constitutionality. If there is a limitation to Congress's power to tax, the fiscal impact is not a relevant factor.

One might call the majority's reasoning a form of tax consequentialism. "Consequentialism" is a term from academic philosophy, but its usage is helpful here. The *Stanford Encyclopedia of Philosophy* describes consequentialism as "the view that normative properties depend only on consequences."[51] Put simply, consequentialism looks to the consequences of something (e.g., an action) as a means of determining if that thing is good or bad, or right or wrong.

Why was the Court in *Moore* particularly concerned with the possible consequences of constraining the federal taxing power? Recall that the Court has invoked the breadth of the congressional power to tax before: as the basis to uphold the constitutionality of the individual mandate in the Patient Protection and Affordable Care Act. In *National Federation of Independent Business v. Sebelius*,[52] the Supreme Court (in an opinion written by Chief Justice Roberts) broadly interpreted the taxing power to uphold the individual mandate portion of the Act. Although the mandate was not a valid exercise of congressional power under the Commerce Clause, the Chief Justice's decisive opinion held that it was a valid exercise of Congress's taxing power. In effect, the Court interpreted the Taxing Clause as the broad power that it needed to justify Congress's law.

In *Moore*, the consequences of overturning the tax were clearly important to the Court's analysis. The Court was concerned with both the potential fiscal effect and the perceived, if misguided, notion that such a ruling would jumpstart a parade of horribles. In light of these concerns, Justice Thomas responded to the majority that "if Congress invites calamity by building the tax base on constitutional quicksand, the judicial Power afforded to this Court does not include the power to fashion an emergency escape."[53]

He's right. Insofar as you agree with the premise that there are constitutional limitations on Congress's taxing power, the fact that

---

[51] Walter Sinnott-Armstrong, *Consequentialism*, STAN. ENCYCLOPEDIA OF PHIL. (Oct. 4, 2023), https://plato.stanford.edu/entries/consequentialism/.

[52] 567 U.S. 519 (2012).

[53] *Moore*, 144 S. Ct. at 1726 (Thomas, J., dissenting) (cleaned up).

overturning a tax would have fiscal consequences cannot be a proper rationale for upholding an unconstitutional tax. Otherwise, an *actual* constitutional parade of horrors could conceivably follow. Any exercise of power by Congress, however much in excess of the power provided for under the Constitution, could be justified under the taxing power so long as invalidating the action would have significant fiscal consequences. This would be a failure of the core function of judicial review: to review and to provide a check on Congress's exercise of its own power.

In any event, the Moores were very clear that they conceded the constitutionality of those other income taxes—which was never really in question. There was no need to fear a parade of horribles whereby every tax would be held unconstitutional on a new attribution theory or a complicated constitutional analysis about the nature of the tax. The question before the Court was simple: Does the MRT tax income? If the answer is yes, then the MRT is constitutional (subject to due process limitations). The devil, of course, is in the details as to what is "income." But all sides agreed that partnership income, S corporation income, and Subpart F income are, in fact, income. And if the MRT had been held unconstitutional on the ground that there was not a realizable event at the time the tax was levied on the taxpayer, such a ruling would have done absolutely nothing to change the clearly constitutional nature of these other taxes.

C. The Question of "Realization"

Left outstanding after *Moore* is the question of whether realization is a constitutional requirement for an income tax. The Court could have—and should have—addressed this question. And it would have if it had reached the real issue in the case: whether the MRT is an income tax. But by assuming away that question, the Court was also able to punt on the question of whether it is fundamental to the nature of an income tax that the income be realized.

So what does it mean for a tax (like the MRT) to be an *income* tax? Does an income tax require realization? And could Congress impose a tax putatively called an "income" tax that taxed Americans' accumulated wealth, whether or not the amounts being taxed were "earned" in a given year?

As previously noted, the concept of realization is fundamental to the definition of "income," particularly in the context of a tax on income. The standard dictionary definition of "income" requires "a coming in" and defines income as "a gain or recurrent benefit usually measured in money that derives from capital or labor; also: the amount of such gain received in a period of time."[54] And as Justice Barrett accurately noted in her concurrence, when we say "realization," we effectively mean the same thing as "derived."[55] For instance, traders realize income from a sale when they derive gains from that sale, and workers realize income from their labor when they derive a wage from that labor. In both instances, the tax regime separates taxing the *income* of something from taxing the thing itself. This has always been how the taxation of income has been understood in a legal sense, from *Macomber* to the present day.

And while some might try to obscure what is "income" by asserting that income ought to be measured through consumption and the net worth of the assets (i.e., the definition of Haig-Simons income), this argument is without constitutional import. The Haig-Simons definition, however useful as a measure of change in wealth, has never been a legal understanding of the base of an income tax. When the Constitution, the tax code, and the courts use the term "income," they are all using a definition of "income" that intrinsically includes a realization requirement. To redefine income along the lines of the Haig-Simons definition would mandate an entirely different constitutional analysis.[56]

Although the majority opinion in *Moore* is silent as to whether realization is a constitutional requirement, the concurrences and dissent bring this issue to the forefront. Justice Barrett's concurrence makes a helpful point: The Moores have not realized the income from their shares in KisanKraft. Justice Barrett expressly noted that there is no difference between the concept of realization and the concept of derivation. As her concurrence explains, the Sixteenth Amendment's "reference to 'derived' income presupposes that the income belongs to the taxpayer. . . . Otherwise the taxpayer's property . . . could be taxed

---

[54] *Supra* note 19.

[55] *Moore*, 144 S. Ct. at 1701 (Barrett, J., concurring in the judgment).

[56] Whether it would be constitutional to tax an individual using a base composed of that individual's Haig-Simons income lies outside the scope of this article. That said, it seems clear that this would not be an "income" tax as that term is used in the Constitution and in Supreme Court precedent. *See, e.g.*, Ivan Allen Co. v. United States, 422 U.S. 617, 621–25 (1975).

without apportionment just because it was once *somebody else's* income."[57] The Moores "have not 'derived' income from their shares because nothing has *come in*."[58] The remainder of Justice Barrett's concurrence considers whether the income of a CFC such as KisanKraft can be attributed to the Moores, an inquiry that (as discussed earlier) is beside the point.

On the other hand, Justice Jackson's sole concurrence (consistent with the Ninth Circuit's reasoning below) rejects the realization requirement altogether. To Justice Jackson, the realization requirement is nothing more than a "Court-created limit on Congress's power." But again, this fails to assess the basic point: The idea of realization is inextricable from the definition of "income" as it is used in the Constitution and the tax code. Justice Jackson believes that this issue is best left to the courts. Her concurrence concludes by directly quoting from Justice John Marshall Harlan's dissent in *Pollock*: "I have no doubt that future Congresses will pass, and future Presidents will sign, taxes that outrage one group or another. . . . However, *Pollock* teaches us that this Court's role in such disputes should be limited. '[T]he remedy for such abuses is to be found at the ballot-box. . . .'"[59]

Justice Thomas, as to be expected, was blunt in his reasoning that realization is necessary for there to be income. "Because the Sixteenth Amendment requires a way to distinguish between income and source, it includes a realization requirement."[60] Justice Thomas argued that the Sixteenth Amendment's enactment in direct response to *Pollock* is evidence in favor of this reading.[61] Justice Thomas's dissent clearly understands that the Court sidestepped the issue—the dissent suggests that it did so to avoid ruling on the realization doctrine. The result is the majority's focus (wrongly, in Justice Thomas's view) on the question of attribution. The majority opinion cites multiple cases about whether taxpayers can "sidestep" income in their attempts to evade tax liability. But Justice Thomas argued that these citations miss the point. He's right. And he's correct that

---

57 *Moore*, 144 S. Ct. at 1708 (Barrett, J., concurring in the judgment).

58 *Id.* at 1702.

59 *Id.* at 1699 (Jackson, J., concurring) (quoting *Pollock*, 158 U.S. at 680 (Harlan, J., dissenting)).

60 *Id.* at 1721 (Thomas, J., dissenting).

61 *Id.* at 1722.

realization cannot be severed from the concept of income, at least insofar as that term has been used in Supreme Court case law, the tax code, and the Constitution.

As for Supreme Court doctrine, the question of realization is left for another day. But at least four Justices are clearly against a tax without realization, and only a single Justice appeared to write in favor of fully abolishing the realization requirement. Given the strong opinions signaled by many on the Court, it appears unlikely that the realization requirement will go away. This is absolutely the correct approach. Realization is an inextricable part of income as income has always been understood. And when the IRS is asked in a novel context (such as virtual currencies) to consider what is within the scope of income, it looks to a standard that expressly includes the notion of clear realization.[62] No sophistry or twisting of the definition can change its common, plain understanding. Such a change in definition would be the only way to bring taxes that clearly do not tax income (but instead tax property itself, such as a wealth tax) within the scope of Congress's taxing power. The Court should have considered this issue in the context of the MRT and set a clear standard for what taxes are permissible as income taxes under the Constitution. Unfortunately, the Court instead assumed the question away.

Conclusion

In 2011, the Supreme Court held that there was not a separate and unique standard of review for tax cases only.[63] That decision ended an era that scholars had called "tax exceptionalism," whereby the uniqueness of the tax field and a perception that tax was "different" or "special" resulted in the application of a different standard of administrative review for tax rules.[64] Under the principles of that 2011 ruling, courts were to review tax regulations like any other, using the same administrative law principles as in any other case.

But here, faced with a fundamental question about the nature of an income tax as applied to the MRT, the Court abandoned its typical

---

[62] *See, e.g.,* I.R.S. Rev. Rul. 2023-14 (citing *Glenshaw Glass,* 348 U.S. 426).

[63] Mayo Found. v. United States, 562 U.S. 44 (2011).

[64] *See, e.g.,* Kristin E. Hickman, *The Need for* Mead: *Rejecting Tax Exceptionalism in Judicial Deference,* 90 Minn. L. Rev. 1537 (2006).

careful constitutional analysis. The majority simply assumed away the underlying issue of whether the MRT was an income tax.

With *Moore* and Chief Justice Roberts's majority opinion in *Sebelius*, the Court has ushered in what we might call an era of tax consequentialism. Rather than analyzing the technical tax issues and making key determinations about income, the Court looked to the consequences of the tax. Specifically, the Court gave significant weight to the fear that constitutional limitations on the MRT would be too expensive to uphold. Chief Justice Roberts and Justice Kavanaugh seem to have no issues in using the perceived breadth of the taxing power as a means to justify congressional action, whether or not the action has anything to do with tax. The words of Justice Thomas thus offer a cautionary tale about reasoning to fiscal consequences: "[I]f the Court is not willing to uphold limitations on the taxing power in expensive cases, cheap dicta will make no difference."[65]

And sadly, the Court lacked the opportunity to clarify its position on retroactive taxation set forth in *Carlton*. Thus, the most interesting question about the constitutionality of the MRT wasn't even discussed in *Moore*.

---

[65] *Moore*, 144 S. Ct. 1727 (Thomas, J., dissenting).

"Speech Nirvanas" on the Internet: An Analysis of the U.S. Supreme Court's *Moody v. NetChoice* Decision

*Eric Goldman**

Overview

Following the January 6, 2021, insurrection and the widespread shutdown of President Donald Trump's Internet[1] accounts, Florida[2] and Texas[3] both enacted "social media censorship laws." The laws purport to restrict "social media platforms"[4] from "censoring" user content, but they do so by overriding the services' editorial policies and choices. Ironically, the laws' titles brazenly admit that the legislatures aspired to censor social media platforms.

Two industry associations, NetChoice and the Computer & Communications Industry Association (CCIA), challenged the social media

---

* Associate Dean for Research, Professor of Law, and Co-Director of the High Tech Law Institute, Santa Clara University School of Law. Email: egoldman@gmail.com. Website: http://www.ericgoldman.org. I appreciate the comments of Mary Rose Finnigan, Lisa Goldman, Brad Joondeph, Daphne Keller, Edward Lee, Mark Lemley, Jess Miers, Amanda Reid, Pam Samuelson, and Rebecca Tushnet.

In the *Moody* appeal, I filed an amicus brief supporting the challengers regarding mandatory editorial transparency and *Zauderer*. *See* Brief of Professor Eric Goldman as Amicus Curiae in Support of NetChoice and CCIA, Moody v. NetChoice, LLC, 144 S. Ct. 2383 (2024) (No. 22-277), https://papers.ssrn.com/sol3/papers.cfm?abstract_id=4655464.

[1] This article intentionally capitalizes the Internet. *See* Wikipedia, *Capitalization of Internet*, https://en.wikipedia.org/wiki/Capitalization_of_Internet (last visited Sept. 3, 2024).

[2] S.B. 7072 (Fla. 2021).

[3] H.B. 20 (Tex. 2021).

[4] Both laws define the term "social media platform" to exclude smaller services. However defined, "social media platforms" is a problematic term. There is not a shared understanding of what constitutes a "platform," and the broad statutory definitions undoubtedly reach services that look nothing like "social media." This chapter sometimes uses the term "Internet service" as a more inclusive descriptor than "social media platform."

censorship laws. In July 2024, the Supreme Court issued its opinion in *Moody v. NetChoice* (along with its companion case *NetChoice v. Paxton*). But the Court didn't definitively resolve the laws' constitutionality. Instead, the Court unanimously remanded both cases for a more detailed analysis of the constitutional questions. These further proceedings surely will be appealed to the Supreme Court again, and final resolution of these cases is likely years away.

Although the Court's remand was anti-climactic, Justice Elena Kagan's majority opinion was a rousing celebration of the First Amendment online. Critically, the majority said that the First Amendment protects social media platforms' content moderation efforts. This conclusion jeopardizes much of the Florida and Texas laws as well as many other laws being enacted around the country.

Meanwhile, the Court will be asked to review other state laws regulating Internet services. Indeed, the day after issuing the *Moody* decision, the Supreme Court granted certiorari for a case challenging a Texas law that requires pornography websites to age-authenticate their users.[5] That case, and others that will soon follow, will give the *Moody* majority more opportunities to reiterate, or qualify, their commitment to protecting Internet speech.

This article proceeds in three parts. The first part describes the prelude to the Supreme Court decision, including passage of the laws and the prior court proceedings. The second part summarizes the Court's opinions. The third part discusses some implications of the Court's decision. The conclusion contextualizes this ruling as part of the Supreme Court's ongoing Internet law jurisprudence.

I. Background

This part describes why Florida and Texas enacted their social media censorship laws, what the laws say, and how the court challenges proceeded prior to the Supreme Court's decision.

A. Path to Passage

Overall, regulators took surprisingly deferential approaches to Internet regulation during the 1990s and early 2000s.[6] Notably, in

---

[5] Free Speech Coal., Inc. v. Paxton, No. 23-50627 (*cert. granted* July 2, 2024).

[6] Several 1990s-era laws to restrict minor access to online pornography were struck down as unconstitutional, including the Communications Decency Act, Child Online Protection Act, and state law equivalents.

47 U.S.C. § 230 (Section 230), Congress affirmatively eliminated Internet services' liability for third-party content in many circumstances, including civil and criminal regulations of third-party content at the state level.[7] As a result, state legislatures largely avoided Internet regulations during the 1990s and 2000s.

The deregulatory zeitgeist broke down in the mid-2010s for several reasons, including:

- The largest Internet services reached breathtaking levels of size, profitability, and market share,[8] which provoked consumer and regulatory pushback.
- The largest Internet services had several high-profile gaffes that eroded public trust in them, such as Google's Wi-Fi sniffing[9] and Facebook's Cambridge Analytica data leakage.[10]
- President Trump relentlessly criticized the media, accusing Internet services in particular of systematically favoring liberals' content over conservatives' content. The facts didn't support those allegations of bias,[11] but perceptions of bias nevertheless became accepted truth among conservatives.[12]

---

[7] Eric Goldman, *An Overview of the United States' Section 230 Internet* Immunity, in THE OXFORD HANDBOOK OF ONLINE INTERMEDIARY LIABILITY. 155 (Giancarlo Frosio ed., 2020).

[8] *See, e.g.*, Jasper Jolly, *Is Big Tech Now Just Too Big to Stomach?*, GUARDIAN (Feb. 6, 2021), https://www.theguardian.com/business/2021/feb/06/is-big-tech-now-just-too-big-to-stomach; Shira Ovide, *How Big Tech Won the Pandemic*, N.Y. TIMES (Apr. 30, 2021), https://www.nytimes.com/2021/04/30/technology/big-tech-pandemic.html.

[9] *See e.g.*, Joffe v. Google, Inc., 746 F.3d 920 (9th Cir. 2013); *In re* Google Inc. Street View Elec. Commc'ns Litig. 21 F.4th 1102 (9th Cir. 2021); David Kravets, *An Intentional Mistake: The Anatomy of Google's Wi-Fi Sniffing Debacle*, WIRED (May 2, 2012), https://www.wired.com/2012/05/google-wifi-fcc-investigation/.

[10] *Facebook–Cambridge Analytica Data Scandal*, WIKIPEDIA, https://en.wikipedia.org/wiki/Facebook%E2%80%93Cambridge_Analytica_data_scandal (last visited July 30, 2024).

[11] *See e.g.*, Paul M. Barrett & J. Grant Sims, *False Accusation: The Unfounded Claim That Social Media Companies Censor Conservatives*, N.Y.U. STERN CTR. FOR BUS. & HUM. RTS. (Feb. 2021), https://static1.squarespace.com/static/5b6df958f8370af3217d4178/t/6011e68dec2c7013d3caf3cb/1611785871154/NYU+False+Accusation+report_FINAL.pdf.

[12] *See e.g.*, Monica Anderson, *Americans' Views of Technology Companies*, PEW RSCH. CTR. (Apr. 29, 2024), https://www.pewresearch.org/internet/2024/04/29/americans-views-of-technology-companies-2/ ("93% of Republicans say it's likely that social media sites intentionally censor political viewpoints that they find objectionable").

Conservatives' antipathy toward Internet services boiled over in 2020 when Twitter "fact-checked" President Trump for the first time.[13] In retaliation, President Trump issued an (unsuccessful) executive order attempting to eviscerate Section 230.[14] After the insurrection of January 6, 2021, several Internet services terminated President Trump's accounts, including Twitter.[15]

The Florida and Texas social media censorship bills were driven by conservatives' anger at "Big Tech" and guided by Justice Clarence Thomas's non-precedential musings about Section 230 and free speech.[16] However, these were "messaging bills" intended to rally the base;[17] they were never meant as serious policy proposals. Their "messaging bill" statuses partially explain why they were poorly drafted, contained a smorgasbord of undertheorized policy ideas, included mockably unserious provisions,[18] and were supported with public declarations that admitted partisan and censorial motivations.[19]

---

[13] See e.g., Katie Paul & Elizabeth Culliford, *Twitter Fact-Checks Trump Tweet for the First Time*, REUTERS (May 26, 2020), https://www.reuters.com/article/us-twitter-trump/twitter-fact-checks-trump-tweet-for-the-first-time-idUSKBN232389/.

[14] Exec. Order No. 13925, 85 Fed. Reg. 34079 (May 28, 2020) (Preventing Online Censorship). President Biden quickly repealed that order. Exec. Order No. 14029, 86 Fed. Reg. 27025 (May 14, 2021) (Revocation of Certain Presidential Actions and Technical Amendment).

[15] See, e.g., Sara Fischer & Ashley Gold, *All the Platforms That Have Banned or Restricted Trump So Far*, AXIOS (Jan. 11, 2021), https://www.axios.com/2021/01/09/platforms-social-media-ban-restrict-trump.

[16] Malwarebytes, Inc. v. Enigma Software Grp. USA, LLC, 141 S. Ct. 13 (2020) (Thomas, J., respecting the denial of certiorari); Biden v. Knight First Amend. Inst. at Colum. Univ., 141 S. Ct. 1220, 1224 (2021) (Thomas, J., concurring); Doe v. Facebook, Inc., 142 S. Ct. 1087, 1088 (2022) (Thomas, J., respecting the denial of certiorari). The day after the *Moody* decision, Justice Thomas issued a fourth anti–Section 230 statement. Doe v. Snap, Inc., 144 S. Ct. 2493, 2494 (2024) (Thomas, J., dissenting from the denial of certiorari).

[17] See, e.g., Aram Sinnreich et al., *Performative Media Policy: Section 230's Evolution from Regulatory Statute to Loyalty Oath*, 27 COMM. L. & POL'Y 167 (2023).

[18] As discussed below, Texas's law hobbled email spam filters. Florida's law initially exempted theme park operators. Dominick Reuter, *The New Florida Law That Fines Tech Platforms for Removing Politicians Has a Huge Loophole for Companies That Own Theme Parks in the State*, BUS. INSIDER (May 25, 2021), https://www.businessinsider.com/florida-censorship-law-loophole-for-theme-park-operators-2021-5. Florida subsequently repealed the theme park exemption to punish Disney for disagreeing with Gov. Ron DeSantis. S.B. 6-C (Fla. 2022).

[19] See Moody v. NetChoice, LLC, 144 S. Ct. 2383, 2407 (2024) (enumerating some examples of the bill supporters' partisan rhetoric).

Normally, messaging bills languish in the legislative process. But with Republicans in control of the Florida and Texas executive and legislative branches,[20] these messaging bills passed.

B. Summaries of the Laws

This subpart selectively summarizes the laws, a lengthy chore because the laws were packed with policy ideas.

1. Florida S.B. 7072

Section 2 says social media platforms cannot "deplatform" known political candidates during their candidacy.[21]

Section 3 (which constitutes about half of the bill's length) creates an "antitrust violator vendor list" (a blocklist) of entities restricted from transacting with the state.[22] Social media platforms may be placed on the list if they have been accused or found guilty (civilly or criminally) of antitrust violations. NetChoice and CCIA did not challenge this provision in court. As of July 2024, Florida apparently has not named any entities to the blocklist.[23]

Section 4 regulates social media platforms' content moderation efforts in multiple ways.[24]

- (2)(a) requires social media platforms to publish their editorial criteria for content removal or downranking.
- (2)(b) requires social media platforms to apply those editorial criteria "in a consistent manner."
- (2)(c) requires social media platforms to notify users of their publication criteria before implementing them. Social media platforms cannot change their editorial criteria more than once every 30 days.

---

[20] "Trifecta" states have single-party control over the legislative and executive branches. Following the 2023 elections, 40 states were trifectas (23 Republican, 17 Democratic). *State Government Trifectas*, BALLOTPEDIA, https://ballotpedia.org/State_government_trifectas (last visited July 30, 2024).

[21] FLA. STAT. § 106.072 (2021).

[22] FLA. STAT. § 287.137 (2022).

[23] *Antitrust Violator Vendor List*, FLA. DEP'T OF MGMT. SERVS., https://www.dms.myflorida.com/business_operations/state_purchasing/state_agency_resources/vendor_registration_and_vendor_lists/antitrust_violator_vendor_list (last visited July 30, 2024). On July 30, 2024, the page said, "There are currently no vendors on this list."

[24] FLA. STAT. § 501.2041 (2024).

- (2)(d) requires social media platforms to notify users when removing/downranking their content or deplatforming users (unless the content is obscene).
- (2)(e) requires social media platforms to provide viewership statistics to posting users.
- (2)(f) requires social media platforms to "[c]ategorize algorithms used for post-prioritization and shadow banning" and allow users to opt out of those algorithms "to allow sequential or chronological posts and content."
- (2)(g) requires social media platforms to annually notify users about those algorithms and reoffer the opt-out opportunity.
- (2)(h) restricts social media platforms from applying their "post-prioritization and shadow banning" algorithms to content from or about political candidates.
- (2)(i) requires social media platforms to give deplatformed users access to their content for at least 60 days.
- (2)(j) restricts social media platforms from removing or downranking content from journalistic enterprises based on their content (except for obscene content).
- (3)(c) requires that notices of removal/downranking include "a thorough rationale explaining the reason that the social media platform censored the user."
- (3)(d) requires that those notices also provide "a precise and thorough explanation of how the social media platform became aware of the censored content or material," including a thorough explanation of any algorithms the platform used to identify the content.
- (5) gives enforcement authority to the Florida Attorney General's office.
- (6) creates a private right of action—including potential statutory damages of up to $100,000, punitive damages, injunctive relief, and attorneys' fees—for alleged violations of the provisions requiring consistent content moderation and user notifications about content removal/downranking.
- (7) characterizes out-of-state social media platforms as doing business in Florida if they make any content moderation decisions affecting Florida users or Florida political candidates.
- (8) allows the Florida Attorney General's office to subpoena "any algorithm used by a social media platform related to any alleged violation."

2. Texas H.B. 20

Sections 120.051–120.053 impose multiple disclosure obligations regarding social media platforms' editorial practices. Social media platforms must publish an "acceptable use policy" that conforms to statutory specifications. They must also publish numerous very detailed transparency reports about their editorial operations and decisions.

Sections 120.101–120.102 require social media platforms to provide users with an easy way to submit complaints about other users' content. The platforms then must "evaluate the legality of the content or activity" within 48 hours of receiving a user complaint.

Sections 120.103–120.104 impose several "procedural due process" obligations on social media platforms when they remove user content for violating their acceptable use policies (with limited exceptions). Platforms must notify the user of the removal; provide an explanation of the removal decision; allow the user to appeal the removal decision (in some cases, within 14 days); and notify appealing users of the appeals decision. If the platform reverses the removal decision, it must explain the reversal.

Section 120.151 authorizes the Texas Attorney General's office to seek injunctions and enforcement costs.

Section 321.054 restricts an electronic mail service provider (such as Gmail) from "intentionally imped[ing] the transmission" of email except for (1) commercial spam if it "provides a process for the prompt, good faith resolution of a dispute" by the sender, and (2) other email if it "has a good faith, reasonable belief that the message contains malicious computer code, obscene material, material depicting sexual conduct, or material that violates other law." This provision includes a private right of action with statutory damages of the lesser of $10 per impeded email or $25,000 per day of impeded email. NetChoice and CCIA did not challenge this provision in court, but I am not aware of any enforcement attempts to date.

Sections 143A.002–143A.008 restrict social media platforms from "censoring" (a defined term) "a user, a user's expression, or a user's ability to receive the expression of another person based on: (1) the viewpoint of the user or another person; (2) the viewpoint represented in the user's expression or another person's expression; or (3) a user's geographic location in this state or any part of this state," whether the viewpoints are expressed online or off. Users cannot waive this protection contractually. The provisions extend to any user who "shares or receives expression," and to "expression that is shared or received," in Texas. The anti-"censoring" provisions have several statutory exclusions, including exceptions for expression that

- "is the subject of a referral or request from an organization with the purpose of preventing the sexual exploitation of children and protecting survivors of sexual abuse from ongoing harassment;"
- "directly incites criminal activity or consists of specific threats of violence targeted against a person or group because of their race, color, disability, religion, national origin or ancestry, age, sex, or status as a peace officer or judge;" or
- "is unlawful expression."

The anti-"censoring" provisions provide a private right of action for declaratory relief (plus enforcement costs) and injunctive relief. The court must enforce injunction violations using "all lawful measures to secure immediate compliance with the order, including daily penalties sufficient to secure immediate compliance." The Texas Attorney General's office can seek injunctions and enforcement costs.

Although the Florida law was enacted first, the Texas law didn't appear to copy verbiage from the Florida law. Still, the laws share some common themes. Both laws override platforms' content moderation discretion (e.g., Florida requires "consistent" moderation, Texas requires viewpoint-neutral moderation). Both laws require platforms to explain content moderation actions to users. And both laws authorize enforcement via private rights of action. However, the laws also have significant differences. For example, Florida created the antitrust blocklist and prioritized journalists' and politicians' content; while Texas banned email filtering, compelled a wider range of editorial transparency, and created appellate rights for content moderation decisions.

C. Court Proceedings Leading up to the Supreme Court's Review

Two industry trade associations, NetChoice and CCIA, challenged both laws (with some exceptions) in federal court. Both district court judges preliminarily enjoined enforcement of the challenged provisions.[25]

---

[25] NetChoice, LLC v. Moody, 546 F. Supp. 3d 1082 (N.D. Fla. 2021); NetChoice, LLC v. Paxton, 573 F. Supp. 3d 1092 (W.D. Tex. 2021).

On appeal, the Eleventh Circuit upheld most of the injunction against Florida's law, except with respect to certain disclosure obligations that qualified for less stringent review under the Supreme Court's *Zauderer* precedent.[26] The Eleventh Circuit panel summarized its conclusions with this chart:[27]

Provision	Fla. Stat. §	Likely Constitutionality	Disposition
Candidate deplatforming	106.072(2)	Unconstitutional	Affirm
Posts by/about candidates	501.2041(2)(h)	Unconstitutional	Affirm
"Journalistic enterprises"	501.2041(2)(j)	Unconstitutional	Affirm
Consistency	501.2041(2)(b)	Unconstitutional	Affirm
30-day restriction	501.2041(2)(c)	Unconstitutional	Affirm
User opt-out	501.2041(2)(f),(g)	Unconstitutional	Affirm
Explanations (per decision)	501.2041(2)(d)	Unconstitutional	Affirm
Standards	501.2041(2)(a)	Constitutional	Vacate
Rule changes	501.2041(2)(c)	Constitutional	Vacate
User view counts	501.2041(2)(e)	Constitutional	Vacate
Candidate "free advertising"	106.072(4)	Constitutional	Vacate
User-data access	501.2041(2)(i)	Constitutional	Vacate

Both sides cross-appealed the Eleventh Circuit opinion to the Supreme Court.

---

[26] Zauderer v. Off. of Disciplinary Couns., 471 U.S. 626 (1985).

[27] NetChoice, LLC v. Att'y Gen. of Fla., 34 F.4th 1196 (11th Cir. 2022).

With respect to the Texas law, the Fifth Circuit initially lifted the district court's injunction without issuing an opinion.[28] The challengers made an emergency appeal to the Supreme Court.[29] The Supreme Court (voting 5–4) restored the injunction pending the Fifth Circuit's opinion.[30] Justice Samuel Alito and two other Justices dissented and said the case's legal questions raised "issues of great importance that will plainly merit this Court's review."[31]

A few months later, the Fifth Circuit issued its decision lifting the injunction.[32] Judge Andrew Oldham wrote the lead opinion, with which Judge Edith Jones mostly concurred. Judge Leslie Southwick concurred with the court's decision to lift the injunction on the mandatory transparency obligations, but he dissented on the rest. Judge Oldham's opinion expressly rejected the Eleventh Circuit's prior decision: "The Platforms urge us to follow the Eleventh Circuit's *NetChoice* opinion. We will not."[33] The challengers again appealed the case to the Supreme Court.

Although it seemed certain that the Supreme Court would accept both cases, the Court invited the Solicitor General's views about granting certiorari. This move delayed the cases from the 2022–2023 Term to the 2023–2024 Term. The Solicitor General recommended narrowing the Questions Presented to "1. Whether the laws' content-moderation restrictions comply with the First Amendment [and] 2. Whether the laws' individualized-explanation

---

[28] NetChoice, LLC v. Paxton, No. 21-51178, 2022 U.S. App. LEXIS 13434 (5th Cir. May 11, 2022) (order granting motion to stay preliminary injunction), https://digitalcommons.law.scu.edu/cgi/viewcontent.cgi?article=3669&context=historical. The Fifth Circuit ironically upheld a law requiring platforms to provide individualized explanations for their decisions—without providing an individualized explanation for its decision.

[29] Emergency appeals like this are sometimes called the Supreme Court's "shadow docket."

[30] NetChoice, LLC v. Paxton, 142 S. Ct. 1715 (2022).

[31] *Id.* at 1716 (Alito, J., dissenting from grant of application to vacate stay).

[32] NetChoice, LLC v. Paxton, 49 F.4th 439 (5th Cir. 2022).

[33] *Id.* at 488.

requirements comply with the First Amendment."[34] The Supreme Court accepted this recommendation and granted certiorari for both cases.

II. The Supreme Court Decision

On July 1, 2024 (the last day of its 2023–2024 Term), the Supreme Court issued its decision in *Moody v. NetChoice*,[35] which also resolved the *NetChoice v. Paxton* appeal. The Justices unanimously agreed to vacate the Fifth and Eleventh Circuit opinions and remand the cases back to the lower courts for reexamination of the facial First Amendment challenges.

The Justices' unanimity was only superficial. The Justices wrote five opinions totaling 96 pages and nearly 28,000 words. Justice Kagan wrote the majority opinion on behalf of herself and four other Justices (John Roberts, Sonia Sotomayor, Brett Kavanaugh, and Amy Coney Barrett). Justice Ketanji Brown Jackson joined Parts I, II, and III-A of Justice Kagan's opinion. Justices Barrett and Jackson wrote concurrences that qualified their support for Justice Kagan's opinion (Justice Jackson's concurrence was partially in the judgment). Justice Alito wrote an opinion concurring in the judgment that was joined by Justices Thomas and Neil Gorsuch. According to CNN reporter Joan Biskupic, Justice Alito was originally slated to write a majority opinion, but he lost the votes of Justices Barrett and Jackson.[36] Justice Thomas wrote his own concurrence in the judgment. In total, six Justices supported First Amendment protection for content moderation and three Justices disagreed.

[34] Brief for the United States as Amicus Curiae, Moody v. NetChoice, LLC, NetChoice, LLC v. Moody, & NetChoice, LLC v. Paxton, 144 S. Ct. 2383 (2024) (Nos. 22-277, 22-393 & 22-555) (on petitions for writs of certiorari), https://www.supremecourt.gov/Docket PDF/22/22-277/275249/20230814145135723_NetChoice%20Invitation%20Brief%20 8.9%20—%20For%20Final.pdf.

[35] Moody v. NetChoice, LLC, 144 S. Ct. 2383 (2024).

[36] Joan Biskupic, *Exclusive: How Samuel Alito Got Canceled from the Supreme Court Social Media Majority*, CNN (July 31, 2024), https://www.cnn.com/2024/07/31/politics/ samuel-alito-supreme-court-netchoice-social-media-biskupic/index.html.

A. Justice Kagan's Majority Opinion

Beyond vacating the lower court rulings and remanding the cases for further consideration, the majority opinion accomplished four major things. First, it specified how facial constitutional challenges should be reviewed. Second, it stated that social media platforms' content moderation decisions qualify for First Amendment protection. Third, it indicated that the Florida and Texas laws probably violate the First Amendment. Fourth, it reviewed and distinguished several key speech-related precedents. A closer look at these four points, as well as a brief discussion of dicta, follows:

1. The opinion specified the review standard for facial First Amendment challenges

   The majority said that the Fifth and Eleventh Circuits did not conduct their facial challenge reviews properly. A facial First Amendment challenger must show that "a substantial number of [the law's] applications are unconstitutional, judged in relation to the statute's plainly legitimate sweep."[37] On remand, the courts "must determine a law's full set of applications, evaluate which are constitutional and which are not, and compare the one to the other."[38] The majority provided a two-step process:

   Step 1: The courts must "assess the state laws' scope. What activities, by what actors, do the laws prohibit or otherwise regulate?"[39]

   Step 2: The courts must "decide which of the laws' applications violate the First Amendment, and [] measure them against the rest. For the content-moderation provisions, that means asking, as to every covered platform or function, whether there is an intrusion on protected editorial discretion. And for the individualized-explanation provisions, it means asking, again as to each thing covered, whether the required disclosures unduly burden expression. . . . [T]he courts below must explore the laws' full range of applications—the

---

[37] Ams. for Prosperity Found. v. Bonta, 594 U.S. 595, 615 (2021).

[38] *Moody*, 144 S. Ct. at 2394.

[39] *Id.* at 2398.

constitutionally impermissible and permissible both—and compare the two sets."[40]

Thus, on remand, the lower courts will need to consider how dozens of statutory provisions could apply to dozens of potentially regulated entities that each have multiple communication modalities—a daunting multidimensional project for all involved. As the majority said, "NetChoice chose to litigate these cases as facial challenges, and that decision comes at a cost."[41]

2. Content moderation received First Amendment protection

The Florida and Texas laws overrode the editorial and publication policies and decisions of social media platforms. The majority clearly and emphatically rejected this legislative objective. The majority stated, "To the extent that social-media platforms create expressive products, they receive the First Amendment's protection."[42] The majority then explained that social media platforms' content moderation, including algorithmic presentations of content, cause the outputs to be "expressive products": "In constructing certain feeds, those platforms make choices about what third-party speech to display and how to display it. They include and exclude, organize and prioritize—and in making millions of those decisions each day, produce their own distinctive compilations of expression."[43]

Later, the majority wrote, "That Facebook and YouTube convey a mass of messages does not license Texas to prohibit them from deleting posts with, say, 'hate speech' based on 'sexual orientation.' It is as much an editorial choice to convey all speech except in select categories as to convey only speech within them."[44]

The majority analogized the expressive products created by social media platforms to the work of "traditional publishers

---

[40] *Id.*

[41] *Id.* at 2398.

[42] *Id.* at 2406.

[43] *Id.* The majority called social media platforms "compilers" rather than "publishers."

[44] *Id.* Justice Jackson did not join this part of the opinion.

and editors."[45] In both cases, "government efforts to alter an edited compilation of third-party expression are subject to judicial review for compliance with the First Amendment."[46]

The majority also wrote that "social-media platforms do not lose their First Amendment protection just because no one will wrongly attribute to them the views in an individual post."[47] The opinion explains that the audience may attribute to the platform the overall viewpoints expressed in its publicly accessible corpus;[48] and the First Amendment applies even if the audience doesn't misattribute anything.

However, not every electronic communications modality will receive favorable levels of constitutional protection. For example, the majority suggested that "transmitting direct messages," such as email or chat, might be treated differently from "[c]urating a feed."[49] This implies that private messaging services might receive less First Amendment protection than other content disseminators. However, this perceived distinction may fade once the Court understands how private messaging services undertake extensive and socially important curatorial and trust-and-safety efforts (such as sorting incoming email into folders and deploying anti-spam filters).

3. The Florida and Texas laws likely restrict First Amendment–protected content moderation

The majority opinion said,

> [T]he current record indicates that the Texas law does regulate speech when applied in the way the parties focused on below—when applied, that is, to prevent Facebook (or YouTube) from using its content-moderation

---

[45] *Id.* at 2393. Justice Kagan confirmed that platforms' "house rules" act as editorial policies. *Id.* at 2406 ("When the platforms use their Standards and Guidelines to decide which third-party content those feeds will display, or how the display will be ordered and organized, they are making expressive choices."). *See generally* Eric Goldman & Jess Miers, *Online Account Terminations/Content Removals and the Benefits of Internet Services Enforcing Their House Rules*, 1 J. FREE SPEECH L. 191 (2021).

[46] *Moody*, 144 S. Ct. at 2393.

[47] *Id.* at 2406. Justice Jackson did not join this part of the opinion.

[48] "[P]latforms may indeed 'own' the overall speech environment." *Id.*

[49] *Id.* at 2398.

standards to remove, alter, organize, prioritize, or disclaim posts in its News Feed (or homepage). The law then prevents exactly the kind of editorial judgments this Court has previously held to receive First Amendment protection. It prevents a platform from compiling the third-party speech it wants in the way it wants, and thus from offering the expressive product that most reflects its own views and priorities. Still more, the law—again, in that specific application—is unlikely to withstand First Amendment scrutiny.[50]

Later, the majority wrote, "Texas's law profoundly alters the platforms' choices about the views they will, and will not, convey. And we have time and again held that type of regulation to interfere with protected speech."[51]

Florida and Texas cannot justify their efforts based on a purported goal to "de-bias" the media: "[I]t is no job for government to decide what counts as the right balance of private expression—to 'un-bias' what it thinks biased, rather than to leave such judgments to speakers and their audiences. That principle works for social-media platforms as it does for others."[52]

Later still, the majority added:

States (and their citizens) are of course right to want an expressive realm in which the public has access to a wide range of views. That is, indeed, a fundamental aim of the First Amendment. But the way the First Amendment achieves that goal is by preventing *the government* from "tilt[ing] public debate in a preferred direction." *Sorrell v. IMS Health Inc.*, 564 U.S. 552, 578–579 (2011). It is not by licensing the government to stop *private actors* from speaking as they wish and preferring some views over

---

[50] *Id.* at 2394.

[51] *Id.* at 2405. Justice Jackson did not join this part of the opinion.

[52] *Id.* at 2394. Justice Barrett reinforced that the First Amendment protects any political bias by social media platforms: "Assume that human beings decide to remove posts promoting a particular political candidate or advocating some position on a public-health issue. If they create an algorithm to help them identify and delete that content, the First Amendment protects their exercise of editorial judgment—even if the algorithm does most of the deleting without a person in the loop." *Id.* at 2410 (Barrett, J., concurring).

> others.... [I]t cannot prohibit speech to improve or better
> balance the speech market. On the spectrum of dangers
> to free expression, there are few greater than allowing
> the government to change the speech of private actors in
> order to achieve its own conception of speech nirvana.[53]

The majority didn't decide whether strict or intermediate
scrutiny applies to Texas' law; it suggested that the law would
not pass either.[54] The majority wrote that Texas sought "to
correct the mix of speech that the major social-media platforms present,"[55] but "the interest Texas has asserted cannot
carry the day: It is very much related to the suppression of
free expression, and it is not valid, let alone substantial."[56]
Thus, "Texas does not like the way those platforms are se-
lecting and moderating content, and wants them to create a
different expressive product, communicating different values and priorities. But under the First Amendment, that is a
preference Texas may not impose."[57]

4. The opinion cleaned up precedent

The majority reviewed seven First Amendment precedents stretching back over a half-century: *Miami Herald*,[58]
PG&E,[59] the two *Turner* rulings,[60] *Hurley*,[61] *PruneYard*,[62] and
Rumsfeld.[63] The majority distilled three lessons from these
precedents:

First, "the First Amendment offers protection when an
entity engaging in expressive activity, including compiling
and curating others' speech, is directed to accommodate

---

[53] *Id.* at 2407 (majority opinion). Justice Jackson did not join this part of the opinion.

[54] *Id.* Justice Jackson did not join this part of the opinion.

[55] *Id.*

[56] *Id.* If the interest is invalid, the law would not survive rational basis review.

[57] *Id.* at 2408. Justice Jackson did not join this part of the opinion.

[58] Miami Herald Publ'g Co. v. Tornillo, 418 U.S. 241 (1974).

[59] Pac. Gas & Elec. Co. v. Pub. Util. Comm'n of Cal., 475 U.S. 1 (1986).

[60] Turner Broad. Sys., Inc. v. FCC, 512 U.S. 622 (1994); Turner Broad. Sys., Inc. v. FCC, 520 U.S. 180 (1997).

[61] Hurley v. Irish-Am. Gay, Lesbian & Bisexual Grp. of Bos., Inc., 515 U.S. 557 (1995).

[62] PruneYard Shopping Ctr. v. Robins, 447 U.S. 74 (1980).

[63] Rumsfeld v. F. for Acad. & Inst. Rts., Inc., 547 U.S. 47 (2006).

messages it would prefer to exclude. . . . And that is as true when the content comes from third parties as when it does not. . . . When the government interferes with such editorial choices—say, by ordering the excluded to be included—it alters the content of the compilation."[64]

Second, the first principle applies even if "a compiler includes most items and excludes just a few."[65]

Third, the "government cannot get its way just by asserting an interest in improving, or better balancing, the marketplace of ideas. . . . [I]n case after case, the Court has barred the government from forcing a private speaker to present views it wished to spurn in order to rejigger the expressive realm."[66]

At times, pro-regulatory advocates have cherrypicked parts of these precedents in attempts to validate government censorship of social media platforms. The principles set out in the majority opinion should end those efforts.

5. Does the majority opinion's dicta matter?

To vacate the Fifth and Eleventh Circuit opinions, the majority opinion could have simply explained why the lower courts' analyses of the facial constitutional challenges were incorrect and stopped there. Because the opinion goes further, the extra discussion becomes dicta.

Critics will use that dicta status to marginalize the majority opinion's significance. It won't work.[67] The majority opinion is a major First Amendment precedent.[68]

---

[64] *Moody*, 144 S. Ct. at 2401–02.

[65] *Id.* at 2402.

[66] *Id.*

[67] *See* Cathy Gellis, *In the* NetChoice *Cases, Alito and His Buddies Are Wrong, but Even if They Were Right It May Not Matter, and That's Largely Good News*, TECHDIRT (July 1, 2024), https://www.techdirt.com/2024/07/01/in-the-netchoice-cases-alito-and-his-buddies-are-wrong-but-even-if-they-were-right-it-may-not-matter-and-thats-largely-good-news/.

[68] Professor Noah Feldman called the decision a "blockbuster" and "the *Brown v. Board of Education* of the emerging field of social media law." Noah Feldman, *Social Media Ruling Is a Free-Speech Landmark: Noah Feldman*, BLOOMBERG (July 1, 2024), https://news.bloomberglaw.com/us-law-week/social-media-ruling-is-a-free-speech-landmark-noah-feldman.

It demonstrates that six Justices, spanning the Court's "conservative" and "liberal" wings, will not tolerate censorial messaging bills. It also provides essential guidance on a fundamental topic—does the First Amendment protect content moderation?—that's currently at the nexus of substantial legislative activity. After reading the majority opinion, many legislators ought to rethink their censorial agendas toward Internet services. Otherwise, those laws will be invalidated.

B. Justice Barrett's Concurrence

Justice Barrett's opinion makes three key points. First, emphasizing the majority's skepticism of facial constitutional challenges, she suggested that facial review may not be available here: "[D]ealing with a broad swath of varied platforms and functions in a facial challenge strikes me as a daunting, if not impossible, task. . . . A facial challenge to either of these laws likely forces a court to bite off more than it can chew."[69]

Second, Justice Barrett spun some hypotheticals involving algorithms:

> [W]hat if a platform's algorithm just presents automatically to each user whatever the algorithm thinks the user will like—e.g., content similar to posts with which the user previously engaged? The First Amendment implications of the Florida and Texas laws might be different for that kind of algorithm. And what about [artificial intelligence (AI)], which is rapidly evolving? What if a platform's owners hand the reins to an AI tool and ask it simply to remove "hateful" content? If the AI relies on large language models to determine what is "hateful" and should be removed, has a human being with First Amendment rights made an inherently expressive choice . . . ? In other words, technology may attenuate the connection between content-moderation actions (e.g., removing posts) and human beings' constitutionally protected right to "decide for [themselves] the ideas and beliefs deserving of expression, consideration, and adherence."[70]

[69] *Moody*, 144 S. Ct. at 2409–11. (Barrett, J., concurring).

[70] *Id.* at 2010. (internal quotation mark omitted).

These purported distinctions don't make sense. In her examples, publishers make difficult and nuanced decisions about what content is appropriate for their audiences. For example, personalized algorithms necessarily reflect a service's editorial judgment (1) that the chosen algorithm will better cater to its audience than other algorithms, and (2) about how to define similarity, which is not a binary assessment at all.[71] Similarly, in her AI example, some human editor chose to (1) deprioritize hateful content, (2) define what "hateful" content means, an exceedingly difficult task filled with judgment calls,[72] and (3) pick a method to identify and exclude "hateful" content consistent with its editorial agenda. The First Amendment shouldn't care what technological means the publisher chooses to implement these editorial goals.

Third, Justice Barrett gave another hypothetical:

> Corporations, which are composed of human beings with First Amendment rights, possess First Amendment rights themselves. . . . But foreign persons and corporations located abroad do not. *Agency for Int'l Development v. Alliance for Open Society Int'l, Inc.*, 591 U.S. 430, 433–436 (2020). So a social-media platform's foreign ownership and control over its content-moderation decisions might affect whether laws overriding those decisions trigger First Amendment scrutiny. What if the platform's corporate leadership abroad makes the policy decisions about the viewpoints and content the platform will disseminate? Would it matter that the corporation employs Americans to develop and implement content-moderation algorithms if they do so at the direction of foreign executives?[73]

Justice Barrett is clearly anticipating the Court's review of Congress's efforts to ban TikTok.[74] Three constitutional challenges are

---

[71] Content-ordering algorithms are *never* neutral because they inherently prioritize certain attributes over others, and deciding which attributes to preference is an editorial decision. *See* Eric Goldman, *Search Engine Bias and the Demise of Search Engine Utopianism*, 8 YALE J.L. & TECH. 188 (Spring 2006).

[72] *See, e.g., Hate Speech*, STAN. ENCYC. OF PHIL. (Jan. 25, 2022), https://plato.stanford.edu/entries/hate-speech/ ("the concept of hate speech" raises "many difficult questions").

[73] *Moody*, 144 S. Ct. at 2410 (Barrett, J., concurring) (citations omitted).

[74] Protecting Americans from Foreign Adversary Controlled Applications Act, Pub. L. No. 118-50 (2024).

pending before the D.C. Circuit on their way to the Supreme Court.[75] Barrett left open the possibility of distinguishing the TikTok ban from this ruling. However, the "foreign persons and corporations located abroad" exclusion may not apply to TikTok given its extensive U.S. presence.[76]

C. Justice Jackson's Concurrence in Part/Concurrence in the Judgment

Justice Jackson reinforced the majority's concerns about facial challenges: "[C]ourts must . . . carefully parse not only what entities are regulated, but how the regulated activities actually function before deciding if the activity in question constitutes expression and therefore comes within the First Amendment's ambit."[77]

D. Justice Alito's Concurrence in the Judgment

Justice Alito's concurrence in the judgment[78] criticizes Justice Kagan's majority opinion extensively. Justice Alito called the majority's discussion of the First Amendment's application to content moderation "nonbinding dicta."[79] He wrote that the majority's description of the laws and the litigation "leaves much to be desired," that it provides an "incomplete" summary of the Court's precedents,

---

[75] TikTok, Inc. v. Garland, No. 24-1113 (D.C. Cir. complaint filed May 7, 2024); Firebaugh v. Garland, No. 24-1130 (D.C. Cir. complaint filed May 14, 2024); BASED Politics Inc. v. Garland, No. 24-1183 (D.C. Cir. complaint filed June 6, 2024).

[76] See Bridges v. Wixon, 326 U.S. 135, 148 (1945) ("Freedom of speech and of press is accorded aliens residing in this country."); Free Speech Coal., Inc. v. Colmenero, 689 F. Supp. 3d 373 (W.D. Tex. 2023), rev'd, Free Speech Coal., Inc. v. Paxton, 95 F.4th 263 (5th Cir. 2024), cert. granted, 2024 WL 3259690 (U.S. July 2, 2024) ("[T]he does not read AOSI to abrogate First Amendment protection for speech occurring in the United States and directed at the United States but hosted by foreign entities[.]").

[77] Moody, 144 S. Ct. at 2411–12 (Jackson, J., concurring in part and concurring in the judgment); accord Eric Schlachter, Cyberspace, the Free Market, and the Free Marketplace of Ideas: Recognizing Legal Differences in Computer Bulletin Board Functions, 16 HASTINGS COMMC'NS & ENT. L.J. 87 (1993).

[78] A reminder that Justice Alito initially drafted a majority opinion. Biskupic, supra note 36. For additional critiques of Justice Alito's concurrence, see Eric Goldman, Everything You Wanted to Know about the Moody v. NetChoice Supreme Court Opinion, TECH. & MKTG. L. BLOG (July 25, 2024), https://blog.ericgoldman.org/archives/2024/07/everything-you-wanted-to-know-about-the-moody-v-netchoice-supreme-court-opinion.htm.

[79] Moody, 144 S. Ct. at 2422 (Alito, J., concurring in the judgment).

that its discussions about Facebook's newsfeed and YouTube's home page are "unnecessary and unjustified," that it "inexplicably singles out a few provisions and a couple of platforms for special treatment," and that it "unreflectively assumes the truth of NetChoice's unsupported assertion" that social media platforms can be analogized to newspapers.[80] He added that the majority opinion "rests on wholly conclusory assumptions that lack record support."[81]

Justice Alito's opinion focuses on whether social media platforms warrant First Amendment protection for their "compilation" decisions. He articulated three prerequisites for such protection: (1) the entity must "exercise 'editorial discretion in the selection and presentation' of the content it hosts"; (2) "the host must use the compilation of speech to express 'some sort of collective point'—even if only at a fairly abstract level"; and (3) "a compiler must show that its 'own message [is] affected by the speech it [is] forced to accommodate.'"[82]

Applying that test, Justice Alito wrote that NetChoice did not adequately establish "*which entities* the statutes cover," "what kinds of content appear on all the regulated platforms," and "how websites moderate content."[83]

E. Justice Thomas's Concurrence in the Judgment

Justice Thomas's concurrence in the judgment revisits several of his longstanding pet topics, with 18 self-citations to his prior opinions. Consistent with his anti–Section 230 statements from a few years ago, Justice Thomas again evangelized a common carriage regulatory approach to social media platforms.[84] The majority opinion never expressly engages with this argument or mentions the terms "common carrier" and "common carriage." Nevertheless, because

---

[80] *Id.*

[81] *Id.* at 2438.

[82] *Id.* at 2431–32.

[83] *Id.* at 2433–36.

[84] Justice Thomas bizarrely claimed that, in *Moody*, "the Eleventh Circuit appropriately strove to apply the common-carrier doctrine." *Moody*, 144 S. Ct. at 2413 (Thomas, J., concurring in the judgment). The Eleventh Circuit actually said that "social-media platforms are not—in the nature of things, so to speak—common carriers." NetChoice, LLC v. Att'y Gen. of Fla., 34 F.4th 1196, 1220 (11th Cir. 2022).

social media platforms are analogous to publishers, the majority opinion clearly rejects arguments that social media platforms can be regulated like common carriers.[85]

F. What's Next?

On remand, the challengers must decide whether to continue with their facial challenges despite the Supreme Court's strong cautions. However, as-applied challenges pose several problems. Most important, the challengers may run into pre-enforcement standing problems. In the *Murthy* case,[86] also issued this Term, a Court majority said, "plaintiffs must demonstrate a substantial risk that, in the near future, they will suffer an injury that is traceable to a Government defendant and redressable by the injunction they seek." Will challengers of the Florida and Texas laws have the requisite evidence of that "substantial risk" before the laws are enforced? Or must the challengers defy the law and wait to make their constitutional challenges after enforcement actions have been brought?

It's unclear how the Supreme Court's vacatur of the appellate opinions affected the preliminary injunctions issued by the district courts. If injunctions are not in place, the Texas and Florida Attorney General's offices could bring enforcement actions. Given the majority opinion's clear skepticism of the laws' constitutionality, that would be highly unwise. But wisdom has always been in short supply in defending the laws. Also, a few individual litigants have already brought private claims to enforce the laws, even while the injunctions were in place. The vacatur of the appellate opinions might encourage more ill-advised private suits.

In the district courts, the challengers raised a range of objections to the laws, of which the First Amendment was just one. The Texas court blocked the Texas law solely on First Amendment grounds.[87] The Florida court blocked the Florida law on both First Amendment

---

[85] *See e.g.*, *Moody*, 144 S. Ct. at 2399 (("[O]rdering a party to provide a forum for someone else's views implicates the First Amendment [if] the regulated party is engaged in its own expressive activity, which the mandated access would alter or disrupt[.]"). Feldman says the majority opinion makes common carriage analogies "passé." Feldman, *supra* note 68.

[86] Murthy v. Missouri, 144 S. Ct. 1972, 1981 (2024).

[87] NetChoice, LLC v. Paxton, 573 F. Supp. 3d 1092 (W.D. Tex. 2021).

and Section 230 grounds,[88] though the Eleventh Circuit didn't affirm the Section 230 discussion. The challengers could ask the district courts to reconsider their objections beyond the First Amendment.

Regardless of the further proceedings, Florida and Texas at any time can enforce the unchallenged parts of their laws (including the antitrust blocklist in Florida and the email filtering ban in Texas), but doing so would likely trigger as-applied constitutional challenges.

III. Some Additional Implications

This part highlights four implications of the decision: how it interplays with the venerable *Reno v. ACLU* precedent; some consequences for First Amendment challenges; the unresolved questions about the laws' compelled editorial transparency; and the need for ongoing Supreme Court supervision of the Fifth Circuit.

A. The Silent Shadow of Reno v. ACLU

In 1997, in *Reno v. ACLU*,[89] the Supreme Court struck down the Communications Decency Act,[90] a law that required websites to prevent minors from accessing pornography. That decision called the Internet "a unique and wholly new medium of worldwide human communication."[91] As a result, unlike the broadcasting and telephony media, the Supreme Court's "cases provide no basis for qualifying the level of First Amendment scrutiny that should be applied to" the Internet.[92]

Although the *Reno* decision has been the Court's flagship Internet First Amendment case for the past quarter-century, it got only a single citation across the five *Moody* opinions.[93] Nevertheless, the majority opinion quietly pays homage to the *Reno* precedent.

Like *Reno*, the majority opinion does not downgrade the level of First Amendment scrutiny applied to social media platforms. The majority rejected (sometimes expressly, sometimes implicitly)

---

[88] NetChoice, LLC v. Moody, 546 F. Supp. 3d 1082 (N.D. Fla. 2021).

[89] Reno v. Am. Civ. Liberties Union, 521 U.S. 844 (1997).

[90] Communications Decency Act of 1996, Pub. L. No. 104-104 tit. V, 110 Stat. 133 (Feb. 8, 1996) (codified at 47 U.S.C. § 223).

[91] *Reno*, 521 U.S. at 845.

[92] *Id.* at 870.

[93] *See Moody*, 144 S. Ct. at 2393.

analogies between social media platforms and other entities that sometimes receive reduced First Amendment protection, including common carriers, shopping mall owners, law schools, cable broadcasters, and private actors who become state actors.

Instead, the majority opinion accepts the analogy between social media platforms and traditional offline publishers like newspapers. This analogy holds despite the unique attributes of social media publishers compared with other publishers. These unique attributes include that social media publishers have a high volume of published content;[94] publish mostly third-party content rather than first-party content;[95] decline to publish only a small percentage of the content submitted to them;[96] primarily exercise editorial discretion through post-publication content moderation rather than pre-publication review;[97] use automated algorithms to organize and present content;[98] and don't necessarily have consumers attribute third-party content to them.[99]

Like *Reno*, the majority opinion simultaneously embraces and rejects Internet exceptionalism. The majority rejected the exceptionalist arguments seeking to treat social media platforms as something less publisher-like than traditional publishers,[100] such as Justice

[94] *Id.* (social media platforms make millions of decisions per day).

[95] *Id.* at 2402 (the principle that content selection and presentation is an expressive activity "is as true when the content comes from third parties as when it does not").

[96] *Id.* at 2402, 2405 (it doesn't matter if "a compiler includes most items and excludes just a few. . . . That those platforms happily convey the lion's share of posts submitted to them makes no significant First Amendment difference"). Justice Kagan added, "The individual messages may originate with third parties, but the larger offering is the platform's. It is the product of a wealth of choices about whether—and, if so, how—to convey posts having a certain content or viewpoint. Those choices rest on a set of beliefs about which messages are appropriate and which are not (or which are more appropriate and which less so). And in the aggregate they give the feed a particular expressive quality." *Id.* at 2405.

[97] The majority opinion repeatedly treats content "removal" as an editorial function.

[98] *Id.* at 2393 ("In constructing certain feeds, those platforms make choices about what third-party speech to display and how to display it.").

[99] *Id.* at 2406 ("[S]ocial-media platforms do not lose their First Amendment protection just because no one will wrongly attribute to them the views in an individual post.").

[100] *Id.* ("[L]aws curtailing [publishers' and editors'] editorial choices must meet the First Amendment's requirements. The principle does not change because the curated compilation has gone from the physical to the virtual world.").

Thomas's common carriage analogy. At the same time, like the *Reno* court's valorization of Internet publication, the majority reiterated that Internet services deserve an unqualified level of constitutional protection, unlike broadcasting or telephony. In that way, *Reno*'s spirit pervades the majority opinion.

B. The Future of First Amendment Challenges to Government Censorship

The *Moody* case will require challengers to spend more money and do more upfront case preparation to bring facial First Amendment challenges. Some censorial laws won't be prospectively challenged simply because of those burdens. Regulators can also intentionally overstuff policy ideas into a censorial law as another way of discouraging facial challenge.[101]

With respect to as-applied First Amendment challenges, Article III standing often plays a critical gatekeeping role, as evidenced by *Murthy*'s dismissal of the challengers' suit.[102] Together, the *Moody* and *Murthy* cases are a one-two punch for challengers of government censorship. *Moody* drives challengers away from facial challenges and toward as-applied challenges, but *Murthy* highlights potential standing difficulties with as-applied challenges.

C. Can Governments Compel Editorial Transparency?

The Florida and Texas social media censorship laws made a historically unprecedented move of compelling substantial affirmative disclosures from publishers about their editorial operations

---

[101] David Greene, *Platforms Have First Amendment Right to Curate Speech, As We've Long Argued, Supreme Court Said, but Sends Laws Back to Lower Court to Decide If That Applies to Other Functions Like Messaging*, EFF (July 14, 2024), https://www.eff.org/deeplinks/2024/07/platforms-have-first-amendment-right-curate-speech-weve-long-argued-supreme-1 ("This decision thus creates a perverse incentive for states to pass laws that by their language broadly cover a wide range of activities[.]").

Bounty-based private enforcement is another technique legislatures are intentionally using to thwart facial constitutional challenges. *See, e.g.,* Free Speech Coal., Inc. v. LeBlanc, 2023 WL 6464768 (E.D. La. Oct. 4, 2023).

[102] Murthy v. Missouri, 144 S. Ct. 1972 (2024).

and decisions.[103] Historically, legislatures have not demanded similar disclosures from traditional publishers. And that's for good reasons, including the obvious chilling effects of such laws.[104] Despite this novelty, the Fifth and Eleventh Circuits agreed that the relaxed *Zauderer*[105] standards of constitutional review applied. Both courts held that many of the disclosure requirements survived constitutional review, except for the Eleventh Circuit's rejection of the individualized explanations obligation.

The Supreme Court granted review of the compelled individualized explanations disclosures, but its decision didn't invest much energy in the topic.[106] The majority instructed that on remand, the lower courts should ask "whether the required disclosures unduly burden expression."[107] In a footnote, the majority reinforced the point that individualized explanations "violate the First Amendment if they unduly burden expressive activity."[108] And the Court clarified that its "explanation of why Facebook and YouTube are engaged in expression when they make content-moderation choices in their main feeds should inform the courts' further consideration of that issue."[109]

---

[103] Brief of Amici Curiae Prof. Eric Goldman and TechFreedom in Support of Appellees and Affirmance, Volokh v. James, No. 23-356 (2d Cir. filed Sept. 25, 2023) ("Prior to the Internet, legislatures apparently never attempted to impose mandatory disclosure requirements like Section 394-ccc on publishers of newspapers, magazines, books, music, and other printed materials."). *See also* Brief of Professor Eric Goldman, *supra* note *. In addition, I published two articles on this topic: Eric Goldman, *The Constitutionality of Mandating Editorial Transparency*, 73 HASTINGS L.J. 1203 (2022) [hereinafter Goldman, HASTINGS]; and Eric Goldman, *Zauderer and Compelled Editorial Transparency*, 108 IOWA L. REV. ONLINE 80 (2023) [hereinafter Goldman, Zauderer]. *See also* Daphne Keller, *Platform Transparency and the First Amendment*, 4 J. FREE SPEECH L. 1 (2023), https://www.journaloffreespeechlaw.org/keller2.pdf.

[104] Goldman, HASTINGS, *supra* note 103. For example, "[t]here is no law that subjects the editorial process to private or official examination merely to satisfy curiosity or to serve some general end such as the public interest; and if there were, it would not survive constitutional scrutiny as the First Amendment is presently construed." Herbert v. Lando, 441 U.S. 153, 174 (1979).

[105] Zauderer v. Off. of Disciplinary Couns., 471 U.S. 626 (1985).

[106] The five opinions reference *Zauderer* by name a total of 16 times.

[107] *Moody*, 144 S. Ct. at 2398.

[108] *Id.* at 2399 n.3.

[109] *Id.*

This decision leaves open critical questions about the individualized explanations, *Zauderer*, and editorial transparency mandates more generally.

First, do the individualized explanations provisions qualify for relaxed *Zauderer* scrutiny, and if so, why?[110] Over nearly 40 years, the Supreme Court has upheld only two compelled commercial disclosure laws using *Zauderer*, both of which sought to prevent deceptive omissions in ad copy.[111] The majority implied that *Zauderer* applies but never explained why, even though individualized explanations are quite different from the only two laws that the Supreme Court has upheld using *Zauderer*. Perhaps *Moody* and *NIFLA*[112] imply that the *Zauderer* test applies to every type of compelled corporate speech.

Second, if *Zauderer* scrutiny applies, what factors will courts use to evaluate the individualized explanations provisions? In *Zauderer*, the Court said that a disclosure obligation would survive scrutiny if it (1) is not unjustified, (2) is not unduly burdensome, and (3) reasonably relates to preventing consumer deception.[113] In its brief discussion of *Zauderer*, the majority silently omitted the first and third considerations, implicitly leaving only a single-factor *Zauderer* evaluation of whether the disclosure obligations "unduly burden expressive activity." Did the majority permanently reduce the *Zauderer* evaluative factors from three to one without explaining why the stricken considerations no longer apply? Or will lower courts revert back to using all three evaluative factors as initially articulated in the *Zauderer* opinion?[114]

With respect to the Florida and Texas individualized explanations, the majority's truncated recapitulation of the *Zauderer* factors may not matter. The Eleventh Circuit has already concluded that Florida's

---

[110] Justice Alito said that because "these regulations provide for the disclosure of 'purely factual and uncontroversial information,' they must be reviewed under *Zauderer*'s framework." *Moody*, 144 S. Ct. at 2439 (Alito, J., concurring in the judgment). That incompletely enumerates *Zauderer*'s prerequisites and assumes without analysis or citations that the mandated disclosures are "purely factual" and "uncontroversial," but they really are not. *See* Goldman, Zauderer, *supra* note 103.

[111] Goldman, Zauderer, *supra* note 103.

[112] Nat'l Inst. of Fam. & Life Advocs. v. Becerra, 585 U.S. 755 (2018).

[113] *Zauderer*, 471 U.S. 626.

[114] The Supreme Court also garbled the *Zauderer* factors in *NIFLA*. *See* Goldman, Zauderer, *supra* note 103.

individual explanations provision is "particularly onerous."[115] As the court put it, the provision is also

> unduly burdensome and likely to chill platforms' protected speech. The targeted platforms remove millions of posts per day; YouTube alone removed more than a billion comments in a single quarter of 2021. For every one of these actions, the law requires a platform to provide written notice delivered within seven days, including a "thorough rationale" for the decision and a "precise and thorough explanation of how [it] became aware" of the material. This requirement not only imposes potentially significant implementation costs but also exposes platforms to massive liability. . . . Thus, a platform could be slapped with millions, or even billions, of dollars in statutory damages if a Florida court were to determine that it didn't provide sufficiently "thorough" explanations when removing posts. It is substantially likely that this massive potential liability is "unduly burdensome" and would "chill[] protected speech"—platforms' exercise of editorial judgment—such that § 501.2041(2)(d) violates platforms' First Amendment rights.[116]

The Supreme Court did not accept review of the challenge to Texas's detailed statistical and operational disclosures, and Florida's law did not have an analogous provision. However, Texas's additional disclosure requirements also pose serious threats to free speech.[117] They impose substantial operational burdens and costs, and they require services to make many judgment calls about how to classify the data. In any enforcement action, regulators can second-guess both those classification decisions and the underlying editorial decisions. And regulators will exercise their prosecutorial discretion to maximize their censorial or partisan goals.[118] For those reasons, mandatory statistical and operational disclosures also should be deemed to "unduly burden expression" and should fail accordingly.

Third, if the lower courts determine that other parts of the social media censorship laws violate the First Amendment, will that

---

[115] NetChoice, LLC v. Att'y Gen. of Fla., 34 F.4th 1196, 1203 (11th Cir. 2022).

[116] *Id.* at 1230–31.

[117] Goldman, Zauderer, *supra* note 103.

[118] *Id.*; Goldman, HASTINGS, *supra* note 103.

affect the constitutional analysis of the individualized explanations requirement? The majority wrote that social media platforms' engagement in expressive activities "should inform the courts' further consideration" of the *Zauderer* issue. This gives courts another basis to strike down the disclosure mandates.

The *Zauderer* issues understandably got overshadowed by the more blatant censorship components of the Florida and Texas laws, but the disclosure issues have critical implications for the First Amendment as well. Given their significance, the *Zauderer* issues deserve the Court's full attention when it sees these cases again.

D. The Fifth Circuit Has Gone Rogue

In the Supreme Court's 2023–2024 Term, the Fifth Circuit had an underwhelming record of three affirmances and seven vacaturs or reversals.[119] This low 30 percent batting average should surprise no one. The Fifth Circuit routinely disregards binding Supreme Court precedent and opinions from other circuits, causing jurisprudential chaos. Unless that changes, the Supreme Court's docket will be clogged with appeals from the Fifth Circuit for the foreseeable future.[120]

Judges Oldham and Jones ought to feel embarrassed by the Supreme Court's assessment of their work. The majority called their positions "wrong" at least four times.[121] As Justice Barrett succinctly put it, "the Eleventh Circuit's understanding of the First Amendment's protection of editorial discretion was generally correct; the Fifth Circuit's was not."[122] Indeed, the majority provided its First

---

[119] Supreme Court Cases, October Term 2023–2024, BALLOTPEDIA, https://ballotpedia.org/Supreme_Court_cases,_October_term_2023-2024 (last visited July 30, 2024).

[120] The day after the Supreme Court issued the *Moody* opinion, it agreed to review another Fifth Circuit Internet Law case, *Free Speech Coalition v. Paxton*. In that case, the Fifth Circuit applied rational basis scrutiny to mandatory online age authentication by citing a 50-year-old opinion (*Ginsberg*), even though the Supreme Court had subsequently twice applied strict scrutiny to mandatory age authentication laws (*Reno v. ACLU* and *Ashcroft v. ACLU*) and expressly rejected the *Ginsberg* case's application to online age authentication (in *Reno*).

[121] *Moody*, 144 S. Ct. at 2399, 2403, 2406. Justice Kagan added, "Contrary to what the Fifth Circuit thought, the current record indicates that the Texas law does regulate speech when applied in the way the parties focused on below." *Id.* at 2394.

[122] *Id.* at 2409 (Barrett, J., concurring). Justice Jackson echoed, "the Eleventh Circuit at least fairly stated our First Amendment precedent, whereas the Fifth Circuit did not." *Id.* at 2411 (Jackson, J., concurring in part and concurring in the judgment).

Amendment dicta to help the Fifth Circuit do its job better.[123] Will that succeed? As the Magic 8 ball might respond, "Don't count on it."

The Fifth Circuit and the Supreme Court's Internet law "dialogue" is just beginning. The Court has already granted review of the challenge to Texas's age-authentication law, *Free Speech Coalition v. Paxton*. The legislatures in the Fifth Circuit's geographic territory will keep enacting censorial messaging bills. And the Fifth Circuit will keep analyzing constitutional challenges to those laws without regard for binding precedent.

Conclusion

We've entered a new phase of Internet law jurisprudence at the Supreme Court. After a long stretch where the Supreme Court took zero or one Internet law cases a year, this Term the Court took five[124]—and the count will continue to grow in future years as states pass more censorial laws that lead to court challenges. Justice Kagan once joked that the Justices "are not, like, the nine greatest experts on the internet,"[125] but they will need to become more Internet savvy to review the censorial Internet laws flooding their docket.

So far, Supreme Court review has worked out OK for the Internet. For example, in the 2022–2023 Term, *Twitter v. Taamneh*[126] was a significant win for Internet services, and *Gonzalez v. Google* didn't destroy Section 230.[127] In 2023–2024, *Moody* validated the services' First Amendment protection (though it made facial First Amendment challenges harder), and the *Murthy* case further acknowledged that Internet services have editorial discretion to deny government censorship requests.

---

[123] As the majority opinion says, "there has been enough litigation already to know that the Fifth Circuit, if it stayed the course, would get wrong at least one significant input into the facial analysis." *Id.* at 2409. Justice Kagan added that the need for additional guidance "is especially stark for the Fifth Circuit." *Id.* at 2399.

[124] Moody v. NetChoice LLC, 144 S. Ct. 2383 (2024) (including the *NetChoice v. Paxton* case combined with it); Murthy v. Missouri, 144 S. Ct. 1972 (2024); Lindke v. Freed, 601 U.S. 187 (2024); O'Connor-Ratcliff v. Garnier, 601 U.S. 205 (2024); Coinbase, Inc. v. Suski, 144 S. Ct. 1186 (2024) (involving an Internet industry defendant but focusing on contract and arbitration law).

[125] Transcript of Oral Argument at 46, Gonzalez v. Google LLC, 598 U.S. 617 (2023) (No. 20-1333).

[126] Twitter, Inc. v. Taamneh, 598 U.S. 471 (2023).

[127] Gonzalez v. Google LLC, 598 U.S. 617 (2023).

Nonetheless, many reasons to worry about the future of Internet law at the Supreme Court remain. First, Justices Thomas, Alito, and Gorsuch subscribe to a radically different vision of Internet free speech compared with the other Justices, and those three Justices seemingly have little concern about *stare decisis*. If this bloc ever assembles a majority, the outcomes could be shocking.[128]

Second, the sheer volume of Internet law cases on future Supreme Court dockets poses its own risk. It takes only one ruling going sideways to dramatically affect the Internet. As the Court hears more such cases, the odds increase that a case *will* go sideways. In effect, the Internet must bat 1.000 across all these cases to preserve its status quo.

Finally, censorship-minded legislators will exploit any ambiguous wording or hypothetical musings in the Court's opinions, even if the case outcome favors the Internet overall. For example, Justice Barrett's *Moody* concurrence expressed caveats regarding foreign ownership, highly personalized algorithms, and AI. State legislators may use her musings as inspiration for new censorial policy proposals. Even if the Supreme Court ultimately strikes down those new efforts, the laws will cause chaos (and impose huge costs on challengers) in the interim.

Both Democrats and Republicans favor censorial restrictions of the Internet; it's a rare topic that brings together legislators across the aisle. This leaves the Supreme Court as the last line of defense for Internet freedoms of speech and press. Will it fulfill that role? The *Moody* decision did, for now, but we'll have to see how long the Court's resolve will last.

---

[128] As Biskupic observed, Justice Alito's "tactics could have led to a major change in how platforms operate" had he not lost his majority in Moody. Biskupic, *supra* note 36.

The Jawboning Cases End with a Bang Disguised by a Whimper

*Derek E. Bambauer**

Introduction

Jawboning is government "enforcement through informal channels, where the underlying authority is in doubt."[1] Jawboning debuted[2] at the Supreme Court in a pair of cases this Term, *National Rifle Association of America v. Vullo*[3] and *Murthy v. Missouri*.[4] Commentators had hoped that the Court would establish an analytical framework to evaluate when jawboning violates the First Amendment.[5] They were disappointed, although not

*Irving Cypen Professor of Law, University of Florida Levin College of Law. I owe thanks for helpful suggestions and discussion to Enrique Armijo, Jane Bambauer, Katherine Bass, Ashutosh Bhagwat, Anupam Chander, Daphne Keller, Jameel Jaffer, Thinh Nguyen, Kari Niedermaier, Dave Schwartz, and the participants at the jawboning convening at the Knight First Amendment Institute at Columbia University in 2023. I welcome comments at <bambauer@law.ufl.edu>.

[1] *See* Derek E. Bambauer, *Against Jawboning*, 100 MINN. L. REV. 51, 61 (2015) (defining jawboning related to speech, especially online).

[2] The issue debuted this Term in at least its modern form, involving indirect pressure by government officials on internet entities such as social media platforms. All sides seemed to agree that *Bantam Books, Inc. v. Sullivan*, 372 U.S. 58 (1963), also constituted indirect governmental pressure through devolution of state authority to a putatively private commission that pushed booksellers to stop selling certain content.

[3] 602 U.S. 175 (2024) (*"Vullo"*).

[4] 144 S. Ct. 1972 (2024) (*"Murthy"*).

[5] *See, e.g.*, Mayze Teitler, *Doctrinal Disarray*, KNIGHT FIRST AMEND. INST. AT COLUM. UNIV. (Mar. 15, 2024), https://knightcolumbia.org/blog/doctrinal-disarray (noting the "justices [faced] a fractious landscape of proposed legal tests and allegedly unconstitutional communications to navigate").

necessarily surprised.[6] The Court disposed of *Vullo* on procedural grounds, holding that the Second Circuit had failed to credit the well-pleaded allegations in the complaint of the National Rifle Association of America (NRA).[7] And the Court interred *Murthy* by finding that none of the plaintiffs had standing to bring suit.[8] The opinions did not set out a methodology for evaluating future jawboning cases, and Justice Neil Gorsuch wrote a concurrence in *Vullo*[9] suggesting that the Court would be unwise to do so—the courts will evidently know jawboning when they see it.[10] Hence, the outcomes seemed unsatisfying to everyone but the NRA, which will get the chance to prove its allegations in court.

However, upon closer inspection, there is far more bang than whimper in *Vullo* and *Murthy*. The cases offer examples of what a successful jawboning claim looks like and what an unsuccessful claim lacks. Thus, jawboning as a species of First Amendment violation is alive and well. Moreover, as Justice Samuel Alito noted in his *Murthy* dissent,[11] one can discern the outline of a methodology for such claims in *Vullo* despite Justice Gorsuch's warning. Ironically, this methodology resembles the multifactor tests previously applied by lower courts of appeals.[12] Lastly, the Court's standing analysis in *Murthy* is, in fact, an assessment of the merits of the plaintiffs' claims: Whether an alleged jawboning victim has standing is inextricably linked to the substantive First Amendment analysis. For once, at least, standing doctrine is not simply a "get out of jail free" card when a court wants to avoid a hard problem. It instead requires diving into whether and how the plaintiffs have suffered a cognizable injury to their freedom of expression.

---

[6] *See* Michael Macagnone, *Supreme Court to Weigh Government Role in Online Misinformation*, ROLL CALL (Mar. 14, 2024), https://rollcall.com/2024/03/14/supreme-court-to-weigh-government-role-in-online-misinformation/; Derek Bambauer (@dbambauer), X (Mar. 15, 2024, 9:41 AM), https://x.com/dbambauer/status/1768633536645320717 (stating "I hope they reach the merits [in *Murthy*], rather than dumping it on standing grounds").

[7] *Vullo*, 602 U.S. at 194–95.

[8] *Murthy*, 144 S. Ct. at 1981.

[9] *Vullo*, 602 U.S. at 200 (Gorsuch, J., concurring).

[10] *See* Jacobellis v. Ohio, 378 U.S. 184, 197 (1964) (Stewart, J., concurring).

[11] *See Murthy*, 144 S. Ct. at 2010 (Alito, J., dissenting).

[12] *See Vullo*, 602 U.S. at 189–91 (listing examples of tests).

This article has three components. First, it briefly describes the opinions in *Vullo* and *Murthy*. Second, it assesses the guidance that the cases provide about jawboning for future plaintiffs, scholars, and courts. Lastly, it argues for a more explicit test for jawboning violations. The proposed test has three factors: the threat made by a government actor, the authority that the government actor possesses to justify this threat, and the power at the actor's disposal to implement that threat. This three-part test would both guide courts in determining when jawboning occurs and focus attention on the most problematic instances of the phenomenon.

I. The Opinions

The Court issued the opinion in *Vullo* first; it was unanimous, with Justice Sonia Sotomayor writing for the Court. The opinion in *Murthy* came out on the final day of the Term. Justice Amy Coney Barrett's majority opinion commanded six votes, with Justices Clarence Thomas and Gorsuch joining a sharp dissent by Justice Alito.

A. National Rifle Association of America v. Vullo

The NRA is a prominent gun rights advocacy organization that offers various benefits to members, including access to affinity insurance programs.[13] One such insurance program, Carry Guard, compensated policyholders for costs incurred from licensed firearm use—including for murder. Unsurprisingly, that coverage violates (at least) New York State law. A complaint from a gun advocacy group in fall 2017 led to an enforcement action brought by the New York Department of Financial Services (DFS). DFS oversees insurance firms operating in New York and was then headed by superintendent (and named defendant) Maria Vullo. DFS found both that the coverage was unlawful and that the NRA promoted Carry Guard without the required license. Other NRA affinity insurance programs had similar flaws. The firms offering and administering Carry Guard suspended the program in late 2017.

In February 2018, a former student of Marjory Stoneman Douglas High School in Parkland, Florida, attacked students and staff at the

---

[13] This summary of *Vullo*'s facts is taken from the majority opinion; critically, the opinion draws upon the well-pleaded allegations in the NRA's complaint and treats them as true given the procedural posture of the case. *See Vullo*, 602 U.S. at 181–86.

school with a semiautomatic weapon, killing 17 people and wounding 17 others. In the wake of the murders, which caused a wave of public anger at the NRA, Vullo met with one of the insurance firms to explain that it was in violation of certain aspects of New York's insurance laws. She explained that DFS would be willing to forgo enforcement if the firm stopped providing insurance to gun groups—and the NRA in particular. The firm agreed to have its subsidiaries stop underwriting gun-related insurance, and to reduce business with the NRA, in exchange for regulatory forbearance.

Two months later, Vullo issued guidance letters to DFS-regulated firms about risk management related to the NRA and similar organizations. The letters encouraged regulated entities to consider whether they faced any reputational or other risks from dealings with such firms. She was also quoted in a press release issued by New York's governor urging insurance companies and banks to cease doing business with the NRA and similar organizations. Shortly thereafter, two of the firms involved in Carry Guard entered into consent decrees with DFS. The firms admitted liability and agreed not to provide NRA-endorsed programs, but they retained the ability to sell corporate insurance to the Association. They also paid multimillion-dollar fines. A third Carry Guard firm entered into a similar consent decree in December 2018. The NRA sued Vullo (among others), alleging that Vullo violated the First Amendment by coercing entities regulated by DFS to cease doing business with the organization. The federal district court denied Vullo's motion to dismiss, but the Second Circuit reversed.

Justice Sotomayor's opinion focused immediately on the core issue in the case: Were Vullo's actions and statements protected as persuasive government speech, or barred as impermissible coercion? The opinion quickly reviewed the most relevant precedent, *Bantam Books, Inc. v. Sullivan*.[14] In *Bantam Books*, the state of Rhode Island had set up a commission to review books and magazines offered by distributors. The commission advised these outlets if any such offerings were, in the body's judgment, either obscene or unsuitable for consumption by anyone under age 18. While the commission had no formal enforcement powers, its advisory letters inevitably reminded

---

[14] *Vullo*, 602 U.S. at 188–90 (summarizing Bantam Books, Inc. v. Sullivan, 372 U.S. 58 (1963)).

distributors that it could make recommendations to the attorney general for prosecution. In addition, recipients of commission notices were usually visited by law enforcement, who would inquire what actions the distributor had taken based on the notice. In its opinion, the Supreme Court found that Rhode Island had crafted an unlawful system of prior administrative restraint, without sufficient constitutional safeguards, even though enforcement authority was at one remove from the commission itself. As Justice Sotomayor's majority opinion in *Vullo* concluded, *Bantam Books* "stands for the principle that a government official cannot do indirectly what she is barred from doing directly: A government official cannot coerce a private party to punish or suppress disfavored speech on her behalf."[15]

In a jawboning case, the core claim is that the government suppressed speech indirectly via pressure on a third party. As the Court explained, the ultimate inquiry is thus whether the plaintiff has "plausibly allege[d] conduct that, viewed in context, could be reasonably understood to convey a threat of adverse government action in order to punish or suppress the plaintiff's speech."[16] On its own, that formulation restates the core question without offering much assistance in answering it. However, the Court moved on to offer some lodestars in the analysis. First, it considered Vullo's authority, since "the greater and more direct the government official's authority, the less likely a person will feel free to disregard a directive from the official."[17] Vullo and DFS had directly regulated the insurance firms involved in Carry Guard and similar programs. Next, the Court assessed the content of Vullo's communications with these regulated entities. Based on the NRA's well-pleaded allegations, Vullo had offered to overlook a set of technical infractions that are evidently common in the industry, so long as the targeted firms cut ties with the NRA. Then, the majority opinion evaluated how these firms reacted: with alacrity, in the direction Vullo indicated. Overall, the NRA's complaint, "assessed as a whole, plausibly alleges that Vullo threatened to wield her power against those refusing to aid her campaign to punish the NRA's gun-promotion advocacy."[18]

[15] *Id.* at 190.
[16] *Id.* at 191.
[17] *Id.* at 191–92.
[18] *Id.* at 194.

In the Court's view, the Second Circuit went astray by "taking the allegations in isolation and failing to draw reasonable inferences in the NRA's favor."[19] Neither the illegal nature of Carry Guard and similar programs, nor Vullo's move to target nonexpressive conduct for enforcement, insulated her actions from First Amendment scrutiny. The Court was attentive to the insidious nature of jawboning that targets intermediaries. After all, intermediaries have fewer incentives to defend speech that is not their own, and they may be subject to multiple regulators, any of whom could leverage that oversight to suppress speech. Based on the NRA's well-pleaded allegations, the Supreme Court reversed the Second Circuit, holding that the NRA's allegations, if true, would make out a First Amendment violation.[20]

B. Murthy v. Missouri

Unlike the straightforward lineup in *Vullo*—one plaintiff, one defendant, one issue—*Murthy* involved a hodgepodge of actors and allegations. The plaintiffs included five individuals and two states, Missouri and Louisiana. They sued a panoply of federal agencies and officials, including the Federal Bureau of Investigation (FBI), Centers for Disease Control and Prevention (CDC), and the Surgeon General, among others. The intermediaries involved in the case comprised most of the major social media platforms, including Facebook, X (formerly Twitter), and YouTube. According to the plaintiffs, the Biden administration, writ large, had pressured these platforms to censor speech, particularly related to the COVID-19 pandemic and to election-related misinformation. A Louisiana federal district court agreed. It granted a wide-ranging injunction barring communication between the administration and platforms and extending even to entities that were not parties to the lawsuit. The Fifth Circuit largely affirmed the injunction, although it trimmed back its scope somewhat. In determining whether content moderation by the

---

[19] *Id.*

[20] Justice Ketanji Brown Jackson wrote a brief concurrence highlighting the necessity of distinguishing between coercion and First Amendment violations—the existence of the former does not automatically prove the latter, in her view. *See id.* at 201 (Jackson, J., concurring). She distinguished between indirect censorship and retaliation, arguing that the second theory of jawboning was the better fit with the facts in *Vullo*. *See id.* at 202–03.

platforms counted as state action, the Fifth Circuit held that "a private party's conduct may be state action if the government coerced or significantly encouraged it."[21] The resulting injunction, though, covered platforms beyond the ones used by the plaintiffs, and was not limited by topic.[22]

The complexities in the case also included the different approaches and methods that the platforms themselves deployed to implement their various content moderation policies. It is often difficult to distinguish between voluntary, private initiatives and coerced ones. And it becomes far more challenging with the range of actors and time in play in *Murthy*.[23]

The majority opinion cut straight to standing (an approach harshly criticized by Justice Alito's dissent). Justice Barrett recounted the familiar elements of standing—concrete and particularized injury that is actual or imminent; traceability to the complained-of conduct; and redressability—in a way that emphasized the challenges faced by the *Murthy* plaintiffs. First, since the states and individuals sought forward-looking injunctive relief, they needed to show "that the third-party platforms 'will likely react in predictable ways' to the defendants' conduct."[24] Second, they had to show a "real and immediate threat of repeated injury."[25] In short, the plaintiffs needed to demonstrate that the platforms were likely to censor them as a result of governmental pressure. And, to support a preliminary injunction, the plaintiffs needed to make a "clear showing" that they were likely to establish each element of standing—based not on allegations, but on the factual evidence obtained during discovery.[26] This framing played up the difficult task that confronted the plaintiffs.

The majority's standing analysis was unsparing. While past instances of harm could serve as evidence of a likelihood of similar

---

[21] Missouri v. Biden, 83 F.4th 350, 380 (5th Cir. 2023) (internal citation omitted).

[22] *See Murthy*, 144 S. Ct. at 1985.

[23] It didn't help that both the district court and the Fifth Circuit relied on made-up facts in their decisions; Justice Barrett devoted a long footnote to explicating some of these findings that "unfortunately appear to be clearly erroneous." *Id.* at 1988 n.4; *see* Derek Bambauer, *Be Careful What You Ask For*, KNIGHT FIRST AMEND. INST. AT COLUM. UNIV. (Oct. 30, 2023), https://knightcolumbia.org/blog/be-careful-what-you-ask-for.

[24] *Murthy*, 144 S. Ct. at 1986 (internal citation omitted).

[25] *Id.* (internal citation omitted).

[26] *Id.* (internal citation omitted).

future injury, the "lack of specific causation findings with respect to any discrete instance of content moderation" meant that the plaintiffs would "essentially have to build [their] case from scratch" and demonstrate that they had new cause to fear government-driven censorship of their particular speech.[27] Even the factual flights of fancy in the district court and Fifth Circuit opinions did not offer any direct links between government pressure and platform decisionmaking. The Court expressly rejected the Fifth Circuit's highly general approach to standing, which "attribute[ed] *every* platform decision at least in part to the" government based upon broad views of how the administration and the platforms interacted.[28] The core problem for showing traceability is that the social media platforms had begun limiting or removing COVID-19 and election misinformation well before the Biden administration came to office, and certainly before the alleged jawboning occurred. Moreover, the complexity of the case (multiple plaintiffs, defendants, platforms, topics, and alleged injuries) made showing causation all the more difficult.

The Court made short work of the States' standing claims and those of four of the individual plaintiffs (three doctors and a citizen journalist). It gave greater credence to claims by Jill Hines, an activist who published and promoted materials skeptical of COVID-19 vaccine and mask mandates. However, even her claims were too tenuous to confer standing. The evidence showed that Facebook had acted to deplatform one of her groups before the White House had made any relevant requests. Nor could she adduce proof that the Biden administration sought to suppress those who reposted content (as opposed to creating it initially). And it was not clear that any of her posted material actually ran contrary to requests from the CDC about COVID-19 misinformation.

Finally, none of the plaintiffs made a sufficient showing that they were likely to suffer future harm from jawboning. In particular, the Biden administration had dramatically scaled back its interactions with and pressure on social media platforms over COVID-19 as the pandemic gradually waned in severity by 2022. And redressability posed a challenge: Even if the social media services originally adopted or enforced content curation policies under governmental

---

[27] *Id.* at 1987.

[28] *Id.* at 1988 (emphasis in original).

duress, the waning of that pressure left the platforms free to maintain or abandon those practices with little fear of repercussion. Thus, an injunction against jawboning by the administration would have scant capacity to prevent future harm to the plaintiffs.

The majority opinion closed with a nod to the complexities of the case and the concomitant problems for proving standing: The burden rests on the plaintiffs, and the Court was not willing to trawl through the voluminous record in a search for connections that the plaintiffs had failed to establish.

Justice Alito's dissent exceeds the majority opinion in length and heat. It characterized *Murthy* as "one of the most important free speech cases to reach this Court in years."[29] Unlike the majority, the dissent cited *Vullo* to reinforce the principle that "government officials may not coerce private entities to suppress speech."[30] Like the majority, the dissent narrowed the field of actors and claims to focus on pressures by the White House and the CDC toward Facebook about content posted by Hines. In the dissent's view, the factual record is clear: The administration "continuously harried and implicitly threatened Facebook with potentially crippling consequences" if it did not comply with demands regarding COVID-19 content.[31] The dissent argued that Hines was "indisputably injured, and due to the officials' continuing efforts, she was threatened with more of the same."[32] The dissent attacked the majority's unwillingness to grapple with the merits of Hines's First Amendment claims. Although that criticism is not entirely accurate, it raised a cogent worry about the distinction between the two jawboning cases: "Officials who read today's decision together with *Vullo* will get the message. If a coercive campaign is carried out with enough sophistication, it may get by."[33]

Justice Alito also convincingly reinforced the concerns about jawboning intermediaries that the Court described in *Vullo*. Such intermediaries may be uniquely susceptible to government pressures (especially from the executive branch) because they depend on the statutory protections of 47 U.S.C. § 230 (popularly known as

[29] *Id.* at 1997 (Alito, J., dissenting).

[30] *Id.* at 1998. The majority opinion did not reference *Vullo* at all.

[31] *Id.*

[32] *Id.*

[33] *Id.* at 1999.

"Section 230"). They are also vulnerable because they are potential targets for antitrust scrutiny and because they rely on American intervention to counteract aggressive European Union (EU) regulators.

The dissent spent nearly 10 pages recounting the oft-dramatic interactions between Biden administration officials and Facebook, perhaps culminating in President Biden's extravagant claim that the social media service was "killing people."[34] Next, the dissent turned to standing and argued for a different standard for traceability. In the dissent's view, it sufficed for Hines to "show that one predictable effect of the officials' action was that Facebook would modify its censorship policies in a way that affected her."[35] The dissent also contended that "it is reasonable to infer . . . that the efforts of the federal officials affected at least some of Facebook's decisions to censor Hines."[36] And, Justice Alito also took issue with the claim that jawboning had diminished by the summer of 2022, since the effects of that jawboning likely lingered and threats can carry force even if not expressly renewed. Finally, the dissent contended that redressability is effectively the mirror image of causation, and thus an injunction was likely to have at least some effect in reducing the future risk of harm to Hines.

After taking the majority to task on standing, Justice Alito's dissent turned to the merits of Hines's First Amendment claim. Here, the dissent articulated three guideposts that it discerned from *Vullo* for distinguishing "permissible persuasion [from] unconstitutional coercion."[37] These three factors are "(1) the authority of the government officials who are alleged to have engaged in coercion, (2) the nature of statements made by those officials, and (3) the reactions of the third party alleged to have been coerced."[38] The dissent emphasized the power of the President to influence all three of the intermediary weak points identified earlier—for example, by seeking legislative alteration of Section 230, by undertaking antitrust enforcement

[34] *Id.* at 2000. The majority opinion disagreed with Justice Alito's characterization of the facts. *See id.* at 1991–92 nn. 7 & 8; 1995 n.10 (majority opinion).

[35] *Id.* at 2006 (Alito, J., dissenting). The majority opinion also disagreed on traceability. *See id.* at 1992 (majority opinion).

[36] *Id.* at 2008 (Alito, J., dissenting).

[37] *Id.* at 2010.

[38] *Id.*

against Facebook, and by negotiating a deal with EU regulators over platforms' transfers of personal data to non-EU jurisdictions (such as the United States).[39] For the dissent, all three analytical factors plainly pointed toward coercion, not persuasion:

> In sum, the officials wielded potent authority. Their communications with Facebook were virtual demands. And Facebook's quavering responses to those demands show that it felt a strong need to yield.[40]

II. The Guidance

At first glance, the opinions in *Murthy* and *Vullo* are a letdown: The former disposes of the case on standing grounds, and the latter remands the case based on civil procedure issues. On the surface, then, the cases make no new First Amendment law. Neither opinion engages with, or even mentions, the other social media and free speech case from this Term, *Lindke v. Freed*.[41] That case addressed how to distinguish when government officials who use social media speak in their personal capacity versus their official capacity.[42] This omission is strange, because *Lindke* grappled directly with the state action doctrine—which is vitally important to jawboning—and because that case established a clear two-part test while simultaneously acknowledging the complexities inherent in analyzing social media cases.[43] *Murthy* and *Vullo* feel like a disappointment and a missed opportunity.

However, the jawboning opinions offer much more when read carefully.

First, and perhaps most important, jawboning remains alive and well as a species of First Amendment violation or claim. *Bantam Books* has always been a bit of an outlier: an oddly constructed oversight

---

[39] *Id.* at 2010–11.

[40] *Id.* at 2015.

[41] 601 U.S. 187 (2024).

[42] *See generally id.*

[43] The *Lindke* test has two parts for determining whether a government official's speech constitutes state action; each prong of the test must be met (in sequential order) for there to be a potential First Amendment violation. *See id.* at 198 (holding that "such speech is attributable to the State only if the official (1) possessed actual authority to speak on the State's behalf, and (2) purported to exercise that authority when he spoke on social media").

scheme in the midst of one of many moral panics about the materials to which minors had access. Two technological shifts have since made the power and risks of jawboning much more potent.[44] The first, of course, was the rise of digitized information, sophisticated discovery mechanisms such as recommendation algorithms, and ubiquitous high-speed connectivity—in short, the modern internet. The second was the debut of popular intermediaries, such as social media platforms, that feature principally (if not almost exclusively) user-generated content rather than material created by the intermediaries themselves. The first trend led many internet consumers to depend on the medium for news, entertainment, and so forth. Control over that medium meant control over consumers' information environment. The second development reduced the incentives of these new intermediaries to defend access to any particular piece of content—after all, any particular topic or story would have only a vanishingly small effect on that platform's revenue stream. These two developments made jawboning, especially of internet intermediaries, both more effective and more attractive for regulators as an approach to control content.

Second, the cases provide exemplars for a successful and unsuccessful jawboning suit. The Court's analysis of *Vullo*, for example, paints a fairly straightforward case of improper regulatory pressure. Infractions by entities regulated by the New York Department of Financial Services were common (although one wonders how many violations involved murder insurance). And the DFS superintendent offered to overlook, or at least treat leniently, misconduct by firms that were willing to sever ties with an organization whose speech she disliked: the NRA.[45] Again, these facts are drawn from the NRA's complaint, and the organization will have to adduce proof in subsequent proceedings below. On this account, though, the threat is clear. If the insurance firms did not cooperate, DFS could have launched investigations that were likely to find malfeasance—indeed, all three firms settled with an admission of guilt. This demonstrates the considerable power that DFS wielded. And, while DFS possesses legitimate authority over some forms of communication

---

[44] *See* Bambauer, *supra* note 1, at 102–05.

[45] *See* Nat'l Rifle Ass'n v. Vullo, 602 U.S. 175, 194–95 (2024). Interestingly, the Fifth Circuit opinion in *Missouri v. Biden* viewed the facts in *Vullo* as "complex and sprawling." Missouri v. Biden, 83 F.4th 350, 378 (5th Cir. 2023).

by insurance entities (for example, over the accuracy of their representations to customers), it has no legitimate remit to dictate which business partners firms should choose based on their views on social issues such as gun control.[46]

Murthy, by contrast, is at best a weak jawboning claim. The facts are frankly a mess. The record is tens of thousands of pages long; some of the facts were outright fictions invented by the district court; and some of the defendants (such as the Surgeon General) lacked any authority or power over the social media platforms. Moreover, the platforms themselves were willing, often eager, to curate controversial content such as COVID-19 and election misinformation. While the platforms consulted various administration agencies and officials for guidance, they did not always follow that advice—as the frustration of Biden administration officials makes plain. Finally, the plaintiffs simply could not show causal links between administration pressure and moderation or removal of their content. As the dissent argued, this could perhaps be due to a subtle, coordinated campaign of pressure undertaken by the Biden administration. But in the midst of the chaos of a deadly pandemic and foreign interference in American elections, the simpler and more likely answer is that federal officials were working haphazardly and under pressure to try to limit the spread of information they viewed as dangerous.[47] To be sure, there seems little question that the administration would have liked to jawbone platforms into removing some of this content. But it is not clear that the platforms were unwilling participants, nor is it clear that the plaintiffs in the case suffered any harm from the government's efforts.

Third, the dissenting opinion in *Murthy* offers far more than a list of purported errors or a catalog of grievances. Justice Alito has discerned at least the outlines of the elements of the test for determining when jawboning is permissible speech and when it is impermissible coercion.[48] The Alito dissent may prove more influential than most dissents precisely because it undertakes the hard work of explaining what the majorities in the two cases seem to be doing.

---

[46] *See Vullo*, 602 U.S. at 176.

[47] This view had excellent empirical support in the case of COVID-19 falsehoods.

[48] *See Murthy*, 144 S. Ct. at 2010 (Alito, J., dissenting). Why the Court was unwilling to set out more precise parameters for jawboning claims in either *Vullo*—a unanimous opinion—or *Murthy* is a mystery, and a frustrating one.

And the dissent sounds a valuable note of warning: Jawboning is least likely to violate the First Amendment when it is subtle and indirect,[49] which are precisely the characteristics that make jawboning so hard to cabin in the first place. The *Vullo* scenario may turn out to be the exception rather than the rule. Government actors with more time and guile than Ms. Vullo may be able to craft jawboning schemes that are sufficiently covert and complex to evade liability, but sufficiently threatening to coerce their targets to comply. Here, too, the lack of a clear test for jawboning liability makes defending against such schemes difficult. Trial courts will have to reason from basic, core First Amendment principles to distinguish coercion from persuasion, without much in the way of guidance from the Supreme Court to assist them in that difficult task.

Fourth, not all members of the Court are in line behind Justice Alito's methodology for jawboning—or any methodology, for that matter. Justice Gorsuch's concurrence in *Vullo* explicitly rejects any of the existing tests utilized by the courts of appeals. Indeed, his concurrence strongly suggests that no such test can even be elucidated. In Gorsuch's view, the question is ultimately whether a suit has "plausibly allege[d] conduct that, viewed in context, could be reasonably understood to convey a threat of adverse government action in order to punish or suppress the plaintiff's speech."[50] That summary is fine descriptively, but it provides zero guidance on how lower courts ought to approach that question. And that is unsatisfying, because unbridled discretion undercuts uniformity and invites ends-driven reasoning. Gorsuch's concurrence also suggests that even if the other eight members of the Court were to come to consensus on a jawboning methodology, Justice Gorsuch would continue to hold out.

Finally, the *Vullo* decision reinforces that state governments are just as capable of jawboning as the federal one—and indeed may have greater power to do so effectively.[51] Federal government actions tend to draw more attention from media, plaintiffs, and commentators. But in many ways, state and local governments have greater

---

[49] *See id.* at 1999.

[50] *Vullo*, 602 U.S. at 200 (Gorsuch, J., concurring).

[51] *See, e.g.*, Bambauer, *supra* note 1, at 53–57 (describing role of state attorneys general in pressure on Google).

daily sway over the lives of most citizens. *Vullo* shows that the Court is attentive to this dynamic, and the set of cases it cites are principally ones from lower levels of government.

III. A Better Test: Threats, Authorization, Power

A better methodology for jawboning considers three variables: threats, authorization, and power.

A. Threats

The existence of a threat from a governmental actor that involves speech is the triggering condition for jawboning analysis.[52] Jawboning is in play if there is a plausible threat, whether direct or indirect, explicit or implicit, latent or implemented. If there is a plausible threat, then a court should move on to the next steps in the analysis. But if there is no threat, then the communication is permissible government speech, not coercion. If the Surgeon General gives a speech noting false COVID-19 information on a social media platform and saying it ought to be removed, that's simply performing the job of being Surgeon General. Like private entities, the government is free to speak and to advocate for policy positions. Moral suasion differs from compulsion, and room for the former is required both by current First Amendment doctrine and the practical realities of governance. Governments are free to complain about what private entities say and how they act; indeed, it's difficult to conceive of how state officials could advocate for policy without so doing. Legitimate government speech may embarrass its target or cause citizens to change how they interact with that entity, but it does not suggest or imply that the state will deploy its regulatory authority to compel such a change.

Whether the state has issued a threat is not always easy to determine. Several courts of appeals use the reaction of the targeted entity

---

[52] Threats that have nothing to do with speech don't implicate the First Amendment. If the government threatens to initiate a Federal Trade Commission investigation of Google unless the firm switches to green energy, that might be a legally impermissible threat for other reasons, but it would not be a First Amendment issue. And threats emanating from direct regimes of prior restraint generate standard First Amendment claims. *See, e.g.,* Packingham v. North Carolina, 582 U.S. 98 (2017) (overturning ban on use of social media sites by registered sex offenders).

as one guidepost,[53] and the *Vullo* opinion does so as well (although without identifying this as part of the formal analysis).[54] However, the target's subjective reaction is a poor indicator of whether jawboning has occurred; an objective analysis is preferable. A weak target—or, perhaps more charitably, one that is highly risk averse—will overreact to even mild government pressure, including government speech. A strong target, with nerves of steel, won't cave even under obvious regulatory threats. Both extremes illustrate the problem with a subjective test: It will generate too many false positive and false negative results. Society should expect the subjects of speech to endure at least some criticism before they rush into court to bring suit—indeed, that is the lesson of defamation doctrine, among other examples. On the other side of the coin, targets of regulatory threats who successfully steel themselves against pressure should not be barred from redress. Instead of a subjective test based on how the *actual* target reacted, an objective test that looks at how a *reasonable* target would react could offer useful guidance on what constitutes governmental disapprobation versus governmental threats.

B. Authorization and Power

Once the recipient establishes that a threat was made, courts should assess two factors together: whether the actor making the threat is authorized to regulate the speech at issue in some fashion, and how much power the actor has to carry the threatened consequences into effect. Not all threats have equal force to compel. Courts should scrutinize most closely instances in which the government actor has little or no authorization to regulate but has considerable power to inflict harm for failure to follow its commands. This combination of factors makes government least legitimate and most menacing. Conversely, when a government entity has clear authorization over the speech and target at issue, and little capacity to make good on threats, courts should allow the state more leeway.

As ever, the hard cases are in the middle. In some of these cases, the threat may come from a government actor with clear authorization and significant power—for example, the Federal Communications

---

[53] *See Vullo*, 602 U.S. at 189 (citing case from the Second Circuit); *see also id.* at 190 (citing cases from the Third, Fifth, Seventh, and Ninth Circuits).

[54] *See Murthy*, 144 S. Ct. at 2010 (Alito, J., dissenting).

Commission (FCC) in the context of broadcast television regulation. In others, the threat may come from a government actor with questionable authorization but little clout—for example, the small-town clerk who threatens to travel across state lines and arrest a social media CEO. In the first type of middle case, as with the FCC, it is difficult to distinguish between legitimate enforcement and illegitimate pressure.[55] In the second type of middle case, it is hard to see how the government actor could carry out the threat. This new methodology does not have straightforward implications for those two combinations of authorization and power; the outcomes are likely to be context specific. Nonetheless, the model helpfully concentrates attention on the worst and most consequential instances of jawboning.

1. Authorization

The second variable pertains to authorization: Is the governmental entity authorized to engage in the conduct that it uses as a threat? The greater the authorization, the less likely that a threat will be jawboning. For example, American legal doctrines make it deliberately difficult to challenge a prosecutor's broad discretion to bring or withhold charges. By contrast, the Federal Trade Commission (FTC) may only declare a particular business practice unlawfully unfair if that practice meets a searching three-part test defined by statute.[56] FTC threats to investigate or bring charges are cabined by that limited authorization, and courts should thus be more willing to treat threats that *aren't* clearly authorized as jawboning. In some instances, courts will still need to play a counter-majoritarian role as a check on the political branches; otherwise, statutes might effectively insulate government entities from jawboning liability by conferring broad discretion upon them. However, unfettered regulators will inevitably generate political opposition. Courts assessing authorization should therefore begin with a presumption of deference to an agency's remit. Employing authorization in the analysis can helpfully constrain jawboning, along with governmental interference with speech more broadly, by pushing the state toward formal

---

[55] For example, the FCC's ability to impose sanctions on broadcasters for fleeting expletives and indecent images remains uncertain. *See* Lyle Denniston, *"Wardrobe Malfunction" Case Finally Ends*, SCOTUSBLOG (June 29, 2012, 11:51 AM), https://www.scotusblog.com/2012/06/wardrobe-malfunction-case-finally-ends/.

[56] 15 U.S.C. § 45(n).

speech-regulating mechanisms.[57] Such mechanisms are more transparent and more subject to state challenge than informal pressures that occur behind closed doors.

2. Power

The third variable in the new methodology is power. As explained above, there are many reasons that a governmental threat might be effective, from a long-shot risk of destruction to the sure risk of being metaphorically nibbled to death by ducks. "Bet the company" decisions are always sobering for executives. But the risk of death by a thousand cuts is also serious; the many Lilliputians managed to tie down Gulliver despite their tiny stature.[58]

This power analysis should have two components: the consequences of the threat that a government actor can plausibly make (outcome) and the likelihood that the actor can bring about that outcome (probability). Unlike the *Lindke* analysis—where the two steps are sequential and an insufficient level of either vitiates a claim of state action—outcome and probability interact and are always in play. Low-probability consequences may be a powerful threat if the potential outcome is severe—for example, the risk that Congress might pass legislation that would force the sale of a popular internet platform such as TikTok. And even a seemingly minimal outcome, such as receiving a stream of civil investigative demands, may be enough to push speakers and platforms into grudging compliance. That result is more likely when the government actor is virtually certain to be able to inflict that penalty, especially in an ongoing fashion.[59] Probability should also measure the constraints, practical and legal, that operate to limit the power of jawboning. Prosecutors often have largely unfettered discretion to open criminal investigations and bring charges. Modern legislators, on the other hand, typically must persuade a significant number of colleagues to pass legislation, even if they have the support of their President or governor. The more steps, or intervening entities, that lie between the actor who makes the threat and its instantiation, the less probable that outcome and thus the less likely that the pressure is jawboning.

---

[57] *See* Derek E. Bambauer, *Orwell's Armchair*, 79 U. Chi. L. Rev. 863, 868 (2012).

[58] Jonathan Swift, Gulliver's Travels (1726).

[59] *See* Bambauer, *supra* note 1, at 54.

In diagram form, the proposed methodology looks like Figure 1:

Figure 1
Jawboning Variables

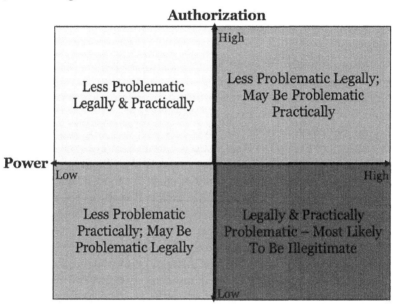

Authorization

This methodology helps considerably in winnowing down jawboning cases. When a governmental entity is operating within its authorized remit (high authorization) but has relatively low capacity to inflict significant consequences (low power), courts should be less willing to impose jawboning liability. In parallel, we do not need to be as concerned about such threats. But this isn't an exemption: Courts should still treat jawboning claims seriously, if only because punishing a threatening regulator from time to time discourages the others.

By contrast, when a government actor is operating outside its authorization but has real power to inflict harm for disobedience, courts should be most alert to potential jawboning and most willing to find that threats violate the First Amendment.

As already mentioned, the intermediate zones pose the most difficulty: when a government actor has both scant authorization to act and little power, or has real power and genuine authorization. The former is less likely to generate controversy or litigation because private entities probably will not fear or heed threats from a renegade but ineffectual regulator. The latter is less likely to prompt challenges because the regulator's facial authority is strong. The latter, however, is the combination where the courts' counter-majoritarian role may be most important, since the political branches may have turned loose a "Mechanical Hound" that transgresses constitutional limits.[60]

Like all models, this one for jawboning simplifies the analysis needed, but hopefully it simplifies in useful fashion. It usefully concentrates attention on the most problematic instances of the phenomenon. But it leaves open a few questions that deserve attention.

First, both the Louisiana district court and the Fifth Circuit bought the argument that some "suggestions" are inherently coercive when made by government officials. For example, the FBI possesses wide-ranging investigative powers and has close ties to the Department of Justice. For this reason, both courts believed that the FBI automatically engages in jawboning when it makes suggestions about content moderation to platforms.[61] In their estimation, it didn't matter that the FBI never threatened or attempted to impose any consequences for failing to follow its advice. But this view is too categorical; a more sensible analysis would place the interactions between the FBI and platforms outside jawboning altogether, because jawboning requires a threat. The FBI never made one—probably because the agency is aware of its power and reputation and hence admirably cautious about pressure.

Still, the concept of an inherent threat shouldn't be rejected out of hand. Consider Darth Vader: No one is actually honored by his presence; he is there to realign activity with governmental wishes.[62] He is there, in short, to put things back on schedule. American government has no immediate analog (fortunately), but Senator Joe McCarthy came close in the 1950s.

Second, regulation by raised eyebrow is a real concern. The Motion Picture Association (formerly the Motion Picture Association of America) adopted its putatively voluntary system of movie ratings

---

[60] *See* RAY BRADBURY, FAHRENHEIT 451 54–55 (Simon & Schuster 2003) (1953).

[61] *See, e.g.*, Missouri v. Biden, 83 F.4th 350, 388–89 (5th Cir. 2023).

[62] *See* RETURN OF THE JEDI, at 03:56 (Twentieth Century Fox 1983).

and content moderation—effectively enforced by a triopoly of movie theater chains at present—to preempt state and local censorship laws that interfered with motion picture distribution.[63] The major movie studios opted to conform to prevailing political preferences rather than to challenge them. However, they did so against the backdrop of a legal system that imposed significant costs and legal risks on everyone involved in distributing a film. Put differently, a presidential whisper is louder than anyone else's shout. It's not clear that courts can or should take account of voluntary, perhaps craven, decisions to go along to get along. If they do not, however, the concern is that risk-averse entities may be pressured outside the bounds of jawboning liability, to the detriment of free expression. The informal blacklisting that occurred in many industries during the McCarthy-era witch hunts for supposed Communists is one example. And it was also part of the dynamic in *Bantam Books v. Sullivan*, which combined outsourcing of government power with public enforcement of private arrangements, thereby resulting in the worst of all possible worlds. Both hard and soft censorship cast long shadows.[64]

Third, the subject matter involved in alleged jawboning likely matters and probably should. Some of the purported coercion in *Murthy* involved the Biden administration attempting to combat dangerous, and in some instances deadly, misinformation about the COVID-19 pandemic, which to date has killed over a million Americans. These efforts occurred against the backdrop of widespread false information about the illness and measures to combat it—false information that had been endorsed in many instances by former President Donald Trump and his administration. Pressure about speech related to COVID-19 seems similar to pressures about speech related to national security matters. In that context, the government formally operates under the same First Amendment standards as in all other contexts, but informally it enjoys more relaxed judicial scrutiny. The Constitution is not a suicide pact, and some deference seems due when the government articulates a reasonable, grounded threat to the polity that is separate from the speech at issue itself

---

[63] *See* E. Judson Jennings, *Show & Tell on the Internet? Will Jane & George Set the Standard? FCC Censorship and Converging Technologies*, 17 SETON HALL J. SPORTS & ENT. L. 1, 13 (2007).

[64] *See* Bambauer, *supra* note 57.

(not bogus threats like Communist propaganda in the mail).[65] With that said, courts ought to ask the government to bring receipts. The federal government often invokes national security to justify regulation of speech, and its track record of accuracy and candor is quite poor.[66] National security should not be a high card in the jawboning analysis.

In the opposite direction, courts ought to be more skeptical about jawboning that seeks to affect democratic processes such as elections. This is essentially a second-order authorization problem. If jawboning can increase the ease with which the government can obtain authorization for regulatory regimes, then authorization will be less useful as a guidepost. Put differently, courts ought to be alert to the risk that jawboning may entrench a set of political actors. This is why the allegations about White House pressures on social media platforms to remove information about the controversy over Hunter Biden's laptop are so worrisome.

Lastly, the jawboning discourse to date has focused almost exclusively on executive branch actors. This is too narrow. Congress has significant power to engage in jawboning. In fact, the House Judiciary Committee in the current session of Congress has essentially provided an ongoing exemplar of the problem. Committees can subpoena documents, compel witnesses to testify, threaten anyone who challenges their authority with contempt or referral to the Department of Justice, and generally impose regulatory costs on speakers and speech with which they disagree. The courts have typically been reluctant to interfere with Congress as a coequal branch, and they normally reject attempts to quash subpoenas via mechanisms such

---

[65] *See* Lamont v. Postmaster General, 381 U.S. 301 (1965).

[66] *See* Geoffrey R. Stone, *Free Speech and National Security*, 84 IND. L.J. 939, 939 (2009) ("In the national security setting, however, the United States has a long and checkered history of allowing fear to trump constitutional values."); N.Y. Times Co. v. United States, 403 U.S. 713, 719 (1971) (Black, J., concurring) ("[National] 'security' is a broad, vague generality whose contours should not be invoked to abrogate the fundamental law embodied in the First Amendment."). The current attempt to force a sale of TikTok, on pain of banning the app, is an excellent example. *See* Brief of First Amendment Law Professors as *Amici Curiae* in Support of Petitioners 20–25, TikTok Inc. v. Garland, No. 24-1113 (D.C. Cir. June 27, 2024), https://storage.courtlistener.com/recap/gov.uscourts.cadc.40861/gov.uscourts.cadc.40861.2062101.0.pdf. (The author is a signatory and co-author of the brief).

as the political question doctrine. But that deference ought to be more limited. The judicial branch has slowly recognized the ways in which the executive branch can interfere with First Amendment rights through misuse of putatively unrelated formal mechanisms and through informal ones. Courts should similarly be more active in reviewing challenges to congressional pressures on speech. And scholars and courts alike should be attentive to jawboning at state and local levels, which attracts less attention but which may be more potent given its concentrated focus. Jawboning, in short, should be a doctrine that constrains governmental pressures on speech at all levels and across all branches. By analyzing threats, authorization, and power, courts can identify the most problematic instances of such pressure and separate protected speech from improper intimidation.

Conclusion

For the first time, jawboning in its modern incarnation came to the Supreme Court this Term. At first blush, the results may seem disappointing: One case failed for lack of standing, and the second was remanded because the Second Circuit neglected to follow the proper approach to evaluating a motion for summary judgment. Those outcomes may please scholars of civil procedure and federal courts, but First Amendment observers can be forgiven for feeling pangs of disappointment.

However, when read closely, the cases end with a bang, not a whimper. Jawboning remains an important constraint upon government attempts to block speech—indeed, the doctrine has been revitalized. *Vullo*, in particular, demonstrates that the Court is attentive to indirect pressures at all levels of government. As bookends, the *Murthy* and *Vullo* decisions show what a viable jawboning claim does, and does not, need to include. While the Justices were not able to agree on a methodology for evaluating jawboning claims (and Justice Gorsuch disagreed even with the attempt to do so), Justice Alito's dissent in *Murthy* reveals the nascent outlines of such an approach. And that dissent contains an important cautionary tale: The courts must be alert to attempts to circumvent any framework they do establish.

This article makes an initial attempt at setting out an analytical method for weighing jawboning claims. The method is admittedly incomplete because the question of "how much government pressure is too much?" resists easy formulation. But it draws upon threads in *Murthy* and *Vullo* and concentrates judicial attention on the most problematic instances of this phenomenon. These two decisions are sure to launch a thousand suits—or, at least, a significant number of them—and their importance in the skein of First Amendment precedent will only grow with time.

Third Time's the Charm: The Supreme Court's Clarification of the Retaliatory Arrest Standards in *Gonzalez v. Trevino*

*Anya Bidwell and Patrick Jaicomo**

Three times in the last seven years, the Supreme Court has grappled with the role that probable cause plays in First Amendment retaliation claims involving arrests.[1] It's an unenviable job.

On the one hand, if an arrest was made with probable cause, then all the boxes would seem to be checked, making an arrest, at least objectively, justifiable. And if the arrest was justifiable, why allow plaintiffs a collateral challenge through a retaliation lawsuit? On the other hand, allowing probable cause to trump evidence of retaliation would leave a backdoor in the First Amendment. Our current expansive kludge of criminal laws means "almost anyone can be arrested for something,"[2] giving petty tyrants an opportunity to silence their critics with minimal creativity and a pair of handcuffs.

The Court's overall approach has been to adopt a compromise so that no one is fully satisfied but both sides can claim a victory of sorts. Government officials who make arrests supported by probable cause have a presumption of good faith, but plaintiffs can present evidence of retaliation at the threshold stage to overcome that presumption. The question that divided the courts before *Gonzalez v. Trevino* was what kind of evidence of retaliation was allowed. After *Gonzalez*, any evidence will suffice, as long as it is objective and

---

* Bidwell and Jaicomo are senior attorneys at the Institute for Justice, leading its Project on Immunity and Accountability. They represented Sylvia Gonzalez at the U.S. Supreme Court in *Gonzalez v. Trevino*.

[1] Gonzalez v. Trevino, 144 S. Ct. 1663 (2024); Nieves v. Bartlett, 587 U.S. 391 (2019); Lozman v. Riviera Beach, 585 U.S. 87 (2018); *see also* Reichle v. Howards, 566 U.S. 658 (2012).

[2] *Nieves*, 587 U.S. at 412 (Gorsuch, J., concurring in part and dissenting in part).

"makes it more likely that an officer *has* declined to arrest someone for engaging in such conduct in the past."[3]

For two reasons, *Gonzalez v. Trevino* is an encouraging development for free speech and bad news for those looking to use the power of arrest to silence their critics. First, the Supreme Court clarified that the only evidence that must be excluded at the threshold stage is state-of-mind evidence. Like the Fifth Circuit in *Gonzalez*, lower courts had interpreted the previous rule to exclude everything but specific examples of individuals who engaged in the same conduct but avoided arrest. They can't do that anymore. Second, the Supreme Court rejected the defendants' request for a sweeping rule that would have rubberstamped all retaliatory arrests supported by warrants.

This article proceeds in four parts. The first part sets up the problem that the Supreme Court faced when grappling with the presence of probable cause in retaliatory arrest claims. The second part examines *Nieves v. Bartlett*, the Supreme Court's first attempt to announce a general rule about retaliatory arrests. The third part discusses the Supreme Court's most recent retaliatory arrest decision, *Gonzalez v. Trevino*, which clarified the rule announced in *Nieves*. The article concludes by looking to the future of these issues.

I. The Pre-*Nieves* Debates: Considering Whether Probable Cause Is a Barrier to Retaliatory Arrest Lawsuits

Arrests are an important law enforcement tool. They protect the public by removing dangerous individuals from the streets, and they deter future lawbreakers from committing crimes. But arrests are also an incredibly effective tool for silencing political opponents. The barrier to arrests is low—arguable probable cause[4] of some crime[5] is all that's required. And the effects of arrests are particularly chilling—when the choice is "shut up or go to jail," most people

---

[3] *Gonzalez*, 144 S. Ct. at 1667.

[4] Probable cause is not a high bar. It will "frequently" be based on "innocent behavior." Illinois v. Gates, 462 U.S. 213, 243 n.13 (1983).

[5] *See* HARVEY A. SILVERGATE, THREE FELONIES A DAY: HOW THE FEDS TARGET THE INNOCENT xxxvi (2011); *see also* JAMES R. COPLAND & RAFAEL A. MANGUAL, MANHATTAN INST., OVERCRIMINALIZING THE SOONER STATE 6 (2016) (explaining that between 2010 and 2015, the South Carolina legislature enacted an average of 60 new crimes annually, followed by Minnesota with 46, Michigan with 45, North Carolina with 34, and Oklahoma with 26).

will choose to forgo their First Amendment rights. No wonder autocrats around the world find arrests to be such an attractive form of "opposition management."[6]

In this country, we've been rightly wary of retaliatory arrests. As the Supreme Court observed 37 years ago, the right to criticize the government, "without thereby risking arrest is one of the principal characteristics by which we distinguish a free nation from a police state."[7]

At the same time, we've also given law enforcement officials substantial deference, especially when their actions are justified by the presence of probable cause. The Court has repeatedly explained that the subjective intent of the officer is simply "irrelevant" and provides "no basis for invalidating an arrest."[8] "[E]venhanded law enforcement is best achieved by the application of objective standards of conduct, rather than standards that depend upon the subjective state of mind of the officer."[9]

So what to do, then, with cases in which a plaintiff admits (or a court decides) that there was probable cause for the arrest but claims that the true cause of the arrest was the plaintiff's political views or speech criticizing the government? Does it make sense to let the suit proceed even though the conduct of the government officials responsible for the arrest was objectively reasonable? Or should such suits be barred even when a complaint presents compelling facts showing that probable cause was merely a laundering mechanism for a First Amendment violation? And are these the only two options?

A. Option One: Probable Cause Is No Barrier to Retaliatory Arrest Suits

The Court has never seriously entertained allowing First Amendment plaintiffs to proceed unencumbered in the face of probable cause.

---

[6] For example, since the start of the war in Ukraine in February 2022, Russia has arrested more than 20,000 Russians who criticized the invasion. These arrests are often made under laws—such as skipping patriotism classes—that are designed to make it look like the arrest was caused by the defendants' activities rather than the substance of their speech. *See* Ann M. Simmons, *Ordinary Russians Feel Wrath of Putin's Repression*, WALL ST. J. (Nov. 11, 2023), https://perma.cc/8MVTLQYV.

[7] City of Houston v. Hill, 482 U.S. 451, 463 (1987).

[8] Devenpeck v. Alford, 543 U.S. 146, 153, 155 (2004).

[9] Kentucky v. King, 563 U.S. 452, 464 (2011) (internal quotation marks and citation omitted).

Even Justices Ruth Bader Ginsburg and Stephen Breyer were leery of this possibility, convinced that probable cause should be dispositive in at least some cases.

Consider Justice Ginsburg's concurrence (joined by Justice Breyer) in *Reichle v. Howards*. In *Reichle*, a secret service officer was sued by a protester after the officer arrested him for lying to a federal official.[10] The situation unfolded when Vice President Dick Cheney visited a shopping mall in Colorado. The protester—Steven Howards—walked up to the Vice President and told him that his "policies in Iraq are disgusting."[11] As the Vice President moved along, Howards touched his shoulder.[12] Following this encounter, one of the agents—Gus Reichle—approached Howards and asked whether he had touched the Vice President. After Howards said no, Reichle arrested him.[13]

Howards sued, arguing that he was arrested not because he had lied about touching the Vice President, but because he had criticized the Iraq War. The Supreme Court ultimately dismissed Howards's claim by granting Reichle qualified immunity. Justice Ginsburg concurred. Going beyond qualified immunity, Ginsburg explained that the presence of probable cause, in her view, meant that Reichle should not be exposed "to claims for civil damages" at all.[14] "Officers assigned to protect public officials must make singularly swift, on the spot, decisions whether the safety of the person they are guarding is in jeopardy. In performing that protective function, they rightly take into account words spoken to, or in the proximity of, the person whose safety is their charge."[15] Because Secret Service officers are "duty bound to take the content of [the suspect's] statements into account" to determine the level of threat, "[r]etaliatory animus cannot be inferred from the assessment they made in that regard."[16]

---

[10] *See* 566 U.S. 658, 662 (2012).

[11] *Id.* at 661.

[12] *See id.*

[13] *See id.*

[14] *Id.* at 672 (Ginsburg, J., concurring in the judgment).

[15] *Id.* at 671.

[16] *Id.* at 672.

Thus, even Ginsburg and Breyer—at the time the second and third most pro-plaintiff Justices on the bench[17]—thought that probable cause was an essential variable in solving the equation of retaliatory arrests. In the process, they zeroed in on something—the public-safety need to take speech into account while making arrests—that would eventually drive the entire Court's thinking.[18]

B. Option Two: Probable Cause Is a Full Barrier to Retaliatory Arrest Suits

Similarly, the Court has never seriously considered barring all retaliatory arrest claims in the face of probable cause. Only Justice Clarence Thomas has made this argument, citing two reasons.

1. Common law

According to Thomas, the three closest analogues to retaliatory arrest claims are false arrest, malicious imprisonment, and malicious prosecution.[19] Because all three required a showing of no probable cause, that's what a retaliatory arrest claim should also require.[20]

2. Thomas's disagreement with Monroe v. Pape

Thomas "adhere[s] to the view that *no* intent-based constitutional tort would have been actionable under the § 1983 that Congress enacted."[21] On this telling, officers can only be sued if they act pursuant to an unconstitutional state or local law. If they act in a rogue manner—for example, by intending to retaliate against an opponent—then that is not covered by § 1983 and should not be actionable in federal court. *Monroe v. Pape* recognized such intentional

---

[17] The most pro-plaintiff Justice on the bench was of course Sonia Sotomayor. The absence of her signature on that concurrence is telling and consistent with her subsequent statements on the issue. *See infra* Part II.

[18] *See infra* Part II.

[19] *See* Lozman v. Riviera Beach, 585 U.S. 87, 105 (2018) (Thomas, J., dissenting).

[20] *See id. But see* Nieves v. Bartlett, 587 U.S. 391, 414 (2019) (Gorsuch, J., concurring in part and dissenting in part) (disagreeing with Thomas because "the *First* Amendment . . . seeks not to ensure lawful authority to arrest but to protect the freedom of speech," so the common-law analogues to the Fourth Amendment should not control) (emphasis in original).

[21] *Lozman*, 585 U.S. at 104 n.2 (Thomas, J., dissenting) (cleaned up).

actions,[22] so according to Thomas it was wrongly decided. As a result, Thomas—along with Justice Antonin Scalia in his time—would deny constitutional remedies altogether.[23]

C. Option Three: Probable Cause Is a Partial Barrier to Retaliatory Arrest Suits

Other members of the Court have openly struggled to chart a middle course that filters out insubstantial cases without catching (too many) meritorious ones. At oral argument in *Nieves v. Bartlett*,[24] Justice Samuel Alito explained the difficulty of crafting a rule to govern a range of cases:

> At one end there is a case where you've got the disorderly person situation. A police officer arrives at the scene where two people are shouting at each other, and one of them says something insulting to the officer, and ends up getting arrested. . . . At the other end, you have a case like a journalist has written something critical of the police department and then a week later is given a citation for driving 30 miles an hour in a . . . 25-mile-an-hour zone.[25]

Justice Alito's question illustrates two competing considerations in retaliatory arrest suits. The first is that, in many of these cases, officers must take protected speech into account to determine whether the speaker should be arrested. As Justice Ginsburg explained in *Reichle*, this need presents a causal complexity: Speech can simultaneously be political (telling Dick Cheney you don't like his Iraq policies) and provide a justification for a valid arrest (a potential motive for intent to harm the Vice President). If considering protected speech can be legitimate—indeed, officers are often "duty bound" to take it into account[26]—then exposing officers to liability on that

---

[22] *See* Monroe v. Pape, 365 U.S. 167, 172 (1961) (concluding that "Congress, in enacting § 19[83], meant to give a remedy to parties deprived of constitutional rights, privileges and immunities by an official's abuse of his position").

[23] *See* Crawford-El v. Britton, 523 U.S. 574, 612 (1998) (Scalia, J., dissenting).

[24] *See infra* Part II.

[25] Transcript of Oral Argument at 9–10, Nieves v. Bartlett, 587 U.S. 391 (2019) (No. 17-1174) (edited for clarity).

[26] Reichle v. Howards, 566 U.S. 658, 672 (2012) (Ginsburg, J., concurring in the judgment).

ground seems not just unfair to the officer, but also detrimental to public safety concerns. Subjecting officers to suits, on this view, would chill legitimate law enforcement and freeze suspect-officer communications at the time when they are most needed.

But the second consideration—which must be weighed against the first—is that pretextual arrests can be easy. Probable cause is a low barrier, and opportunities to find a crime to pin on a critic are increasingly abundant.[27]

At the Institute for Justice, we receive potential case submissions involving retaliatory arrests on a weekly basis. This area has become one of our most frequently litigated. Most fact patterns we hear about do not involve on-the-spot arrests, as in *Reichle*. Instead, they center on premeditation arising from a long-brewed animosity, akin to the second scenario discussed by Justice Alito.

Here are some examples just from the last year:

- In Escambia County, Alabama, a newspaper publisher and reporter were arrested for publishing a story—based on their confidential sources—on a school superintendent's misuse of COVID-19 funds. Media accounts later revealed that the superintendent was very close with the district attorney and the sheriff.[28]
- In Surfside, Florida, a teenage activist spent 27 hours in jail for allegedly pushing the vice mayor during a debate. The original affidavit relied on the vice mayor's account, but later interviews revealed that the confrontation never took place.[29]
- In Trumbull County, Ohio, a local politician spent a day in jail after she refused to apologize for her criticism of the sheriff for abominable jail conditions.[30]

---

[27] *See Nieves*, 587 U.S. at 412 (Gorsuch, J., concurring in part and dissenting in part).

[28] *See* Paul Farhi, *Local Journalists Arrested in Small Alabama Town for Grand Jury Story*, WASH. POST (Nov. 1, 2023), https://www.washingtonpost.com/style/media/2023/11/01/atmore-alabama-journalists-arrested-grand-jury/.

[29] *See* Martin Vassolo, *Surfside Arrest Further Divides Town Ahead of Election*, AXIOS (Mar. 15, 2024), https://www.axios.com/local/miami/2024/03/15/surfside-arrest-divides-town-election.

[30] *See* Amanda Holpuch, *Arrest Violated County Official's Free Speech Rights, Judge Rules*, N.Y. TIMES (Jan. 18, 2024), https://www.nytimes.com/2024/01/18/us/ohio-niki-frenchko-arrest.html.

In all of these cases, charges were quickly dismissed. But by then, the powers-that-be had already forced their critics behind bars—however temporarily—sending chills down their spines and across their communities. Preventing these types of bogus criminal cases from proceeding is insufficiently protective of the First Amendment.

II. *Nieves*: The Court Makes Probable Cause a Partial Barrier to Retaliatory Arrest Lawsuits

After sidestepping this dilemma in *Reichle* and then *Lozman*,[31] the Supreme Court took a direct shot at it in *Nieves*. Balancing these two considerations, the Court held that probable cause is a barrier to a retaliation suit but not an insurmountable one. The Court explained that a plaintiff must plead and prove the absence of probable cause, unless he alleges "objective evidence that he was arrested when otherwise similarly situated individuals not engaged in the same sort of protected speech had not been."[32] The Court did not flesh out the definition of the term "objective" other than to say that evidence must go beyond allegations of state of mind.[33] Nor did the Court address the meaning of the phrase "similarly situated" other than to cite *United States v. Armstrong*.[34] That case had held that to properly state a defense against a racially biased criminal prosecution, criminal defendants must point to specific comparators—that is, individuals who were not Black and who could have been prosecuted, but were not.[35]

---

[31] *Lozman v. Riviera Beach* came out one Term before *Nieves v. Bartlett*. Riviera Beach had had enough of Fane Lozman's opposition to its policies, so one of its councilmembers "suggested that the City use its resources to 'intimidate' Lozman." Lozman v. Riviera Beach, 585 U.S. 87, 91 (2018). As a result of this "premeditated plan," Lozman was arrested. *Id.* at 100. When he sued, the Court set out to answer generally "whether the existence of probable cause defeats the First Amendment claim for retaliatory arrest." *Id.* at 102 (Thomas, J., dissenting) (internal quotation marks and citation omitted). But just as the Court did in *Reichle*, it ended up punting on this question. *See id.* at 99 (majority opinion) The Court instead announced that its rule, which allowed Lozman's suit to move forward, was limited to an official municipal policy of retaliation. *See id.* at 101.

[32] *Nieves*, 587 U.S. at 407 (citing United States v. Armstrong, 517 U.S. 456, 465 (1996)).

[33] *Id.* at 403.

[34] *Id.* at 407.

[35] *See Armstrong*, 517 U.S. at 465.

Nieves arose out of Alaska's Arctic Man festival, "known for both extreme sports and extreme alcohol consumption."[36] When Russell Bartlett crossed paths with officers Bryce Weight and Luis Nieves, it was "around" 1:30 a.m.[37] The two encounters at issue in the case involved the officers explaining to Arctic Man attendees that they should move their beer kegs inside their RVs and also asking those who were underage whether they'd been drinking.[38] Bartlett intervened in both of those encounters, yelling at the officers and commanding his fellow Arctic Man aficionados not to talk to them. When the latter encounter escalated into what appeared to be a confrontation between Bartlett and Weight, Nieves arrested Bartlett for disorderly conduct. After Nieves handcuffed Bartlett, he reportedly said: "[B]et you wished you would have talked to me now."[39]

Bartlett sued both officers, claiming that he was arrested not because of his belligerent behavior but because the officers did not like the content of his speech. Although the district court found that Bartlett's arrest was supported by probable cause,[40] Bartlett pointed to Nieves's comments during the arrest as evidence of retaliation.[41]

There was no question that Bartlett's speech criticizing the officers was protected. By the time the case reached the Supreme Court, there was also no question that Bartlett was arrested at least in part because of his speech. The question before the Court was whether the officers' consideration of Bartlett's speech permitted Bartlett to bring a First Amendment claim, given the existence of probable cause.

A. General Rule: Probable Cause Bars Retaliatory Arrests

Channeling Justice Ginsburg's discussion of causal complexity in *Reichle*,[42] the Supreme Court held that "probable cause should generally defeat a retaliatory arrest claim."[43] This holding was based

---

[36] *Nieves*, 587 U.S. at 395.

[37] *Id.*

[38] *See id.* at 395–96.

[39] *Id.* at 397.

[40] *See id.*

[41] *See id.*

[42] *See supra* Part I; *see also* Reichle v. Howards, 566 U.S. 658, 671 (2012) (Ginsburg, J., concurring in the judgment).

[43] *Nieves*, 587 U.S. at 406.

on the Court's concern that "retaliatory arrest cases . . . present a tenuous causal connection between the defendant's alleged animus and the plaintiff's injury."[44] The causal connection is tenuous because "protected speech is often a wholly legitimate consideration for officers when deciding whether to make an arrest."[45] "Officers frequently must make split-second judgments when deciding whether to arrest, and the content and manner of a suspect's speech may convey vital information—for example, if he is ready to cooperate or rather presents a continuing threat."[46] "Indeed, that kind of assessment happened in this case. The officers testified that they perceived Bartlett to be a threat based on a combination of the content and tone of his speech, his combative posture, and his apparent intoxication."[47]

B. Exception: Objective Evidence That Nonretaliatory Grounds Are Insufficient to Explain the Arrest Can Overcome Probable Cause

But the Court's reliance on causal complexity could go only so far. In the second part of *Nieves*, the Court announced that a plaintiff may show that "non-retaliatory grounds were in fact insufficient to provoke the adverse consequences" through an "objective inquiry that avoids the significant problems that would arise from reviewing police conduct under a purely subjective standard."[48] If a plaintiff can make such a showing, then the plaintiff's retaliation claims should be allowed to proceed "in the same manner as claims where the plaintiff has met the threshold showing of the absence of probable cause."[49]

For some retaliatory arrests, "probable cause does little to prove or disprove the causal connection between animus and injury."[50] For example, "if an individual who has been vocally complaining about police conduct is arrested for jaywalking" at a busy intersection where such arrests are rare, it's a safe bet that the arrest was

---

[44] *Id.* at 401 (internal quotation marks and citation omitted).

[45] *Id.* (cleaned up).

[46] *Id.* (cleaned up).

[47] *Id.*

[48] *Id.* at 407 (cleaned up).

[49] *Id.* at 407–8.

[50] *Id.* at 407.

motivated by the jaywalker's complaints, not his crime.[51] If a plaintiff can make a similar showing, a retaliatory arrest claim should be able to proceed regardless of probable cause.

Still, the Court announced the jaywalking exception in mystifying terms: "[T]he no-probable-cause requirement should not apply," it said, "when a plaintiff presents objective evidence that he was arrested when otherwise similarly situated individuals not engaged in the same sort of protected speech had not been."[52] The Court did not define the term "objective" other than to explain that purely subjective evidence, such as allegations of the officer's state of mind, do not come in.[53] Nor did the Court explain the meaning of "similarly situated."[54] Instead, it cited to a selective prosecution case, *United States v. Armstrong*, as an example of what it had in mind.[55]

In *Armstrong*, Black individuals were indicted on charges of conspiring to possess and distribute crack cocaine.[56] In their attempt to throw out the indictments, these individuals raised a defense of selective prosecution. As evidence, they presented a study showing that the defendants were Black in all of the 24 relevant closed cases in the previous year.[57] That fact, they claimed, tended to show that they were prosecuted only because of their race, entitling them to further discovery on the defense of selective prosecution.[58] But what they didn't have was evidence that white people were accused of similar crimes without being indicted. That, in the Court's view, was a death blow to this argument. Because the criminal defendants could not point to "individuals who were not black and could have been prosecuted for the offenses for which respondents were charged, but were not so prosecuted," the district attorney could proceed with the indictments.[59]

---

[51] *Id.*

[52] *Id.*

[53] *Id.* at 403–04 (rejecting "Bartlett's purely subjective approach").

[54] *Id.* at 407.

[55] *See id.*

[56] *See* United States v. Armstrong, 517 U.S. 456, 458 (1996).

[57] *See id.* at 459.

[58] *See id.*

[59] *Id.* at 470.

As Justice Sonia Sotomayor pointed out in her *Nieves* dissent, there might as well have been no jaywalking exception at all if this standard applied. In selective prosecution cases, statistical evidence of nonprosecutions is available through a comparison of those who were arrested for a crime against those who were subsequently prosecuted for that crime.[60] But such comparative statistics do not exist in retaliatory arrest cases.[61] "And unlike race, gender, or other protected characteristics, speech is not typically sorted into statistical buckets that are susceptible of ready categorization and comparison."[62] If *Armstrong* applies, then "comparison-based evidence is the sole gateway" through which plaintiffs can avoid the general no-probable-cause rule.[63] But such "fetishiz[ation of] one specific type of motive evidence . . . at the expense of other modes of proof" is "arbitrar[y]" and "ration[s] First Amendment protection in an illogical manner."[64]

Unlike Justice Sotomayor, Justice Neil Gorsuch did not see the *Nieves* majority as taking the *Armstrong* argument that far. "[E]nough questions remain about *Armstrong*'s potential application," he explained, "that I hesitate to speak definitively about it today."[65] Moreover, "[s]ome courts of appeals have argued that *Armstrong* should not extend, at least without qualification, beyond prosecutorial decisions to arrests by police."[66] Justice Gorsuch explained that in his view *Nieves* did not "adopt[] a rigid rule . . . that First Amendment retaliatory arrest plaintiffs who can't prove the absence of probable cause must produce 'comparison-based evidence' in every case."[67] He "retain[ed] hope that lower courts" would apply *Nieves* "'commonsensically,' and with sensitivity to the competing arguments about whether and how *Armstrong* might apply in the arrest setting."[68]

---

[60] *See Nieves*, 587 U.S. at 429 (Sotomayor, J., dissenting).

[61] *See id.* ("[W]hile records of arrests and prosecutions can be hard to obtain, it will be harder still to identify arrests that never happened.").

[62] *Id.*

[63] *Id.*

[64] *Id.* at 427–28.

[65] *Id.* at 418 (Gorsuch, J., concurring in part and dissenting in part).

[66] *Id.*

[67] *Id.* at 419.

[68] *Id.* (internal citation omitted).

III. *Gonzalez*: The Court Clarifies That Probable Cause Can Be Overcome with Any Objective Evidence of Retaliation

It did not take long for circuit courts to split over the meaning of *Nieves*'s "similarly situated" standard.[69] According to the Seventh Circuit, *Nieves* "does not appear to be adopting a rigid rule that requires, in all cases, a particular form of comparison-based evidence."[70] Instead, courts "must consider each set of facts as it comes to [them], and in assessing whether the facts supply objective proof of retaliatory treatment," the Seventh Circuit "surmise[d] that Justices Gorsuch and Sotomayor are correct—common sense must prevail."[71]

According to the Fifth Circuit, on the other hand, "the plain language of *Nieves* requires comparative evidence, because it require[s] 'objective evidence' of 'otherwise similarly situated individuals' who engaged in the 'same' criminal conduct but were not arrested."[72] The Fifth Circuit acknowledged that "one of [its] sister circuits ha[d] taken a broader view" but stated that it did "not adopt this more lax reading of the exception."[73]

A. Proceedings Below

Consistent with its narrow view of comparative evidence, the Fifth Circuit rejected a First Amendment retaliation claim by a 72-year-old city councilwoman, Sylvia Gonzalez, who was arrested weeks after she championed a petition calling for the resignation of the city manager in her hometown of Castle Hills, Texas. Gonzalez was arrested under a statute criminalizing tampering with a government record. Two months earlier, during a city council meeting when the petition was introduced, she had taken what she thought was a copy of the petition and placed it in her binder at the dais. As soon as the

---

[69] *Id.* at 407 (majority opinion).

[70] Lund v. City of Rockford, 956 F.3d 938, 945 (7th Cir. 2020) ("agree[ing] with Justice Gorsuch's interpretation of the majority opinion in *Nieves*").

[71] *Id.*

[72] Gonzalez v. Trevino, 42 F.4th 487, 492 (5th Cir. 2022), *vacated and remanded*, 144 S. Ct. 1663 (2024).

[73] *Id.* at 492–93.

mayor pointed out that this was the actual petition and not a copy, Gonzalez had given it back.[74]

The question in the case, like in *Nieves*, was whether Gonzalez could sue the mayor and other allies of the city manager for retaliation. Gonzalez claimed that the defendants had organized her arrest to punish her oppositional speech. But because a magistrate had signed a warrant for her arrest—making the existence of probable cause virtually unassailable—the defendants argued that she should be prevented from asserting a retaliation claim.[75]

Because this case was filed on the heels of *Nieves*, Gonzalez knew that she needed to plead objective evidence in her complaint showing that government officials normally use their discretion not to arrest in these types of situations. To do this, she reviewed 10 years' worth of felony and misdemeanor data in Bexar County (where Castle Hills is located), showing that the anti-tampering statute "had never been used in the county 'to criminally charge someone for trying to steal a nonbinding or expressive document.'"[76] "[T]he typical indictment" involved "'accusations of either using or making fake government identification documents.'"[77] And "[e]very misdemeanor case, according to Gonzalez, involved 'fake social security numbers, driver's licenses, [or] green cards.'"[78]

In addition to this survey, Gonzalez presented "*other* types of objective evidence" to show that in cases like hers government officials "typically exercise their discretion not to [arrest]."[79] For example, Gonzalez "pointed to . . . details about the anomalous procedures used for her arrest," like the fact that 72-year-old councilmembers wanted for nonviolent misdemeanors are typically issued summonses and not arrest warrants.[80] Moreover, the warrant affidavit itself contained "statements . . . suggesting a retaliatory motive,"[81]

---

[74] *See* Gonzalez v. Trevino, 144 S. Ct. 1663, 1666 (2024).

[75] *See id.* at 1667.

[76] *Id.* at 1666 (quoting the complaint).

[77] *Id.* at 1667 (quoting the complaint).

[78] *Id.* (quoting the complaint).

[79] *Id.* at 1677 (Jackson, J., concurring) (emphasis in original).

[80] *Id.* at 1678. *See also id.* at 1666 (majority opinion) ("[A] local Magistrate granted a warrant for Gonzalez's arrest.").

[81] *Id.* at 1678 (Jackson, J., concurring).

such as observations that Gonzalez was "openly antagonistic to the city manager" and "desperately [wanted] to get him fired."[82]

For the Fifth Circuit, none of this objective evidence mattered. The Fifth Circuit did not even engage with the nonsurvey evidence, such as the unusual procedures employed by the defendants to ensure an arrest or their statements in the affidavit. With respect to the survey evidence, the Fifth Circuit simply stated that "Gonzalez does not offer evidence of other similarly situated individuals who mishandled a government petition but were not prosecuted under Texas Penal Code § 37.10(a)(3). Rather, the evidence she offers is that virtually everyone prosecuted under § 37.10(a)(3) was prosecuted for conduct different from hers."[83] The Court thus threw out Gonzalez's claim because she couldn't find another councilmember who similarly put a nonbinding petition in her binder and was *not* arrested for it.

Judge Andrew Oldham dissented from the Fifth Circuit's decision. According to his opinion, "such *comparative* evidence is not required. *Nieves* simply requires objective evidence. And evidence is '[s]omething (including testimony, documents, and tangible objects) that tends to prove or disprove the existence of an alleged fact.'"[84] Judge Oldham stated that as long as a plaintiff provides objective evidence that "tend[s] to connect the officers' animus to the plaintiff's arrest," the plaintiff should be able to proceed with her claims.[85] "Such evidence could be comparative. But as far as [Judge Oldham could] tell, nothing in *Nieves* requires it to be so."[86]

B. The Supreme Court Ruling

The Supreme Court full-throatedly agreed with Judge Oldham's view. In reversing the Fifth Circuit, it stated that (1) the Fifth Circuit's interpretation of the *Nieves* exception was "overly cramped"; (2) "specific comparator evidence" is not required; and (3) "the demand for virtually identical and identifiable comparators goes

---

[82] *Gonzalez*, 42 F.4th at 490 (internal quotation marks omitted).

[83] *Id.* at 492.

[84] *Id.* at 502 (Oldham, J., dissenting) (quoting *Evidence*, BLACK'S LAW DICTIONARY (11th ed. 2019)).

[85] *Id.*

[86] *Id.*

too far."[87] Instead, "[t]he only express limit [the Court] placed on the sort of evidence a plaintiff may present . . . is that it must be objective in order to avoid the significant problems that would arise from reviewing police conduct under a purely subjective standard."[88]

This reference to "objective" evidence echoed the Court's *Nieves* decision, where it emphasized the importance of evaluating an officer's conduct under the objective standard of reasonableness.[89] So long as the plaintiff provides objective evidence that "makes it more likely that an officer *has* declined to arrest someone for engaging in such conduct in the past," this requirement is met.[90]

The Supreme Court further clarified that when it asked for evidence of similarly situated individuals in *Nieves*, it did not limit that evidence to specific comparator evidence as it had in *Armstrong*. Any objective evidence that officers have in the past used their discretion not to arrest would do.[91] In other words, the Seventh Circuit was right: Courts must commonsensically assess whether the facts supply objective proof of retaliatory treatment, without tying themselves in statistical knots to figure out what does and does not constitute a direct comparator.[92] As Justice Alito explained in his concurrence:

> Our jaywalking example in *Nieves* plainly proves this point. We did not suggest that a vocal critic of the police charged with jaywalking had to produce evidence that police officers knowingly refused to arrest other specific jaywalkers. And we certainly did not suggest that this jaywalker had to find others who committed the offense under the same conditions as those in his case—for example, on a street with the same amount of traffic traveling at the same speed within a certain distance from a crosswalk at the same time of day.[93]

Crucially, the Court did not give any credence to the defendants' argument that a warrant short-circuits the analysis, barring a claim of retaliation. While having a warrant is a defense in cases where the existence

---

[87] *Gonzalez*, 144 S. Ct. at 1667.

[88] *Id.* (internal quotation marks omitted).

[89] *See supra* Part II.

[90] *Gonzalez*, 144 S. Ct. at 1667.

[91] *See id.*

[92] *See* Lund, 956 F.3d at 945.

[93] *Gonzalez*, 144 S. Ct. at 1673 (Alito, J., concurring).

of probable cause is at issue,[94] once probable cause is not disputed, the fact that defendants obtained a warrant is immaterial. The Court's unwillingness to entertain arguments about the protective power of warrants is consistent with its general deference to those officers who are pressed to make warrantless arrests in dangerous settings.[95]

Justice Alito's concurrence provides additional guidance. For example, he explained that objective evidence means anything other than evidence regarding an officer's state of mind—"*e.g.*, evidence of bad blood between the officer and the plaintiff."[96] Valid objective evidence also includes Gonzalez's evidence that elderly councilmembers with no criminal records typically aren't arrested for nonviolent misdemeanors. Alito further clarified that the threshold question "asks whether the plaintiff engaged in the type of conduct that is unlikely to result in arrest or prosecution," which is different from the merits question of "whether the defendant's adverse decision was influenced by the plaintiff's constitutionally protected speech."[97] By this definition, objective evidence of the defendant surveying the plaintiff's house for several weeks does not come in, because that evidence is still dealing with that particular defendant's motivations.[98] But objective evidence of "an affidavit from an officer testifying that no one has been prosecuted in the jurisdiction for engaging in similar conduct" does come in.[99] Such evidence shows not the state of mind of the defendant, but rather the overall practice of not arresting these types of individuals. This is consistent with Justice Ketanji Brown Jackson's concurrence (joined by Justice Sotomayor), which emphasized that objective evidence also includes statements in the arrest affidavit suggesting a retaliatory motive.[100] Even an objective

[94] Franks v. Delaware, 438 U.S. 154, 171 (1978) (discussing the presumption of validity for government action supported by a warrant).

[95] *E.g.*, Kisela v. Hughes, 584 U.S. 100, 103 (2018) (extending extra deference to "police officers" because they are "often forced to make split-second judgments—in circumstances that are tense, uncertain, and rapidly evolving—about the amount of force that is necessary in a particular situation") (internal quotation marks omitted).

[96] *Gonzalez*, 144 S. Ct. at 1672 (Alito, J., concurring).

[97] *Id.*

[98] *See id.* ("[E]vidence regarding an officer's state of mind . . . does not qualify [as objective evidence].").

[99] *Id.*

[100] *See id.* at 1677–78 (Jackson, J., concurring).

inquiry can take the defendants' statements into account, as long as they go to show not the defendants' state of mind but rather the objective fact that a reasonable official in their shoes could have declined to arrest under similar circumstances in the past.[101]

Justice Thomas wrote the sole dissent.[102] Thomas was concerned that the Court in *Gonzalez* had expanded the *Nieves* exception, which now applies "if a plaintiff presents evidence of *any* objective fact that makes it more likely that an officer has declined to arrest someone for engaging in such conduct in the past."[103] Consistent with Thomas's previous statements on this issue,[104] he emphasized that he would erect a full barrier to suit when there is probable cause because "[t]here is no basis in either the common law or our First Amendment precedents for the exception created in *Nieves* and expanded upon [in *Gonzalez*]."[105]

IV. The Future of Retaliatory Arrest Claims

In her *Nieves* dissent, Justice Sotomayor wrote that "[w]hat exactly the Court means by 'objective evidence,' 'otherwise similarly situated,' and 'the same sort of protected speech' is far from clear."[106] *Gonzalez* mostly clarified these terms. We now know that *Nieves*, unlike *Armstrong*, does not require specific comparator evidence to overcome the presence of probable cause. We now know that all the plaintiff must present is objective evidence, which is anything other than evidence regarding an officer's state of mind. And we now know that the evidence need only show that a person taking similar action *without* the speech would have avoided arrest.

This type of objective evidence of meaningfully differential treatment can take many forms, including unusual timing or procedures, statistical evidence, anecdotal evidence, and even statements by

---

[101] *See id.*

[102] Justice Brett Kavanaugh wrote separately to opine that the grant of certiorari was "ill-advised," but he concurred in full because in his view the opinion "does not seem to say anything that is harmful to the law." *Id.* at 1677 (Kavanaugh, J., concurring).

[103] *Id.* at 1679 (Thomas, J., dissenting) (internal quotation marks omitted) (emphasis in original).

[104] *See supra* Part I.B.

[105] *Gonzalez*, 144 S. Ct. at 1679 (Thomas, J., dissenting) (internal quotation marks omitted).

[106] *Nieves*, 587 U.S. at 432 (Sotomayor, J., dissenting).

government officials. That means police reports and arrest affidavits can come in. It also means that statements by police officers *after* the arrest can come in too. So, for example, bodycam footage of a police officer's statement to a colleague that "we usually don't arrest people for this minor offense" or "I see people do this all the time, but this is the only time I arrested someone" must be allowed in. Such statements show differential treatment and therefore are sufficient to overcome the presence of probable cause.

The upshot: Retaliatory arrest claims—extremely difficult to bring before *Gonzalez*—now stand a chance. In this age of increased polarization, this outcome is most welcome. It means that government officials cannot count on arrests as a retaliatory weapon of choice to silence their opponents. Even when an arrest is supported by probable cause, a plaintiff can now bring a retaliation lawsuit. And the plaintiff does not have to point to a specific individual who engaged in the same conduct, did not criticize the government, and was not arrested. In *Gonzalez*, common sense prevailed. Let's hope it prevails in the future choices made by our government officials, too.

In Denial about the Obvious: Upending the Rhetoric of the Modern Second Amendment

George A. Mocsary*

[T]here be nothing new, but that, which is, Hath been before.[1]

Introduction

Sixteen years ago, before the U.S. Supreme Court decided *District of Columbia v. Heller*,[2] I published a student note which argued that one had to "explain[] away the obvious" to conclude that the Second Amendment did not protect an individual arms right.[3] The penchant to deny the historical evidence[4] that the Second Amendment protects an individual right ran deep among those believing that "guns are bad"[5] or that "ordinary people are too careless and stupid to own guns."[6]

* Professor of Law, University of Wyoming College of Law; Director, University of Wyoming Firearms Research Center. Fordham University School of Law, JD, summa cum laude, 2009; University of Rochester Simon School of Business, MBA, 1997. I thank Leo Bernabei, Joseph G.S. Greenlee, Nicholas J. Johnson, Donald Kilmer, David B. Kopel, Robert Leider, Jamie G. McWilliam, and Matthew Wright for their valuable insights and feedback.

[1] WILLIAM SHAKESPEARE, THE POEMS OF WILLIAM SHAKESPEARE 45 (William Jones ed., 1791) (Sonnet 59).

[2] 554 U.S. 570 (2008).

[3] George A. Mocsary, *Explaining Away the Obvious: The Infeasibility of Characterizing the Second Amendment as a Nonindividual Right*, 76 FORDHAM L. REV. 2113 (2008).

[4] As relevant to *Bruen's* method, "evidence" is not "proof." George A. Mocsary, *Statistically Insignificant Deaths: Disclosing Drug Harms to Investors (and Patients) Under SEC Rule 10b-5*, 82 GEO. WASH. L. REV. 111, 113 n.7, 138–56 (2013). Much information can evidence a claim, but little can definitively prove it. *See id.*

[5] N.Y. State Rifle & Pistol Ass'n v. Bruen, 597 U.S. 1, 78 (2022) (Alito, J., concurring).

[6] Silveira v. Lockyer, 328 F.3d 567, 569 (9th Cir. 2003) (Kozinski, J., dissenting from denial of rehearing en banc).

During the first 114 years after the Second Amendment's ratification, for example, all but one court held that arms rights were individual.[7] Nevertheless, 20th-century courts selectively relied on cases that were likewise rife with selective citations routinely to hold that the Second Amendment protected a collective right.[8] In 2008, after a century of abuse, *Heller* affirmed the individual right to arms.[9] In 2010, the Court incorporated *Heller* against the states in *McDonald v. City of Chicago*.[10] With two smaller exceptions,[11] the Court did not issue another Second Amendment decision until the 2022 case of *New York State Rifle & Pistol Ass'n v. Bruen*, which invalidated New York's may-issue public-carry regime and set forth a test for Second Amendment adjudications.[12]

In this Term's *United States v. Rahimi*, a criminal defendant with a history of violence asserted a Second Amendment right to possess firearms while under a domestic violence restraining order. The Court rejected his challenge and upheld the defendant's conviction by an 8–1 vote.[13] In so doing, the Court illustrated that its Second Amendment jurisprudence is a straightforward application of the centuries-old practice of common-law reasoning that is taught to first-year law students.

Part I of this article surveys the denial that took place between *Heller* and *Bruen*. Part II distills *Rahimi*'s seven opinions. Section II.A discusses the Court's majority opinion, showing that *Rahimi* is a textbook example of common-law adjudication. Section II.B reviews the dissent, which also applies the common-law method but sees *Bruen* differently. Section II.C analyzes *Rahimi*'s *Bruen*-protesting

---

[7] Mocsary, *supra* note 3, at 2148, 2157 (citing sources and noting that the first instance occurred in 1905).

[8] Nicholas J. Johnson, Heller *as* Miller, *in* 1 Guns and Contemporary Society: The Past, Present, and Future of Firearms and Firearm Policy 83 (Glenn H. Utter ed., 2016).

[9] *See generally Heller*, 554 U.S. 570.

[10] 561 U.S. 742 (2010).

[11] *See infra* notes 19–28 and accompanying text.

[12] *Bruen*, 597 U.S. 1.

[13] United States v. Rahimi, 144 S. Ct. 1889 (2024). The Court also granted certiorari, vacated, and remanded (GVR'd) the remaining Second Amendment cases on its docket. *See* Leo Bernabei, *Thoughts on the Supreme Court's End-of-Term Second Amendment Dispositions*, Firearms Rsch. Ctr. (July 3, 2024), https://firearmsresearchcenter.org/forum/thoughts-on-the-supreme-courts-end-of-term-second-amendment-dispositions/.

concurrences, which acknowledge that *Rahimi* applied *Bruen* correctly but nonetheless find *Bruen* to be unworkable. Section II.D, elaborating on *Rahimi's* originalism concurrences, discusses the importance of the Constitution's role as a hands-tying document that protects minority rights by restraining government's majoritarian propensities.

I. Post-*Heller* Denial

Soon after *McDonald*, lower courts began applying the "Two-Part Test" to Second Amendment challenges. Under that test, courts first asked whether the regulated activity was within the Second Amendment's scope as determined by history and tradition.[14] If it was not, the challengers lost. If it was, courts applied means-end scrutiny to determine whether the government's regulation was important enough to justify depriving the challengers of their rights.[15] In theory, strict scrutiny applied to regulations at the core of the right. In practice, courts held almost nothing to be within the core of the right and thus usually applied what they called "intermediate scrutiny." This form of intermediate scrutiny was often as or more deferential to the government than rational-basis review. Thus began a quiet defiance of *Heller*.[16] Nearly every regulation was upheld, with judges going as far as to undermine decades of fundamental-rights jurisprudence rather than rule in Second Amendment plaintiffs' favor.[17] The judges often did not hide their contempt for *Heller*.[18]

The Supreme Court did not consider another Second Amendment case until the 2016 case of *Caetano v. Massachusetts*.[19] Jaime Caetano had been convicted of possessing a stun gun that she had acquired after her abusive boyfriend put her into the hospital and she became

---

[14] *See Bruen*, 597 U.S. at 18–19.

[15] *See* NICHOLAS J. JOHNSON ET AL., FIREARMS LAW AND THE SECOND AMENDMENT: REGULATION, RIGHTS, AND POLICY 976 (3d ed. 2021).

[16] George A. Mocsary, *Treating Young Adults as Citizens*, 27 TEX. REV. L. & POL. 607, 610–13 (2023) [hereinafter Mocsary, *Young Adults*]; George A. Mocsary, *A Close Reading of an Excellent Distant Reading of* Heller *in the Courts*, 68 DUKE L.J. ONLINE 41, 55 (2018) [hereinafter Mocsary, *Distant Reading*].

[17] Mocsary, *Young Adults*, *supra* note 16, at 612–14.

[18] *See* Mocsary, *Distant Reading*, *supra* note 16, at 42 & n.10 (citing sources).

[19] 577 U.S. 411 (2016) (per curiam).

homeless.[20] She used it to scare off her abuser one day after work, when he was waiting for her and screaming at her that she should have been caring for the kids that they had together.[21]

The Massachusetts high court upheld her conviction, rejecting her Second Amendment argument.[22] That court reasoned that stun guns are not protected arms because (1) they "were not in common use at the time of the Second Amendment's enactment"; (2) they are "dangerous and unusual"—dangerous because they are weapons and unusual because they are a "modern invention"; and (3) they are not useful in the military.[23]

A unanimous Court reversed that decision, easily applying *Heller*. The Court reasoned that (1) *Heller* had rejected as "bordering on the frivolous" the argument "that only those arms in existence in the 18th century are protected by the Second Amendment"; (2) guns are also considered dangerous in Massachusetts and *Heller* protects those; and (3) *Heller* rejected the proposition that only military weapons are protected by the Second Amendment.[24]

The trend of judicial defiance continued in *New York State Rifle & Pistol Ass'n v. City of New York*, in which the plaintiffs challenged certain restrictions on New York City's premises handgun licenses. The restrictions barred licensees from taking licensed firearms anywhere except in-city shooting ranges. They could not take licensed firearms to second homes in or outside the City, or to shooting ranges outside the City.[25] The City implausibly argued that it had limited firearm transport to only in-City ranges because it wanted fewer guns on *the City's* streets. This proffered justification survived the trial court and Second Circuit.[26] When the Supreme Court granted certiorari, many of the law's defenders lobbied for its repeal.[27]

---

[20] *See id.* at 412–13 (Alito, J., concurring).

[21] *See id.* at 413.

[22] *See* Commonwealth v. Caetano, 26 N.E.3d 688, 695 (Mass. 2015).

[23] *See id.* at 692–94.

[24] *See Caetano*, 577 U.S. at 411–12.

[25] 590 U.S. 336, 345–46 (2020) (Alito, J., dissenting).

[26] *See id.* at 348–49.

[27] *See id.* at 349–51; *see also* Suggestion of Mootness, N.Y. State Rifle & Pistol Ass'n v. City of New York, 590 U.S. 336 (2020) (No. 18-280), 2019 WL 3451573.

The law was indeed changed, and the Court then granted the City's request for a dismissal on mootness grounds.[28]

New York State Rifle & Pistol Ass'n. v. Bruen[29] can be viewed as the Court acting to rein in this abuse. *Bruen* rejects the Two-Part Test's second step, the tiered-scrutiny review. *Bruen* instead instructs that when courts determine the constitutionality of firearm regulations, they must base their review on text, history, and tradition.[30] Complaints about *Bruen*'s alleged deficiencies began with its dissenting opinion, appeared online within hours, and have continued since.[31] Based on these complaints—from judges,[32]

---

[28] *N.Y State Rifle & Pistol Ass'n*, 590 U.S. at 339 (per curiam).

[29] 597 U.S. 1 (2022).

[30] *Id.* at 17–22.

[31] *See* Lisa Vicens & Samuel Levander, *The* Bruen *Majority Ignores Decision's Empirical Effects*, SCOTUSBLOG (July 8, 2022, 1:14 PM), https://www.scotusblog.com/2022/07/the-bruen-majority-ignores-decisions-empirical-effects/; Esther Sanchez-Gomez, *The Right to Fear, in Public: Our Town Square after* Bruen, SCOTUSBLOG (June 29, 2022, 1:44 PM), https://www.scotusblog.com/2022/06/the-right-to-fear-in-public-our-town-square-after-bruen/; *see also* Ry Rivard & Daniel Han, *Murphy Vows to 'Do Everything in Our Power to Protect' New Jerseyans after Supreme Court's Gun Ruling*, POLITICO (June 23, 2022, 3:24 PM), https://www.politico.com/news/2022/06/23/murphy-new-jersey-supreme-court-strikes-down-gun-laws-00041745 (New Jersey governor calling *Bruen* a "deeply flawed" and "dangerous decision" that "will make America a less safe country"); *Mayor Adams' Statement on Bruen Supreme Court Decision*, NYC (June 23, 2022), https://www.nyc.gov/office-of-the-mayor/news/426-22/mayor-adams-on-bruen-supreme-court-decision (New York City mayor arguing that *Bruen* "will put New Yorkers at further risk of gun violence"); Gavin Newsom (@GavinNewsom), X (June 23, 2022, 11:27 AM), https://twitter.com/GavinNewsom/status/1539993469644447744 [https://perma.cc/H2HN-W5A6] (California governor implying that the decision would lead to people "being gunned down" in public).

[32] *See, e.g.*, Barris v. Stroud Township, 310 A.3d 175, 215 (Pa. 2024) (Dougherty, J.) ("[T]o many, the *Bruen* Court's word that the Second Amendment is meant 'to be adapted to the various crises of human affairs' largely rings hollow since the Court has frozen its meaning in time[.]") (quoting *Bruen*, 597 U.S. at 28); State v. Wilson, 543 P.3d 440, 453 (Haw. 2024) (Eddins, J.) (arguing that the Court "distorts and cherry-picks historical evidence" and "shrinks, alters, and discards historical facts that don't fit"); United States v. Bullock, 679 F. Supp. 3d 501, 530–31 (S.D. Miss. 2023) (Reeves, J.) (arguing that *Bruen* contains "no accepted rules for what counts as evidence," that it "remains susceptible to accusations of political bias," and that "the Justices who decided *Bruen* wrote off the history they didn't like by declaring it 'ambiguous at best'") (quoting *Bruen*, 597 U.S. at 39); United States v. Love, 647 F. Supp. 3d 664, 670 (N.D. Ind. 2022) (Brady, J.) (referring to "*Bruen*'s game of historical Where's Waldo").

legal scholars,[33] and historians[34]—one would think it no longer possible to adjudicate Second Amendment cases. The defiance also continued.[35]

Part II discusses *Rahimi*'s seven opinions and shows that *Rahimi* proved wrong the allegations that *Bruen* could not be administered.

II. *Rahimi*

In February 2020, Zackey Rahimi was made subject to a temporary civil restraining order for allegedly assaulting and battering his

---

[33] *See, e.g.,* Brief of Second Amendment Law Scholars as Amici Curiae in Support of Petitioner at 4, United States v. Rahimi, 144 S. Ct. 1889 (2024) (No. 05-1631) ("To date, the lower courts' application of *Bruen*'s approach has not produced consistent, principled results"); Eric J. Segall, *Originalism,* Bruen, *and Constitutional Insanity*, 51 FORDHAM URB. L.J. ONLINE 1, 1 (2024) (calling *Bruen* "the most aggressive, consequential, and hopelessly anti-originalist decision interpreting the Second Amendment in American history").

[34] *See, e.g.,* Saul Cornell, *Cherry-Picked History and Ideology-Driven Outcomes:* Bruen's *Originalist Distortions*, SCOTUSBLOG (June 27, 2022; 5:05 PM), https://www.scotusblog.com/2022/06/cherry-picked-history-and-ideology-driven-outcomes-bruens-originalist-distortions/ (opining that "the Bizarro constitutional universe inhabited by Thomas is bonkers," that "[t]he court's right-wing originalist supermajority, including Thomas, Alito, and their ideological co-conspirators, are making up the rules of evidence and historical interpretation on the fly," and that Justices "Gorsuch and Barrett" are "ideological warriors and political hacks" for perpetuating a "historical charade").

[35] Mocsary, *Young Adults, supra* note 16, at 616–17 & nn.61–62 (citing cases). The first case citing *Bruen* dismissed via a footnote its applicability to a California law barring persons confined to a mental-health facility within the previous five years from possessing firearms. The court merely cited Justice Brett Kavanaugh's concurrence, which restated *Heller*'s blessing of laws that disarm the mentally ill. *See* Pervez v. Beccerra, No. 18-CV-2793, 2022 WL 2306962, at *2 n.2 (E.D. Cal. June 27, 2022). Many courts have dismissed *Bruen*'s applicability to 18 U.S.C. § 922(g)(1)'s lifelong felon-in-possession ban on the ground that *Bruen* concerned law-abiding citizens, while convicted felons are not law abiding. *See, e.g.,* United States v. Riley, 635 F. Supp. 3d 411, 424 (E.D. Va. 2022). Other courts have adhered to pre-*Bruen* circuit precedent that did not rely on history and instead treated *Heller*'s "presumptively lawful" regulations, such as laws disarming felons and the mentally ill, as *unrebuttably* lawful. *See, e.g.,* United States v. Dubois, 94 F.4th 1284, 1293 (11th Cir. 2024); Vincent v. Garland, 80 F.4th 1197, 1202 (10th Cir. 2023), *cert. granted, judgment vacated*, No. 23-683, 2024 WL 3259668 (U.S. July 2, 2024); *cf. infra* note 78 and accompanying text.

Post-*Rahimi*, the U.S. Court of Appeals for the Tenth Circuit again concluded that its post-*Heller* decision categorically upholding § 922(g)(1) remained valid despite its lack of historical analysis. *See* United States v. Curry, No. 23-1047, 2024 WL 3219693, at *4 n.7 (10th Cir. June 28, 2024). The Supreme Court GVR'd *Vincent* for reconsideration in light of *Rahimi*, effectively forcing the Tenth Circuit to consider § 922(g)(1)'s validity with more than a citation to *Heller*'s "presumptively lawful" language.

girlfriend, the mother of his child.[36] When he noticed a bystander observing the incident, he retrieved a firearm from his car and fired toward his girlfriend and the bystander.[37] He later called his girlfriend and threatened to shoot her if she reported the incident.[38]

The restraining order included a finding that Rahimi committed "'family violence'" that was "'likely to occur again'" and that he "posed 'a credible threat' to the 'physical safety'" of his girlfriend and child.[39] The order explicitly prohibited him from "'[c]ommitting family violence,'" "possessing a firearm," or engaging in various other harassing behaviors.[40]

Between November 2020 and January 2021, Rahimi allegedly assaulted another woman with a gun and was involved in five rage-driven shootings (none of which apparently resulted in injury).[41] After a lawful search of his home, police discovered firearms. Rahimi was then indicted and convicted for violating 18 U.S.C. § 922(g)(8), which bars firearm possession by one who is subject to a court order that—

    (A) was issued after a hearing of which such person received actual notice, and at which such person had an opportunity to participate;

    (B) restrains such person from harassing, stalking, or threatening an intimate partner of such person or child of such intimate partner or person, or engaging in other conduct that would place an intimate partner in reasonable fear of bodily injury to the partner or child; and

    (C)

        (i) includes a finding that such person represents a credible threat to the physical safety of such intimate partner or child; or

        (ii) by its terms explicitly prohibits the use, attempted use, or threatened use of physical force against such intimate partner or child that would reasonably be expected to cause bodily injury.[42]

---

[36] *See Rahimi*, 144 S. Ct. at 1894–95.

[37] *Id.* at 1895.

[38] *Id.*

[39] *Id.* (quoting order)

[40] United States v. Rahimi, 61 F.4th 443, 449 (5th Cir. 2023) (quoting order).

[41] *Rahimi*, 144 S. Ct. at 1895; *Rahimi*, 61 F.4th at 449.

[42] 18 U.S.C. § 922(g)(8); *Rahimi*, 144 S. Ct. at 1895–96.

A. The Opinion of the Court

Chief Justice John G. Roberts authored the opinion for the Court, writing for every Justice except Justice Clarence Thomas. The Court's opinion first notes some basic propositions from *Heller*, *McDonald*, and *Bruen*: The Second Amendment was a fundamental right applicable to the states through the Fourteenth Amendment, it protected ordinary citizens, it was not unlimited, regulations are lawful under the Second Amendment if they fit within the "historical tradition of firearm regulation," and the burden is on the government to justify its regulations.[43]

1. Common-law "principles"

The Court's opinion characterizes some lower courts as having "misunderstood" the Court's Second Amendment methodology. Using a phrase that is already catching on, the opinion notes that historical regulations did not create "law trapped in amber."[44] Rather, as *Bruen* dictates, adjudicating a Second Amendment challenge requires examining whether "'relevantly similar'" analogous regulations were permitted by the American tradition of firearm regulation.[45] Importantly, a court must determine whether "the challenged regulation is consistent with the *principles* that underpin our regulatory tradition. . . . The law must comport with the *principles* underlying the Second Amendment," but it need not be a clone of a permissible earlier regulation.[46] The Court repeated that such analogizing is "a commonplace task for any lawyer or judge."[47] As it did in *Bruen*, the Court declined to opine on the relative weights of comparator laws from around the Founding (when the Second Amendment was ratified in 1791) or Second Founding (when the Fourteenth Amendment was ratified in 1868).[48]

---

[43] *Rahimi*, 144 S. Ct. at 1897.

[44] *Id. Cf. Bruen*, 597 U.S. at 27–28, 30.

[45] *Rahimi*, 144 S. Ct. at 1898 (quoting *Bruen*, 597 U.S. at 29).

[46] *Id.* (emphases added).

[47] *Id.* (quoting *Bruen*, 597 U.S. at 28).

[48] *See id.* at 1898 n.1. The Justices referred to both eras in their analyses. For an early discussion of this potential difference in interpretation, see Clayton E. Cramer et al., 'This Right Is Not Allowed by Governments That Are Afraid of the People': The Public Meaning of the Second Amendment When the Fourteenth Amendment Was Ratified, 17 GEO. MASON L. REV. 823, 824 (2010) ("[T]he public understanding in 1866 of the right to arms protected by the Fourteenth Amendment might be different from the public understanding in 1791[.]").

The Court's reference to "principles," coupled with its reminder that modern laws need not be twins of earlier laws, reflects a straightforward common-law method to Second Amendment adjudication.[49] As Professors William Baude and Robert Leider have shown, common-law adjudication involves discerning the "scope of the right as reflected in legal materials such as statutes and court decisions."[50] A common-law judge looks to a wide range of such materials from different jurisdictions, sets aside outliers, and distills general principles.[51]

Bruen instructs courts to use a method of interpolation and extrapolation,[52] and *Rahimi* applies this method. It is nothing new. "[A]pplying old law to new facts . . . is the stuff of first-year law classes the world over."[53] *Bruen's* "how and why" are "*at least* two [of the] metrics" that go into a Second Amendment common-law analysis.[54] But as the Court's words suggest, these need not be the only metrics. How long regulations have burdened one's right to armed self-defense can also matter, for example. This is basic common-law reasoning.

Bruen dictates that comparator laws from the First and Second Foundings merit particular attention. That is appropriate when interpreting constitutional provisions, which *are* supposed to be trapped in amber. Doing so removes majoritarian decision-making from future legislators and judges.[55] It is also appropriate that the 1791-versus-1868 question has not yet been resolved, given that the common law is built out by cases as they arise in

---

[49] William Baude & Robert Leider, *The General Law Right to Bear Arms*, 99 Notre Dame L. Rev. 1466, 1486 (2023).

[50] *Id.* at 1484; *accord id.* at 1485.

[51] *See id.* at 1470–73, 1485–86.

[52] *See id.* at 1483–96. It's also what gun-rights scholars have been doing for decades.

[53] William Baude & Stephen E. Sachs, *Originalism and the Law of the Past*, 37 Law & Hist. Rev. 809, 817–18 (2019).

[54] *Bruen*, 597 U.S. at 29 (emphasis added).

[55] *Id.* at 34–38; *Rahimi*, 144 S. Ct. at 1908 (Gorsuch, J., concurring); *see also* Mocsary, *Young Adults*, *supra* note 16, at 608 (discussing the Constitution's anti-majoritarian function).

a system where judicial authority is bounded by actual cases or controversies.[56]

The "historical" analysis required by *Bruen* is lawyer's work. It is entirely within lawyerly competence to look at constitutional provisions and statutes and any cases that interpreted them.[57] These are legal questions, not esoteric historical inquiries requiring historians. These cases do not require determining whether King Arthur actually existed or what happened to the vanished Roanoke colonists.[58] The Court, unsurprisingly, did not need to rely on expert reports or testimony.

Of course, common-law analogizing can be done too loosely. Analogizing necessarily requires reliance on principles. One cannot properly analogize without some basis for determining what are the relevantly similar analogical metrics. One way to analyze *Rahimi*, then, is to ask whether it properly applied common-law reasoning as cabined by the rules set forth in *Bruen*.

That the decision was 8–1 exemplifies the proposition. The eight in the majority represent the common (law) view. The one is the outlier. As is normal in common-law adjudication, each side asserted that the other was wrong about the law that they believe to be "out there," as defined by original meaning, precedent, treatises, scholarship, and the like.[59]

As offered below, both the majority's and the dissent's common-law analyses fit within *Bruen*'s boundaries. But one prevailed. *Rahimi*, in other words, is an example of the common law working as it should. *Bruen* is a natural step in the Second Amendment's development, albeit one giving more instruction on common-law analysis than jurists should need.

---

[56] *See* U.S. Const. art. III, § 2, cl. 1; Aetna Life Ins. Co. v. Haworth, 300 U.S. 227, 240–41 (1937).

[57] Regulations may also be part of this inquiry, though the regulatory state arose well after the dates of constitutional relevance to the Second Amendment.

[58] *See* Owen Jarus, *20 Biggest Historical Mysteries That Will Probably Never Be Solved*, LiveScience (Mar. 18, 2024), https://www.livescience.com/11361-history-overlooked-mysteries.html.

[59] *See* Baude & Leider, *supra* note 49, at 1466–68, 1470–72.

2. The facial challenge standard

The *Rahimi* Court first noted that under its *Salerno* precedent, a facial challenge can only succeed if the challengers show that the law fails in all its applications.[60] Interestingly, few merits-stage briefs cited this basic rule, and the Fifth Circuit glossed over arguments about whether the *Salerno* rule has "fallen out of favor."[61]

This point is important because it allowed the court to begin and end its analysis at § 922(g)(8)(C)(i). That subsection prohibits possession of a firearm if the defendant is subject to a restraining order that made an explicit finding that the defendant was a danger to an intimate partner or child. This dangerousness requirement puts this subsection on relatively firm starting ground in the constitutional analysis, at least given *Rahimi*'s analysis.[62] But the next subsection, § 922(g)(8)(C)(ii), provides an alternate ground for prohibiting firearm possession by the subject of a restraining order. It does so if the restraining order prohibits the use of physical force likely to cause bodily injury.[63] This subsection is infirm because, as Fifth Circuit Judge James Ho pointed out, protective orders are often issued in divorce proceedings in the absence of perceived danger. They are often issued simply because "[f]amily court judges may face enormous pressure to grant [and] no incentive to deny" such orders.[64]

---

[60] *Rahimi*, 144 S. Ct. at 1898–99 (citing United States v. Salerno, 481 U.S. 739, 745 (1987)).

[61] *See* United States v. Rahimi, 61 F.4th 443, 453 (5th Cir. 2023) (citations omitted), *rev'd* 144 S. Ct. 1889 (2024); *see also, e.g.*, Brief of Amici Curiae Professors of Second Amendment Law et al. in Support of Respondent and Affirmance, United States v. Rahimi, 144 S. Ct. 1889 (2024) (No. 05-1631) (joined by this author) [hereinafter Professors' Brief]. Exceptions were the government's Reply, Texas Advocacy Project, Prosecutors Against Gun Violence, American Civil Liberties Union, and California Legislative Women's Caucus briefs, out of 70 accepted briefs. All briefs are available on the Supreme Court's website, https://www.supremecourt.gov/search.aspx?filename=/docket/DocketFiles/html/Public/22-915.html.

[62] *See generally* Joseph G.S. Greenlee, *The Historical Justification for Prohibiting Dangerous Persons from Possessing Arms*, 20 Wyo. L. Rev. 249 (2020).

[63] *See, e.g.*, United States v. Perez-Gallan, 640 F. Supp. 3d 697, 699 & n.2 (W.D. Tex. 2022), *aff'd*, 2023 WL 4932111 (5th Cir. Aug. 2, 2023), *cert. granted, judgment vacated*, 2024 WL 3259665 (U.S. July 2, 2024) (challenge brought under (C)(ii)).

[64] United States v. Rahimi, 61 F.4th 443, 465–67 (Ho, J., concurring); Professors' Brief, *supra* note 61, at 29.

3. Surety and "going armed" laws

The *Rahimi* Court began its analysis of historical laws with an important point: Although English and colonial law routinely disarmed political opponents who were characterized as dangerous, such practices were not proper grounds for justifying modern disarmament.[65] By implication, other laws that were later made unconstitutional by equal-protection doctrines, such as those targeting oppressed racial minorities, would be similarly inappropriate.[66]

The majority found historical support for § 922(g)(8) in surety and "going armed" laws "[t]aken together."[67] To the Court, these laws established a tradition of disarming those who "pose a clear threat of physical violence to another." These laws were relevant even though they were not the twins of § 922(g)(8), which the majority believed the dissent and lower court wrongly demanded.[68]

Surety laws allowed magistrates, "upon complaint of any person having reasonable cause to fear an injury, or breach of the peace," to require the subject of the complaint to appear and post a good-behavior bond. Exceptions could be made if the subject of the complaint had "reasonable cause to fear an assault or other injury, or violence to his person, or to his family or property."[69] Sureties were available in domestic-abuse situations.[70] Failure to post the bond resulted in the subject of the complaint being jailed for up to six months.[71] At the next term of court, the subject of the complaint could appeal the magistrate's decision or be required to post further

---

[65] *Rahimi*, 144 S. Ct. at 1899.

[66] *See* JOHNSON ET AL., *supra* note 15, at 210–12, 455–77; Mocsary, *Young Adults*, *supra* note 16, at 615 (stating that *Bruen*'s "why" inquiry "should cause laws passed for later unconstitutional reasons . . . to face a greater hurdle in their justification").

[67] *Rahimi*, 144 S. Ct. at 1901.

[68] *Id.* at 1901, 1903.

[69] *Id.* at 1899–1900 (citing 4 WILLIAM BLACKSTONE, COMMENTARIES ON THE LAWS OF ENGLAND 251–53 (10th ed. 1787)); *e.g.*, Mass. Rev. Stat., ch. 134, § 16; *see id.* §§ 1–15 (codifying the common-law surety powers of justices of the peace).

[70] *See Rahimi*, 144 S. Ct. at 1900.

[71] *See* Mass. Rev. Stat., ch. 134, §§ 2, 16.

sureties for a longer term, as the court decreed.[72] Several states adopted such statutes, including around the time of the Fourteenth Amendment's adoption.[73]

"Going armed" laws, a subset of affray laws, prohibited going about with "dangerous and unusual weapons in such a manner, as will naturally cause a terror to the people."[74] Conviction under such laws resulted in "forfeiture of arms . . . and imprisonment."[75]

The Court found in these laws a "relevantly similar" legal tradition of temporarily prohibiting arms possession by those judicially determined to be a violent threat to others on the basis of their past conduct.[76] The burden imposed was also similar. Like sureties, § 922(g)(8) imposed only a temporary restriction on Rahimi. Indeed, "going armed" laws allowed for *imprisonment*, so § 922(g)(8)'s lesser penalty of temporary disarmament was acceptable.[77]

The Court thus elucidated for jurists the level of generality for this inquiry (as common-law courts do). Laws that disarm people based on their being found dangerous can comply with the Second Amendment. And the finding of dangerousness can come from a civil proceeding, without proof beyond a reasonable doubt. Future cases before the Supreme Court and lower courts will determine questions like how much evidence and what kind of determination of dangerousness is required. In the process, they will create common-law data points for future adjudications. The majority's analysis also

---

[72] *See id.*

[73] *E.g., Rahimi*, 144 S. Ct. at 1900; 1869 Wyo. Terr. Laws, ch. 74, §§ 1–12.

[74] *Rahimi*, 144 S. Ct. at 1901; State v. Huntly, 25 N.C. 418, 420–23 (N.C. 1843) ("For any lawful purpose—either of business or amusement—the citizen is at perfect liberty to carry his gun."). Huntly's conduct resembles Rahimi's outrageous post-restraining order behavior. *See id.* at 418–19. Presumably, only Rahimi's pre-order conduct is relevant to whether he can be disarmed under § 922(g)(8).

[75] *Rahimi*, 144 S. Ct. at 1901 (quoting 4 BLACKSTONE, *supra* note 69, at 149) (ellipsis in *Bruen*).

[76] *Id.* at 1901–2.

[77] *Id.* at 1902.

strengthened the perhaps-obvious intuition that as-applied challenges can rebut *Heller's* "presumptively lawful" regulations.[78]

The Court made four points about what it was *not* doing. First, it was not opining (appropriately, since the question was not before it) on whether the Second Amendment allowed legislatures to ban arms possession by groups they deem especially dangerous (presumably subject to other constitutional limits).[79] Second, it distinguished the law stricken in *Bruen*, which presumptively barred public carry by nearly everyone, with severe penalties for carry violations.[80] Third, it rejected the proposition that Rahimi could be disarmed because he was not "responsible," noting that this term was vague.[81] As recognized by the dissent, the government could classify practically anyone as dangerous under such a standard. Fourth, it made clear that due-process questions were not before the Court and thus not addressed (but one detects a strong undercurrent of due-process considerations).[82] These questions are likely to return in similar cases or later iterations of this case.

---

[78] District of Columbia v. Heller, 554 U.S. 570, 626–27 & n.26 (2008); *see In re* Cendant Corp. Litig., 264 F.3d 201, 282 (3d Cir. 2001) ("Saying that there is a presumption necessarily assumes that it can be overcome in some cases."); *Presumption*, BLACK'S LAW DICTIONARY (11th ed. 2019) (noting that an adversely affected party may "overcome[] [a presumption] with other evidence"); *see* Catherine L. Carpenter, *Panicked Legislation*, 49 J. LEGIS. 1, 43 (2022) (noting that the Supreme Court has "invalidated statutes that relied on false irrebuttable presumptions to confer or deny a right to a specific group of people"); *cf.* 4 JOHN HENRY WIGMORE, EVIDENCE § 1353 (4th ed. 1972) ("[C]onclusive evidence is not a rule of evidence at all, but rather a rule of substantive law[.]"). *But see* United States v. Jackson, 69 F.4th 495, 505 n.3 (8th Cir. 2023), *cert. granted, judgment vacated*, No. 23-6170, 2024 WL 3259675 (U.S. July 2, 2024) ("Some have taken the phrase 'presumptively lawful' to mean that the Court was suggesting a presumption of constitutionality that could be rebutted on a case-by-case basis. That is an unlikely reading, for it would serve to cast doubt on the constitutionality of these regulations in a range of cases despite the Court's simultaneous statement that 'nothing in our opinion should be taken to cast doubt' on the regulations. . . . We think it more likely that the Court presumed that the regulations are constitutional because they are constitutional, but termed the conclusion presumptive because the specific regulations were not at issue in *Heller*.") (quoting *Heller*, 554 U.S. at 626, 627 n.26).

[79] *See Rahimi*, 144 S. Ct. at 1901; *id.* at 1902 (discussing *Heller's* "presumptively lawful" regulations); *supra* text accompanying notes 65–66.

[80] *Rahimi*, 144 S. Ct. at 1901–2.

[81] *Id.* at 1903.

[82] *See id.* at 1903 n.2.

B. The Dissent

Justice Thomas's disagreement with the majority was about *Bruen's* application, not *Bruen's* method. The dissent's theme is protectiveness of the right to arms from governmental—including judicial—overreach. Stating that the Second Amendment "is a barrier, placing the right to keep and bear arms off limits to the Government," it reminds readers that the government bears the burden of justifying arms restrictions.[83] This approach is unsurprising given earlier defiance of the right, Justice Thomas's earlier life amidst Jim Crow violence, and this nation's history of Black disarmament.[84]

Due-process concerns are a strong undercurrent in the dissent. It notes, for example, that § 922(g)(8) does not require a criminal conviction or a finding that the defendant committed domestic violence. It notes that the law provides no due process other than that provided for the issuance of the underlying order, which can vary wildly.[85] It notes that despite this lack of a due-process guarantee, violation of the law is a felony punishable by 15 years' imprisonment and permanent disarmament.[86]

The dissent thus would hold that, while modern laws need not be "exact cop[ies]" of historical analogues (despite what the majority asserted Justice Thomas demands), the comparators proffered by the government were "worlds—not degrees—apart from § 922(g)(8)."[87]

1. Holding the government to its burden

Justice Thomas noted that § 922(g)(8) touches core Second Amendment conduct, and that Rahimi is among "the people" protected by

---

[83] *Rahimi*, 144 S. Ct. at 1931 (Thomas, J., dissenting).

[84] *See* Clarence Thomas, My Grandfather's Son: A Memoir 161 (2008); Johnson et al., *supra* note 15, at 195–96, 439–42, 455–77.

[85] California, for example, has varying evidentiary standards for issuing restraining orders that result in the suspension of arms rights. The dissent's example, Cal. Civ. Proc. Code Ann. § 527.6(i)—*Rahimi*, 144 S. Ct. at 1943 (Thomas, J., dissenting)—is to a civil harassment regime aimed at rowdy disputes between neighbors and the like. It requires the relatively stiff standard of clear-and-convincing evidence to disarm one's neighbor. The more relevant analogue from California is Cal. Fam. Code §§ 6251 (emergency orders) and 6300(a) (*ex parte* and orders after hearing), which merely require the party seeking an order to prove "to the satisfaction of the court, reasonable proof of a past act or acts of abuse."

[86] *See Rahimi*, 144 S. Ct. at 1930–31 (Thomas, J., dissenting).

[87] *Id.* at 1941; *accord id.* at 1943; *see supra* text accompanying note 68.

that amendment because he is a citizen who possessed a firearm. With this in mind, Justice Thomas then examined the evidence proffered by the government to justify its statute. Citing *Bruen's* instructions, he concluded that none of the government's comparators were "relevantly similar"—none "'impos[ed] a comparable burden' that [was] 'comparably justified.'"[88]

Justice Thomas's analysis of English laws disarming those deemed "'dangerous' to the peace of the kingdom"[89] illustrates his skepticism of citizen disarmament and, more generally, government monopolies on implements of violence. He correctly noted that the Second Amendment was an explicit response to English monarchs' disarming of political enemies, religious undesirables (which varied with the sovereign's religion), and other nonconformists via wanton dangerousness classifications.[90] Because these laws were about rendering enemies of the Crown helpless rather than about "preventing interpersonal violence," they were inapposite support for § 922(g)(8).[91]

The dissent also rejects comparisons to a pair of failed Bill of Rights proposals from Massachusetts and Pennsylvania and to Civil War–era Union disarmament orders. All of these sources referred to both "peaceable" citizens' right to be armed and to the legitimate disarmament of those who, for example, presented "a real danger of public injury."[92] The dissent levels a similar criticism against the Union orders as it does against the English dangerousness laws, although it acknowledges that the Union orders targeted the violent.[93] But the commentary and failed amendments, although not regulations or judicial opinions on them, are evidence of the Second Amendment's original meaning.[94] *Heller* appropriately relied on such commentary.[95]

The dissent dispenses with the government's remaining comparators, like early firearm storage laws and laws targeting minors and the intoxicated. Justice Thomas argues that these fail *Bruen's* "how"

---

[88] *Rahimi*, 144 S. Ct. at 1933 (Thomas, J., dissenting) (quoting *Bruen*, 597 U.S. at 29).

[89] *Id.*

[90] *See id.* at 1933–35.

[91] *Id.* at 1935.

[92] *Id.* at 1936.

[93] *See id.* at 1936–37.

[94] *See supra* text accompanying notes 44–59.

[95] *See* District of Columbia v. Heller, 554 U.S. 570, 598–604 (2008).

and "why" tests, particularly focusing on the burdens those comparator laws placed on the arms right.[96] There is a difference between regulating and eliminating the right: "between having *no* Second Amendment rights and having *some* Second Amendment rights."[97]

2. Surety and "going armed" laws

Justice Thomas implicitly included surety and "going armed" laws among the rejected comparators. This rejection demonstrated his commitment to *Bruen's* requirement that courts properly enforce the Second Amendment by holding the government to its burden. Although the government did reference these laws in its brief, its discussion of them was strikingly short—a paragraph and a sentence—and was intertwined with its discussion of disarming the "irresponsible."[98] Although a brisk discussion was arguably sufficient given the extent to which the laws were discussed in *Bruen* and the brief's citations to that case for the surety laws (but not the "going armed" laws), the brief said practically nothing about the "how" and "why" of these laws.

Justice Thomas added that while "surety laws shared a common justification with § 922(g)(8)," they "imposed a materially different burden," and thus did not survive *Bruen's* "how" requirement.[99] Sureties allowed accused individuals *who posted bonds* to continue to exercise the full panoply of Second Amendment rights.[100] If they then breached the peace, they forfeited the surety. Section 922(g)(8), by comparison, is a complete right deprivation that punishes violations with up to 15 years of imprisonment and lifetime disarmament.[101] And § 922(g)(8) is made the worse by zealous courts in behavior reminiscent of *Heller*-to-*Bruen*-era judicial defiance. Courts have, for example, upheld its applicability when someone sat on a firearm or cohabited with someone who possessed ammunition.[102] Justice Thomas's analysis would have been more complete if he had noted that accused

[96] *See Rahimi*, 144 S. Ct. at 1937–38 & n.5 (Thomas, J., dissenting).

[97] *Id.* at 1937.

[98] *See* Brief for the United States at 23–24, United States v. Rahimi, 144 S. Ct. 1889 (2024) (No. 22-915); *see also supra* note 81 and accompanying text; Mocsary, *Young Adults, supra* note 16, at 615–16 (describing *Bruen* as the Court policing lower-court defiance of *Heller*).

[99] *Rahimi*, 144 S. Ct. at 1939 (Thomas, J., dissenting).

[100] *See id.* at 1939, 1941.

[101] *Id.* at 1939–41.

[102] *See id.* at 1939–40.

individuals who did not post sureties were jailed, and thus disarmed of *all* civil rights, while § 922(g)(8) revokes only the arms right of those subject to a restraining order covered by § 922(g)(8).[103]

Justice Thomas argued, first, that "going armed" laws failed *Bruen's* "why" mandate. Unlike § 922(g)(8), they applied only to public conduct involving actual violence or going about with dangerous and unusual weapons so as to cause "'terror to the people.'"[104] Second, their "how" burdens were markedly different, leaving in-home possession and peaceable public carry untouched, and providing self-defense exceptions, unlike § 922(g)(8)'s total prohibition.[105] Relatedly, affray laws' penalties could only be imposed after a criminal conviction, providing defendants with all the constitutional protections required in criminal cases, like proof beyond a reasonable doubt, confrontation rights, double jeopardy, and hearsay bans. None of these protections are mandated in hearings to determine whether to issue a restraining order, "which are not even about § 922(g)(8)."[106]

Finally, Justice Thomas objected to the Court's use of surety laws to satisfy *Bruen's* "why"—protecting against future interpersonal violence—and affray laws to provide the "how"—disarmament as a lesser included penalty of imprisonment.[107] He feared that, because imprisonment existed at the Founding, the government need only find a "why"-satisfying law to disarm someone, taking the law back to its pre-*Bruen* "'regulatory blank check'" state.[108] This concern has merit if one agrees with Justice Thomas that affray laws address a different societal problem from § 922(g)(8). But the majority, despite its "[t]aken together" language, saw both the surety and "going armed" laws as meeting *Bruen's* "why" and at least some of the "how" at the level of generality it selected: laws disarming individuals "found to threaten the physical safety of another" to mitigate threats of physical violence.[109]

---

[103] *See supra* text accompanying note 71.

[104] *Rahimi*, 144 S. Ct. at 1942 (Thomas, J., dissenting) (quoting 1 RICHARD BURN, THE JUSTICE OF THE PEACE, AND PARISH OFFICER 13 (2d ed. 1756)).

[105] *See id.* at 1942–43.

[106] *Id.* at 1943.

[107] *Id.* at 1943–44; *see supra* text accompanying note 77.

[108] *Rahimi*, 144 S. Ct. at 1944 (Thomas, J., dissenting) (quoting N.Y. State Rifle & Pistol Ass'n v. Bruen, 597 U.S. 1, 30 (2022)).

[109] *Id.* at 1899–1901 (majority opinion).

Determining what a legislature considered a single act versus multiple acts may be difficult. For example, a legislature addressing bad public behavior might have passed separate surety and affray laws. Or it might instead have passed a single law, with two components, to secure good behavior: a surety component for one type of behavior with a peace bond sanction, and an affray component with an imprisonment penalty for truly bad behavior.[110] Such a unified comparator should neither automatically validate nor automatically invalidate a challenged modern law. A "more nuanced,"[111] analysis would be required, in which the court should ask the difficult questions about levels of generality, applicability of other constitutional rights, and the like. These questions were asked and answered by all the Justices in *Rahimi*.

3. Majoritarian dangerousness determinations

Justice Thomas, in closing, agreed with the Court's rejection of the government's argument that Congress can disarm anyone it deems not responsible or law abiding.[112] As with ancient English dangerousness determinations, he noted that such reasoning was used against "freed blacks following the Civil War" to make them helpless. Justice Thomas recognized these to be easy cover for policy choices (at best) or majoritarian attacks against outgroups (more likely).[113] His thorough analysis rightly captured the Second Amendment's essence, nicely stated by the Fifth Circuit in another case, that "the legislature cannot have unchecked power to designate a group of persons as 'dangerous' and thereby disarm them."[114]

It would have been nice to see such a thorough explication in the majority opinion. Such a discussion would have gone a long way toward allaying the worry expressed in the dissent and in multiple concurrences (and shared by this author) that the mere

---

[110] Going out on multiple rides armed "with pistols, guns, knives, and other dangerous and unusual weapons" while declaring an intent "to beat, wound, kill, and murder" someone is a good candidate for such behavior. State v. Huntly, 25 N.C. 418, 418 (N.C. 1843). Something less extreme might justify only a surety.

[111] *Bruen*, 597 U.S. at 27.

[112] *See supra* text surrounding notes 81–82.

[113] *Rahimi*, 144 S. Ct. at 1944–47 (Thomas, J., dissenting).

[114] *See id.* at 1945–46; United States v. Daniels, 77 F.4th 337, 353 (5th Cir. 2023), *cert. granted, judgment vacated*, No. 23-376, 2024 U.S. LEXIS 2910 (U.S. July 2, 2024).

mention of principles might one day countenance judicial enforcement of "unenacted policy goals lurking behind the Second
Amendment."[115]

C. The Bruen-*Protesting Concurrences*

Justice Sonia Sotomayor filed a concurrence, joined by Justice
Elena Kagan. Justice Ketanji Brown Jackson also filed a concurrence,
writing only for herself. Both concurrences agree that the majority
opinion "fairly applies" *Bruen* in a way "calibrated to reveal something useful and transferable to the present day."[116] In applying
Second Amendment "principles" and "clarifying" *Bruen*, they assert,
the Court correctly concluded "that 'the Second Amendment permits the disarmament of individuals who pose a credible threat to
the physical safety of others.'"[117] The dissent's rigid approach would
be "a too-sensitive alarm" that invalidates too many modern laws
not "identical to ones that could be found in 1791."[118]

So far, one might read the concurrences as acknowledging that
Bruen is a workable precedent. After all, *Bruen*'s common-law
method does not require "a critical mass of historical firearm regulations that look precisely (or almost precisely) like the challenged
law."[119] *Bruen* makes clear that the presence or absence of a given
historical law or precedent is "evidence"—not proof—of the challenged law's constitutionality.[120] Rather, *Bruen* repeatedly says that
its test requires a "historical *analogue*, not a historical *twin*";[121] that
comparators need not be "dead ringer[s]" of modern laws; that "cases
implicating unprecedented societal concerns or dramatic technological changes may require a more nuanced approach";[122] that the
Second Amendment was "intended to endure for ages to come, and,
consequently, to be adapted to the various crises of human affairs";[123]

---

[115] *Daniels*, 77 F.4th at 353.

[116] *Rahimi*, 144 S. Ct. at 1904 (Sotomayor, J., concurring); *id.* at 1926 (Jackson, J.,
concurring).

[117] *Id.* at 1904–5 (Sotomayor, J., concurring); *id.* at 1926 (Jackson, J., concurring).

[118] *Id.* at 1904–5 (Sotomayor, J., concurring); *id.* at 1926 (Jackson, J., concurring).

[119] Baude & Leider, *supra* note 49, at 1489–90.

[120] *Bruen*, 597 U.S. *passim*; *see supra* note 45.

[121] *Bruen*, 597 U.S. at 30; *see also Rahimi*, 144 S. Ct. at 1898.

[122] *Bruen*, 597 U.S. at 27.

[123] *Id.* at 28.

and that "the Constitution can, and must, apply to circumstances beyond those the Founders specifically anticipated."[124] These quotations and others like them in *Bruen* are basic statements of what a constitution must be able to accommodate. There is no clarifying happening in *Rahimi* other than that which normally happens as new cases and controversies are adjudicated under the common law.

Recognizing that "history has a role" in Second Amendment adjudication, both concurrences nevertheless proceed to criticize *Bruen*'s rejection of means-end scrutiny. Justice Sotomayor wrote that means-end scrutiny properly gives "full consideration to the real and present stakes of the problems facing our society today."[125] Justice Jackson added that *Bruen*'s history-and-tradition method is too difficult to apply, leaves too many "unresolved questions," and creates inconsistent judicial outcomes—"chaos," in short.[126]

1. Getting to Bruen

Two meta points are apt before addressing the concurrences in detail.

First, *Bruen* likely turned out as it did because lower courts were so openly abusing means-end scrutiny to uphold firearm restrictions.[127] Some judges essentially admitted their defiance.[128] The propriety of applying heightened scrutiny in Second Amendment cases may never have been questioned had courts applied it in a way that respected plaintiffs' rights. Before the Two-Part Test's abuse, gun-rights advocates regularly considered the Second Amendment in terms of the First Amendment's means-end-scrutiny categories. The Court did away with this implement of abuse and set forth basic rules about analogizing and constitutional adjudication. Lower courts, in other words, *worked for Bruen*.

---

[124] *Id.*

[125] *Rahimi*, 144 S. Ct. at 1905–6 (Sotomayor, J., concurring); *id.* at 1928 (Jackson, J., concurring).

[126] *Rahimi*, 144 S. Ct. at 1927–29 & n.3 (Jackson, J., concurring). Justice Sotomayor's concurrence suggests this about the dissent's approach but otherwise opines that means-end scrutiny is better because it is more flexible. *See id.* at 1905–7 (Sotomayor, J., concurring).

[127] *See* Mocsary, *Young Adults*, *supra* note 16, at 610–11 & nn.24–26 (citing sources from commentators, academics, Congress, and Justices); *see also supra* Part I.

[128] *See* Mocsary, *Distant Reading*, *supra* note 16, at 42 & n.10 (citing examples of open judicial hostility to arms rights).

Second, no one complaining post-*Bruen* about the allegedly insurmountable problems of relying on history and tradition[129] had criticized the use of history under the pre-*Bruen* Two-Part Test. Before *Bruen*, the Two-Part Test's history-based step served only to filter out cases from Second Amendment protection. One explanation for the newfound protests is that many judges and scholars favor narrower gun rights. Now that history is a basis for *affirming* gun rights and upsetting gun regulation, critics claim that it is unmanageable.

If a history-and-tradition guidepost is truly unworkable, as many now claim, then it should also be unworkable in at least some applications of the Two-Part Test. One would expect someone now criticizing *Bruen*'s method to have made similar complaints before it was divorced from step two. The closest pre-*Bruen* complaints were courts "assuming without deciding" (and similar language) that the conduct at issue was protected by the Second Amendment, before ruling that the regulation passed step two.[130]

2. Misunderstandings, inconsistency, confusion, and madness?

Justice Jackson expressed concern that lower courts' "'misunderst[andings]'" evinced "'confusion'" among lower courts about "*Bruen*'s [methodological] madness" that is manifesting itself in inconsistency among Second Amendment adjudications.[131] But claims of "chaos" and inconsistency among lower courts "struggl[ing]" to apply *Bruen* are, at best, overstated.[132] More likely, they are efforts, sometimes by the struggling courts themselves, to undermine arms rights by undermining *Bruen*. "[T]he blame" for lower court "misunderstandings"—often, but not always, a courteous characterization by the majority—does not lie with *Bruen*.[133]

---

129 *See, e.g., Rahimi*, 144 S. Ct. at 1928–29 (Jackson, J., concurring) (citing sources); *supra* notes 31–34 and accompanying text (same).

130 *See* Joseph Greenlee, *Text, History, and Tradition: A Workable Test That Stays True to the Constitution*, DUKE CTR. FIREARMS L. (May 4, 2022), https://firearmslaw.duke.edu/2022/05/text-history-and-tradition-a-workable-test-that-stays-true-to-the-constitution.

131 *Rahimi*, 144 S. Ct. at 1926–27 (Jackson, J., concurring) (quoting sources, including the majority; first alteration in original).

132 *Id.* at 1927, 1929 n.3

133 *Id.* at 1926 ("[T]he blame may lie with us, not with them[.]"); *see United States v. Duarte*, 108 F.4th 786, 788 (9th Cir. 2024) (VanDyke, J., dissenting from denial of rehearing en banc).

To set the baseline, lower courts have been quite consistent in applying *Bruen*. A well-known 2018 study showed that under the two-part test, Second Amendment claims succeeded in 19 percent of strict-scrutiny claims and 10 percent of intermediate-scrutiny claims, with an overall success rate of 9 percent.[134] For other rights, one study found a 70 percent success rate for strict-scrutiny claims, and another found success rates of 88 and 74 percent for strict and intermediate scrutiny.[135] A newer 2023 study of the first year of post-*Bruen* claims found that 12 percent of Second Amendment claims succeeded.[136]

A comparison of the types of claims examined in the 2018 and 2023 studies shows that challenges to laws disqualifying firearm possession based on criteria like criminality, false statements in firearm purchases, the federal prohibited-person criteria in § 922(g), and machineguns—together a supermajority of the claims in both data sets—succeeded at similar single-digit rates pre- and post-*Bruen*.[137] Similar results were found in a collection of post-*Bruen* cases created for a continuing-legal-education program in April 2023.[138] Courts are not merely agreeing with each other on the main issues post-*Bruen*; they are agreeing with their pre-*Bruen* selves.

---

[134] *See* Eric Ruben & Joseph Blocher, *From Theory to Doctrine: An Empirical Analysis of the Right to Keep and Bear Arms after Heller*, 67 DUKE L.J. 1433, 1496, 1472 (2018) (finding that, between the date *Heller* was decided and February 2016, only 108 of 1,153 Second Amendment challenges "were not rejected, for an overall success rate of 9 percent"). These figures likely overestimate the number of successful challenges because they measure claims rather than final case outcomes. *See* Mocsary, *Distant Reading, supra* note 16, at 49–52. They also do not speak to how far the laws being challenged infringe the core of the right.

[135] *See* Mocsary, *Distant Reading, supra* note 16, at 54 (citing sources).

[136] *See* Jacob D. Charles, *The Dead Hand of a Silent Past*: Bruen, *Gun Rights, and the Shackles of History*, 73 DUKE L.J. 67, 126 (2023).

[137] *Compare id.* at 126–27 & n.349 (citing spreadsheet with detailed data), *with* Ruben & Blocher, *supra* note 134, App. C at xxiv–xxvi. Although parsing all data to a low level is difficult because the studies' categories do not overlap, some categories, like machinegun bans, are succeeding at a *lower* rate post-*Bruen*.

[138] *See* David B. Kopel, *Second Amendment Cases after* Bruen *Part I: Prohibitions on Types of People and Types of Arms*, LAWLINE (May 1, 2023), https://www.lawline.com/course/second-amendment-cases-after-bruen-part-i-prohibitions-on-types-of-people-and-types-of-arms.

The claims with larger changes pre- versus post-*Bruen*, and with less consistency between courts post-*Bruen*—with success rate ranges going from zero to 17 percent, to 33 to 60 percent— include age-based restrictions, license requirements, "assault weapon" bans, and location restrictions.[139] This is to be expected and shows that *Bruen* has been at least partially successful in curbing decisions based on judicial hostility to arms rights. Age-based restrictions, for example, are especially unjustified and morally questionable.[140] The term "assault weapon" was popularized by a 1980s strategy report by a gun-control group to leverage some "weapons' menacing looks coupled with the *public's confusion*" about whether they were machineguns to garner support for banning those weapons.[141]

More likely, that the success rates for these types of claims are not higher is a sign that *Bruen* has been only partially successful in curbing post-*Heller* defiance.[142] Some post-*Bruen* inconsistency has been the result of "uncivil obedience," in which "lower courts 'take the Supreme Court's opinions at face value and pursue the logic of the opinions to their ends'" to arrive at unreasonable and attention-grabbing results to criticize those opinions.[143] Defiant and uncivilly obedient opinions, combined with good-faith attempts to apply *Bruen*, create decisional inconsistency by design.

---

[139] *Compare* Charles, *supra* note 136, at 126–27 & n.349 (citing spreadsheet with detailed data), *with* Ruben & Blocher, *supra* note 134, App. C at xxiv–xxviii.

[140] *See* Mocsary, *Young Adults, supra* note 16, at 621–25 (citing sources and statistics).

[141] Robert J. Cottrol & George A. Mocsary, *Guns, Bird Feathers, and Overcriminalization: Why Courts Should Take the Second Amendment Seriously*, 14 GEO. J.L. & PUB. POL'Y 17, 35–36 (2016) (citing Josh Sugarman, *Assault Weapons and Accessories in America: Conclusion*, VIOLENCE POLICY CTR. (1988), https://www.vpc.org/studies/awaconc.htm).

[142] *See* Brannon P. Denning & Glenn H. Reynolds, *Retconning* Heller: *Five Takes on* New York State Rifle & Pistol Association, Inc. v. Bruen, 65 WM. & MARY L. REV. 79, 112–16 (2023) (citing cases); Mocsary, *Young Adults, supra* note 16, at 616–17 & nn.61–62 (same); *supra* note 35 (same).

[143] Denning & Reynolds, *supra* note 142, at 120 (quoting Brannon P. Denning, *Can Judges Be Uncivilly Obedient?*, 60 WM. & MARY L. REV. 1, 14 (2018)); *see also id.* at 120–25 (citing cases).

In addition, some inconsistent and unusual decisions in developing areas of law are to be expected.[144] As is normal, much of the (actual, but not necessarily manufactured) inconsistency between district courts will be resolved by appeals courts. Unusual and outlier decisions from appeals courts are eventually resolved by the Supreme Court. This is the common law settling. *Rahimi* is a case in point. The district court upheld Rahimi's conviction, as most thought it would. The Fifth Circuit, surprisingly, reversed. The Supreme Court reversed 8–1, easily applying *Bruen* to correct an unusual decision. This is the opposite of "a prime example of the pitfalls of *Bruen*'s approach."[145]

---

[144] *Cf.* Leo Bernabei, *Bruen as Heller: Text, History, and Tradition in the Lower Courts*, 92 FORDHAM L. REV. ONLINE 1, 21 (2024) ("Inevitably, some degree of confusion in the lower courts is to be expected after the Supreme Court announces a new legal standard."). One example occurred after the Third Circuit granted relief from § 922(g)(1)—the felon-in-possession ban—to an individual whose predicate offense was a decades-old conviction for food stamp fraud committed to feed his family. The dissent and commentators then claimed that the majority's standard would prove unworkable and render § 922(g)(1) unconstitutionally vague. *See* Range v. Att'y Gen. U.S., 69 F.4th 96, 129 (Krause, J., dissenting) (claiming that the majority's approach was "so standardless as to render [the ban] void for vagueness in any application"), *vacated sub nom.* Garland v. Range, No. 23-374, 2024 WL 3259661 (U.S. July 2, 2024); Andrew Willinger, *Litigation Highlight: En Banc Third Circuit Holds Felon Prohibitor Unconstitutional in Certain Applications*, DUKE CTR. FIREARMS L. (June 21, 2023), https://firearmslaw.duke.edu/2023/06/litigation-highlight-en-banc-third-circuit-holds-felon-prohibitor-unconstitutional-in-certain-applications ("I ultimately don't believe that the majority's approach is tenable.").

But far from causing an avalanche of successful challenges to § 922(g)(1), district courts in the Third Circuit have had no trouble distinguishing *Range*. One court, rejecting a vagueness challenge, noted that "any confusion regarding the scope of the statute following *Range* is undermined by the near unanimous treatment of the issue in this circuit." *See* United States v. Hedgepeth, No. CR-22-377, 2023 WL 7167138, at *9 (E.D. Pa. Oct. 31, 2023). Out of the hundreds of challenges to § 922(g)(1) in the Third Circuit since *Range*, only two (before the same judge) appear to have succeeded. *See* United States v. Harper, 689 F. Supp. 3d 16 (M.D. Pa. 2023); United States v. Quailes, 688 F. Supp. 3d 184 (M.D. Pa. 2023). And their rationale has been rejected by other Third Circuit district courts. *See, e.g.*, United States v. Laureano, No. 23-CR-12, 2024 WL 838887, at *8 (D.N.J. Feb. 28, 2024); United States v. Dockery, No. CR-23-068, 2023 WL 8553444, at *8 (E.D. Pa. Dec. 11, 2023) (referring to them as "outlier opinions"); United States v. Santiago, No. 23-CR-00148, 2023 WL 7167859, at *4 n.8 (E.D. Pa. Oct. 31, 2023).

[145] *Rahimi*, 144 S. Ct. at 1928 (Jackson, J., concurring).

Neither *Bruen* nor *Heller* emerged "in a vacuum," demanding historical evidence (which all Justices agree "has a role") in Second Amendment cases by "conscript[ing] parties and judges into service as amateur historians."[146] As discussed, lawyers are better suited to the task than historians.[147] Moreover, over 40 years of scholarship has elucidated the matter and will continue to do so.[148] *Rahimi* shows that judges are perfectly capable of interpreting and applying the evidence required by *Bruen.* So did *Heller,* which did not "newly unearth[]" an individual Second Amendment right after "'over two centuries,'" but rather synthesized cases and other legal sources (appropriately rejecting outliers) from around the First and Second Foundings which, on the whole, evince an individual right.[149] A non-individual Second Amendment is a 20th-century invention.[150]

A charitable view of the "confusion" surrounding the application of *Bruen*'s common-law method to novel regulations is that judges no longer know how to do it.[151] The more realistic view is that the "confusion" is an exercise in willful blindness manifested through defiance, uncivil obedience, and "concern trolling"[152] about what *Bruen* has (appropriately[153]) not yet answered.[154]

D. The Originalism Concurrences

Separate concurrences by Justices Neil M. Gorsuch, Brett M. Kavanaugh, and Amy Coney Barrett discuss originalism and achieving a constitution's role of tying the government's hands to protect minorities in a common-law system.

---

[146] *Id.* at 1926, 1928 n.2; *see supra* text accompanying note 125. *See generally Rahimi,* 144 S. Ct. 1889.

[147] *See supra* text following notes 56–58.

[148] Don B. Kates, Jr., *Handgun Prohibition and the Original Meaning of the Second Amendment,* 82 Mich. L. Rev. 204 (1983), is famous for being the first major Second Amendment law review article. Today at least two law school centers are devoted to developing the field. *See* Firearms Rsch. Ctr., https://firearmsresearchcenter.org; *see also* Duke Ctr. Firearms L., https://firearmslaw.duke.edu.

[149] *Rahimi,* 144 S. Ct. at 1928 (Jackson, J., concurring) (quoting *Heller,* 554 U.S. at 676 (Stevens, J., dissenting)); *Heller,* 554 U.S. at 598–604.

[150] *See supra* notes 77–88 and accompanying text.

[151] *See* Baude & Leider, *supra* note 49, at 1491.

[152] The author thanks Martin Edwards for this poignant phrase.

[153] *See supra* note 56 and accompanying text.

[154] *See Rahimi,* 144 S. Ct. at 1929 (Jackson, J., concurring).

The Constitution is an anti-majoritarian instrument that protects rights by restraining the "tyranny of the majority" by "tak[ing] certain policy choices off the table."[155] Judges, like the political branches, are not immune to majoritarian impulses.[156] Alexander Hamilton hoped that judges would resist this impulse via "an uncommon portion of fortitude."[157] In the case of Second Amendment adjudication, they have often fallen short.[158]

These Justices—especially Gorsuch and Kavanaugh—believe that a test to determine original meaning using text, history, and tradition is better than interest balancing at preventing judicial majoritarianism or acquiescence to legislative majoritarianism.[159] The Constitution would not be an anti-majoritarian document if judges' policy preferences controlled, and balancing "is policy by another name."[160] Balancing is a majoritarian exercise that "forces judges to act more like legislators who decide what the law should be, rather than judges who 'say what the law is,'" because balancing "requires judges to weigh the benefits of a law against its burdens— a value-laden and political task."[161]

Instead, "[c]onstitutional interpretation should reflect 'the principles adhered to, over time, by the American people, rather than those favored by the personal (and necessarily shifting) philosophical dispositions of a majority of this Court.'"[162] A historical approach focuses on "laws, practices, and understandings" from the relevant periods to discern textual meaning and embodied principles, thus

---

[155] *Heller*, 554 U.S. at 636; JOHN STUART MILL, ON LIBERTY 13 (London, John W. Parker & Son 1859); *accord* THE FEDERALIST NO. 10 at 42 (James Madison) (George W. Carey & James McClellan eds., 2001) ("[M]easures are too often decided, not according to the rules of justice, and the rights of the minor party, but by the superior force of an interested and overbearing majority[.]").

[156] *See* Mocsary, *Young Adults*, *supra* note 16, at 629–30 & n.148 (discussing and citing sources).

[157] THE FEDERALIST NO. 78 at 406 (Alexander Hamilton).

[158] *See Rahimi*, 144 S. Ct. at 1909 (Gorsuch, J., concurring); *see also supra* note 127 (citing sources).

[159] *See Rahimi*, 144 S. Ct. at 1907–09 (Gorsuch, J., concurring); *id.* at 1912 (Kavanaugh, J., concurring); *id.* at 1924 (Barrett, J., concurring).

[160] *Id.* at 1920–21 (Kavanaugh, J., concurring).

[161] *Id.*

[162] *Id.* at 1917.

excluding from consideration the judge's biases—at least to where human fortitude permits.[163]

Yet "a court must be careful not to read a principle at such a high level of generality that it waters down the right."[164] Too far an extrapolation risks replacing the right that the provision in question was "originally understood to protect"—that which was important enough to make immune to future policy determinations—with judges' values.[165]

Of course, complex questions inherent in common-law adjudication do come up.[166] But "[p]ulling principle from precedent, whether case law or history, is a standard feature of legal reasoning, and reasonable minds sometimes disagree about how broad or narrow the controlling principle should be."[167] Judicial precedent, although not all from the relevant historical time frames, includes judges' "accumulated wisdom" about a legal point—a kind of Burkean adherence to tradition, tempered by text and history.[168] But none of this countenances judges substituting their policy preferences, in the guise of balancing, for common-law analysis.[169] Similarly, "evidence of 'tradition' unmoored from original meaning is not binding law."[170]

Some have nevertheless argued that *Bruen*'s test gives too much discretion to judges.[171] No test is immune to interpretation, but a history-based one is more constraining than means-end scrutiny. That is especially true of the watered-down version of intermediate scrutiny used as part of the Two-Part Test, which allowed judges to include in their balancing anything they wanted, including history.[172]

---

[163] *Id.* at 1912; *see supra* text accompanying note 157.

[164] *Rahimi*, 144 S. Ct. at 1926 (Barrett, J., concurring); *accord id.* at 1908 (Gorsuch, J., concurring).

[165] *Id.* at 1908 (Gorsuch, J., concurring); *see id.* at 1909.

[166] *See id.* at 1916 n.4 (Kavanaugh, J., concurring); *id.* at 1925 (Barrett, J., concurring).

[167] *Rahimi*, 144 S. Ct. at 1926 (Barrett, J., concurring).

[168] *Id.* at 1920 (Kavanaugh, J., concurring); *see generally* EDMUND BURKE, REFLECTIONS ON THE REVOLUTION IN FRANCE (1790) (making the case for gleaning wisdom from long-lasting traditions).

[169] *See Rahimi*, 144 S. Ct. at 1923–24 (Kavanaugh, J., concurring).

[170] *Id.* at 1925 (Barrett, J., concurring).

[171] *See, e.g.*, Joseph Blocher & Eric Ruben, *Originalism-by-Analogy and Second Amendment Adjudication*, 133 YALE L.J. 99, 105 (2023) (arguing that *Bruen*'s method is "wildly manipulable"); *supra* notes 32–34 (citing sources).

[172] *See Rahimi*, 144 S. Ct. at 1909 (Gorsuch, J., concurring); Mocsary, *Distant Reading*, *supra* note 16, at 53.

"[H]istory tends to narrow the range of possible meanings"[173] because it is grounded in *what is* (or was) rather than judges' varying and changing proclivities.

One might rejoin that a history-based test, to the extent that it relies on the absence of a historical twin as *proof* of a modern regulation's unconstitutionality, can too easily result in legislatures losing authority that they originally had, but did not exercise.[174] But as *Rahimi* shows, *Bruen* neither requires a twin nor makes the absence (or presence) of a historical analog conclusive.[175]

Courts have good reasons, in the nature of Madisonian liquidation and desuetude,[176] to consider the absence of legislation in the past as evidence of unconstitutionality. Or preferably, such absence would establish a presumption of unconstitutionality, which would "favor liberty."[177] The Constitution is a tyranny-control document that exists to protect individuals from overbearing government. A legislature's nonexercise of an alleged power to restrict freedom is evidence that it does not need that power. Moreso if no "governments (local, state, or federal) ever extended their power . . . to the extent the government currently being challenged has."[178]

Allowing a legislature a given power provides it with another tool to make people less free. When the legislation invokes the sanction of criminal law, as firearm regulations typically do, the potential for destructive consequences to individuals is all the greater. Although "no one acquires a vested or protected right in violation of

---

[173] *Rahimi*, 144 S. Ct. at 1922 (Kavanaugh, J., concurring).

[174] *See id.* at 1925 (Barrett, J., concurring); Charles, *supra* note 136, at 111.

[175] *See supra* notes 4, 120 and surrounding text.

[176] Madisonian liquidation is the settlement of constitutional text's meaning in post-Founding practices. *See generally* William Baude, *Constitutional Liquidation*, 71 STAN. L. REV. 1 (2019); *see also, e.g.*, Anderson v. Magistrates, Mor. 1842, 1845 (Ct. Sess. 1749) ("[A] statute can be abrogated . . . by a contrary custom, inconsistent with the statute, consented to by the whole people; . . . When we say, therefore, that a statute is in desuetude, the meaning is, that a contrary universal custom has prevailed over the statute[.]").

[177] Greenlee, *supra* note 130 (challenging the proposition that historical analogizing should "be based on evidence of widespread understanding that a past practice was *protected as a right*, not simply that it existed without regulation" on the ground that this would inappropriately "[p]lace[] the burden on the people to prove the existence of their constitutional rights").

[178] *Id.*

the Constitution by long use . . . '[i]f a thing has been practised for two hundred years by common consent,'" in right-protecting fashion, it "is not something to be lightly cast aside" in constitutional interpretation.[179]

Conclusion

Rahimi shows that *Bruen* is easy to apply if one does so in good faith. Post-*Heller* denial and defiance may have done more for the advancement of originalism than anything else since originalism became a distinct legal theory. To channel Winston S. Churchill, "No one pretends that [originalism] is perfect or all-wise. Indeed . . . [originalism] is the worst form of [constitutional interpretation] except for all those other forms that have been tried."[180]

---

[179] Walz v. Tax Comm'n of N.Y.C., 397 U.S. 664, 677 (1970) (quoting Jackman v. Rosenbaum Co., 260 U.S. 22, 31 (1922)).

[180] Winston S. Churchill, Prime Minister, Address at the House of Commons (Nov. 11, 1947) (replacing "democracy" with "originalism" and "government" with "constitutional interpretation").

Law, Politics, and the Eighth Amendment

John F. Stinneford*

In *City of Grants Pass v. Johnson*,[1] the Supreme Court held that an Oregon city's anti-camping ordinance did not violate the Eighth Amendment's Cruel and Unusual Punishments Clause. The ordinance authorized fines or short prison terms for violations. The Ninth Circuit had previously found this ordinance unconstitutional on the ground that it effectively criminalized the "status" of homelessness. If a homeless person in Grants Pass, Oregon, did not have access to adequate indoor accommodations, the Ninth Circuit reasoned, her decision to sleep in a public park was "involuntary" and thus the ordinance punished her "status" rather than her "conduct." For this reason, the Ninth Circuit had held that the case was controlled by the Supreme Court's previous decision in *Robinson v. California*,[2] which had held that it is cruel and unusual to punish someone for the status of being a drug addict.

The Ninth Circuit's decision, like so many Ninth Circuit decisions, was constitutionally dubious and its reversal surprised no one. But *Grants Pass* is an important case nonetheless, for the Supreme Court's reasoning demonstrates a key uncertainty about the current Court: Will it be a serious originalist Court or merely a conservative political one? If the former, its decisions may endure. If the latter, they will be written in sand. As we will see below, the *Grants Pass* opinion gives us some reasons to be hopeful, but also significant reasons to worry.

---

* Edward Rood Eminent Scholar Chair and Professor of Law, University of Florida Levin College of Law.

[1] 144 S. Ct. 2202 (2024).

[2] 370 U.S. 660 (1962).

Grants Pass in the Lower Courts

Homelessness is a serious problem.[3] By some accounts, more people lack housing today than at any point in the last 15 years. The causes of homelessness are complicated. A large majority of homeless people suffer from mental illness and/or drug addiction. Others become homeless because of a temporary financial or health crisis, or because of a lack of affordable housing.

Cities have responded to this crisis in a variety of ways: through social services, mental health and addiction treatment, homeless shelters, and housing subsidies. Many of these services are provided through private, often religious, charitable organizations.

Nonetheless, large homeless encampments have cropped up in many American cities, particularly on the West Coast. Some homeless people join these encampments for a sense of safety or companionship. Many others join because the camps provide ready access to illegal drugs. And some join because the camps allow them to engage in other criminal activity (for example, sexual assault or theft) with relative impunity. As a result, these encampments have become a danger to public health and safety, both to those living in the encampments and to others who work or live in the city.

Cities have encouraged these encampments to disperse by offering social services and shelters, but these efforts have not been successful. Many encampment dwellers prefer to live on the street rather than in a shelter because the street offers a greater sense of freedom and does not require them to seek medical treatment, stop using illegal drugs, or follow other rules.

To reinforce the "carrot" of shelter and social services, a number of cities have turned to the "stick" of anti-vagrancy laws. Laws like these have been widely used in the English and American legal systems since at least the 14th century. They allow cities to impose trespass orders on people who occupy public property or public spaces contrary to city law, and to enforce such orders with arrest. In other words, anti-vagrancy laws allow municipalities to forcibly clear homeless encampments when the encampments' residents refuse to leave voluntarily.

---

[3] The following factual discussion is derived from the Supreme Court's majority opinion in *Grants Pass*.

Grants Pass is among these cities. It has passed laws prohibiting sleeping "on public sidewalks, streets, or alleyways," "occupying a campsite" on public property, and "[c]amping" or [o]vernight parking" in city parks. The ordinance defines a campsite as any place in which bedding or a fire has been placed "for the purpose of maintaining a temporary place to live." Penalties for violating these laws escalate from fines, to orders banning repeat violators from city parks, to criminal trespass with a maximum sentence of 30 days in prison and a $1,250 fine.

The *Grants Pass* plaintiffs filed suit to enjoin enforcement of these statutes on the ground that they impose cruel and unusual punishments on those homeless people against whom they are enforced. Both the district court and the Ninth Circuit agreed, holding that these statutes criminalized the status of homelessness because they prohibited homeless people from camping in public without providing "adequate indoor accommodations." This holding was based on two prior Supreme Court cases (*Robinson v. California* and *Powell v. Texas*) and a prior Ninth Circuit case (*Martin v. City of Boise*).[4]

Background Cases

The Eighth Amendment prohibits the infliction of "cruel and unusual punishments."[5] In *Robinson v. California*,[6] the Supreme Court held that it would be cruel and unusual to punish a defendant for the "status" of being addicted to drugs. The majority opinion contained no analysis of the text or history of the Cruel and Unusual Punishments Clause. In fact, it contained little legal analysis of any kind. Rather, the Court simply asserted:

> It is unlikely that any State at this moment in history would attempt to make it a criminal offense for a person to be mentally ill, or a leper, or to be afflicted with a venereal disease. . . . [I]n the light of contemporary human knowledge, a law which made a criminal offense of such a disease would doubtless be universally thought to be an infliction of cruel

---

[4] Martin v. City of Boise, 920 F.3d 584 (9th Cir. 2019), *abrogated by Grants Pass*, 144 S. Ct. at 2226.

[5] U.S. CONST. amend. VIII.

[6] 370 U.S. 660 (1962).

and unusual punishment in violation of the Eighth and Fourteenth Amendments.[7]

The Court held that because addiction was a disease like mental illness or leprosy, a person could not be punished for having this status: "Even one day in prison would be a cruel and unusual punishment for the 'crime' of having a common cold."[8]

Justice Byron White dissented, faulting the majority for elevating its own moral intuition over both the terms of the Constitution and the judgment of state and federal legislatures:

> I deem this application of "cruel and unusual punishment" so novel that I suspect the Court was hard put to find a way to ascribe to the Framers of the Constitution the result reached today rather than to its own notions of ordered liberty. If this case involved economic regulation, the present Court's allergy to substantive due process would surely save the statute and prevent the Court from imposing its own philosophical predilections upon state legislatures or Congress. I fail to see why the Court deems it more appropriate to write into the Constitution its own abstract notions of how best to handle the narcotics problem, for it obviously cannot match either the States or Congress in expert understanding.[9]

Six years later, in *Powell v. Texas*,[10] the Court was forced to deal with the logical implications of its decision in *Robinson*. In *Powell*, the defendant was a chronic alcoholic who had been convicted of public drunkenness. He argued that alcoholism was a disease, like drug addiction, and that his compulsion to drink robbed him of the free will necessary for criminal responsibility. Thus, he argued, it was cruel and unusual to punish him for being drunk in public. Justice Thurgood Marshall wrote the plurality opinion rejecting this argument. His opinion distinguished *Robinson* on the ground that public drunkenness required an act—appearing in public while drunk—while the crime of addiction did not. He also rejected the defendant's attempt to create a constitutional mens rea standard

---

[7] *Id.* at 666.

[8] *Id.* at 667.

[9] *Id.* at 689 (White, J., dissenting).

[10] 392 U.S. 514 (1968).

based on modern psychology, for this would be inconsistent with "[t]raditional common-law concepts of personal accountability and essential considerations of federalism."[11] He wrote that the Court could not "cast aside the centuries-long evolution of the collection of interlocking and overlapping concepts which the common law has utilized to assess the moral accountability of an individual for his antisocial deeds."[12]

Justice White concurred in the result. Although he had dissented in *Robinson*, he believed that the logic of *Robinson* prohibited punishment not only for a "status" like drug addiction or alcoholism, but also for conduct compelled by that status. Thus, he opined that *Robinson* might well prohibit punishing an alcoholic for getting drunk, and if the alcoholic were homeless, it might prohibit punishing him for public drunkenness: "For [homeless alcoholics] I would think a showing could be made that resisting drunkenness is impossible and that avoiding public places when intoxicated is also impossible. As applied to them this statute is in effect a law which bans a single act for which they may not be convicted under the Eighth Amendment—the act of getting drunk."[13] But because there was no showing that the defendant's alcoholism compelled him to appear in public while drunk, White agreed that it was constitutional to punish him for doing so.[14]

In *Martin v. City of Boise*,[15] the Ninth Circuit held that an anti-camping ordinance was cruel and unusual under *Robinson* and *Powell*. It treated Justice White's opinion in *Powell* as controlling because both White and the four *Powell* dissenters had agreed that it was unconstitutional to punish a homeless alcoholic for public drunkenness.[16] Similarly, the Ninth Circuit held, it was unconstitutional to punish homeless people for sleeping in public "so long as there is a greater number of homeless individuals in a jurisdiction

---

[11] *Id.* at 535 (plurality opinion).

[12] *Id.* at 535–36.

[13] *Id.* at 551 (White, J., concurring in the judgment).

[14] *See id.*

[15] 920 F.3d 584 (9th Cir. 2019), *abrogated by Grants Pass*, 144 S. Ct. at 2226.

[16] *Id.* at 616. This was an odd position to take, since a Supreme Court majority had subsequently endorsed *Powell*'s plurality opinion in a number of cases. *See, e.g.,* Kahler v. Kansas, 589 U.S. 271, 280 (2020).

than the number of available beds in shelters."[17] Since sleep is a universal human necessity, the court held, it was cruel and unusual to punish those who slept outside due to lack of access to adequate indoor shelter.

In *City of Grants Pass v. Johnson*, the Ninth Circuit applied this reasoning to a similar anti-camping ordinance and found the ordinance unconstitutional.[18] Before we discuss what the Supreme Court did with all of this, let's take a step back and look at the Court's Eighth Amendment jurisprudence more generally.

The Court's Anti-originalist Approach to the Cruel and Unusual Punishments Clause

Recall the *Robinson* Court's assertion that "at this moment in history" and "in the light of contemporary human knowledge," a law that punished disease "would doubtless be universally thought" cruel and unusual.[19] Two things stand out about this assertion: First, the Court appeals to contemporary rather than traditional standards to determine the constitutionality of a given punishment. Second, the Court uses no data other than its own imagination ("it would doubtless be thought") to determine the content of contemporary standards.

This reasoning is characteristic of the approach the Supreme Court took to the Cruel and Unusual Punishments Clause in the second half of the 20th and the beginning of the 21st centuries. This approach was first set forth in 1958, when a plurality opinion in *Trop v. Dulles* announced that the Court would not interpret the Clause in light of its original meaning, but according to the "evolving standards of decency that mark the progress of a maturing society."[20] History is inherently progressive, the *Trop* plurality seemed to believe, and if history is progressive then the Constitution should be as well. We should not be tied to the barbaric standards of our primitive

---

[17] *Martin*, 920 F.3d at 617 (internal citations and punctuation omitted).

[18] 72 F.4th 868 (9th Cir. 2023). In reaching this conclusion, the *Grants Pass* panel interpreted *Martin* as excluding shelters with a "mandatory religious focus" from the count of available beds on the ground that including these shelters would violate the Establishment Clause. *Id.* at 877 (quoting *Martin*, 920 F.3d at 609–10).

[19] *Robinson*, 370 U.S. at 666.

[20] Trop v. Dulles, 356 U.S. 86, 101 1958 (plurality opinion).

and superstitious past. We should focus instead on the enlightened standards of today.

The evolving standards of decency test has some surface appeal, and not just for progressives. A number of punishments used at the time of the Founding seem inconsistent with current cultural norms. For example, branding and nostril slitting were sometimes used to mark an offender and warn others that he was dangerous. The ducking stool and the pillory were used to publicly humiliate some offenders, including poor, elderly women convicted of the now-unpalatable crime of being a "common scold." "The First Congress authorized the death penalty for crimes we now consider relatively minor, such as counterfeiting."[21] Sometimes cultural standards really do change over time. For this reason, Justice Antonin Scalia once described himself as a "faint-hearted originalist" and publicly doubted whether he could uphold punishments such as branding or bodily mutilation, were a legislature to revive them.[22]

The evolving standards of decency test suffers from three fatal flaws, however: It is based on a mistaken view of history; it fails to specify how current "standards of decency" are to be determined; and it violates basic separation of powers principles.

First, history. Perhaps it was possible in the 1950s to assume that history inevitably moves in the direction of greater enlightenment and that a "mature" society will treat criminal offenders with greater kindness and "decency" than in the past. But anyone familiar with American history since the 1960s knows that this simply isn't true. We have had a wave of crime panics—first about crime rates generally, then drug crime, then "juvenile superpredators," and most recently sex offenders. Legislatures have responded by ratcheting up the harshness of punishment to demonstrate that they are in control

---

[21] John F. Stinneford, *The Original Meaning of 'Unusual': The Eighth Amendment as a Bar to Cruel Innovation*, 102 Nw. U. L. Rev. 1739, 1742 (2008).

[22] *See* Antonin Scalia, *Originalism: The Lesser Evil*, 57 U. Cin. L. Rev. 849, 864 (1989). Later in his career, Justice Scalia became less faint hearted. *See* Marcia Coyle, The Roberts Court: The Struggle for the Constitution 165 (2013); Jennifer Senior, *In Conversation: Justice Scalia*, N.Y. Mag., Oct. 14, 2013, at 24 ("[W]hat I would say now is, yes, if a state enacted a law permitting flogging, it is immensely stupid, but it is not unconstitutional.").

of the problem. As a result, we now imprison more people, and for longer periods of time, than at any prior point in our history. There certainly are punishments from the 1790s that we would consider cruel today, but overall, the criminal punishment system is much harsher now than it was then.

Second, data sources. The Supreme Court has never specified any authoritative data set to determine current standards of decency. Sometimes it has looked to jury verdicts and legislative actions, because these two bodies might be thought reliable indicators of current standards of decency. After all, juries are composed of a cross section of the people, and legislatures are elected by the people to represent their values. But the Court has never limited itself to these sources. Sometimes it has looked to the opinion of professional associations like the American Bar Association, sometimes it has looked to international opinion, and sometimes—as in *Robinson*—it has simply relied on its own imagination.

Third, separation of powers. As punishment became harsher—with strong public support—in the final decades of the 20th century, the Supreme Court found itself in a bind. Under the evolving standards of decency test, strong public support for a punishment meant, ipso facto, that the punishment was constitutional. The only punishments that could be invalidated were those that were already unpopular. But of course, these were the punishments least likely to be imposed in the first place. What was the Court to do if the government sought to impose a punishment that was both extremely harsh and broadly popular?

The Court responded to this problem with subterfuge, finding increasingly implausible ways to pretend that public opinion was opposed to a punishment that it actually supported. Sometimes, as in *Robinson*, the Court appealed to a hypothetical public opinion of its own imagining. Sometimes it engaged in creative state-counting to find a "trend" against a given punishment.[23] Sometimes (as noted above) it appealed to public opinion among

---

[23] *E.g.*, Roper v. Simmons, 543 U.S. 551, 588 (2005) (O'Connor, J., dissenting); *id.* at 609 (Scalia, J., dissenting) ("Words have no meaning if the views of less than 50% of death penalty States can constitute a national consensus.").

professional elites, or in foreign countries.[24] As this approach became increasingly untenable, the Court started openly asserting its right to use "independent judgment" to find punishments unconstitutional.[25] In practice, that meant judgment independent of any external constitutional standard, including current societal consensus.[26]

The "independent" turn in Eighth Amendment jurisprudence made the Court's decisions obviously illegitimate. It is one thing for the Court to enforce a standard that comes from the Constitution, or even from current public opinion. It is quite another thing for the Court to strike down democratically authorized punishments in the name of its own moral intuitions. To use a now-hackneyed term, such a move turns the Court into a "superlegislature," contrary to Articles I and III of the Constitution.

Paradoxically, the Court's unconstitutional arrogation of authority to itself resulted in *less* protection for criminal offenders than would a standard based on original meaning. Although the Court sometimes used the "evolving standards of decency" test to strike down applications of the death penalty that it didn't like, it declared an almost-total "hands off" policy concerning prison sentences.[27] The Court seems to have realized that a decision putting thousands of offenders on the street, based on nothing other than the Court's will, could turn public opinion decisively against the Court itself. Ultimately, less than one-thousandth of one percent of criminal offenders benefited from the evolving standards of decency test, as the Court contented itself with occasional virtue signaling concerning the death penalty.

[24] *E.g., Trop,* 356 U.S. at 102 (plurality opinion) (referencing "the international community of democracies").

[25] *E.g., Roper,* 543 U.S. at 564.

[26] *See generally id.* at 587–607 (O'Connor, J., dissenting); *id.* at 607–30 (Scalia, J., dissenting).

[27] "[F]ederal courts should be reluctant to review legislatively mandated terms of imprisonment, and . . . successful challenges to the proportionality of particular sentences should be exceedingly rare." Hutto v. Davis, 454 U.S. 370, 374 (1982) (internal quotation marks and citations omitted) (citing Rummel v. Estelle, 445 U.S. 263, 272, 274 (1980)).

Conservative Responses to the Evolving Standards of Decency Test

The "evolving standards" regime lasted over half a century, despite being both unprincipled and ineffectual. One reason for this was conservatives' failure to present a well-grounded, principled alternative. Sometimes conservatives responded to the left's willingness to make up new constitutional standards by making up new standards of their own, and sometimes they presented "originalist" arguments that were not well-grounded in text or history. These arguments seemed mainly designed to limit the reach and effectiveness of the Cruel and Unusual Punishments Clause.

The most egregious example of a made-up conservative constitutional standard is what I call the "pick your poison" requirement. During the first decade and a half of this century, anti-death-penalty activists sought to make executions impossible by persuading courts to declare the three-drug lethal injection protocol unconstitutional. Their argument was not frivolous. The three-drug protocol typically involves a barbiturate to make the offender unconscious, a paralyzing agent to render the offender (including the offender's lungs) immobile, and a heart-stopping agent to cause cardiac arrest.[28] The argument against this protocol was that if the barbiturate were improperly administered, the remaining drugs would make the offender feel like he was being simultaneously drowned and burned to death from the inside. Death by torture is a classic example of a cruel and unusual punishment. Ultimately, however, the Supreme Court found that the risk of improper administration was not significant enough to invalidate the three-drug protocol.

Anti-death-penalty activists responded to this defeat by instituting a largely successful campaign to pressure drug manufacturers to stop providing barbiturates for use in capital punishment.[29] The idea was that if states were denied barbiturates, they would have to either stop executing people or substitute a less-effective drug

---

[28] *See* Baze v. Rees, 553 U.S. 35, 44 (2008) (plurality opinion) (describing the three-drug protocol).

[29] By May 2016, "every FDA-approved drug company [had] ban[ned] the sale of drugs for such purposes," Pfizer having "clos[ed] off the last remaining open-market source of drugs used in executions." STEPHEN A. SALTZBURG ET AL., CRIMINAL LAW: CASES AND MATERIALS 391 (4th ed. 2017) (quoting Erik Eckholm, *Pfizer Prohibits Use of Its Drugs for Executions*, N.Y. TIMES (May 13, 2016), https://www.nytimes.com/2016/05/14/us/pfizer-execution-drugs-lethal-injection.html).

to render offenders unconscious. If a state chose the latter course, activists could then challenge the new three-drug protocol with the less-effective drug as cruel and unusual. This is precisely what happened. Faced with an inability to obtain barbiturates, Oklahoma announced a new protocol that used an anesthetic called midazolam to eliminate pain.[30] When a challenge to the new punishment reached the Supreme Court in the 2015 case *Glossip v. Gross*, the Court held that, to successfully challenge a method of execution, an offender must "identify an alternative that is feasible, readily implemented, and in fact significantly reduce[s] a substantial risk of severe pain."[31] Under this requirement, the state could order the cruelest method of punishment imaginable—for example, it could order than an offender be chased down and torn to death by wild beasts—and the offender would not be permitted to challenge that punishment unless he could devise an alternative means for his own execution that the courts considered both "feasible" and "readily implemented."[32]

This "pick your poison" requirement has no basis in the text or history of the Eighth Amendment, nor in any precedent. The requirement was first articulated in 2008 in an opinion that attracted the support of only three Justices.[33] The requirement's real justification was political: By forcing offenders to identify an acceptable method of execution, the *Glossip* Court checkmated death penalty abolitionists' effort to eliminate the death penalty by eliminating all acceptable methods of execution. But the price of this victory was the forfeiture of any claim to be more principled than advocates of the evolving standards of decency test.[34]

Conservatives have also advanced "originalist" interpretations of the Cruel and Unusual Punishments Clause based on incomplete textual and historical analysis. The focus of these interpretations has been to impose bright-line rules limiting the scope of the Clause. For example, in *Harmelin v. Michigan*,[35] Justice Scalia argued that the

---

[30] *See id.* at 393.

[31] Glossip v. Gross, 576 U.S. 863, 877 (2015).

[32] *Id.*

[33] *See Baze*, 553 U.S. at 52 (plurality opinion).

[34] This discussion is drawn from John F. Stinneford, *The Original Meaning of 'Cruel,'* 105 Geo. L.J. 441, 451–56 (2017).

[35] 501 U.S. 957 (1991).

original meaning of the Clause contained no proportionality principle. Under that view, the Clause prohibited only those methods of execution that would have been considered cruel at the end of the 18th century. Justice Clarence Thomas opined in *Baze v. Rees* that a method of execution could only be cruel and unusual if it were "deliberately designed to inflict pain"[36] beyond the pain inherent in death itself. Justice Thomas also argued in *Hudson v. MacMillian*[37] and *Helling v. McKinney*[38] that poor prison conditions could not violate the original meaning of the Cruel and Unusual Punishments Clause because the conditions were not "part of the sentence for a crime."[39] As I have shown elsewhere, these opinions are characterized by a highly selective (and sometimes nonexistent) review of the historical record combined with a hefty dose of abstract policy-oriented reasoning.[40]

These opinions appear to use historical analysis instrumentally, to further the policy goal of limiting judicial discretion. If proportionality analysis has permitted free-floating judicial lawmaking, then it is useful to read the Clause as excluding proportionality analysis. If botched execution or prison conditions cases have allowed courts to improperly invade the province of the executive branch, then it is useful to limit the Clause to cover only sentences whose explicit terms exhibit cruel intent. But as we will see below, and as I discuss extensively in other articles,[41] the best evidence indicates that the original meaning of the Clause *does* contain a proportionality principle, does *not* require a showing of cruel intent, and likely governs at least some prison conditions cases. Properly understood, the Clause also constrains judicial discretion in these areas sufficiently to eliminate the danger of judicial lawmaking.

---

[36] *Baze*, 553 U.S. at 94 (Thomas, J., concurring in the judgment).

[37] 503 U.S. 1, 17 (1992) (Thomas, J., dissenting).

[38] 509 U.S. 25, 37 (1993) (Thomas, J., dissenting).

[39] *Hudson*, 503 U.S. at 18 (Thomas, J., dissenting).

[40] *See, e.g.*, Stinneford, *supra* note 21, at 1763–65; John F. Stinneford, *Rethinking Proportionality under the Cruel and Unusual Punishments Clause*, 97 VA. L. REV. 899, 934–38 (2011); Stinneford, *supra* note 34, at 453 n.61, 475 n.197, 481 n.239. In addition to providing extensive textual and historical analysis, I have been informed that these articles are excellent sleep aids.

[41] *See, e.g.*, articles cited *supra* note 40.

The Original Meaning of the Cruel and Unusual Punishments Clause

As I have shown in prior articles, the phrase "cruel and unusual punishments" was a legal term of art at the end of the 18th century. "Cruel" meant "unjustly harsh," and "unusual" meant "contrary to long usage." Thus, the phrase "cruel and unusual" originally meant "unjustly harsh in light of longstanding prior practice."[42]

The word "unusual" is key to the meaning and application of this phrase. To understand this word, we need to understand what the common law is—or at least, what the Founding generation thought it to be. Today, most lawyers are taught that judges "make" the common law based on their views of public policy. We think this because Justice Oliver Wendell Holmes said it.[43] His long bushy mustache and talent for aphorisms have cast a spell over the American legal community. But prior to Holmes, no one claimed that judges had the authority to make law. The common law was not considered judge-made law, but rather customary law: the law of "custom and long usage."[44] The basic idea was that the customs of a free people are likely to conform to natural law—to be "just" and "reasonable"—and therefore can be enforced as law. In fact, customary law was considered normatively superior to legislatively enacted law because "long usage" had shown customary law to be just and reasonable, and to enjoy the consent of the people. A new law that violated rights established through long usage was called "unusual," a term used in both England and America as a synonym for "unconstitutional."[45] For example, during the American Revolution, colonists used the terms "unusual"

---

[42] This discussion is based on the articles cited *supra* note 40, as well as John F. Stinneford, *Death, Desuetude, and Original Meaning*, 56 Wm. & Mary L. Rev. 531, 536, 577 (2014), and John F. Stinneford, *Experimental Punishments*, 95 Notre Dame L. Rev. 39, 48 (2019).

[43] *See* Oliver Wendell Holmes, Jr., The Common Law 1 (Little Brown & Co. 1923) (1881) ("[T]he intuitions of public policy, avowed or unconscious . . . have had a good deal more to do than the syllogism in determining the rules by which men should be governed."); *id.* at 5 (describing the process by which the common law developed at a high level of generality).

[44] Stinneford, *supra* note 21, at 1790.

[45] Stinneford, *supra* note 34, at 471 & n.179 (citing Stinneford, *supra* note 21, at 1799–800).

and "unconstitutional" interchangeably to describe British efforts to tax Americans without giving them representation in parliament and to deprive Americans of the right to a jury trial.[46] Both of these efforts violated longstanding common-law rights.

The Supreme Court's dilemma in adjudicating cases under the Eighth Amendment arises in part because the very purpose of punishment is to inflict pain. How do we draw the line between acceptable punishments and unconstitutional ones? Under the original meaning of the Clause, the answer is to compare the challenged punishment to those traditionally given for the same or similar crimes. If the challenged punishment is not significantly harsher than the traditional baseline, it is constitutional. If it is significantly harsher, it may be cruel and unusual.

Although this standard does not reduce Eighth Amendment cases to the certainty of a math problem, it significantly constrains judicial discretion and deprives the Supreme Court of the ability to remake the criminal punishment system in its own image. Moreover, the insight behind this standard seems a good one: The multigenerational consensus reflected in longstanding practice is more likely to be just than the public opinion of a given moment, whether that moment occurs in 1790 or today.

The original meaning of the Cruel and Unusual Punishments Clause has several additional implications for current jurisprudence.

First, the original meaning of the Clause allows for legal development over time, albeit development driven by the people rather than by judges. The great common-law thinker Edward Coke wrote, "custome loses its being if usage failes."[47] To put this idea in modern terms, when traditional punishments fall out of usage for a period of multiple generations, they have failed the test of time. If a legislature seeks to reintroduce them, they will be considered new punishments and will be judged in light of the tradition as it has survived up to that moment. This reasoning solves Justice Scalia's "faint-hearted originalist" problem.[48]

---

[46] See Stinneford, supra note 21, at 1778, 1795.

[47] Id. (cleaned up) (quoting EDWARD COKE, THE COMPLEAT COPYHOLDER (1630), reprinted in 2 THE SELECTED WRITINGS & SPEECHES OF SIR EDWARD COKE 563, 564 (Steve Sheppard ed., 2003)).

[48] See articles cited supra note 23.

Second, the original meaning of the Clause covers disproportionate punishments as well as inherently cruel methods of punishment. The evidence in both England and Founding-era America demonstrates that imposing a major punishment for a minor crime could be considered cruel and unusual. Indeed, the phrase "cruel and unusual punishments" was first written into the English Bill of Rights in response to a disproportionate punishment (life imprisonment, whippings, the pillory, a huge fine, and defrocking) inflicted on a very bad man (Titus Oates) who did a very bad thing (frame innocent people for a capital offense), but whose crime of conviction (perjury) was a mere misdemeanor. The punishment inflicted on Oates would not have been disproportionate to the crime of treason, but because it was unprecedentedly harsh for the crime of perjury, it was cruel and unusual.[49]

Notice that this standard constrains judicial discretion. Judges do not determine proportionality by relying on their own moral intuitions, but by comparing the challenged punishment to traditional punishments for the same or similar crimes.

Third, the original meaning of the Clause does not require a showing of cruel intent, and likely covers at least some prison conditions cases. Prison was invented as a mode of punishment after the ratification of the Eighth Amendment, so prison conditions were not discussed in the debate over that Amendment. But Founding-era cases make clear that when a given punishment significantly increases the risk of disproportionate suffering beyond the risk entailed by traditional punishments, that punishment may be considered cruel and unusual. For example, a Virginia court held in 1799 that it would be cruel and unusual to impose a joint fine in a criminal case. The court noted that the common law prohibited joint fines in criminal cases because default on a fine could result in incarceration. If one defendant defaulted on his portion of the joint fine, the other defendants could be incarcerated or forced to pay his portion, resulting in disproportionate punishment. It did not matter that the disproportionate penalty was neither intended by the sentencer nor a formal part of the sentence. Because the punishment departed from tradition in

---

[49] For further discussion of the Titus Oates case and its historical importance, see Stinneford, *supra* note 21, at 1759–63, and JOHN H. LANGBEIN, RENEE LETTOW LERNER, & BRUCE P. SMITH, HISTORY OF THE COMMON LAW: THE DEVELOPMENT OF ANGLO-AMERICAN LEGAL INSTITUTIONS 649–52 (2009).

a manner that significantly increased the risk of unjust suffering, it was cruel and unusual. The same principle would apply in prison conditions cases. If a given prison condition—extreme overcrowding, for example—significantly heightened the risk of violence or disease, it might be considered cruel and unusual.

Grants Pass in the Supreme Court

Grants Pass is an easy case under the original meaning of the Cruel and Unusual Punishments Clause. Anti-vagrancy laws like the one at issue in *Grants Pass* have been used in England and America since at least the 14th century.[50] Their use has been widespread throughout American history, up to and including today. Such laws have traditionally imposed much harsher punishments than the modest fines and prison sentences at issue in *Grants Pass*. There is thus no plausible argument that the anti-camping laws in *Grants Pass* are "unjustly harsh in light of longstanding prior practice."[51]

The Supreme Court did not engage in this originalist analysis in *Grants Pass*, possibly because the Court's main focus was deciding whether to overrule, limit, or extend *Robinson*.[52] The Court was particularly skeptical of the argument that the Cruel and Unusual Punishments Clause might limit the conduct that a legislature could make criminal, as opposed to limiting the punishment that might flow from such conduct. Although the Court was highly critical of *Robinson*'s holding to this effect, it opted to limit *Robinson* rather than overrule it.[53] The Court found that because the Grants Pass anti-camping statute required proof of an act, like the public intoxication statute in *Powell*, it did not punish the "status" of homelessness and was distinguishable from *Robinson*.[54]

---

[50] *See* Brief of Professor John F. Stinneford as *Amicus Curiae* in Support of Petitioner at 3, City of Grants Pass v. Johnson, 144 S. Ct. 2202 (2024) (No. 23-175); *Grants Pass*, 144 S. Ct. at 2216.

[51] Stinneford, *supra* note 34, at 464.

[52] *See Grants Pass*, 144 S. Ct. at 2220 (declining "to extend *Robinson* beyond its narrow holding").

[53] *See id.* at 2218.

[54] *Id.*

In dicta, the Court used language that came close to endorsing some of the faulty conservative opinions discussed above. In his majority opinion, Justice Neil Gorsuch wrote that the "Clause has always been considered, and properly so, to be directed at the method or kind of punishment a government may impose for the violation of criminal statutes."[55] This statement could be interpreted to agree with Justice Scalia's view that the Eighth Amendment prohibits only barbaric methods of punishment, not disproportionate punishments.[56] Justice Gorsuch also wrote that the punishments in *Grants Pass* were not cruel because they were not "designed to superadd terror, pain, or disgrace,"[57] echoing Justice Thomas's claim that a constitutional violation requires a showing of cruel intent.[58]

The *Grants Pass* Court also recognized, however, that a punishment can become unusual by falling out of usage. As discussed above, this is a corollary to the original meaning of "unusual," not the original meaning itself. This recognition in *Grants Pass* is not a wholehearted embrace of the original meaning of the Cruel and Unusual Punishments Clause, but it might be a start.

If the Court continues down a politically conservative but textually and historically questionable path, its holdings will disappear as soon as two conservative Justices are replaced by liberals. For example, Justice Scalia's claim that the Clause does not contain a proportionality principle not only runs contrary to text and history but makes the Clause unnecessarily ineffective. What should the Court do when some legislature authorizes a life sentence for a strict liability recordkeeping offense? Is it plausible that the liberty-loving Framers would draft the Clause to exclude such a scenario? It is much more practical and more principled to recognize that when a new punishment is cruelly disproportionate to the crime in light of prior practice, that punishment is cruel and unusual.

---

[55] *Id.* at 2215 (internal quotation marks and punctuation omitted) (quoting Powell v. Texas, 392 U.S. 514, 531–32 (1968) (plurality opinion)).

[56] *See, e.g., Roper*, 543 U.S. at 626 (Scalia, J., dissenting).

[57] *Grants Pass*, 144 S. Ct. at 2216 (cleaned up) (quoting Bucklew v. Precythe, 587 U.S. 119, 130 (2019)).

[58] *See, e.g., Baze*, 553 U.S. at 97 (Thomas, J., concurring in the judgment) ("Embellishments upon the death penalty designed to inflict pain for pain's sake also would have fallen comfortably within the ordinary meaning of the word 'cruel.'").

Takings and Implied Causes of Action

Ann Woolhandler,* Julia D. Mahoney,** and Michael G. Collins***

Introduction

In *DeVillier v. Texas*,[1] a group of property owners asked the Supreme Court to imply a private right of action against the State of Texas to remedy alleged violations of the Fifth Amendment's Takings Clause.[2] Without having compensated the plaintiffs, the state built a highway barrier that led to flooding of the plaintiffs' property.[3] *DeVillier* had the makings of a major property rights decision, because the question of whether the Takings Clause is "self-executing" in the sense of implying a private right of action has long remained unresolved. In the end, however, a unanimous Court determined that there was no need to grapple with this thorny constitutional issue because it had become clear in the course of litigation that "Texas state law provides a cause of action by which property owners may seek just compensation against the state."[4]

* William Minor Lile Professor and Caddell and Chapman Research Professor, University of Virginia School of Law.

** John S. Battle Professor and Joseph C. Carter, Jr., Research Professor, University of Virginia School of Law. Professor Mahoney participated in an amicus brief in *DeVillier* in support of petitioners.

*** Joseph M. Hartfield Professor and John V. Ray Research Professor, University of Virginia School of Law. Professor Collins provided brief advice upon request of an attorney for respondent. The authors thank John Harrison, Richard M. Re, and George Rutherglen for helpful comments. Nimrita Singh and Rajan Vasisht provided outstanding research assistance.

[1] 601 U.S. 285 (2024).

[2] The Takings Clause provides, "nor shall private property be taken for public use, without just compensation." U.S. Const. amend. V. The Takings Clause has been incorporated against the states under the Due Process Clause of the Fourteenth Amendment. Chicago B. & Q. R.R. Co. v. Chicago, 166 U.S. 226 (1897).

[3] 601 U.S. at 288.

[4] *Id.* at 293.

The Court in *DeVillier* thereby declined the opportunity to overhaul constitutional doctrine, opting instead to take a "wait and see" approach toward modifying the existing and highly complicated system of just compensation remedies.[5] The Court's hesitation to recognize a federal Fifth Amendment implied right of action is understandable; an implied action would presumably have allowed inverse condemnation plaintiffs to file compensation claims directly against states in federal court as federal question cases.[6] Such a result would be in tension with traditional state sovereign immunity from monetary relief in the federal courts and would raise other federalism and separation of powers concerns.

I. Procedural Tangles

To understand the stakes in *DeVillier*, it is important to know the extent of existing takings remedies—quite apart from any Fifth Amendment claim that the plaintiffs had asked the Court to create. It is also helpful to understand the procedural posture of *DeVillier* itself.

A. Current Takings Remedies

The Fifth Amendment requires that "private property [shall not] be taken for public use, without just compensation."[7] When governments wish to acquire ownership of private property, they generally meet their just compensation obligations to the property owners by initiating formal eminent domain actions, in which actions the fair market value of the property is awarded against the government.[8] Governments, however, do not always initiate eminent domain proceedings when they invade private ownership. Sovereign immunity, moreover, generally forbids private parties from directly suing a state for monetary relief without its consent.[9]

---

[5] *See* Ann Woolhandler & Julia D. Mahoney, *Federal Courts and Takings Litigation*, 97 NOTRE DAME L. REV. 679 (2022).

[6] 28 U.S.C. § 1331.

[7] U.S. CONST. amend. V.

[8] *See* Thomas W. Merrill, *The Compensation Constraint and the Scope of the Takings Clause*, 96 NOTRE DAME L. REV. 1421, 1422 (2021); *see also* Julia D. Mahoney, *Kelo's Legacy: Eminent Domain and the Future of Property Rights*, 2005 S. CT. REV. 103.

[9] *See* Julia Grant, *A Clash of Constitutional Covenants: Reconciling State Sovereign Immunity and Just Compensation*, 109 VA. L. REV. 1143 (2023).

That contrasts with municipalities, which do not generally enjoy similar sovereign immunity.[10]

Traditionally, property owners could pursue certain actions for monetary and injunctive relief addressing takings against individual governmental officers, including state as well as municipal officers.[11] Owner-initiated claims are generally denominated "inverse condemnation" actions.[12] States, over time, have made inverse condemnation actions for monetary and other relief available against states themselves (as well as against municipalities), at least in the state's own courts.

In addition to the various state-law-based remedies now available, remedies addressing takings can also be pursued under 42 U.S.C. § 1983, a federal civil rights statute which allows actions against every "person" who deprives another of constitutional rights.[13] Individual officers, state as well as local, can be sued for injunctive relief and damages under § 1983. Monetary relief, however, may be difficult to obtain against individual officers with respect to takings because, among other things, individuals can claim "good faith" or qualified immunity from damages.[14]

But this difficulty in obtaining monetary relief against individual officers under § 1983 is not a problem as to local government takings. The Court has held that municipalities are "persons" who are subject

---

[10] In referring to municipalities, we also include counties, which are treated the same as cities with respect to immunities.

[11] Potential nonimmune defendants included state and municipal officers, municipalities, and government contractors.

[12] *See* Knick v. Township of Scott, 588 U.S. 180, 186 (2019) ("Inverse condemnation is a cause of action against a governmental defendant to recover the value of property which has been taken in fact by the governmental defendant.") (internal quotation marks omitted).

[13] 42 U.S.C. § 1983: "Every person who, under color of any statute, ordinance, regulation, custom, or usage of any State . . . subjects, or causes to be subjected, any citizen of the United States or other person within the jurisdiction thereof to the deprivation of any rights, privileges, or immunities secured by the Constitution and laws, shall be liable to the party injured in an action at law, suit in equity, or other proper proceeding for redress. . . ."

[14] Under the current judge-made law of good faith or qualified immunity, mostly developed since the 1970s, an individual is not liable unless he "violate[d] clearly established statutory or constitutional rights of which a reasonable person would have known." *See, e.g.,* Harlow v. Fitzgerald, 457 U.S. 800 (1982) (enunciating this standard in an implied action against a federal official); Davis v. Scherer, 468 U.S. 183 (1984) (applying this standard in a § 1983 action).

to direct suits under § 1983.[15] Municipalities do not enjoy sovereign immunity, nor can they claim the good faith immunity from damages that is available to individual officers.[16] States, however, are doubly protected. They are not suable "persons" under § 1983, and they have sovereign immunity in the federal courts unless properly abrogated by Congress.

B. Procedures in DeVillier

At stake in *DeVillier* was the ability of property owners to pursue inverse condemnation actions for monetary relief against the state of Texas itself in the lower federal courts. But the issue was clouded by the convoluted procedural posture of *DeVillier*. States generally have made inverse condemnation actions available directly against themselves in *state* courts, but property owners cannot initiate inverse condemnation actions directly against states in *federal* courts because of the sovereign immunity and statutory limitations noted earlier. In *DeVillier*, however, Texas had opted to remove the plaintiffs' claims from state courts to a federal court.[17] Texas's removal likely waived sovereign immunity as to state-law claims, since the state did not enjoy such immunity with respect to state-law claims in state courts.[18]

---

[15] Monell v. Dep't. of Soc. Servs., 436 U.S. 658, 690 (1978).

[16] Owen v. City of Independence, 445 U.S. 622, 650 (1980). Municipalities are only liable for their laws, customs, and policies, which will generally be implicated in takings claims.

[17] In oral argument before the Court, the Texas Solicitor General explained that Texas did so because the *DeVillier* litigation comprised "four separate cases, all putative class actions" and there was "no way to put all of them in a single Texas court." Transcript of Oral Argument at 44, DeVillier v. Texas, 601 U.S. 285 (2024) (No. 22-913). In addition, the Texas Solicitor General said Texas's decision was motivated by concerns that, while its own state courts "don't have a lot of experience with implied rights of action," such issues are the "bread and butter" of the federal courts." *Id.* at 44–45.

[18] *See* Lapides v. Bd. of Regents, 535 U.S. 613, 617, 624 (2002) (holding that removal of state-law claims as to which the state had waived sovereign immunity for state-court proceedings waived the state's immunity in federal court); *cf.* Alden v. Maine, 527 U.S. 706, 748 (1999) (holding that as to federal claims, the states can assert in state courts the same sovereign immunity that they would have in federal courts). The plaintiffs sought to sideline the sovereign immunity issue due to Texas's removal. Petition for Writ of Certiorari at 19, *DeVillier*, 601 U.S. 285 (No. 22-913); Brief for Petitioners at 16 n.4, *DeVillier*, 601 U.S. 285 (No. 22-913) ("Petitioners do not concede that a State could ever invoke sovereign immunity in the face of a superior constitutional obligation to pay just compensation, but in all events Texas has waived its immunity here . . .").

In *DeVillier*, the Supreme Court granted certiorari on the following issue:

> May a person whose property is taken without compensation seek redress under the self-executing Takings Clause even if the legislature has not affirmatively provided them with a cause of action?[19]

The reader may be forgiven for concluding from this phrasing of the Question Presented that Texas law did not allow for just compensation claims against itself in state court. Indeed, the Supreme Court seems to have initially so assumed.[20] In the initial complaints and the consolidated complaint filed after removal to federal court, the plaintiffs pleaded an implied action directly under the Fifth Amendment, as well as a claim under the Texas Constitution.[21] Texas sought to dismiss the Fifth Amendment claim, arguing that—as a matter of federal law—such a cause of action did not exist. The district court declined to dismiss the case,[22] certifying to the Fifth Circuit the question of whether there could be an implied Fifth Amendment claim.[23]

The Fifth Circuit panel agreed with Texas that there was no such implied federal takings claim, directing that the plaintiffs' claims be remanded to the state courts.[24] The panel assumed that the plaintiffs could raise both Texas and Fifth Amendment constitutional claims in

[19] *See DeVillier*, 601 U.S. at 287–88; Petition for Writ of Certiorari at i, *DeVillier*, 601 U.S. 285 (No. 22-913).

[20] *See DeVillier*, 601 U.S. at 292 ("The question presented asks what would happen if a property owner had no cause of action to vindicate his rights under the Takings Clause.").

[21] Joint Appendix at 24, 36, *DeVillier*, 601 U.S. 285 (No. 22-913); Brief for the United States as Amicus Curiae Supporting Respondent at 2, *DeVillier*, 601 U.S. 285 (No. 22-913).

[22] DeVillier v. Texas, No. 3:20-CV-00223, 2021 U.S. Dist. LEXIS 165951, at *6 (S.D. Tex 2021) (Magistrate's recommendation), *adopted*, 2021 U.S. Dist. LEXIS 164573 (W.D. Tex. 2021).

[23] *See* 28 U.S.C. § 1292(b); Peter W. Low, John C. Jeffries, Jr. & Curtis A. Bradley, Federal Courts and the Law of Federal-State Relations 207 (9th ed. 2018) ("The Supreme Court has not approved a new *Bivens* claim since 1980."); Bivens v. Six Unknown Fed. Narcotics Agents, 403 U.S. 388 (1971) (implying an action under the Fourth Amendment against individual federal officers).

[24] DeVillier v. Texas, 53 F.4th 904, 904 (5th Cir. 2022).

the state courts.[25] That meant the Fifth Amendment issues could be raised under a state-law cause of action that might include federal-law elements, rather than in the form of a more thoroughly federal cause of action rooted directly in the Fifth Amendment itself.[26]

Fifth Circuit Judge Andrew Oldham, dissenting from the denial of rehearing en banc, nevertheless treated the panel decision as rendering "federal takings claims non-cognizable in state or federal court."[27] The plaintiffs featured this language in a supplemental brief in support of their certiorari petition,[28] and their merits brief made a similar argument.[29]

The Supreme Court, however, determined that a state court inverse condemnation action "provides a vehicle for takings claims based on both the Texas Constitution and the Takings Clause."[30] It therefore declined to decide what the result would be if state-law actions to vindicate plaintiffs' takings rights had been unavailable.[31]

---

[25] "The Supreme Court of Texas recognizes takings claims under the federal and state constitutions, with differing remedies and constraints turning on the character and nature of the taking." *Id.* Two of the panel judges, Judges Patrick Higginbotham and Stephen Higginson, wrote more extensive opinions accompanying the denial of the petition for rehearing en banc. *See* DeVillier v. Texas, 63 F.4th 416, 417, 420 (5th Cir. 2023); *id.* at 417 (Higginbotham, J., concurring in denial of rehearing en banc) ("The pathway for enforcement in takings by the state is rather through the state courts to the [U.S.] Supreme Court); *id.* at 426 (Higginson, J., concurring in denial of rehearing en banc) ("In short, we have long outgrown the *ancien regime* that freely implied rights of action.'") (citation omitted).

[26] The panel also opined that the state-law claim could not stay in federal court as a state-law claim with a federal ingredient because the federal issue must be "necessary to the resolution of the state-law claim." 53 F.4th at 905 n.5 (citing Mitchell v. Advanced HCS, 28 F.4th 580, 588 (5th Cir. 2022)). *See also* Lamar Co. v. Miss. Trans. Comm'n, 976 F.3d 524, 529 (5th Cir. 2022).

[27] DeVillier v. Texas, 63 F.4th 416, 426 (5th Cir. 2023) (Oldham, J., dissenting from the denial of rehearing en banc).

[28] Supplemental Brief in Support of Certiorari at 2, DeVillier v. Texas, 601 U.S. 285 (2024) (No. 22-913); *id.* (also quoting language that the "the Takings Clause [is] a dead letter" with respect to the states in the Fifth Circuit).

[29] Brief for Petitioners at 10, *DeVillier*, 601 U.S. 285 (No. 22-913) ("[T]he consequence of ruling for Texas is not that claims for compensation under the Fifth Amendment will proceed in state court. It is that they will not proceed.").

[30] *DeVillier*, 601 U.S. at 293.

[31] *Id.*

II. Traditions of Takings Remedies

By many criteria, takings claims present a strong argument for implied constitutional remedies, including monetary relief. While the Court in recent years has been reluctant to imply damages actions directly from the Constitution,[32] the Takings Clause arguably provides an explicit textual basis for such claims.[33] What is more, claims to remedy takings are well supported by the traditions of common law actions and other remedies.[34]

A. Actions in State Courts

As noted earlier, governments have long initiated proceedings to acquire property in eminent domain actions, in which property owners could obtain determinations of how much just compensation they were due as defendants to the government-initiated action.[35] Even though property owners in such proceedings were litigating against the state, sovereign immunity was no bar to compensation, because the government entity seeking condemnation had made itself amenable to the award by initiating the action as a plaintiff.

Even when the government had not initiated such an action, the property owner was not without remedies.[36] Historically, causes of action addressing governmental takings were the same as those available against private parties for invasions of property interests—actions in trespass,[37] in ejectment,[38] and for

---

[32] *See, e.g.,* Egbert v. Boule, 596 U.S. 482 (2022).

[33] *See also* U.S. CONST. art. I, § 9, cl. 2 ("The Privilege of the Writ of Habeas Corpus shall not be suspended, unless when in Cases of Rebellion or Invasion the public Safety may require it.").

[34] *See* Woolhandler & Mahoney, *supra* note 5, at 684–86.

[35] *See* Robert Brauneis, *The First Constitutional Tort: The Remedial Revolution in Nineteenth-Century State Just Compensation Law,* 52 VAND. L. REV. 57, 69–70 (1999) (indicating that sometimes legislatures provided actions only the condemnor could initiate). The account of various types of state-law claims in this section draws heavily on Brauneis's article.

[36] *See id.* at 69–72 (describing some such actions).

[37] *Id.* at 65 (describing common law actions). Trespass refers to actions for invasions of persons and property.

[38] Ejectment is a common law action to recover property from a defendant in possession.

injunctive relief.[39] These claims typically ran against individual officers, including state officers involved in the taking,[40] rather than directly against the state.[41] Officers were sued as individuals, and officers would defend by claiming that their actions were justified by law. But the defense would fail if their actions were not indeed authorized by law, or if the law was unconstitutional. In either instance, officers could not claim sovereign immunity nor good faith immunity from damages and injunctive remedies.[42] Suits against individual officers thereby accommodated the rule of law to sovereign immunity.[43]

Over time, the state courts supplemented these common law actions with additional remedies,[44] aided by various state statutory and state constitutional provisions.[45] While state sovereign immunity doctrines continued to provide some hurdles to actions directly against the states,[46] the early 20th century saw state courts increasingly willing to allow actions in state courts directly against the states, including for monetary relief.[47] Virtually all states now allow

[39] *See* Brauneis, *supra* note 35, at 98 (discussing the use of injunctions and ejectment).

[40] Government contractors and municipalities also could be subject to suits. *See id.* at 75 (indicating private corporations generally could be held liable); *id.* at 72 (discussing some immunities that municipalities could claim).

[41] *See id.* at 72 (noting states' general acceptance that states could not be sued without consent).

[42] *See id.* at 72, 79, 82–83, 109.

[43] Private bills in the legislature were also a means for receiving compensation. *See* William Michael Treanor, *The Original Understanding of the Takings Clause and the Political Process*, 95 COLUM. L. REV. 782, 783 (1995).

[44] Brauneis, *supra* note 35, at 133 (indicating that increasingly courts were allowing permanent damages, although this might make the courts more reluctant to grant injunctions).

[45] *Id.* at 69 (noting statutory actions); *id.* at 119–20 (discussing "taking or damage" provisions in state constitutions); *cf.* Brief for Professors James W. Ely, Jr., and Julia D. Mahoney and the Buckeye Institute as Amici Curiae in Support of Petitioners at 2, DeVillier v. Texas, 601 U.S. 285 (2024) (No. 22-913) ("State courts took the lead in fashioning takings jurisprudence and affirmed the just compensation principle.").

[46] Brauneis, *supra* note 35, at 135–37.

[47] *See id.* at 138–39 ("But beginning in the 1920s and 1930s, many state courts began to hold that state just compensation provisions did abrogate state sovereign immunity. . . .").

compensatory remedies against the states in state courts to address takings.[48]

B. Actions in Federal Courts

Federal courts have long entertained actions for takings against state (and local) officials under theories of individual officer liability,[49] including actions at law in trespass and ejectment and suits in equity for injunctions. But the federal courts did not entertain actions brought against the states themselves, even when states had allowed inverse condemnation actions against themselves in state courts.[50]

It should be noted that the federal government, like the states, enjoys sovereign immunity from monetary claims to which it has not consented. But the federal courts have sustained common law actions in takings claims implicating the United States when those actions were brought against federal officers as individuals—for example, by ejectment.[51] In addition to suits against individual officers, eminent domain proceedings and private bills in Congress addressed federal government takings.[52] And in 1946, the Supreme

---

[48] *See* Knick v. Township of Scott, 588 U.S. 180, 186 & n.1 (2019). Ohio is sometimes listed as an exception, but a property owner can bring a mandamus action to compel the government to initiate an eminent domain case. *See id.* Louisiana is sometimes listed as an exception, but inverse condemnation suits against governments are allowed. *Cf.* Watson Mem'l Spiritual Temple of Christ v. Korban, 387 So.3d 499 (La. 2024) (holding that mandamus would lie to compel a local governmental entity to satisfy an inverse condemnation award); *id.* (remanding to the district court to tailor a plan for the satisfaction of the judgment within a reasonable time); *cf.* Libr. of Cong. v. Shaw, 478 U.S. 310, 316 n.3 (1986) ("Prior to the creation of the Court of Claims, a citizen's only means of obtaining recompense from the Government was by requesting individually tailored waivers of sovereign immunity, through private Acts of Congress.").

[49] Woolhandler & Mahoney, *supra* note 5, at 684–86. Federal courts also entertained some eminent domain actions at the instance of landowners seeking review of certain commission determinations against local governments and government contractors. *See id.* at 686.

[50] *Cf.* Smith v. Reeves, 178 U.S. 436, 445 (1900) (holding that the state could limit its consent to be sued for tax refunds to its own courts, subject to Supreme Court review).

[51] *See, e.g.*, United States v. Lee, 106 U.S. 196 (1882).

[52] *See* Brief for the United States as Amicus Curiae Supporting Respondent at 5, 15, DeVillier v. Texas, 601 U.S. 285 (2024) (No. 22-913) (discussing private bills and tort actions).

Court interpreted a federal statute called the Tucker Act to provide for taking claims directly against the United States.[53]

All of the above state and federal remedies indirectly support the view that governments must provide adequate remedies for takings claims. But the examples also support at least two qualifications to arguments supporting an implied Fifth Amendment takings action. First, federal courts did not provide remedies directly against the sovereign states. And second, the tradition of remedies suggests that an implied action is not necessary.[54]

III. Federal Courts' Nonprovision of Remedies Directly against Sovereigns

When sovereign entities—the state or federal government—were involuntary parties, the federal courts did not allow monetary remedies against them.[55] To the extent that the Supreme Court has implied the availability of monetary remedies, it has been against individual officers or nonsovereign entities.[56] Even where states allowed such claims in *state* courts through their judge-made law, statutes, and constitutions, the state was not treated as having consented to suit in the *federal* courts.[57] And federal-court actions directly against the federal government for monetary liability required statutory authorization to abrogate sovereign immunity.[58]

---

[53] *Id.* at 18–20 (citing United States v. Causby, 328 U.S. 256 (1946)); 28 U.S.C. § 1491(a)(1). The Court had previously interpreted the Tucker Act to require some form of express or implied contract. Brief for the United States as Amicus Curiae Supporting Respondent at 18–19, *DeVillier*, 601 U.S. 285 (No. 22-913).

[54] In addition, the traditional view is that Article III does not require that lower federal courts be created. *See* Richard H. Fallon et al., Hart and Wechsler's The Federal Courts and the Federal System 307 (7th ed. 2015) [hereinafter Hart and Wechsler].

[55] There are certain exceptions, such as when the federal government properly sues a state, or a state properly sues another state. *See id.* at 921.

[56] *See* FDIC v. Meyer, 510 U.S. 471 (1994) (holding that an implied action under *Bivens v. Six Unknown Federal Narcotics Agents*, 403 U.S. 388 (1971), was not available against a federal agency).

[57] *See* Brauneis, *supra* note 35, at 139; *cf.* Richard H. Seamon, *The Asymmetry of State Sovereign Immunity*, 76 Wash. L. Rev. 1067, 1102–13 (2001) (arguing that due process should be seen as requiring state courts, if the states' other remedies are inadequate, to supply compensation remedies directly against the states in state courts).

[58] To be sure, the Court has at times employed a somewhat liberal interpretation of the Tucker Act to allow for inverse takings remedies. *See, e.g.*, United States v. Causby, 328 U.S. 256, 267 (1946).

There are two possible avenues for suing the states as defendants in federal court: state consent and congressional abrogation. As noted, the states can consent to being sued in their own courts. But consent to being sued in *state* court has not been treated as consent to being sued in the lower *federal* courts.[59] The notion of consent, however, does allow for Supreme Court review of state-court decisions in which the state has waived sovereign immunity. On direct review of state-court decisions, the Supreme Court generally takes the state courts and their causes of action as it finds them, correcting errors of federal law within the state-recognized cause of action. Where the state has substituted suits against itself for remedies that the Court might have found to be constitutionally required against an individual officer,[60] the Court has filled in remedies against the state that the Court could have compelled against the individual officer.[61]

Another possible avenue for making states involuntarily suable at the initiative of individuals is congressional abrogation. The Court has held that, within certain limitations, Congress can abrogate state sovereign immunity when acting under Section 5 of the Fourteenth Amendment, which provides that "Congress shall have power to enforce, by legislation" the provisions of the Fourteenth Amendment.[62] In some instances, the Court has required that Congress produce evidence of systemic failures of state remedies for alleged constitutional violations in order to legislatively abrogate state sovereign immunity.[63]

---

[59] *See* HART AND WECHSLER, *supra* note 54, at 919. The state can, by removal, waive its immunity with respect to claims as to which it could not assert immunity in state court. *See* cases cited *supra* note 18.

[60] *See* Carlos Manuel Vázquez, *What Is Eleventh Amendment Immunity?*, 106 YALE L.J. 1683, 1770 (1997) (discussing a right to damages from individuals as to certain mandatory federal obligations).

[61] *See id.* at 1771–73 (indicating that remedies that can run against the state are based on the state's designating itself rather than the officer as the proper party defendant); Ann Woolhandler, *The Common Law Origins of Constitutionally Compelled Remedies*, 107 YALE L.J. 77, 152–54 (1997) (providing a similar interpretation).

[62] *See* Fitzpatrick v. Bitzer, 427 U.S. 445, 452–56 (1976).

[63] For example, in *Florida Prepaid Postsecondary Education Expense Board v. College Savings Bank*, 527 U.S. 627 (1999), the Court held Congress could not make the states liable for patent violations without a showing of a pattern of unremedied patent violations by the state. But it is not clear that systemic failures are required if the legislation merely forbids what the Court has recognized as a violation of the Fourteenth Amendment and provides remedies that are congruent and proportional to the violation. *See* HART AND WECHSLER, *supra* note 54, at 959.

In any event, Congress has not abrogated state sovereign immunity for takings claims. And relatedly, Congress has not provided that states should be considered suable "persons" directly subject to compensatory or other remedies under § 1983.[64] Thus, implying an action, and an action that abrogated sovereign immunity, would run counter to Congress's prerogative to provide remedies for constitutional violations and to abrogate sovereign immunity.

IV. The Nonnecessity of an Implied Takings Remedy

Thus, despite the long tradition of takings remedies, there is no tradition of federal-court abrogation of state sovereign immunity in takings claims. In addition, the long tradition of takings remedies in both state and federal courts undermines an argument for the necessity of implying a Fifth Amendment action against states for takings. In the Supreme Court's recent implied remedies cases involving federal officials, the Court has suggested that alternative remedies obviate the need for implied actions.[65] And indeed, it was the existence of such alternative remedies that led the Court in *DeVillier* to decline to address the Fifth Amendment implied right-of-action claim.

One might argue that an implied action would bring desirable uniformity to takings compensation as against state entities. There are, however, alternative avenues for uniformity respecting Fifth Amendment requirements that do not require courts to develop an implied right of action. The absence of a thoroughly federalized implied action does not mean that the states do not consider Fifth Amendment issues, and the Supreme Court has used direct review of state-court decisions to outline major requirements for remedies. In addition, § 1983 claims against municipalities and individuals,

---

[64] Will v. Mich. Dep't. of State Police, 491 U.S. 58, 71 (1989).

[65] *See, e.g.*, Egbert v. Boule, 596 U.S. 482, 497 (2022) (reasoning that the existence of alternative remedies for alleged misconduct of border patrol agents counted against the Court's extending an implied remedy). In addition, the federalism concerns involved in implying an action directly against the state in federal court counsel hesitation. *Cf. id.* at 492 (indicating that the Court looks to whether special factors counsel hesitation in implying a remedy). Also counselling hesitation is that when Congress created a fairly comprehensive remedy for constitutional violations in 42 U.S.C. § 1983, it elected not to include states as defendants for takings claims or other constitutional violations. *See* Bush v. Lucas, 462 U.S. 367, 378, 385–86 (1983) (indicating that Congress's providing a comprehensive remedial civil service scheme weighed against implying an action under the First Amendment against individual officers).

and Tucker Act claims against the federal government, provide avenues for lower federal courts to develop takings doctrine.

What is more, the course of state takings remedies demonstrates certain benefits of disuniformity. States over time have expanded the types of compensable damages recoverable, and they have provided remedies against the states themselves.[66]

A closely analogous area illustrating the values of disuniformity and federalism involves remedies for overpayment of taxes. Similar to takings claims, a person who has been subject to an illegal tax has a strong claim to a monetary remedy. The government, after all, may be intentionally internalizing a specific amount of money that belongs to another.[67]

Similar to actions against officers as individuals for takings of land, common law actions against tax collectors as individuals were traditionally available in the state and federal courts. As against state officers sued as individuals, the federal courts allowed injunctions[68] and various forms of monetary relief such as in assumpsit and trespass.[69] But the federal courts did not provide monetary remedies against the state itself,[70] given sovereign immunity.

Over time, the states made actions for overpayments available against themselves in state courts. But even these actions directly against the state were not available in the federal courts.[71]

What is more, the Supreme Court has more generally channeled refund remedies against state and local governments to state-law causes of action even when the taxpayer alleges that the taxes violated the federal Constitution. The Tax Injunction Act of 1937 disallowed most federal-court injunctions against the enforcement of

---

[66] *See supra* notes 44–48; Brief of Minnesota et al., as *Amici Curiae* in Support of Respondent at 14–17, DeVillier v. Texas, 601 U.S. 285 (2024) (No. 22-913).

[67] *See* Ann Woolhandler & Michael G. Collins, *State Jurisdictional Independence and Federal Supremacy*, 72 FLA. L. REV. 73, 107 (2020).

[68] *See* Osborn v. Bank of the U.S., 22 U.S. (9 Wheat.) 738, 844–46 (1824) (allowing an injunction action against the state collector).

[69] *See, e.g.*, Atchison, T. & S.F. Ry. Co. v. O'Connor, 223 U.S. 280, 285 (1912) (allowing a common law assumpsit action against a state collector).

[70] *Cf.* Ford Motor Co. v. Dep't. of Treasury of Ind., 323 U.S. 459, 463–65, 470 (1945) (holding that authorization of a refund action against the state waived immunity only with respect to the state courts, not the lower federal courts, but did not foreclose Supreme Court review of the state-court decisionmaking).

[71] *See, e.g.*, Burrill v. Locomobile Co., 258 U.S. 34, 37–38 (1922).

taxes so long as a "plain, speedy, and efficient remedy" exists in state courts.[72] And the Court declined to read § 1983 as allowing monetary relief against suable parties (such as municipalities and individual collectors) where state refund remedies are available, even though such monetary remedies are not explicitly barred by the Tax Injunction Act.[73]

In many ways, the state remedies exceed likely constitutional minima. Remedies could be sought directly against the states, payment under protest generally is not required, and taxpayer mistake rather than government illegality is commonly a ground for relief. As for these remedies that must be pursued in the state courts, direct review by the Supreme Court has been available to correct constitutional errors.[74] As with takings, there is no compelling need to federalize tax remedies with respect to state taxes even when the tax is alleged to be unconstitutional.

One similarly sees useful variation in the area of habeas corpus. The federal courts supply remedies for certain constitutional violations, but federal statutes and federal courts impose numerous hurdles to obtaining relief.[75] States provide a somewhat different set of postconviction remedies. Some such remedies exceed those that the federal courts supply, including claims for innocence based on new evidence.[76] All states provide for postconviction DNA testing by statute, and the states may provide more leniency as to procedural defaults and statutes of limitation than the federal courts.[77]

To the extent that an implied takings action would have to be entertained in both state and federal courts against the states, such actions might tend to undermine state experimentation with their

---

[72] The Tax Injunction Act of 1937, 50 Stat. 738, 28 U.S.C. § 1341. The Johnson Act of 1934, 48 Stat. 775, 28 U.S.C. § 1343, similarly foreclosed many federal-court injunctive suits challenging state and local utility rates.

[73] *See, e.g.,* Fair Assessment in Real Est. Ass'n v. McNary, 454 U.S. 100, 115–16 (1981) (holding that comity barred a § 1983 suit for damages against the county and individual officers).

[74] *See, e.g.,* McKesson Corp. v. Div. of ABT, 496 U.S. 18, 51–52 (1990).

[75] *See* 28 U.S.C. § 2254.

[76] *See* Brandon L. Garrett & Lee Kovarsky, Federal Habeas Corpus 163 (2013); 1 Donald E. Wilkes, Jr., State Postconviction Remedies and Relief Handbook 2017–2018 § 1:4, at 7–8 (2017) (finding 37 states provide such relief under their main postconviction mechanisms).

[77] Woolhandler & Collins, *supra* note 67, at 120–21 (citing authority).

own remedies. States would not be precluded from having differing claims, but the states might tend to restrain their own efforts if compelled to follow the details of a thoroughly federalized claim.[78] As Professor Paul Bator asked, "Do we not derive enormous benefits from having a variety of institutional 'sets' within which issues of federal constitutional law are addressed?"[79]

V. Congressional Power to Control Lower-Federal-Court Jurisdiction

As discussed above, the tradition of takings remedies does not support an implied action against the sovereign state in the federal courts. And the tradition of remedies also suggests that there is no pressing need to imply such an action. What is more, an implied action against the state could undermine the presumptive congressional allocation of jurisdiction between the federal and state courts.

For the most part, federal courts, under their "federal question" jurisdiction (28 U.S.C. § 1331), entertain claims in which federal law provides a cause of action.[80] Generally, such federal actions are statutory, such as lawsuits under the antitrust or employment discrimination laws. But a federal judge-made implied Fifth Amendment action would also command an original federal forum under § 1331.

The *DeVillier* Court did not decide whether to imply such a Fifth Amendment claim, reasoning that state-law claims sufficiently addressed Fifth Amendment issues. But a state-law claim that incorporates a significant and contested issue of federal law[81] could possibly obtain lower-federal-court jurisdiction under § 1331.[82] The Court has sometimes indicated that a plaintiff's state-law claim must "necessarily raise" a federal issue,[83] and the Fifth Circuit has read this as

---

[78] *Id.* at 121–22.

[79] *See* Paul M. Bator, *The State Courts and Federal Constitutional Litigation*, 22 Wm. & Mary L. Rev. 605, 634 (1981).

[80] *See, e.g.*, Am. Well Works Co. v. Layne & Bowler, 241 U.S. 257, 260 (1916).

[81] *See* Grable & Sons Metal Prods., Inc. v. Darue Eng'g & Mfg., 545 U.S. 308, 313 (2005); Hart and Wechsler, *supra* note 54, at 817 ("[J]urisdiction under § 1331 has been upheld in some cases not involving a federal cause of action, on the basis that a state law cause of action incorporates a question of federal law in a fashion that merits the exercise of federal question jurisdiction. . . .").

[82] *See, e.g.*, Smith v. Kan. City Title & Tr. Co., 255 U.S. 180, 199 (1921).

[83] *See, e.g.*, *Grable*, 545 U.S. at 314.

meaning that the federal issue will necessarily have to be decided in the case. Presumably because takings claims often can be resolved on state-law grounds, the Fifth Circuit indicated that *DeVillier* should not receive an original federal forum under § 1331 and therefore should be remanded to state court.[84]

Another requirement for such state-law causes of action with federal ingredients to obtain an original federal forum is that the type of action should not upset Congress's presumptive allocation of jurisdiction to the federal courts.[85] For example, tort claims alleging negligence per se based on violation of a federal law are generally jurisdictionally disallowed,[86] because, inter alia, they might bring in a raft of state-law tort claims as to which Congress did not provide a federal cause of action.

The Supreme Court's remand in *DeVillier* left unclear whether the state-law claim with a federal takings ingredient could proceed in federal court.[87] But sovereign immunity would normally prevent the plaintiff from filing such an action against the state in a federal court. If the state removed an action that could have proceeded against the state in the state court, the state would have waived its immunity in the federal court with respect to that action. Although that sort of removal occurred in *DeVillier*, it is not likely to happen often.

A different matter would be presented, however, if the Court did imply a federal cause of action directly under the Fifth Amendment. If one assumes that the primary reason for implying such an action is to provide a monetary remedy directly against the state without a sovereign immunity bar, then plaintiffs could routinely file inverse condemnation claims for monetary relief in the lower federal courts

---

[84] DeVillier v. Texas, 53 F.4th 904 at n.5 (5th Cir. 2022). The Fifth Circuit's "necessarily decided" requirement may be unduly narrow, given the vagaries of what may be decided in the course of litigation.

[85] *See Grable*, 545 U.S. at 313.

[86] *See, e.g.*, Merrell Dow Pharms. v. Thompson, 478 U.S. 804, 812 (1986).

[87] The Fifth Circuit had reversed the district court's refusal to dismiss the implied Fifth Amendment claim and remanded with directions that the action should proceed in state court. *See* 54 F.4th 904, 904 (5th Cir. 2022). The Supreme Court order states, "The judgment of the Court of Appeals is vacated, and the case is remanded for further proceedings consistent with this opinion." *DeVillier*, 601 U.S. at 293.

against states as an action arising under federal law.[88] As an action deriving directly from the Fifth Amendment, the claim would not need to satisfy the standard of not altering Congress's presumptive allocation of jurisdiction between state and federal courts. Nevertheless, such an implied action would significantly alter lower-federal-court jurisdiction by allowing takings actions directly against the state in federal court in the teeth of sovereign immunity—a result that Congress has not explicitly authorized.

VI. What If States Abrogate Remedies?

The Supreme Court and many amici assumed that *DeVillier* presented the question of whether the Court should imply a takings remedy directly under the Fifth Amendment when the state did not provide adequate state-law remedies. In fact, Texas did provide such remedies, as do the states more generally. Failure of the state courts in meeting Fifth Amendment standards can largely be addressed on direct review by the Supreme Court of state-court decisions. As noted above, the Supreme Court has often corrected state errors on review within the setting of causes of action that the state has provided against itself. But if the state purports to abrogate effective remedies against itself and further attempts to cut off remedies against individual officers, the Supreme Court on direct review could still require states courts to provide tort and injunctive remedies against individual officers.[89]

Not only can the Supreme Court correct errors on direct review, but the federal courts may provide significant remedies under § 1983 even within the strictures of sovereign immunity. Injunction actions that technically run against individual state officers are available. So too are damages actions. Under current doctrine, monetary remedies

[88] The Court, to an extent, has allowed such claims against municipalities under § 1983, although two of this article's authors have suggested that the federal courts might want to limit such actions through an abstention doctrine designed for land-use cases. Woolhandler & Mahoney, *supra* note 5, at 708–11.

[89] *See, e.g.*, Poindexter v. Greenhow, 114 U.S. 270, 302–03 (1884) (holding on direct review that the trespass action against the collector could not be repealed); Chaffin v. Taylor, 114 U.S. 309, 310 (1884) (reinstating a tort action against the collector that the state court had dismissed); *cf.* Ward v. Bd. of Cnty. Comm'rs, 253 U.S. 17 (1920) (requiring the state court to entertain an assumpsit action) (discussed in Woolhandler, *supra* note 61, at 120–21, 137).

against individuals face barriers of qualified immunity. But historically such immunity was unavailable, and the current federal courts could dispense with those immunities to provide just compensation.[90] While individual officers may lack the resources to pay the judgments, the government likely would pay such awards.[91]

Holding individuals liable may strike some as a byzantine way to provide just compensation, but such individual liability long provided constitutionally sufficient remedies for takings. And such remedies leave to the state itself discretion to substitute other constitutionally adequate remedies. For example, in *McKesson Corp. v. Division of Alcoholic Beverages & Tobacco*,[92] the Court on direct review indicated that the state must provide the tax refund remedy that it promised.[93] But it also indicated that going forward, the state might substitute prepayment remedies.[94] And for a discriminatory tax, it could remedy the inequality by imposing higher taxes on others for the relevant tax period.[95]

Conclusion

History and precedent tell us that the just compensation requirement has been implemented by a complex network of remedies providing multiple avenues for redress. To say that the Takings Clause requires adequate remedies is not the same as saying that the Clause requires an implied action directly against the states that can be brought in federal courts. If one operates with a preference for taking constitutional doctrine down to the studs, a cause of action directly against the states under the Fifth Amendment might seem like a clean result. But one must be wary of displacing a network that works reasonably well, and with greater respect for the states and Congress, than would an implied Fifth Amendment action.

[90] *See* Woolhandler, *supra* note 61, at 153.

[91] *Cf.* Joanna Schwartz, *Police Indemnification*, 89 N.Y.U. L. REV. 885 (2014).

[92] 496 U.S. 18, 36–38 (1990).

[93] *Id.* at 31.

[94] *Id.* at 36–37.

[95] *See id.* at 35–36, 40. Similarly, in *Missouri v. Jenkins*, 495 U.S. 33, 51 (1990), the Court held that the district court should not order a specific tax to pay for a desegregation remedy but should rather leave discretion to the School Board to determine how to raise money. *See also id.* (remedies should show "proper respect for the integrity and functions of local government institutions").

Heart of Mootness: *FBI v. Fikre*

Clark Neily*

Imagine you join a socially active church near your home in Portland, Oregon, that strongly opposes illegal wildlife trade and sometimes stages protests outside the embassies of responsible countries. On a trip to investigate elephant poaching in South Africa, you receive an invitation to attend a security briefing at the American Embassy. You arrive at the appointed time, only to be escorted to a small office where two grim-faced men in dark suits are waiting for you. They cut right to the chase: "We're Special Agents Kurtz and Marlow, and we're working on an investigation involving members of your church. We've put you on the No Fly List, which means you're effectively stranded abroad until we remove you—which we will do if you agree to become an FBI informant and spy on your fellow congregants in connection with our investigation. So, what do you say?"

You refuse and spend the next five years in the proverbial wilderness, separated from your family as you try to find a way back home. During this odyssey, you're kidnapped and tortured for several months by another country's secret police (who claim to be acting at the behest of the U.S. government), and your spouse divorces you due to the rigors of the separation and the stigma of your watchlist status. You eventually make it back to America and file suit against the FBI, which then takes you off the No Fly List without explanation and moves to dismiss your case as moot. You fight them up and down the federal court system for nearly a decade on that point until the Supreme Court unanimously slaps down the government's mootness argument, clearing the way for you to finally learn the truth behind the FBI's decision to ruin your life.

* * *

* Senior Vice President for Legal Studies at the Cato Institute.

As difficult as it may be to imagine an American citizen being subjected to such a horrific ordeal—especially by an agency whose official motto is "Fidelity, Bravery, and Integrity"[1]—those are the essential facts of *Federal Bureau of Investigation v. Fikre*,[2] one of several cases this Term in which government officials employed various stratagems designed to forestall judicial review of their alleged misconduct. Overall, the results were mixed.[3]

As the brevity and unanimity of the decision suggest, *Fikre* was neither a close call nor a difficult case to get right. Nor did it break any fresh doctrinal ground or resolve any meaningful split of legal authority among lower courts. So why bother writing (or reading) about it, especially in a Term with so many blockbuster cases? The short answer is because the government tried to pull a fast one on the Supreme Court and got smacked down—gently, but firmly. And despite being unsuccessful in this case, the government's attempt to derail a potentially meritorious case through procedural legerdemain warrants close scrutiny. Because when we catch government officials trying to steal a base—as they've succeeded in doing on this issue in some lower courts and as they tried mightily to do here—we should call attention to it. "If you see something, say something."[4]

Perhaps the most interesting thing about the short and seemingly unremarkable opinion in *Fikre* is how it evokes the so-called "Iceberg Theory" (or "Theory of Omission") often associated

---

[1] FBI, *History*, https://www.fbi.gov/history/seal-motto#.

[2] 601 U.S. 234 (2024). Yonas Fikre's government-authored ordeal began in Sudan, not South Africa, and he was there to sell consumer electronics, not to investigate elephant poaching. Also, he attended a mosque in Portland, not a church. The facts of Fikre's case are otherwise materially identical to the hypothetical. *See id.* at 237–38.

[3] *See, e.g.*, Trump v. United States, 144 S. Ct. 2313 (2024) (establishing broad immunity from criminal prosecution for acts of former Presidents taken while in office); Moody v. NetChoice, 144 S. Ct. 2383 (2024) (remanding challenges to Florida and Texas laws restricting content moderation by social media platforms); Murthy v. Missouri, 144 S. Ct. 1972 (2024) (holding that plaintiffs lacked standing to sue federal officials regarding "jaw-boning" of social media companies); Dep't of Agric. Rural Dev. Rural Hous. Serv. v. Kirtz, 601 U.S. 42 (2024) (denying federal agency's assertion of sovereign immunity as defense to Fair Credit Reporting Act suit); Food & Drug Admin. v. All. for Hippocratic Med., 602 U.S. 367 (2024) (holding that plaintiff-physicians lacked standing to challenge FDA rules regarding approval and availability of abortion-inducing drug mifepristone).

[4] DEP'T OF HOMELAND SEC., *If you see something, say something*, https://www.dhs.gov/see-something-say-something.

with Ernest Hemingway's writing, in which some of the most important characters or actions exist outside the formal narrative and are never explicitly mentioned by the author. In *Fikre*, this unnamed-but-nevertheless-omnipresent character goes by the name of "strategic mooting," an increasingly common (and pernicious) practice that enables rights-violating government officials to shield their unlawful acts from judicial scrutiny and deny their victims the relief to which they are justly entitled.[5] And while the Justices never mention "strategic mooting" by name in their decision, make no mistake—it's the other villain in *FBI v. Fikre*.

I'll begin by describing in more detail what the FBI tried to do here, both in the field and in court, and then explain how an incoherence in the Supreme Court's mootness doctrine has been exploited by government officials to shield their own misconduct from judicial review. I conclude with some thoughts about how judges can more effectively rebuff this unseemly practice and discourage the time- and resource-wasting litigation tactics so vividly on display in this and other cases described below.

The FBI is a domestic law-enforcement organization. So one question that jumps off the page in *Fikre* is why U.S.-based FBI agents traveled all the way to Sudan to meet with a U.S.-domiciled American citizen regarding a U.S.-based investigation when they could just as well have met with him back in Oregon, where he resides and where the mosque in question is located.[6] Presumably, the discovery process will shed further light on that question. But the most plausible explanation right now is that the agents wanted to confront Yonas Fikre in a setting of particular vulnerability for him and exceptional leverage for them in order to maximize the likelihood that he would agree to spy on his fellow congregants back in Portland. Informing a U.S. citizen who has left the protections and comforts of American soil that he will be marooned abroad indefinitely if he refuses to cooperate represents an extraordinary exercise of government power. And the question presented by Fikre's complaint—as in most constitutional litigation—is whether the exercise of that power was legal.

---

[5] For further discussion of "strategic mooting," see Joseph C. Davis & Nicholas R. Reaves, *The Point* Isn't *Moot: How Lower Courts Have Blessed Government Abuse of the Voluntary Cessation Doctrine*, 129 Yale L.J. Forum 325–42 (Nov. 26, 2019), https://www.yalelawjournal.org/pdf/DavisandReaves_ThePointIsntMoot_3f4xopmf.pdf.

[6] *See Fikre*, 601 U.S. at 237–38.

Unsurprisingly, the FBI fought tenaciously to avoid making the disclosures necessary for a reviewing court to assess the lawfulness of the FBI's decision to place Fikre on the No Fly List. As Justice Neil Gorsuch noted somewhat dryly near the beginning of his opinion, "it appears no statute or publicly promulgated regulation describes the standards the government employs when adding individuals to, or removing them from, the list."[7] In other words, the process is a black box.

Also unclear is what doctrinal framework should govern challenges to the government's decision to place someone on the No Fly List. Which factors may the government lawfully consider in making that determination and which factors, if any, are impermissible? May the government include in its decisionmaking calculus traditionally forbidden characteristics such as race, ethnicity, national origin, religion, or gender?[8] And whatever the set of permissible characteristics may be, what quantum of proof, if any, must the government possess in order to legally place someone on the No Fly List? Will a mere scintilla suffice, or must there be reasonable suspicion, probable cause, or something akin to clear and convincing evidence? And does the quantum of proof depend to some extent on the gravity of the suspicion, such that A-list bomb makers or "chemical super-freaks"[9] require a lesser showing than rabble-rousing college students? But these and other questions remain largely unanswered, leaving countless people to wonder why they were put on the No Fly List and what it might take to get themselves removed.

To be clear, there can be perfectly good reasons why an agency like the FBI might be reluctant to explain publicly (or even to a judge alone, *in camera*) why it decided to put a given person on the No Fly List. Among other things, the disclosure of that information could compromise confidential sources and methods of intelligence collection, tip off genuinely bad actors that they're under surveillance, cause those bad actors to upgrade the security of their communications, or prompt them to flee to another country from which extradition or rendition may be impossible.

But there can also be wholly illegitimate reasons for putting people on the No Fly List, including a bare desire, unsupported by any

---

[7] *Id.* at 237.

[8] *See id.* at 239.

[9] *The Rock* (Don Simpson/Jerry Bruckheimer Films 1996).

concrete suspicion of wrongdoing, to pressure them into cooperating with the government in some way. Thus, in Fikre's case, it may well be that the FBI had some law-enforcement or national security interest in the mosque he attended. The FBI may have decided that it would be useful to have an informant inside that mosque, targeting Fikre simply because he happened to be the first congregant to put himself in a vulnerable position by traveling overseas. If so, not only would that be a clear abuse of power, but it would also suggest that the various governmental defendants and their counsel were less than candid when they assured the courts that Fikre "'was placed on the No Fly List in accordance with applicable policies and procedures.'"[10]

Notably, Fikre's complaint cites the notorious case of a woman named Rahinah Ibrahim, a Malaysian graduate student who studied architecture in California and inexplicably found herself on the No Fly List when trying to fly from Kuala Lumpur to San Francisco.[11] After nearly a decade of litigation, during which the government fought tooth and nail not to disclose its reason for placing Ibrahim on the No Fly List, it emerged during the bench trial that one of the FBI agents involved in her case had simply checked the wrong box on the relevant form.[12] Thus, there appears to be at least some basis for Fikre's allegation that the FBI's reasons for putting him on the No Fly List were improper. And its reasons for taking him off the list also deserve skepticism. The FBI's effort to keep those reasons secret may have had more to do with saving face than with national security.

Those concerns are further supported by the ACLU's amicus brief, which presents as comprehensive an accounting as possible of the government's handling of No Fly List litigation.[13] The picture that

---

[10] *See, e.g.,* Petition for Writ of Certiorari at 8, *Fikre,* 601 U.S. 234 (No. 22-1178) (quoting declaration of Acting Deputy Director for Operations of the Terrorist Screening Center Christopher R. Courtright).

[11] *See* Ibrahim v. Dep't of Homeland Sec., 62 F. Supp. 3d 909, 916 (N.D. Cal. 2014).

[12] *See id.; see also* Seventh Amended Complaint, Fikre v. Christopher Wray, et al., No. 3:13-cv-00899-MO (D. Or. Dec. 18, 2019), ECF No. 145 at 13 ¶ 46.

[13] *See* Brief for the American Civil Liberties Union and the ACLU Foundation of Oregon as Amici Curiae in Support of Respondent at 14, *Fikre,* 601 U.S. 234 (No. 22-1178) (noting that of "40 U.S. persons who engaged in litigation over their placement on the No Fly List, 28—i.e., 70%—received confirmation that *they were removed from the List during litigation*") (emphasis added).

emerges, according to the ACLU, is "a pattern in which the government strategically and methodically averts judicial review by taking individual plaintiffs off the No Fly List, declaring the plaintiffs' cases effectively over, and leaving unanswered serious questions about if and how the program will be applied to those plaintiffs in the future."[14] In short, the government persistently seeks to "avoid judicial review" in No Fly List cases "through jurisdictional manipulation"[15]—that is, strategic case mooting.[16]

The opportunity for strategic mooting arises from an approach-avoidance conflict in the Supreme Court's overall jurisprudence for determining which cases are properly before the federal courts. The Court has consistently acknowledged its "virtually unflagging obligation to hear and resolve questions properly before it."[17] Yet the Court has nevertheless churned out a steady profusion of avoidance doctrines that are only tenuously grounded—if grounded at all—in any plausible construction of governing law, including Article III's "case or controversy" provision.[18] These judicially confected litigation off-ramps include (1) prudential standing and ripeness rules,[19] (2) comity-promoting abstention doctrines,[20] (3) heightened pleading requirements,[21] and (4) invented-from-whole-cloth defenses, such as qualified immunity[22]

---

[14] *Id.* at 4.

[15] *Id.* at 16.

[16] *Id.* at 21; *c.f. generally* Davis & Reaves, *Abuse of the Voluntary Cessation Doctrine*, *supra* note 5.

[17] *Fikre*, 601 U.S. at 240 (internal quotation marks omitted).

[18] *See* U.S. CONST. art. III, § 2.

[19] *See* S. Todd Brown, *The Story of Prudential Standing*, 42 HASTINGS CONST. L.Q. 95, 96 (2014) ("Technically speaking, prudential standing is not really 'standing' at all; it is merely a judicially crafted set of exceptions to the obligation to hear and decide matters that are within the court's jurisdiction.").

[20] *See generally* John Harland Giammatteo, *The New Comity Abstention*, 111 CALIF. L. REV. 1705 (2023).

[21] *See* Ashcroft v. Iqbal, 556 U.S. 662 (2009); Bell Atlantic Corp. v. Twombly, 550 U.S. 544 (2007).

[22] *See* Jay Schweikert, *Qualified Immunity: A Legal, Practical, and Moral Failure*, CATO INST. POL'Y ANALYSIS NO. 901 (Sept. 14, 2020), https://www.cato.org/sites/cato.org/files/2020-09/PA%20901_1.pdf.

and absolute prosecutorial immunity.[23] Thus, the Justices assure themselves (and the public) that the doors to federal courthouses are open to people with colorable claims while simultaneously festooning those doors with a slew of case-killing locks, buzzers, and barricades.

These barricades include mootness doctrine, which seeks to prevent courts from issuing impermissible advisory opinions regarding essentially hypothetical questions and also to avoid the pointless expenditure of judicial resources on once-viable legal disputes where there is no longer anything at stake for the parties.[24] As Justice Gorsuch explained in *Fikre*, "Sometimes, events in the world overtake those in the courtroom, and a complaining party manages to secure outside of litigation all the relief he might have won in it."[25] Such cases must be dismissed as moot, the Justices said, because "[t]he limited authority vested in federal courts to decide cases and controversies means that they may no more pronounce on past actions that do not have any 'continuing effect' in the real world than they may shirk decision on those that do."[26]

But the line between a still-viable case where there is enough at stake to merit judicial review and an ostensibly moot case can be vanishingly thin. This was illustrated several years ago in a case called *Uzuegbunam v. Preczewski*, which involved a challenge to the application of a Georgia college's speech code that restricted religious expression on campus.[27] After initially seeking to defend the restriction, the college officials "quickly abandoned that strategy and instead decided to get rid of the challenged policies."[28] This rendered Chike Uzuegbunam's request for injunctive relief superfluous, and the defendants moved to dismiss the case on the grounds that

---

[23] *See* Imbler v. Pachtman, 424 U.S. 409 (1976); *see also* William Bock, *The Idiosyncrasies of Imbler: Absolute Immunity for Prosecutors Makes Absolutely No Sense*, B.U. Sch. of L. Dome (Jan. 26, 2024), https://sites.bu.edu/dome/2024/01/26/the-idiosyncrasies-of-imbler-absolute-immunity-for-prosecutors-makes-absolutely-no-sense/.

[24] For the first Supreme Court decision addressing the mootness doctrine and setting forth its initial impetus, see Mills v. Green, 159 U.S. 651, 653–54 (1895).

[25] *Fikre*, 601 U.S. at 240.

[26] *Id.* at 241.

[27] 592 U.S. 279 (2021).

[28] *Id.* at 284.

his claim for nominal damages "was insufficient by itself to establish standing."[29] The district and circuit courts agreed and dismissed the case.[30]

The Supreme Court reversed in an 8–1 decision, from which only Chief Justice John Roberts dissented.[31] The majority acknowledged that "if in the course of litigation a court finds that it can no longer provide a plaintiff with effectual relief, the case generally is moot."[32] In determining whether a claim for purely nominal damages (like a single dollar) satisfies that standard, the Court "look[s] to forms of relief awarded at common law."[33] And the award of nominal damages was plainly such a remedy. As the majority explained, historically "[t]he award of nominal damages was one way for plaintiffs to 'obtain a form of declaratory relief in a legal system with no general declaratory judgment act.'"[34] Thus, "by permitting plaintiffs to pursue nominal damages whenever they suffered a personal legal injury, the common law avoided the oddity of privileging small-dollar economic rights over important, but not easily quantifiable, nonpecuniary rights."[35]

But that "oddity" asserts itself with breathtaking force in cases like Fikre's. Sometimes a plaintiff like Fikre alleges truly abominable and manifestly injurious conduct but is unable to assert a claim for so much as one dollar in nominal damages because the defendant is wholly immune from suits for money damages. This can occur

---

[29] *Id.* The line between standing and mootness is often indistinct, and the Justices used the terms essentially interchangeably in the majority, concurring, and dissenting opinions. *See id.* at 282 ("[S]tanding generally assesses whether [a concrete legal] interest exists *at the outset* [of the litigation], while . . . mootness considers whether it exists *throughout the proceedings*. . . . And if in the course of litigation a court finds that it can no longer provide a plaintiff with any effectual relief, the case generally is moot.") (emphasis added); *id.* at 293 (Kavanaugh, J., concurring) (nominal damages both "satisfy the redressability requirement" and "keep an otherwise moot case alive"); *id.* at 295–96 (discussing mootness in terms of Article III's redressability requirement).

[30] Uzuegbunam v. Preczewski, 781 Fed. Appx. 824 (11th Cir. 2019); Uzuegbunaivi v. Preczewski, 378 F. Supp. 3d 1195 (N.D. Ga. 2018).

[31] *See generally Uzuegbunam*, 592 U.S. at 279.

[32] *Id.* at 282.

[33] *Id.* at 296 (Roberts, C.J., dissenting).

[34] *Id.* at 285 (majority opinion) (quoting D. LAYCOCK & R. HASEN, MODERN AMERICAN REMEDIES 636 (5th ed. 2019)).

[35] *Id.* at 289.

despite the defendant's having engaged in misconduct for which the common law would certainly have provided compensation. And which class of litigant ends up being the most frequent beneficiary of this mootness-by-mere-happenstance manifestation of judicial formalism? Why, governmental defendants, of course.

Again, courts have been prolific in the creation of legal doctrines that exempt rights-violating government actors from liability in cases where a nongovernmental defendant would pay through the nose. The result is a largely incoherent patchwork of liability and immunity. Some government entities are liable for some misconduct some of the time, whereas other government entities are completely immune from liability across the board, and still other government entities have whatever liability that they have chosen, in their largesse, to create for particular plaintiffs and claims. It has reached the point where any correspondence between a governmental defendant's exposure to financial liability today and what that same defendant's exposure would have been at common law is largely coincidental. Moreover, it seems doubtful that the existence of an Article III "case or controversy" should, in the colorful words of the Chief Justice, "depend on whether the defendant decides to fork over a buck."[36] And yet it does.[37]

Or does it? In fact, mootness doctrine features a number of exceptions that breathe life into cases where there is no money at stake—not even "a buck."[38] This is perhaps not surprising, given the essentially arbitrary distinction between victims who are owed one dollar for the government's misconduct and identically situated victims who are owed zero dollars due to the nonavailability of a nominal-damages claim. But how can a case *not* be moot if it is impossible for the judiciary to do anything more than opine that a particular defendant's past conduct was or was not unlawful? As Professor Matthew Hall explains, it is because "[t]he law of mootness lacks a coherent theoretical foundation."[39] As a result, "courts routinely hear moot cases where strong prudential reasons exist

---

[36] *Id*. at 304 (Roberts, C.J., dissenting).

[37] *Id*. at 291 (majority opinion) ("[N]o federal court has jurisdiction to enter a judgment unless it provides a remedy that can redress the plaintiff's injury.").

[38] *See* Matthew I. Hall, *The Partially Prudential Doctrine of Mootness*, 77 Geo. Wash. L. Rev. 562 (2009).

[39] *Id*.

to do so—a practice that cannot be reconciled with the belief that mootness is a mandatory jurisdictional bar."[40]

Among these prudential exceptions to mootness is the doctrine of "voluntary cessation," which provides that courts may retain jurisdiction over cases where no damages are available for past injury and where the defendant has obviated the need for a forward-looking injunction by ceasing the alleged misconduct.[41] Although it is possible to successfully moot a case through voluntary cessation, the defendant "bears the formidable burden of showing that it is *absolutely clear* the alleged wrongful behavior *could not reasonably be expected* to recur."[42] As the incongruous pairing of the categorical term "absolutely clear" with the more pliable "not reasonably expected" suggests, this is an inherently imprecise standard that puts the party who bears the burden of persuasion at a distinct disadvantage. To be sure, it is certainly possible to imagine situations where a given act could not plausibly happen again, such as if the government has razed a prison that was alleged to be unfit for human habitation. But the vast majority of civil rights claims involve policies or practices that can be commenced, suspended, and recommenced at the drop of a hat.

Moreover, as any experienced litigator knows very well, sometimes the burden of persuasion is everything. Hotly contested issues are often a sufficiently close call that a conscientious adjudicator could go either way. In those situations, there is a strong temptation for judges to simply throw up their hands and find that the party who bore the burden of persuasion fell short of carrying it—especially when the burden itself is couched in such capacious terms that it is not entirely clear what showing would be necessary to satisfy it.

Government lawyers are acutely aware that this puts them at a disadvantage. They have thus initiated a quiet campaign to shift the burden of persuasion from themselves to would-be plaintiffs in voluntary-cessation cases. In case after case, they have asserted that governmental defendants are in effect more trustworthy than "'self-interested private parties'"[43] and are therefore entitled to a

---

[40] *Id.* at 563.

[41] *See* Friends of the Earth, Inc. v. Laidlaw Envtl. Servs. (TOC), Inc., 528 U.S. 167, 189 (2000).

[42] *Id.* at 190 (emphases added).

[43] Davis & Reaves, *Abuse of the Voluntary Cessation Doctrine, supra* note 5, at 326 (quoting Sossamon v. Lone Star State of Tex., 560 F.3d 316, 325 (5th Cir. 2009)).

"'presumption of good faith.'"[44] And that campaign has been remarkably successful in the lower courts. According to Becket Fund litigators Joe Davis and Nick Reaves, as of 2019, six circuits placed a lighter burden on the government than on private litigants to show that a case was moot.[45]

In some cases, including *Fikre*, this burden-lightening/shifting strategy manifested as an explicit request for special treatment under the guise of the so-called "presumption of regularity." According to this presumption, courts will assume—"in the absence of clear evidence to the contrary"—that government actors "have properly discharged their official duties."[46] Notably, the term "presumption of regularity" appears nine times in the government's Supreme Court briefing in *Fikre* (and twice more in its oral argument to the Court), but zero times in the Supreme Court's decision and in the opinions of the courts below.[47] In short, the government was selling it hard, but the courts weren't buying. And it's no mystery why not. As explained and documented in various *Fikre* amicus briefs, the assertion that governmental defendants are more trustworthy than private litigants when disclaiming bad faith in the voluntary-cessation context emphatically fails to withstand scrutiny.

Starting with the theoretical case, the Becket Fund's amicus brief explains that the government-favoring presumption of regularity "gets things exactly backwards" because governmental defendants are "both *readier* and *abler* than private defendants to use voluntary cessation to strategically moot claims."[48] The brief then lists three distinct reasons why the government's burden in voluntary-cessation cases should, if anything, be more stringent than for private parties: (1) governmental defendants have strong incentives to strategically moot a case when faced with the "potentially enormous downstream consequences of an adverse result";[49]

---

[44] *Id.* at 333 (quoting Marcavage v. Nat'l Park Serv., 666 F.3d 856, 861 (3d Cir. 2012)).

[45] *Id.* at 333 & n.50 (citing cases).

[46] United States v. Chemical Found., 272 U.S. 1, 14–15 (1926).

[47] *See* Petition for a Writ of Certiorari at 17, *Fikre*, 601 U.S. 234 (No. 22-1178); Brief for the Petitioners at 18, 20, *Fikre*, 601 U.S. 234 (No. 22-1178); Reply Brief for the Petitioners at 6-7, *Fikre*, 601 U.S. 234 (No. 22-1178).

[48] Brief of the Becket Fund for Religious Liberty as Amicus Curiae in Support of Neither Party at 3, *Fikre*, 601 U.S. 234 (No. 22-1178).

[49] *Id.* at 9.

(2) "far more than the average private defendant, governmental defendants are repeat litigants," which gives them both the opportunity and the incentive to be selective about when to take cases the full distance and when to throw in the towel early;[50] and (3) as previously noted, "governmental defendants enjoy statutory and constitutional immunities that often insulate them from damages claims—making it much easier to strategically moot cases."[51]

Multiple amici in *Fikre* make the empirical case against lessening (or transferring) the government's burden in voluntary-cessation cases. These include the Cato Institute's Pat Eddington, whose amicus brief argues that "the presumption that government officials generally act reasonably and with good faith is not supported by experience"—to the contrary, there have been "numerous examples" of public officials "acting unreasonably and with improper motives in litigation."[52] These examples include (1) New York City's repealing a conversion-therapy law to avoid a First Amendment challenge (and one official's acknowledgment that this was done to avoid creating adverse precedent against similar statutes); (2) the Florida prison system's vigorously contesting pro se challenges to its no-kosher-meals policy but then granting an exception to the policy to a prisoner who was represented by counsel (and thus more likely to effectively challenge the policy); and (3) a similar ploy by the U.S. Bureau of Prisons in litigation over its refusal to provide deaf prisoners with sign language interpreters for religious services.[53]

Perhaps the most notorious example of strategic mooting in recent memory occurred when the Supreme Court granted certiorari in a case challenging New York City's "premises" licensing policy for handguns, which severely restricted the ability of law-abiding citizens to move lawfully owned firearms from one location to another.[54] After defending that policy vigorously—and successfully—in the

---

[50] *Id.* at 10.

[51] *Id.* at 12.

[52] Brief of Patrick G. Eddington as Amicus Curiae in Support of Respondent at 25, *Fikre*, 601 U.S. 234 (No. 22-1178).

[53] *Id.* at 25–26.

[54] *See* N.Y. State Rifle & Pistol Ass'n v. City of New York, 883 F.3d 45, 51–52 (2d Cir. 2018).

lower courts,[55] the City promptly repealed the law following the Supreme Court's cert grant in a blatant (and successful) effort to moot the case and prevent the Court from assessing the constitutionality of the challenged law.[56] As Justice Samuel Alito noted with some asperity in dissent, "Although the City had previously insisted that its ordinance served important public safety purposes, our grant of review apparently led to an epiphany of sorts, and the City quickly changed" its policy.[57]

Finally, the ACLU's amicus brief makes a strong empirical case that there is good reason to suspect that the federal government has made a similarly calculated effort to manipulate No Fly List litigation, and that its indignant denials[58] of strategic mooting are neither persuasive nor credible.[59] After meticulously documenting all of the No Fly List cases it was able to identify and what happened in each of them, the ACLU concluded that a pattern emerges. The sequence

> goes like this: When a plaintiff sues to challenge placement on the List, the government removes the plaintiff from the List and seeks to moot the case before a court has a chance to definitively weigh in on the merits of the plaintiff's challenge. And the government is often successful, even though it provides the thinnest of explanations to the reviewing court—explanations that . . . would not satisfy mootness-by-voluntary-cessation requirements in any other type of case, even one involving the government.[60]

---

[55] *See* N.Y. State Rifle & Pistol Ass'n v. City of New York, 86 F. Supp. 3d 249 (S.D.N.Y. 2015) (rejecting challenges based on the Second Amendment, fundamental right to travel, First Amendment, and dormant Commerce Clause), *aff'd*, 883 F.3d 45 (2d Cir. 2018), *cert. granted*, 139 S. Ct. 939 (2019).

[56] *See* N.Y. State Rifle & Pistol Ass'n v. City of New York, 590 U.S. 336, 338 (2020).

[57] *Id.* at 341 (Alito, J., dissenting).

[58] *See, e.g.*, Brief for the Petitioners, *Fikre*, 601 U.S. 234 (No. 22-1178) at 20 (complaining that the lower court's "uncharitable reading" of key FBI declaration "is at odds with the presumption of regularity and this Court's general acceptance of similar governmental representations").

[59] *See* Brief for the American Civil Liberties Union and the ACLU Foundation of Oregon as Amici Curiae in Support of Respondent at 13–16, *Fikre*, 601 U.S. 234 (No. 22-1178).

[60] *Id.* at 19.

Summarizing the government's litigation strategy, the ACLU echoed other amici in arguing that "unlike any other defendant, the government has managed to moot claims even where it plainly does not meet the 'heavy burden' that voluntary cessation doctrine demands," and it has done so by "invoking the presumption of regularity and the trump card of national security to justify a voluntary cessation standard that does not remotely resemble the standard that this Court has applied to all defendants alike."[61] In other words, the government tried to run a game on the Supreme Court in *Fikre*—the same one it has run successfully on at least half a dozen circuit courts[62]—and got smacked down: gently but unmistakably.

The current mootness doctrine lacks coherence, invites litigation gamesmanship, and employs a variety of half-baked kludges to lessen the violence that the doctrine does to the judiciary's "virtually unflagging obligation" to exercise the full measure of jurisdiction conferred upon it by the Constitution.[63] Nonetheless, the Supreme Court has allocated the burden of persuasion in voluntary-cessation cases with consistency and clarity.[64] It is thus both surprising and unsettling to see how much success the government has had in leading lower-court judges down the primrose path of lightening the government's burden—or even sloughing it off onto hapless plaintiffs like Yonas Fikre.[65] Those judges would do well not just to heed the Justices' unanimous rejection of the government's attempt to rejigger the voluntary-cessation rubric in *Fikre*, but also to better acquaint themselves with the real-world track record of public officials pursuing blatant—and often deeply cynical—efforts at strategic mooting across a wide variety of cases. And they should recognize that if there is a difference between

---

[61] *Id.* at 21. *Cf.* Brief of the Institute for Justice as Amicus Curiae in Support of Respondent at 10–11, *Fikre*, 601 U.S. 234 (No. 22-1178); Brief of Patrick G. Eddington as Amicus Curiae in Support of Respondent at 4, *Fikre*, 601 U.S. 234 (No. 22-1178).

[62] *See* Davis & Reaves, *Abuse of the Voluntary Cessation Doctrine*, *supra* note 5, at 333 & n.50.

[63] *Fikre*, 601 U.S. at 240 (internal quotation marks omitted).

[64] *See, e.g.*, West Virginia v. EPA, 597 U.S. 697, 719 (2022); Trinity Lutheran Church of Columbia, Inc. v. Comer, 582 U.S. 449, 457 & n.1 (2017); Parents Involved in Cmty. Sch. v. Seattle Sch. Dist. No. 1, 551 U.S. 701, 719–20 (2007).

[65] *See* Davis & Reaves, *Abuse of the Voluntary Cessation Doctrine*, *supra* note 5, at 333 & n.50.

governmental litigants and private litigants regarding a propensity for strategic mooting, it cuts exactly opposite from the way the government avers in seeking the benefits of a largely mythical "presumption of regularity" regarding its litigation strategies.

Conclusion

Governmental defendants have become extraordinarily adept at derailing potentially meritorious lawsuits that seek to shed light on their actions, elicit (honest) explanations for their decisions, and ensure accountability for their misconduct. Today, only a handful of public officials and their counsel know for sure whether the FBI had a good reason for what it did to Yonas Fikre. It subjected him to a Kafkaesque five-year odyssey, blew up his marriage by putting him on the No Fly List, and then inexplicably removed him after he filed suit—just as it has done with dozens of other No Fly List litigants. Perhaps the FBI was acting in good faith throughout Fikre's ordeal; perhaps it was not. The FBI repeatedly assured the courts, through counsel, that its decision to remove Fikre from the No Fly List in the midst of litigation was merely a coincidence and not a cynical attempt to frustrate judicial review. Perhaps those assurances were honest, perhaps they were not. Either way, the Justices should be commended for sending a clear and unanimous message that when government actors seek to moot judicial review of their plausibly unlawful policies by suspending those policies after the commencement of litigation, the judiciary will not presume the purity of their motives where no such presumption is remotely warranted.

Presidential Immunity

*Keith E. Whittington**

It is probably not a good sign for the health of the republic that in my lifetime we have developed a body of law regarding presidential immunity from legal proceedings. For most of the nation's history, such doctrines were apparently unnecessary. Presidents might have faced many problems, but the possibility of being dragged into court was not one of them.

But times change. Presidents and former Presidents now face prosecutors and process servers, and thus we have had to contemplate the circumstances in which such individuals are amenable to judicial accountability for their alleged actions. The Department of Justice has concluded that sitting Presidents cannot be criminally prosecuted.[1] The Supreme Court has held that Presidents can be made to disgorge documents for use in criminal investigations.[2] The Court has concluded that civil suits can proceed against a sitting President for his private actions, but that former Presidents cannot be subjected to personal civil suits for their official actions while in office.[3]

It was perhaps inevitable that the Court would eventually have to decide whether a former President could be held criminally liable for his conduct while in office. Inevitable perhaps, but answering the question was never going to be easy. Bromides about how no man is above the law would not get us very far in resolving the complexities involved. Experience does not provide much guidance in assessing how opening or closing the door on prosecutions might work out.

---

* David Boies Professor of Law, Yale Law School; Visiting Fellow, Hoover Institution.

[1] Robert G. Dixon, Jr., Office of Legal Counsel, *Amenability of the President, Vice President and Other Civil Officers to Federal Criminal Prosecution While in Office*, memorandum, Department of Justice (Sept. 24, 1973); Randolph D. Moss, Office of Legal Counsel, *A Sitting President's Amenability to Indictment and Criminal Prosecution*, 22 Op. O.L.C. 222 (Oct. 16, 2000).

[2] United States v. Nixon, 418 U.S. 683 (1974).

[3] Clinton v. Jones, 520 U.S. 681 (1997); Nixon v. Fitzgerald, 457 U.S. 731 (1982).

The experience with independent counsels suggests the need for some caution about assuming that criminal investigations of high officials will be rare and uncontroversial.

It was perhaps also inevitable that when the Court was called on to resolve this issue, no one was particularly happy with the result. Chief Justice John Roberts likely hoped that a consensus could be reached on the Court that might provide a framework on how to proceed while quieting partisan critics. Perhaps we will someday learn whether such a consensus was ever a practical possibility and how the majority opinion in *Trump v. United States* came about.[4] From the published opinions we have before us, it seems unlikely that a unanimous opinion from this Court was ever in the cards for a case addressing whether former President Donald Trump can be criminally prosecuted for his actions while in office. The opinion that the Court has given us, under the nominal authorship of the Chief Justice, bears all the hallmarks of an uneasy negotiation and compromise among the Justices in the majority. It will not be surprising if the Court finds itself having to revisit these issues in the not-too-distant future, when a more fractured majority will offer competing interpretations of what this Court meant. The Court has thrown the hot potato back into the hands of the lower courts, perhaps hoping that the case will not return to the Court too soon or that the circumstances will look rather different when it does.

This article examines *Trump v. United States* in several parts. Part I reviews how this issue made its way to the Court, both politically and procedurally. Part II reviews the rationales for immunity for high government officials that have been offered in other contexts. Part III examines how the majority in *Trump v. United States* attempted to address the issue. Parts IV and V examine the concurring opinion by Justice Amy Coney Barrett and the dissenting opinion by Justice Sonia Sotomayor. Part VI considers the implications of what the Court has done and where we might go from here.

---

[4] A first draft at history can be found in Joan Biskupic, *Exclusive: The Inside Story of John Roberts and Trump's Immunity Win at the Supreme Court*, CNN (July 30, 2024), https://www.cnn.com/2024/07/30/politics/supreme-court-john-roberts-trump-immunity-6-3-biskupic/index.html.

I. How Did We Get Here?

President Donald Trump had a tumultuous term of office, and it became even more so as it ended. He survived an independent counsel investigation focused on how he had won the 2016 presidential election, which expanded to include questions about how he had responded to—or obstructed—the investigation itself. No sooner had he put that investigation behind him than he found himself facing only the third presidential impeachment trial in the history of the U.S. Senate. With the stalwart support of Senate Republicans, he was not convicted on impeachment charges revolving around abuse of his presidential powers. Within weeks of his acquittal, the country was consumed by the global pandemic that defined the rest of the 2020 election year.

If that were not enough, President Trump ended his first term of office calling into question the legitimacy of the election that had brought his presidency to an end. Beyond a comprehensive campaign to sow doubt about the election results, the Trump campaign embarked on a systematic and increasingly desperate and deranged effort to overturn the election results. The effort included fruitless recounts and lawsuits that produced no evidence of the massive fraud or vote stealing that the Trump campaign alleged to have corrupted the election results.

With the clock ticking on the final certification of the election victory of his rival Joe Biden, scheduled to be performed in Congress on January 6, 2021, the Trump campaign looked for a Hail Mary play that might snatch victory from the jaws of defeat. One possibility might be to persuade a state to replace a duly elected slate of presidential electors for Joe Biden with a slate pledged to vote for Donald Trump. This would have to be done before the Electoral College met to cast its ballots on December 14, 2020. Failing that, the Trump campaign hoped that Congress might be persuaded to throw out some Biden ballots and instead count some "alternative" electoral votes in favor of Trump. *In extremis*, perhaps Vice President Mike Pence might be persuaded to unilaterally throw out some Biden ballots when opening the envelopes on January 6 "in the presence of the Senate and the House of Representatives," as the Twelfth Amendment commanded.

All those efforts proved unavailing in the end, but they were not without consequence. The unprecedented effort to overturn the apparent presidential election results by fair means or foul did significantly undermine public confidence in the integrity of American elections and made it a Republican article of faith and loyalty test that the 2020 election had been "stolen." It undoubtedly suppressed Republican voter turnout for the Georgia runoff elections for two Senate seats on January 5, 2021, likely costing the GOP control of the U.S. Senate.

More dramatically, it led to a violent assault on the Capitol Building in an effort to prevent Joe Biden from being declared the winner of the 2020 election and to prevent the peaceful transfer of power. President Trump himself headlined a "Save America March" at the White House Ellipse on the morning of January 6, 2021, promising on social media that the rally "[w]ill be wild."[5] His supporters soon began to promote the event as the "Wild Protest" in which "Patriots" will gather to "Stop the Steal" and "Fight for Trump" and "Fight for your country."[6] Tens of thousands rallied on the Ellipse, and thousands marched to the Capitol where Congress had assembled to certify the election results. Although President Trump did not manage to fulfill his apparent intent of leading the march to the Capitol "to cheer on our brave senators and congressmen and women" so that they would "take back our country," many of his supporters did make their presence known to the assembled members of Congress.[7]

Rioters broke through police lines and stormed the Capitol. As the air rang with chants of "hang Mike Pence," members of Congress fled for their lives. Meanwhile the President hunkered in the White House, glued to the television and taking in the spectacle while making no effort to restore order. Several hours later, police managed to clear the building of the rioters, and Congress finally met

[5] Carol D. Leonnig, Josh Dawsey, Peter Hermann & Jacqueline Alemany, *Trump Call Jan. 6 to "Walk Down to the Capitol" Prompted Secret Service Scramble*, WASH. POST (June 7, 2022), https://www.washingtonpost.com/politics/2022/06/07/trump-pressed-secret-service-for-plan-to-join-march-to-capitol/.

[6] U.S. SECRET SERVICE, PROTECTIVE INTELLIGENCE BRIEF: WILD PROTEST (Dec. 30, 2020), https://www.govinfo.gov/content/pkg/GPO-J6-DOC-CTRL0000101135.0001/pdf/GPO-J6-DOC-CTRL0000101135.0001.pdf.

[7] Charles Cameron & Michael Gold, *Trump Acknowledges He Wanted to Go to the Capitol on Jan. 6*, N.Y. TIMES (Mar. 1, 2024), https://www.nytimes.com/2024/05/01/us/politics/trump-capitol-jan-6.html; Charlie Savage, *Incitement to Riot? What Trump Told His Supporters before Mob Stormed Capitol*, N.Y. TIMES (Jan. 12, 2021), https://www.nytimes.com/2021/01/10/us/trump-speech-riot.html.

and completed its task of ceremonially counting the electoral ballots and declaring Joe Biden to be the President-Elect.

These events led to a second impeachment and trial of Donald Trump, though by the time of the Senate trial Joe Biden had been inaugurated as President and Trump was a private citizen and former President. This time the sole article of impeachment passed by the House charged Trump with the high crime of "inciting violence against the Government of the United States."[8] Trump was once again acquitted in his unprecedented second impeachment trial.

The impeachment verdict did not put the matter to bed. The Department of Justice pursued criminal charges against hundreds of individuals who participated in the Capitol riot. A House Select Committee was appointed to investigate the events of January 6, resulting in damning public testimony and a lengthy report. Local prosecutors began to investigate potential criminal violations associated with the "Stop the Steal" campaign. On November 18, 2022, Attorney General Merrick Garland appointed Jack Smith to be a special counsel to investigate any criminal offenses Trump might have committed associated with the events of January 6 and in relation to his retention of classified documents after leaving the presidency. Ultimately, Donald Trump faced four separate criminal indictments, two in state court and two in federal court. A state indictment in New York involved his actions during the 2016 election, and a federal indictment in Florida involved his post-presidential retention of classified documents. A state indictment in Georgia focused on his campaign to overturn the 2020 election, and a second federal indictment in Washington, D.C., arose from the events of January 6. It is that last indictment which gave rise to the question heard by the Supreme Court in *Trump v. United States*.

On August 1, 2023, Donald Trump was indicted on four counts of violating federal criminal law based on his actions while he held the office of President of the United States. All four counts involved his postelection campaign. They included allegations that he used false claims to attempt to get state officials to change electoral votes, that he organized "fraudulent slates of electors" and caused them to "transmit their false certificates to the Vice President," that he attempted to use the Department of Justice to "conduct sham election

---

[8] H.R. Res. 24, 117th Cong., 1st Sess. (Jan. 25, 2021).

crime investigations," that he attempted to persuade the Vice President "to fraudulently alter the election results," and that he sought to persuade members of Congress to delay the certification of the electoral vote using "false claims of election fraud."[9]

Trump moved to dismiss the indictment on the grounds that the alleged actions "fell within the core of his official duties" as President and that he enjoyed "absolute immunity from criminal prosecution" for such actions.[10] The district court denied the motion to dismiss, holding that "former presidents d[id] not possess absolute federal criminal immunity for any acts committed while in office."[11] On appeal, the D.C. Circuit affirmed that ruling. The circuit court concluded that presidential actions that "violated generally applicable criminal laws" were not "properly within the scope of his lawful discretion" and thus were not entitled to immunity from prosecution.[12]

In a 6–3 decision, the Supreme Court reversed the lower courts and remanded the case back for further proceedings. The opinion of the Court was written by Chief Justice Roberts, and a concurring opinion was written by Justice Amy Coney Barrett that disagreed with parts of the Chief Justice's analysis. A dissent by Justice Sonia Sotomayor was joined by Justices Elena Kagan and Ketanji Brown Jackson. A separate solo concurrence by Justice Clarence Thomas took issue with the legality of the special counsel's appointment, and a separate solo dissent by Justice Jackson discussed the implications of immunity for criminal accountability. For purposes of this essay, I focus on the opinions by Roberts, Barrett, and Sotomayor on presidential immunity.

II. Amenability of High Officials to Judicial Proceedings

Before examining how the Justices grappled with the problem of presidential immunity to criminal prosecution, it is worth noting how the Court and the Office of Legal Counsel (OLC) have approached immunity questions in the past. Over recent decades,

---

[9] Trump v. United States, 144 S. Ct. 2312, 2324–25 (2024).

[10] *Id.* at 2325.

[11] *Id.*

[12] *Id.* at 2326. For a detailed critique of the framework offered by the D.C. Circuit, see Amandeep S. Grewal, *The President's Criminal Immunity*, 77 SMU L. REV. F. 81 (2024).

the Court has constructed an elaborate body of law regarding the immunity of government officials to judicial proceedings, and the rationale for recognizing such immunity has varied depending on the context. In some ways, the problem of presidential criminal immunity is the last puzzle piece to fall into place.

One issue has not yet reached the Court, though perhaps a version of it might do so in the not-too-distant future, and that is the issue of whether a sitting President can be criminally prosecuted.[13] During the presidencies of both Richard Nixon and Bill Clinton, the Office of Legal Counsel produced opinions arguing that they could not be. The presidential immunity contemplated by the OLC turned on the burden that a criminal case would impose on the constitutional office of the presidency. "A necessity to defend a criminal trial and to attend court in connection with it . . . would interfere with the President's unique official duties, most of which cannot be performed by anyone else."[14] Moreover, to the extent that the "President is the symbolic head of the Nation . . . [t]o wound him by a criminal proceeding is to hamstring the operation of the whole governmental apparatus."[15] Notably such considerations are unique to the case of a sitting President, so much so that even a sitting Vice President could not claim a similar immunity from criminal proceedings.[16]

The Clinton OLC explicitly observed that "[r]ecognizing an immunity from prosecution for a sitting President would not preclude such prosecution once the President's term is over or he is otherwise removed from office by resignation or impeachment."[17] The OLC's analysis emphasized a functionalist balancing test. The OLC opinion weighed the interests in *immediate* prosecution and punishment" of a President and found that sitting Presidents were uniquely situated.[18]

---

[13] The OLC opinions effectively precluded the possibility of federal criminal prosecution of a sitting President. But they did not foreclose the possibility that a state prosecutor might seek an indictment against a sitting President, and such an event would then trigger judicial scrutiny of whether such a prosecution could proceed.

[14] Dixon, Jr., *supra* note 1, at 28.

[15] *Id.* at 30.

[16] *Id.* at 40.

[17] Moss, *supra* note 1, at 255.

[18] *Id.*

The OLC opinions on this topic were exclusively concerned with the timing of any presidential prosecution. They did not address or attempt to distinguish among different acts for which a President might be prosecuted. For purposes of a sitting President, the mere fact of indictment and prosecution created the constitutional problem, and it did not matter whether the acts being prosecuted arose from the President's private or public conduct or whether they preceded the President's term in office entirely. Prosecution for any reason triggered the concern, and such burdens on a sitting President's time and prestige would necessarily become irrelevant once the President left office. The particular presidential interests considered by the OLC could provide no basis for post-presidential immunity from criminal prosecution.

The Supreme Court itself has similarly deployed a balancing approach to developing doctrines of immunity. Like the OLC, the Court has not been overly concerned with the lack of textualist or originalist pedigree for such doctrines. In *United States v. Nixon* (also known as the Watergate Tapes case), the Court considered arguments as to whether "the independence of the Executive Branch within its own sphere . . . insulates a President from a judicial subpoena in an ongoing criminal prosecution, and thereby protects confidential Presidential communications."[19] The Court had no difficulty recognizing that "[c]ertain powers and privileges flow from the nature of enumerated powers," notwithstanding "the silence of the Constitution on this score."[20] The structuralist reasoning that the Court had made use of since at least *McCulloch v. Maryland* provided a sufficient basis for extrapolating necessary privileges from the logic of the overarching design of the Constitution and the practical realities of making such a design functional.[21] In the Watergate Tapes case, however, the Court thought that an "absolute privilege as against a subpoena essential to enforcement of criminal statutes" would "upset the constitutional balance of 'a workable government' and gravely impair the role of the courts."[22] Without a more specified presidential interest in refusing a particular subpoena and without a demonstration that the subpoena impinged on important presidential duties, the judiciary's

---

[19] United States v. Nixon, 418 U.S. at 706.

[20] *Id.* at 705, 705 n.16.

[21] McCulloch v. Maryland, 17 U.S. (4 Wheat.) 316 (1819).

[22] United States v. Nixon, 418 U.S at 707.

interest in its own constitutional functions weighed more heavily in the balance.

A few years later, former President Nixon asserted a similar absolute privilege against a civil suit arising from allegedly unlawful official conduct. In *Nixon v. Fitzgerald*, the Court recognized such an immunity.[23] Here it was the nature of the acts in question rather than the timing of the judicial proceeding that did the constitutional work. In contemplating the existence of such an immunity from civil suits, the Court pointed to a long history of judicial recognition "that government officials are entitled to some form of immunity from suits for civil damages."[24] This history extended back to "English cases at common law" and drew upon "'[t]he interests of the people'" in "bold and unhesitating action" by government officials without fear of a countervailing private interest in avoiding future personal liability.[25] The "requisite inquiry," the Court indicated, "may be viewed in terms of the 'inherent' or 'structural' assumptions of our scheme of government."[26] "[O]ur constitutional heritage and structure" required courts to recognize what was "implicit in the nature of the President's office in a system structured to achieve effective government."[27] As Justice Joseph Story contended, there are "incidental powers belonging to the executive department, which are necessarily implied from the nature of the functions, which are confided to it," which at least included immunity from arrest for sitting Presidents and immunity from personal civil liability for their official acts.[28]

Once again, the unique nature of the presidency came into play. In *Fitzgerald*, its unique nature justified an absolute immunity of the type that the Court had held to be enjoyed by judges and prosecutors, rather than a qualified immunity of the type enjoyed by lower executive officers. The "singular importance of the President's duties" weighed against subsequent personal accountability for his official conduct.[29] Presidential decisions are both the most

[23] *See* Nixon v. Fitzgerald, 457 U.S. 731.

[24] *Id.* at 744.

[25] *Id.* at 744–45.

[26] *Id.* at 748 n.26.

[27] *Id.* at 748.

[28] *Id.* at 749.

[29] *Id.* at 751.

controversial and the most important, "the most sensitive and far-reaching . . . entrusted to any official under our constitutional system."[30] It was well settled, the Court thought, that the judiciary "must balance the constitutional weight of the interest to be served against the dangers of intrusion on the authority and functions of the Executive Branch," and only the weightiest of "broad public interests" could justify judicial action.[31]

Likewise, the unique nature of the presidency had implications for the scope of the President's immunity. The Court had often "held that an official's absolute immunity should extend only to acts in performance of particular functions," but the "Court also has refused to draw functional lines finer than history and reason would support."[32] Because the President's "discretionary responsibilities" were vast and sensitive, close judicial inquiries "could be highly intrusive."[33] A President acting "within the 'outer perimeter' of his official responsibility" should be immune from personally answering for such actions in court.[34]

The Court's finding of absolute immunity took civil liability for official acts off the table, but the Court thought its ruling would "not leave the Nation without sufficient protection against misconduct on the part of the Chief Executive."[35] Presidents could still face impeachment, public scrutiny, congressional oversight, electoral pressures, and more. Such "alternative remedies" weighed in the balance in favor of presidential immunity from civil liability for official acts and insured that the President was not "above the law."[36] Notably, the Court did not in *Fitzgerald* list criminal prosecution as among those "alternative remedies," and the dissent in *Fitzgerald* thought the logic of the Court's opinion would in fact naturally extend to at least some criminal protections.[37]

In *Clinton v. Jones*, the Court refused to extend such an absolute immunity to sitting Presidents facing civil suits over their *private* actions.

---

[30] *Id.* at 752.

[31] *Id.* at 754.

[32] *Id.* at 755.

[33] *Id.* at 756.

[34] *Id.*

[35] *Id.* at 757.

[36] *Id.* at 758.

[37] *Id.* at 780.

In doing so, however, the Court again emphasized the importance of the distinction between official and unofficial acts in the balance of constitutional interests that justify immunity.[38] The Court's "central concern was to avoid rendering the President 'unduly cautious in the discharge of his official duties.'"[39] "Immunities are grounded in 'the nature of the function performed, not the identity of the actor who performed it.'"[40] This "functional approach" cut against President Clinton since the acts in question had nothing to do with the presidency.[41] Moreover, the Court thought that the "dominant concern" in previous immunity cases was "the diversion of the President's attention during the decisionmaking process caused by needless worry as to the possibility of damages actions stemming from any particular official decision."[42] The fact that the Clinton litigation involved "questions that relate entirely to the unofficial conduct of the individual who happens to be the President" meant that it "pose[d] no perceptible risk of misallocation of either judicial power or executive power."[43] The Court thought that civil litigation, even when it involved a sitting President, was unlikely to "impair the effective performance of his office."[44] There were "appropriate circumstances" in which the courts could burden "the time and attention of the Chief Executive," such as when the courts entertained suits to "determine whether he has acted within the law."[45] The presidential responsibility "to accomplish [his] assigned mission" must yield to the judiciary's responsibility "to decide whether his official conduct conformed to the law," but such a burden on the executive branch was intrinsic to the constitutional design in which the presidency was one of constitutionally delimited powers.[46]

The Court has repeatedly emphasized that "absolute immunity must be justified by reference to the public interest in the special functions of [an executive official's] office, not the mere fact of high station."[47]

---

[38] Clinton v. Jones, 520 U.S. 681.

[39] *Id.* at 693–94.

[40] *Id.* at 695.

[41] *Id.* at 694.

[42] *Id.* at 694 n.19.

[43] *Id.* at 701.

[44] *Id.* at 702.

[45] *Id.* at 703.

[46] *Id.*

[47] Harlow v. Fitzgerald, 457 U.S. 800, 812 (1982).

Indeed, in many circumstances, the "greater power of such officials affords a greater potential for a regime of lawless conduct," and thus a greater need for judicial accountability.[48] Judicial accountability is most needed, moreover, when officers are not "subject to other checks that help to prevent abuses of authority from going unredressed."[49] Immunity for an officer should only follow from the special "responsibilities of his office" and from a demonstration that the officer "was discharging the protected function when performing the act for which liability is asserted."[50] The judiciary has a special interest in actions that are "lawless," or outside the scope of an officer's authority, and that are unlikely to be redressable by other means. But the judiciary should show restraint when a judicial process is likely to impinge on an officer's willingness and ability to vigorously perform his own public duties.

So where does that leave Trump? The particular question of whether Presidents can be held criminally liable for their official conduct was novel in *Trump v. United States*, but the Court had over several decades developed a conceptual framework for answering such questions. The framework is functional and pragmatic and hardly airtight. But it has put particular emphasis on the uniqueness of the presidency, the conduct in question, and the burdens imposed on an officer's decisionmaking, counterbalanced by the nature of the judiciary's interest in inquiring into an officer's actions.

III. The Roberts Opinion

The Court's critical holding in *Trump* is that,

> under our constitutional structure of separated powers, the nature of Presidential power requires that a former President have some immunity from criminal prosecution for official acts during his tenure in office. At least with respect to the President's exercise of his core constitutional powers, this immunity must be absolute. As for his remaining official actions, he is also entitled to immunity.[51]

None of this disturbs, or endorses, the OLC's opinion that a sitting President is immune from prosecution as a matter of timing.

[48] Butz v. Economou, 438 U.S. 478, 506 (1978).
[49] Mitchell v. Forsyth, 472 U.S. 511, 522 (1985).
[50] *Harlow*, 457 U.S. at 813.
[51] Trump v. United States, 144 S. Ct. 2312, 2327 (2024).

The Court effectively divided presidential actions into three categories, each of which receives a different level of immunity from criminal prosecution. A sitting President engages in some conduct that is entirely personal and private, "unofficial" conduct. The President has no presumptive immunity for any criminal acts he might commit in that personal capacity. At least according to the OLC, prosecution of such acts might have to wait until the President has left office, but a former President can be held criminally liable for such conduct. A President who engages in the same criminal behavior that any other private individual is capable of performing can be held accountable in the same fashion as any other private individual. Thus, a President who shot someone on Fifth Avenue, raped a government employee, tampered with evidence in a criminal investigation, or engaged in fraud in seeking a private loan, among many other actions, can be prosecuted in an ordinary criminal court, at least after he has left office. This, at least, is uncontroversial, though determining what actions by a President are personal and "unofficial" might be difficult in practice.

Roberts did provide two cautions about distinguishing official from unofficial acts. First, courts "may not inquire into the President's motives" to determine that something was an unofficial act.[52] Second, courts may not determine that an act is unofficial "merely because it allegedly violates a generally applicable law."[53] These cautions may harken back to special counsel Robert Mueller's investigation of President Trump. The second volume of Mueller's report was dedicated to documenting the ways in which the President hindered the criminal investigation into Russian interference in the 2016 election. Such actions might well have been impeachable, but Mueller also suggested that they might amount to criminal obstruction of justice. The conduct in question centered around official acts, such as the President removing FBI Director James Comey.

Can such official acts become "unofficial" acts because they were driven by corrupt motives or fell within the scope of a catch-all phrase in an obstruction statute? Special Counsel Mueller argued that they did. Crucially, the special counsel asserted, a "preclusion of 'corrupt'

[52] *Id.* at 2333.
[53] *Id.* at 2334.

official action is not a major intrusion on Article II powers."[54] The President's Article II authority do not properly include actions "for corrupt personal purposes," and thus a congressional and judicial imposition on such actions cannot intrude on the President's constitutional authority.[55] Any danger of intrusion into legitimate executive branch actions would be minimal, Mueller posited.

By contrast, Trump's own personal legal counsel had informed Mueller that in their view, "as a matter of law and common sense, the President cannot obstruct himself or subordinates acting on his behalf by simply exercising [the President's] inherent Constitutional powers" to direct and control the administration of justice.[56] Before being appointed Attorney General, William Barr wrote to Trump's Department of Justice to elaborate on his own objections to "Mueller's 'Obstruction' Theory."[57] In Barr's view, the longstanding position of the Department of Justice is that "the President's authority over law enforcement matters is necessarily all-encompassing, and Congress may not exscind certain matters from the scope of his responsibilities."[58] Actions that are legal in themselves would become criminal if an outside body determined that the official had the wrong subjective motivations when taking the actions. Such disputes about motive and its effect on otherwise lawful actions are a proper matter for political accountability, not criminal accountability. Officials who must labor under the possibility that outside perceptions of their motives might become a sufficient basis for the imposition of criminal punishments will avoid making necessary but controversial decisions. Judges may determine whether an officer has the authority to decide a question, but once it is recognized that discretionary authority has been placed in the hands of a decisionmaker, those

---

[54] U.S. Dept of Just., 2 Report of the Investigation into Russian Interference in the 2016 Presidential Election 174 (2019). For a defense of Mueller's position, see Daniel J. Hemel & Eric A. Posner, *Presidential Obstruction of Justice*, 106 Calif. L. Rev. 1277 (2018).

[55] U.S. Dept of Just., *supra* note 53, at 176.

[56] Marc E. Kasowitz, CEO, Kasowitz Benson Torres, letter to Robert S. Mueller III, Special Counsel, Dept. of Just. (June 23, 2017), https://www.nytimes.com/interactive/2018/06/02/us/politics/trump-legal-documents.html#june-23-2017.

[57] Bill Barr, *Memorandum to Deputy Attorney General Rod Rosenstein and Assistant Attorney General Steve Engel, Re: Mueller's "Obstruction" Theory* (June 8, 2018), https://www.justsecurity.org/wp-content/uploads/2018/12/June-2018-Barr-Memo-to-DOJ-Muellers-Obstruction-Theory-1.2.pdf.

[58] *Id.* at 10.

decisions must be "non-reviewable."[59] "The prospect of review itself undermines discretion."[60]

The Roberts Court came down squarely on the side of Barr in his dispute with Mueller. It held that facially lawful official acts by the President cannot be criminalized or converted into unofficial acts as a result of second parties such as judges or juries questioning the President's motives when taking those actions.

A second category of presidential actions involves "core constitutional powers," official acts that are "within [the President's] 'conclusive and preclusive' constitutional authority."[61] These are the powers that Justice Robert Jackson described as existing at the "lowest ebb" of presidential power, those cases in which the President is relying on his "own constitutional powers minus any constitutional powers of Congress over the matter."[62] These are powers upon which Congress cannot constitutionally encroach. Similarly, "the courts have 'no power to control [the President's] discretion' when he acts pursuant to the powers invested exclusively in him by the Constitution."[63] The specific powers that fall within this "core" would depend on one's constitutional theory, but Roberts listed such examples as the President's pardoning power and power to fire federal officials. These powers are constitutionally vested in the President alone, as distinct from any other private individual or government official. No private individual is capable of taking the same actions that the President can take under these powers. If neither Congress nor the courts can encroach on those powers, then Presidents cannot be criminally prosecuted for their official actions making use of those powers.

A third category of presidential actions involves official acts outside of that core, acts that rest on a legal authority that is shared with Congress. Such acts are taken "pursuant to an express or implied authorization of Congress" or in areas where "[the President]

---

[59] *Id.* at 9, 13.

[60] *Id.* at 13.

[61] *Trump*, 144 S. Ct. at 2328.

[62] Youngstown Sheet & Tube Co. v. Sawyer, 343 U.S. 579, 637 (1952) (Jackson, J., concurring).

[63] *Trump*, 144 S. Ct. at 2327.

and Congress may have concurrent authority."[64] Again, determining which official acts rest on concurrent authority and which rest on exclusive authority depends on the underlying theory of presidential power that one adopts. But discretionary policy decisions of all sorts, particularly in the domestic sphere, are likely to fall within this zone.

The fact that such official acts might rest on a delegated legal authority from Congress suggests that they cannot be as insulated from congressional regulation and control as those resting on the President's exclusive constitutional authority. This possibility of congressional regulation might open space for piercing the absolute immunity that the Court recognized for core powers. Even so, the Court left that question unresolved, saying that the President is entitled to at least "presumptive" immunity in this context. Why might that be so? The Court looked back to *Fitzgerald* and the rationale for immunity from personal civil liability for official acts.[65] Regardless of the source of the discretionary policy authority, the public interest requires that an officer exercise that authority with vigor and not hedge his decisionmaking so as to avoid personal risk. If the threat of personal *civil* liability creates a constitutionally unacceptable risk that an officer might shirk his public duty, a threat of personal *criminal* liability must pose an even greater one. This would seem to suggest that it is up to Congress to choose where to draw the lines on the discretionary authority it has delegated to the President. The Supreme Court may patrol those boundaries to ensure that Presidents do not overstep the limits of their authority, but Congress may not demarcate those boundaries by imposing a *criminal* penalty for presidents who traverse it. Such a draconian penalty creates an inappropriate chilling effect on the ability of the President to take care that the laws be faithfully executed within those bounds. The independence of the chief executive in performing his constitutional responsibilities will be "significantly undermined" if Congress can subject his official acts to the "scrutiny in criminal prosecutions" and cast a "pall" over his exercise of constitutional discretion.[66]

The *Trump* Court borrowed the idea of a "presumptive privilege" from the *Nixon* Court's ruling on executive privilege claims. But the

---

[64] *Youngstown*, 343 U.S. at 635, 637 (Jackson, J., concurring).

[65] *See Trump*, 144 S. Ct. at 2329–30.

[66] *Id.* at 2331.

Court's *Trump* opinion inexplicably elaborates, borrowing from *Fitzgerald*, that at "a minimum, the President must therefore be immune from prosecution for an official act unless the Government can show that applying a criminal prohibition to that act would pose no 'dangers of intrusion on the authority and functions of the Executive Branch.'"[67] That statement marks a significant revision of both *Nixon* and *Fitzgerald*. In *Nixon*, the Court held that a presumptive privilege could be overcome with an adequate showing of the important interests in piercing the privilege. One such sufficient interest was when the allegedly privileged material was "essential to the justice of the [pending criminal] case."[68] In his opinion for the Court in *Trump*, Roberts said nothing about the balance of interests that might help justify overcoming the President's presumptive immunity from criminal prosecution. In *Fitzgerald*, the Court similarly argued that the public interest, such as the interest in an "ongoing criminal prosecution," could counterbalance "the dangers of intrusion on the authority and functions of the Executive Branch."[69] Compared with that approach, the Roberts opinion would seem to up the stakes such that there can be *no* dangers of intrusion on the executive branch. The *Trump* opinion lapses silent on any interests that might be balanced against the President's presumptive immunity. Within this outer perimeter of official presidential action, Roberts borrowed from the functionalist balancing framework of earlier separation of powers cases but downplayed the weighing of interests that those cases had always emphasized. At first blush, "presumptive" immunity appears to be all but absolute in practice.[70]

The Supreme Court remanded the *Trump* case back to the lower courts for further proceedings to determine whether the President's actions at issue are official or not, core or not, immune or not. Nonetheless, it is worth noting that the Court suggested an extremely broad understanding of what falls within the outer perimeter of the President's office for this purpose. In political science terms, a modern President serves many functions within the political system,

---

[67] *Id.*

[68] United States v. Nixon, 418 U.S at 713 (brackets in original).

[69] Nixon v. Fitzgerald, 457 U.S. at 754.

[70] *Cf. Trump*, 144 S. Ct. at 2361 (Sotomayor, J., dissenting) ("It is hard to imagine a criminal prosecution for a President's official acts that would pose no dangers of intrusion on Presidential authority in the majority's eyes.").

only some of which derive from his constitutional office and legal responsibilities.[71] Roberts, however, blurred the distinction between the President's legal and political functions. Thus, in Roberts's telling the President's use of the "bully pulpit" or his efforts to advance a legislative agenda simply become aspects of "Presidential power," apparently indistinguishable from the President's legal obligation to take care that the laws are faithfully executed.[72] The Court still left open the possibility that some of this behavior could be unofficial. But the Court obscured the difference between the President acting as a head of government and the President acting as a political leader in ways that might not be constitutionally justified.

Trump had made an additional argument for presidential immunity grounded in the Constitution's "Impeachment Judgment Clause." The Constitution provides that if an official is impeached and convicted, the judgment "shall not extend further than to removal from Office, and disqualification to hold and enjoy any Office of honor, Trust or Profit under the United States."[73] But "the Party convicted shall nevertheless be liable and subject to Indictment, Trial, Judgment and Punishment, according to Law."[74] Trump argued that this provision means a President may be convicted of a crime *only* if he has previously been impeached by the House and convicted by the Senate.

The Court decisively rejected Trump's argument that the Impeachment Judgment Clause precludes criminal prosecution when the Senate does not convict in its own proceedings. On Trump's reading, a Senate conviction in an impeachment is a necessary condition to penetrating presidential immunity for acts taken in office. But the Court pointed out that Trump's theory is at odds with the text, history, and logic of the impeachment power. In doing so, the Court also correctly observed that "impeachment is a political process" and not a criminal process, and that the two kinds of proceedings should not be conflated.[75]

---

[71] *See, e.g.,* CLINTON ROSSITER, THE AMERICAN PRESIDENCY (1956).

[72] *Trump*, 144 S. Ct. at 2340.

[73] U.S. CONST. art. I, § 3, cl. 7.

[74] *Id.*

[75] *Trump*, 144 S. Ct. at 2342. *See also* KEITH E. WHITTINGTON, THE IMPEACHMENT POWER (2024).

IV. The Barrett Concurrence

Justice Barrett offered a concurring opinion that frames its disagreement with the Chief Justice narrowly but hints at a broader alternative to the scheme the majority opinion lays out. The majority opinion might have done well to have borrowed more of Barrett's framing.

Barrett began by suggesting that we should reconceptualize presidential immunity as two distinct propositions. First, the President (or former President) is entitled to "challenge the constitutionality of a criminal statute as applied to official acts alleged in the indictment."[76] Second, the President "can obtain interlocutory review of the trial court's ruling."[77]

Barrett's first suggestion clarifies the nature of the problem of criminalizing some presidential conduct. When applied to unofficial acts, there is no valid Article II challenge to be made, and thus prosecutions could proceed. When an indictment involves official acts, however, a sitting President would naturally be able to argue that the application of the statute to the President's official actions is unconstitutional. That would be true whether the statute in question sought to impose criminal penalties on a President who violated it or sought to impose some other form of penalty. Moreover, it would be equally true whether the statute in question specifically targeted some presidential conduct (e.g., removing a Cabinet member without Senate approval) or was cast in general terms that arguably include some presidential conduct (e.g., removing a Cabinet member to end a specific criminal investigation). If the application of the statute is delayed by the assumption that a sitting President cannot be criminally prosecuted, then the underlying constitutional issue is still the same when it is eventually applied to the former President. The overriding questions are whether Congress may declare certain presidential actions unlawful and whether the substance or means of how Congress attempts to do so unduly interfere with the constitutional prerogatives of the President. In other words, the question is not whether Presidents are immune from criminal prosecution *as such*, but instead whether particular criminal law provisions are constitutionally infirm as they might be applied to presidential actions.

---

[76] *Trump*, 144 S. Ct. at 2352 (Barrett, J., concurring in part).
[77] *Id.*

The latter is a familiar question within American law. To be sure, the Court might reach a correct or incorrect conclusion about that question in any given case. But the idea that Congress might encroach on presidential powers by way of a statute or that the judiciary has a responsibility in such a case to intervene and declare the law null and void as applied in that context is hardly novel or a threat to democracy or the rule of law.

The prospect of interlocutory review would address a key aspect of a privilege of immunity, which is the ability to avoid full judicial proceedings. If the process of a civil or criminal trial itself imposes an inappropriate burden on an officer who enjoys absolute immunity, then the question of whether a criminal statute can be constitutionally applied to a former officer can be resolved before the process of a trial is undertaken. The concept of immunity cannot avoid the necessity of litigation to determine whether immunity is warranted in specific circumstances. But that litigation process can be channeled through a system of interlocutory review of what is in essence a substantive constitutional issue: the scope of congressional authority. As Barrett recognized, allowing an interlocutory appeal in this context would give the former President a fast-track to resolution of the constitutional issues that other parties who suffer under unconstitutional laws do not have. But that disparity can be examined and addressed separately.

If in a future case the Court finds that a particular criminal statute is unconstitutional as applied, then the President is "immune" from further sanction and the prosecution is at an end. If the Court, by contrast, finds that the particular criminal statute is constitutionally valid as applied to particular presidential actions, then the President is not "immune" from further sanction and the prosecution can proceed. The question of presidential immunity is not a general or stand-alone question; it is ultimately a question about the constitutionality of legislative restrictions on particular presidential actions. That question is both routine and familiar within our constitutional system. There is nothing magical about Congress attempting to place its restrictions on the presidency within the federal criminal code as opposed to elsewhere within the statute books.

Barrett also seemed to take some issue with the Court's opinion over the scope of the President's authority. She would have given more guidance to the lower courts as to how they ought to analyze the indictment at issue in this case. For example, Barrett did not think further proceedings were necessary to know that the President is not taking an official action when he participates in a scheme to organize a slate of fake electors or persuade state legislatures to set aside their presidential election results.[78]

Barrett's explicit disagreement with the majority opinion, however, came on the question of what evidence of presidential conduct may be presented to a jury in a trial regarding unprotected conduct. Because Roberts wanted to exclude any judicial inquiry into presidential motives or any judicial scrutiny of presidential decisionmaking, his opinion for the Court forbade the use of any evidence regarding protected conduct in court. If a President does "not have to answer for his conduct" on those matters, then they should not be laid bare in a courtroom.[79] Juries should not be allowed to "probe official acts for which the President is immune," and the judiciary should not risk that juries might be tainted by political passions raised by such evidence.[80]

By contrast, Barrett was more comfortable with "familiar and time-tested procedure[s]" to deal with such evidentiary problems.[81] Roberts's evidentiary carve-out may point to the fact that the presidential immunity in his framework has a more sweeping character than the two propositions that Barrett suggested. Barrett's approach of as-applied challenges to criminal statutes has no immediate implications for what evidence might be admissible at trial for unofficial acts that are within Congress's authority to regulate. Her limited recognition that executive privilege might be relevant in such cases highlights the extent to which she would prefer to treat the *Trump* case as much more routine. In practice, there might not be much difference between the evidence that Roberts and Barrett would allow into court. But Roberts clearly had a heightened concern about whether, in our hyperpolarized world, prosecutors and jurors can be trusted not to make improper use of evidence relating to presidential motives.

[78] *See id.* at 2353 n.2.
[79] *Id.* at 2340 (majority opinion).
[80] *Id.* at 2341.
[81] *Id.* at 2355 (Barrett, J., concurring in part).

V. The Sotomayor Dissent

Undoubtedly Roberts hoped that the Court would respond to the Trump litigation with the same kind of unanimity that it displayed in *United States v. Nixon* or *Clinton v. Jones*. If so, he was to be disappointed. Instead, the Court came closer to the 5–4 ruling that it issued in *Nixon v. Fitzgerald*. Of course, *Fitzgerald* was the only case that the President won and the closest in its immunity claims to *Trump*. Since we had already seen a preview of the *Trump* case in the debate surrounding the Mueller Report, a clear conservative/liberal divide on whether criminal statutes could be applied to presidential official acts might have been anticipated.

In her dissent, Sotomayor offered a sweeping rejection of presidential immunity for official acts, though she did not clearly say what, if any, limits she might recognize on the congressional authority to criminalize presidential behavior. If Barrett's framework had been adopted by the majority, it might have forced Sotomayor to grapple with that problem more directly. She might then have explained what authority Congress has to regulate how the President conducts his office and where the limits of that authority might be found. But as things stand, Sotomayor did not grapple with that problem. Instead, she focused on the question of whether there is a recognized presidential immunity from criminal prosecution. Unsurprisingly, since the issue is a novel one, she found no text or history establishing such an immunity.

More problematic, however, was that Sotomayor went further and insisted that there is a settled tradition establishing that Presidents "are answerable to the criminal law for their official acts."[82] The evidence here is thin, primarily consisting of the facts that President Gerald Ford pardoned former President Nixon and that independent counsels had investigated Presidents in the past. That is not much of a tradition, and it says little about the specific question of immunity for official acts.

Sotomayor was quick to convert the consensus that a President can be prosecuted for unofficial acts ("of course he can") into a proposition that unofficial acts are whatever acts for which Presidents can be properly prosecuted. Her concern was not that Roberts's vision of official acts included more than the President's role as head

---

[82] *Id.* at 2359–60 (Sotomayor, J., dissenting).

of the government. Her concern was instead that Roberts would immunize "any use of official power for any purpose."[83] In her view, Presidents are effectively above the law if they are "beyond the reach of the federal criminal laws for any abuse of official power."[84] Yet the idea that "abuse" of power can be criminalized is itself an astonishing leap. The identification of abuses of power is a quintessentially political act. It is why the Framers thought we needed elections and impeachments.[85] When officers exceed their power, they can be checked by courts who can declare such acts beyond those officers' authority. And when officers abuse their power, they should be held politically accountable. But if officers can be *imprisoned* for abuse of power, then criminal prosecutions will be the stuff of politics.

Sotomayor would downplay the dangers of the door she would open. Unlike Roberts, she had no concern about politicized prosecutions. In the civil liability context, the Court worried about how easy it would be to find potential parties who might harass controversial political officials through nettlesome litigation. In the criminal context, Sotomayor thought such worries could be put to rest. Who could imagine the possibility of "a baseless criminal prosecution?"[86] The criminal justice process, she assured us, is surrounded by many checks and balances to effectively separate out the guilty from the innocent and filter out meritless cases. The long history of the nation has demonstrated an ample "restraint" on the prosecution of former Presidents.[87] There is no reason to imagine that presidential prosecutions might become a problem in the future.

Sotomayor was also little concerned about the possibility of criminal liability affecting presidential decisionmaking. If she were President, she suggested, she would simply not commit crimes. How hard could that be? Surely Presidents have always acted under the shadow of the criminal law, and yet they have not hesitated to perform their duties.[88] Complying with the criminal law should be no

---

[83] *Id.* at 2361.

[84] *Id.* at 2362.

[85] *See* WHITTINGTON, *supra* note 75.

[86] *Trump*, 144 S. Ct. at 2365 (Sotomayor, J., dissenting).

[87] *Id.* at 2364.

[88] *See id.* at 2364–65.

"great burden."[89] She was "deeply troubled by the idea, inherent in the majority's opinion, that our Nation loses something valuable when the President is forced to operate within the confines of federal criminal law."[90] But Sotomayor did not grapple with the Court's reasoning in *Fitzgerald*, which contended that personal presidential liability for official conduct would have a chilling effect on the President that would skew government decisions and damage the public good. The question is not just whether the President operates within the confines of federal criminal law. It is whether Presidents will hesitate to do their duty for fear that they might accidently step over that line or be perceived by partisan political actors to have stepped over that line. Sotomayor seemed to assume that such lines are so clear that there will be no chilling effect.

At the same time, however, Sotomayor suggested that the criminal law can and does carve out a large hole in presidential powers. Any official acts driven by "corrupt motives and intent," she asserted, can be reached by the criminal law.[91] It is not properly within the President's authority to act with "corrupt purpose," and thus any actions he takes with such wrong purposes must be "unofficial" acts.[92] Ultimately, Sotomayor shared Mueller's view that the scope of the President's constitutional authority is defined, in part, by the President's subjective mental state when he takes an action. Prosecutors must be able to examine the President's motives when he takes putatively official acts, and if they find that those motives were not sufficiently public-spirited they can imprison him.

Running through Sotomayor's dissent is the belief that the threat of criminal prosecution has been a significant component of the checks and balances that have kept Presidents from abusing their powers. By recognizing a presidential immunity from criminal prosecution for official presidential acts, the majority has removed a load-bearing beam from the constitutional framework. Presidents who were previously tempted to order "Seal Team Six to assassinate a political rival" or "organize a coup" or "take a

[89] *Id.* at 2365.
[90] *Id.*
[91] *Id.* at 2361.
[92] *Id.*

bribe" will now be emboldened to do so.[93] There will be, apparently, no other means of redress to prevent, discourage, or counter such presidential conduct.

V. Kicking the Can Down the Road

It was unfortunate that the Court had to hear an argument at all raising the question of presidential immunity from criminal liability. That the Court had to address the question is not the fault of the Justices but the fault of former President Trump and the prosecutors who have pursued him. The country would be better off if the Court had not had to detail the precise contours of presidential immunity and had not incepted into the public consciousness the question of what exactly a sitting President can order Seal Team Six to do. The constitutional system functions better if some hypotheticals are not discussed beyond a seminar room, if some possibilities of how power might be exercised are so far beyond the pale that they are not even imagined, and if the boundaries of legislative and executive authority are not tested and detailed. But if high government officials insist on testing the outer bounds of their powers, law will replace norms and vague sensibilities will be reduced to fine details.

Given that the issue is now being litigated, the Court's opinion says much less than was needed. The Court invited political backlash by insufficiently explaining the logic of its own opinion and refusing to address reasonable concerns about the outer bounds of that logic. By framing the question as one of immunity rather than limits on congressional authority to interfere with Article II powers, the Court opened the door to simplistic solutions in the name of accountability. A constitutional amendment declaring that "No One Is above the Law" and stripping Presidents of immunity from criminal prosecution would be enticing, but it would fail to grapple with the real problems that could be unleashed by a Congress empowered to criminalize presidential conduct at will. The Court could have done more to inform such a public debate, but instead it chose to be oblique. Meanwhile, the Court provided only limited guidance to the lower courts on how to navigate the complexities surrounding a prosecution of a former President. The Court failed to clarify what actions a President might take that would be constitutionally

---

[93] *Id.* at 2371 (cleaned up).

protected from criminal prosecution. Simultaneously, the Court threw into confusion evidentiary issues associated with criminal prosecutions by indicating that some materials relating to presidential conduct are constitutionally off-limits.

The Court's analytical framework is an odd mixture of formalism and functionalism that is unlikely to be satisfying to advocates of either approach and that leaves important issues unresolved. The opinion has all the trappings of a functionalist argument and appeals to the canonical opinion of modern functionalist separation-of-powers jurisprudence in Justice Robert Jackson's concurring opinion in the *Steel Seizure Case*.[94] This in itself is neither surprising nor problematic. The Jackson opinion is the standard starting point for thinking about presidential powers problems, and functionalism undergirds all of the Court's prior opinions regarding constitutional immunity for Presidents and other government officials. Although the *Trump* dissent makes some rhetorical hay out of the Court's minimal engagement with constitutional text and original meaning, there is nothing unusual about how Roberts approached the issue of presidential immunity.

However, Roberts did make two important, unexplained, and undeveloped departures from traditional forms of analysis. First, Roberts borrowed a balancing framework but did not engage in any constitutional balancing. Recent conservative Justices have often been uncomfortable with balancing tests, not least because they often appear to be highly subjective in application. The immunity decisions have relied on balancing tests, however, and Roberts freely borrowed from their language and rationale—at least when it comes to understanding the constitutional interests of the presidency. Criminal scrutiny of presidential actions could corrupt the administration of the executive branch and unduly interfere with the decisiveness and energy of the executive. The structural design of the Constitution creates implications that courts have been willing to recognize in order to preserve the independence of the executive branch. Those structural considerations have given rise to such doctrines as executive privilege and immunity from personal civil liability for official actions.

[94] *See supra* note 62.

But the Court has also thought that there might be circumstances that would justify overcoming those presidential interests. In *Nixon* itself, the Court held that the government's interest in criminal prosecutions could outweigh an absolute executive privilege, though even here the President's interest had to be accommodated through such safeguards as *in camera* review of potentially privileged evidence. In *Trump*, however, Roberts gave no recognition of such counterbalancing constitutional interests. The unwillingness to grapple with *Nixon*'s concerns for criminal justice is particularly notable in the specific context of *Trump*. There might be reasons to think that the balance of constitutional interests is tilted even more heavily toward the President in the context of criminal prosecutions of the President himself, but Roberts did not say so. The functionalist analysis is incomplete, and one suspects that it is unstable.

At the same time, the *Trump* opinion sweeps in some more formalist considerations but without sufficient explanation to provide much guidance for future doctrine. Part of the difficulty is the breadth of the question of presidential immunity as such. In the independent counsel case, Chief Justice William Rehnquist framed the key separation of powers question as whether the statute was "impermissibly interfering with the functions of the Executive Branch."[95] On the one hand, Rehnquist posed the functionalist question of how much and what kind of "interference" might impede the President in the performance of his duties. On the other hand, he largely assumed a formalist background of what counted as among the "functions of the Executive Branch." In the context of the independent counsel statute, the executive duty in question was specific and clear. But in the context of the presidential immunity questions raised by the *Trump* case, the executive duties that might become at issue are infinite. From a formalist perspective, we need to know what the scope of presidential duties under the Constitution might be to know when criminal statutes might impermissibly interfere with those duties. Trying to answer that question at a high level of abstraction stretched the Court's opinion to the breaking point. The Court's distinction between official and unofficial acts and, further, between core and noncore official acts begs more questions than it answers.

---

[95] Morrison v. Olson, 487 U.S. 654, 697 (1988).

Roberts apparently preferred to avoid getting into hypotheticals in his opinion. But avoiding specifics left the door open to the kind of rhetorical reaction that the opinion received both on and off the Court. By its silence, did the Court's majority mean to say that the President is, in fact, some kind of king? That the President could, in fact, order Seal Team Six to assassinate a political rival? That the President could, in fact, initiate a self-coup? It seems likely that the majority did not think so, but the opinion simply does not provide the material for explaining why. Perhaps the various Justices in the majority were not of one mind about which specific acts might be on or off the table, and so getting into specifics would have fractured the majority. Perhaps the various members of the majority were not of one mind about their underlying understanding of the formal scope of presidential power, and so getting into specifics would have broken down an overlapping consensus on the basic questions. Such is the danger of a minimalist opinion. The opinion is so concerned with papering over differences that it says very little that is meaningful.

Things get complicated at the level of specifics. A more thoroughgoing formalist analysis might have said more about where the boundaries of presidential power might be found. A more thoroughgoing functionalist analysis might have said more about where the counter-balancing interests of Congress or the structuralist logic of the overarching constitutional system begin to "[]permissibly intrude[]" on presidential choices.[96]

If we sweep away the idea of presidential immunity entirely, as some Democrats are currently suggesting we should do in the wake of the *Trump* decision, then the consequences for presidential independence are dramatic. Let us distinguish between two kinds of statutory possibilities. One type of statute would criminalize acts that the President alone can take; the other would criminalize acts that the President could take along with ordinary citizens. The former type of statute would, of course, involve the use of presidential powers, whether those powers are rooted in the Constitution, statute, or treaty.

If we conclude that Presidents have no immunity from criminal prosecution for their official actions or that the authority of Congress

---

[96] Commodity Futures Trading Comm'n v. Schor, 478 U.S. 833, 851 (1986).

to adopt criminal laws must always trump whatever constitutional authority a President might have, then Congress would be positioned to gut the independence of the presidency. When the Reconstruction Congress passed the Tenure of Office Act forbidding President Andrew Johnson from removing a Cabinet officer without Senate approval, could it have upped the ante by making it a criminal offense for the President to attempt to do so? Could a former President be prosecuted under a statute that specifically made it a crime to fire the Secretary of Defense or the Attorney General or the director of the FBI? Could Congress have criminalized its disputes with President George W. Bush over the scope of the President's commander-in-chief authority? Could a former President who had ordered "enhanced interrogation" of foreign terrorists or sweeping national security electronic intelligence or the detention of unlawful combatants in security facilities abroad be prosecuted under specific criminal statutes aimed at such presidential conduct? Could President Barack Obama be prosecuted under a Senator Rand Paul–inspired statute imposing criminal penalties for any president who ordered a targeted drone strike on an American citizen under any circumstances? Could Congress authorize the criminal prosecution of a President who insufficiently enforced immigration laws or pardoned sex offenders or withdrew the United States from NATO or NAFTA or exchanged a convicted Russian arms dealer for an American journalist?

If we think some meaningful line can be drawn between a President issuing an order to Seal Team Six to assassinate a domestic political rival and issuing an order to target a drone strike at an American citizen abroad who is actively engaged in terrorist operations, then simply saying there should be no such thing as presidential immunity does not help. But neither does it help to simply say that Presidents enjoy absolute immunity when exercising their core constitutional powers. Both examples involve the President acting in his role as commander-in-chief. Perhaps there is no meaningful line to be drawn. Perhaps assassinating a political rival is just an "abuse" of the commander-in-chief authority rather than an action lying outside of that authority. Perhaps we must simply depend on the good character of a sitting President to know when to order the targeted killing of an American citizen and when not. Or perhaps we must depend on the political checks-and-balances that raise the costs on Presidents making bad calls in such situations.

Or perhaps we need a theory of the proper constitutional scope of the commander-in-chief power that would allow us to distinguish between constitutionally proper and improper presidential orders to the military. Perhaps such a theory might turn on presidential motivations, as the *Trump* dissent suggests. But that seems unlikely to be adequate. If we had clear evidence that a President was concerned about improving his reelection chances or his historical reputation when ordering a military strike, would that be sufficient to move the order outside the President's constitutional authority and make him criminally liable? If a terrorist group kidnapped the President's daughter and the president authorized the release of a terrorist leader to secure the return of his daughter, would he be acting from a corrupt personal motive that would justify his criminal prosecution? If the President chose one military target over another because he once had a nice meal in a city that could have been a target or because he has friends and donors who have substantial property interests in a potential target, is he no longer operating within his proper constitutional authority? If a President working on racist assumptions ordered the detention of American citizens who shared a national heritage with a wartime adversary, could he be held criminally liable for his flawed decisionmaking? By excluding presidential motivation from the equation, the *Trump* majority wanted to take such possibilities off the table. Criminal juries should not be asking whether the President had a good enough reason to order bombs dropped on a particular target.

If the dissent's theory is inadequate for identifying the boundaries of the President's constitutional authority, we still need such a theory and the majority declines to give us one. The impeachment power is aimed at addressing acts incompatible with holding office, but those acts can be either criminal or noncriminal. The Constitution itself lists "treason" as an impeachable offense, and that presumably includes at least cases of literal treason involving a government officer committing the ordinary crime of treason. Surely the President himself could commit treason while in office, just as the President could commit murder, obstruction of justice, or various other criminal acts. But can the President commit treason while exercising his otherwise lawful powers of the presidency? Are there any orders that a President might issue as commander-in-chief that could qualify as treasonous in a criminal sense, not just a political sense? If a President were to order an unconditional surrender to a dominant wartime adversary, there is little question that doing so would be giving aid and comfort to the enemy. But surely the President could not be charged with treason for exercising his constitutional duties as he thought necessary in the circumstances. Could a President order that a nuclear bomb be dropped on New York City so as to avoid an all-out nuclear exchange with a foreign adversary without opening himself to criminal liability? Other cases would presumably be harder. If the President ordered American troops to stand down as an invasion was launched against the United States, would such an order necessarily be protected as within the scope of his lawful powers? If the President ordered the American national security agencies to unilaterally turn over the names of all American covert foreign assets to a hostile foreign nation, could there be criminal sanctions?

Are there circumstances in which the President could purport to be acting under his authority as commander-in-chief, but would in fact be acting unlawfully and outside the scope of that authority? The question could arise not only in the context of a treason statute but in the context of other statutory crimes as well. A vast array of actions would be criminal in ordinary contexts but are regarded as lawful within a military context; but Congress and the President might disagree about the military necessity of various wartime orders. If Congress can back its judgment with criminal sanctions, the President would be deterred from faithfully exercising his constitutional responsibilities as he understands them. But perhaps objective circumstances could be identified that would put some military orders or actions outside the scope of the President's proper constitutional authority.

I think it is obvious that a President could not simply walk across the debate stage and shoot his electoral opponent in the head in the name of national security. If that is "obvious," however, it is presumably because there is no plausible national security rationale for such an action. But I could also presumably add more details to the hypothetical that would overcome that presumption and suggest that perhaps there are circumstances in which Seal Team Six could be ordered to act against a presidential candidate. In ordinary American political circumstances, we do not imagine a plausible scenario in which a major party nominee poses such a threat. That in turn implies there are objective limits to what a President can order the military to do even in wartime. Unfortunately, we do not have anything like a consensus theory of what such a limit might be. President Obama's Department of Justice might suggest, for example, that if an American citizen were involved in the operational planning of violent attacks on the United States and could not be feasibly captured, such an individual could be a legitimate military target notwithstanding that individual's political activities. In a dystopian world in which an American political party had a military wing and sought to gain power through both electoral and terroristic means, a sitting President might well be within his constitutional authority to take lethal action against an electoral foe. Presumably President Abraham Lincoln could not have ordered the assassination of a Democratic "peace candidate" on the grounds that such a candidate posed an existential threat to the nation, but he could have ordered the assassination of Jefferson Davis had he been a contender for the Democratic Party nomination in 1864. Chief Justice Roger Taney feared that he might be detained by Union forces if he issued judicial opinions obstructing Lincoln's wartime actions. Suppose the President were to order the arrest of Supreme Court Justices. Whether the President was acting within the scope of his constitutional authority—and thus properly immune from criminal prosecution—would likely depend on what the Justices had allegedly done. If the Justices had been conspiring with foreign enemies, then their detention would be understandable. If the Justices had disagreed with the President about the scope of his constitutional prerogatives, then their detention would seem much more dubious. The bounds of presidential power may not be determined by the President's subjective motives or even by the action undertaken, but they might well depend on the public reasons for his actions. A President who detains judges because he dislikes their constitutional opinions is acting unlawfully. A President who detains judges because they are behaving criminally is not. A theory that cannot distinguish between a President acting within his constitutional authority and a President purporting to act within his constitutional authority is going to be inadequate.

The Court created more uncertainty within its expansive notion of official presidential acts and its refusal to provide more of a hint as to where those limits are to be found. Take the problem of presidential speech. Presumably Congress cannot criminalize the President's making speeches in public. Even without a theory of presidential speech being part of the President's Article II authority, Congress would encounter some First Amendment limits to an overly broad ban on presidential speechmaking. The *Trump* Court, however, was less focused on the First Amendment than on Article II. It focused on distinguishing between the occupant of the White House speaking to the public as part of his "official responsibilities" and speaking in an "unofficial capacity."[97] When speaking "as a candidate for office or party leader," the President speaks in an "unofficial capacity."[98]

But is it the case that even when Presidents speak in their official capacity, they cannot be brought within the bounds of the criminal law? The exceptions for the First Amendment are narrow, and it would seem strange if Presidents were constitutionally criminally immune when operating within those exceptions. Shoehorning such presidential communications into an "unofficial speech" category just because of their illicit content would seem to be nothing but a legal fiction. If a President were to post child pornography on the White House website or make true threats in a televised speech from the Oval Office, such speech might functionally be within the "outer perimeter of his official responsibilit[ies]" and yet still be criminal under generally applicable law.[99] The speech would not be "otherwise lawful" conduct in Attorney General Barr's framework, but it could perhaps become lawful precisely because the President was doing it while conducting his office. A "fact specific" analysis might help us sort such situations out. But that is less because we could distinguish official from unofficial acts than because we could balance the competing constitutional interests to determine when presidential interests would have to give way to other public concerns.

Imagine that then-President Trump engaged in speech that in fact met the standards for incitement to imminent unlawful action and for being integral to illegal conduct. As a consequence, Trump would have engaged in speech that fell outside the scope of established First Amendment protections and within the scope of established and generally applicable criminal laws. The Court's *Trump* opinion provides a path to prosecuting such speech if Trump engaged in such

[97] *Trump*, 144 S. Ct. at 2340.

[98] *Id.*

[99] *Id.* at 2331.

speech in an unofficial capacity, for example by engaging in such speech as a political candidate. But what if that out is not available? The Court has characterized a wide range of presidential speech as within the "outer perimeter of his official responsibilities," but such speech could be criminal in such a sense. Is a President necessarily immune from criminal prosecution if he gives an "official" speech that incites a riot? *Contra* the dissent, the relevant question would not be whether the President's motives in delivering such speech were corrupt. *Contra* the majority, the relevant question would not be whether the President's speech was delivered in an unofficial capacity. The question is ultimately one of where the balance of constitutional and public interests is to be found. Even if we accept the majority's desire to constitutionalize the President's bully pulpit, the constitutional interest in that bully pulpit is substantially weaker than the constitutional interest in the discretionary authority vested in the commander-in-chief or chief magistrate. At the same time, the public interest in not having elected demagogues go around inciting riots or orchestrating criminal conspiracies is quite substantial.

The *Trump* Court simultaneously said too little and too much, and it would have done better to have framed the constitutional issue differently. As it stands, the Court has invited unnecessary controversy and confusion. The Court has put off until later questions that will eventually have to be answered. If the Court ever gets around to answering those questions, it seems likely that the apparently simple framework outlined in the majority opinion will have to be significantly complicated.

Justice Barrett offered a more promising path forward than Chief Justice Roberts. A criminal statute may impermissibly intrude on the President's constitutional authority, and that is true whether the criminal statute is written in general terms or specifically targets presidential actions. Former Presidents are "immune" from criminal prosecution for their actions as President to the extent that those actions are constitutionally insulated from congressional interference. But to the extent that those actions are properly subject to congressional regulation, Presidents must face the consequences of their actions. There are unavoidably hard problems involved in determining whether a particular presidential action is beyond the reach of congressional statutes, and that is no less true in the context of criminal statutes than in the context of other federal legislation.

The majority could have reserved for a later case the question of where exactly the outer bounds of presidential power might be in any particular circumstance, but it nonetheless could have been clearer about the relevant questions to be asked if Congress is contemplating criminalizing some presidential conduct or a prosecutor is considering pursuing an indictment for some presidential action.

A crucial difference between the majority opinion and the dissent turns on a prediction about the future. The majority worries that a hyperpolarized world will subject former Presidents to questionable criminal prosecutions and undermine the ability of the President to perform his constitutional functions. The dissent imagines that the criminal justice system will rise above such pressures but that a President unconcerned about criminal sanctions will inevitably abuse his powers. Constitutional jurisprudence frequently depends on such assessments about the balance of probabilities and the realities of how institutions will operate. Which opinion currently seems more persuasive depends in part on our intuitions about those political realities and where our country is headed. Which opinion will in the future seem more prescient will depend on how those predictions turn out. If Presidents begin to behave in a more criminal fashion, then Sotomayor will have been vindicated in thinking that the threat of criminal prosecution was doing some real work in deterring presidential misconduct. If politicized lawfare becomes a routine feature of our domestic politics, then we may be thankful that Roberts saw what was coming and constructed some constitutional barriers to Presidents becoming victims of at least some forms of "politics by other means." Do we expect our future Presidents to be petty or not-so-petty criminals, or do we expect our future prosecutors to be partisan zealots? We can hope that neither will be true, but we might have to prepare for the possibility that one or both might be true.

A Lost Opportunity to Protect Democracy Against Itself: What the Supreme Court Got Wrong in *Trump v. Anderson*

*Ilya Somin**

Introduction

In *Trump v. Anderson*,[1] a divided Supreme Court achieved unusual unanimity in an important case. All nine Justices agreed that state governments could not use Section 3 of the Fourteenth Amendment to disqualify former President Donald Trump from running for the presidency in the 2024 election. Section 3, the Court ruled, is not "self-enforcing."[2] Unfortunately, the Court achieved unanimity by making a grave error. In so doing, they went against the text and original meaning of the Fourteenth Amendment and undermined a potentially vital constitutional safeguard of liberal democracy.

Section 3 states that "No person shall be a Senator or Representative in Congress, or elector of President and Vice-President, or hold any office, civil or military, under the United States, or under any State, who, having previously taken an oath, as a member of

* Professor of Law, George Mason University. For helpful suggestions and comments, I would like to thank Will Baude, Thomas Berry, Josh Blackman, Gerard Magliocca, Mike Paulsen, Josh Sarnoff, and Seth Barrett Tillman. I would like to thank Devin Gray and Tyler Lardieri for helpful research assistance. Parts of this article are adapted, with permission, from Ilya Somin, *What the Supreme Court Got Wrong in the Trump Section 3 Case*, LAWFARE (Mar. 8, 2024), https://www.lawfaremedia.org/article/what-the-supreme-court-got-wrong-in-the-trump-section-3-case, and Ilya Somin, *Section 3 Disqualifications for Democracy Preservation*, LAWFARE (Sept. 6, 2023), https://www.lawfaremedia.org/article/section-3-disqualifications-for-democracy-preservation.

[1] 601 U.S. 100 (2024).

[2] *Id.* at 110–17.

Congress, or as an officer of the United States, or as a member of any State legislature, or as an executive or judicial officer of any State, to support the Constitution of the United States, shall have engaged in insurrection or rebellion against the same, or given aid or comfort to the enemies thereof."[3] The plaintiffs in the case argued that Trump had engaged in insurrection by instigating the January 6, 2021, attack on the Capitol in order to stay in power after losing the 2020 presidential election. By focusing exclusively on the self-execution issue, the Court left for another day all the other arguments at stake in the *Trump v. Anderson* case, such as whether the Jan. 6, 2021, attack on the Capitol qualifies as an "insurrection," whether Trump "engaged" in it, whether his actions were protected by the First Amendment, whether Trump received adequate due process, and whether the presidency is an "office . . . under the United States" covered by Section 3. The Justices may hope they can avoid ever having to decide these questions.

In this article, I explain what the Court got wrong. I also consider some of the broader issues raised by the case that the Justices did not address because they disposed of the litigation against Trump on the self-enforcement issue.

Part I provides a brief overview of the history of the Section 3 litigation against Trump. In Part II, I explain why the Court got the issue of self-enforcement badly wrong. In the process, I also address the argument that disqualification required a prior criminal conviction for "insurrection."[4] Part III considers the question of whether the January 6 attack qualifies as an "insurrection," and—more briefly— whether Trump "engaged" in it. The answers to both questions are "yes," though the second is a closer call than the first.

Part IV addresses broader implications of Section 3 for constitutional democracy. There is an obvious tension between respect for democracy and provisions that limit voter choice, as Section 3

---

[3] U.S. CONST. amend. XIV, § 3.

[4] This issue was the subject of an amicus brief I filed in the case. *See* Brief of Amicus Curiae Professor Ilya Somin in Support of Respondent, Trump v. Anderson, 601 U.S. 100 (2024) (No. 23-719) [hereinafter Somin, Amicus Brief], https://www.supreme court.gov/DocketPDF/23/23-719/299426/20240131152417959_23-719%20Amicus %20BOM%20Somin%20PDFA.pdf.

necessarily does. Nonetheless, there is good reason for this and some other constitutional constraints that protect the democratic process against itself. The Supreme Court's effective gutting of Section 3 gravely weakens one of those constraints.

Finally, Part V summarizes the implications of the *Trump v. Anderson* decision for the future. The Court's ruling largely guts enforcement of Section 3 against federal officeholders and candidates for federal office. But it leaves open the possibility that Section 3 can still be enforced against state officials and candidates for state offices.

I do not attempt to address every issue raised by the Section 3 case against Trump, instead focusing on the one on which the Supreme Court based its decision, plus a few others that have broad applicability and on which I have points to make that have, I believe, not been sufficiently covered by previous commentaries on the case.

For those reasons I do not address the much-debated issues of whether the President is an "officer of the United States" and therefore barred from future office-holding if he engages in insurrection, and whether the presidency is an "office . . . under the United States" that insurrectionists are forbidden to hold in the future.[5] Similarly, I do not consider the question of whether the

---

[5] For detailed statements of opposing views on this question, see William Baude & Michael Stokes Paulsen, *The Sweep and Force of Section Three*, 172 U. Pa. L. Rev. 605 (2024) (arguing that the President is covered under both provisions); Mark Graber, *Section Three of the Fourteenth Amendment: Our Questions, Their Answers*, U. Md. Legal Studies Rsch. Paper No. 2023-16 (2023), https://papers.ssrn.com/sol3/papers.cfm?abstract_id=4591133 (same); Josh Blackman & Seth Barrett Tillman, *Sweeping and Forcing the President into Section 3*, 28 Tex. Rev. L. & Politics 350 (2024) (arguing that the President is not "an officer of the United States"), and Kurt Lash, *The Meaning and Ambiguity of Section Three of the Fourteenth Amendment*, 47 Harv. J. L. & Pub. Pol'y 310 (2024) (arguing that the presidency is not an "office. . . under the United States"). I have previously summarized my perspective on the "officer" issue in Ilya Somin, *Why President Trump is an "Officer" who Can be Disqualified From Holding Public Office Under Section 3 of the 14th Amendment*, Reason (Sept. 16, 2024), https://reason.com/volokh/2023/09/16/why-president-trump-is-an-officer-who-can-be-disqualified-from-holding-public-office-under-section-3-of-the-14th-amendment/, and Ilya Somin, *Yes, Trump Is Disqualified from Office*, Bulwark (Nov. 30, 2023), https://www.thebulwark.com/p/trump-disqualified-office-fourteenth-amendment.

Colorado courts gave Trump constitutionally adequate due process; I have previously addressed this latter issue in my amicus brief before the Supreme Court.[6] I also do not go into the argument that Trump's actions qualify as speech protected by the First Amendment.[7]

I. Overview of the Trump Section 3 Litigation

After losing the 2020 presidential election to Joe Biden, then-President Donald Trump refused to concede that he had been defeated, instead falsely claiming that he was a victim of voter fraud. Trump and his political allies filed numerous lawsuits challenging the election results, almost all of which were rejected by the courts or withdrawn by the plaintiffs themselves after it became clear they had no chance of success.[8] Several of the decisions rejecting Trump's election challenges were written by conservative judges who had been appointed by Trump himself.[9]

But Trump refused to concede defeat, even after his legal challenges had failed. Instead, he and various political allies attempted to pressure Vice President Mike Pence into rejecting duly cast electoral votes for Biden, and pressure state officials into falsifying vote totals and substituting fake electors for those duly chosen.[10]

As a result of Trump's continued efforts to overturn the 2020 election result, hundreds of his supporters were inspired to attack

---

[6] See Somin, Amicus Brief, *supra* note 4 at 17–25.

[7] This issue is discussed in detail in the decision of the Colorado Supreme Court ruling that Trump is disqualified under Section 3. *See* Anderson v. Griswold, 543 P.3d 283, 336–42 (Colo. 2023), *rev'd* Trump v. Anderson, 601 U.S. 100 (2024).

[8] For a detailed overview of the litigation following the 2020 election, see John Danforth et al., *Lost, Not Stolen: The Conservative Case that Trump Lost and Biden Won the 2020 Election* (July 2022), https://lostnotstolen.org/.

[9] *See, e.g., id.* at 57 (citing Donald J. Trump for President, Inc. v. Sec'y of Pa., 830 F. App'x 377, 382 (3d Cir. 2020) (Bibas, J.) (expressing that Trump's claims "ha[d] no merit")).

[10] For an extensive overview of these machinations, see H.R. REP. No. 117-663, FINAL REPORT: SELECT COMMITTEE TO INVESTIGATE THE JANUARY 6TH ATTACK ON THE UNITED STATES CAPITOL chs. 2–3 (2022), available at https://www.govinfo.gov/content/pkg/GPO-J6-REPORT/pdf/GPO-J6-REPORT.pdf.

the Capitol on January 6, 2021, the date on which Congress met to certify the electoral vote totals. Their attack was defeated by police and military forces, but only after five people were killed and over 140 police officers injured.[11] After the failure of the assault, Trump was ultimately forced to leave office on January 20, 2021, as required by law. He did not attempt further resistance to the transition of power.

The idea that the January 6 attack qualifies as an "insurrection" requiring Trump's disqualification under Section 3 first emerged soon after the attack itself, advanced by legal scholars Gerard Magliocca and Mark Graber.[12] Proceedings began against a number of lower-level participants in the attack who had previously held public office.[13]

But the idea of disqualifying Trump himself gained new impetus from the circulation of an article advocating that position. The article was written by prominent right-of-center originalist legal scholars William Baude and Michael Stokes Paulsen.[14] Although not published until 2024, the article was posted to the SSRN website on August 14, 2023,[15] and quickly became a major focus of academic and public debate.

---

[11] Alanna Durkin Richer & Michael Kunzelman, *Hundreds of Convictions, But a Major Mystery Is Still Unsolved 3 Years after the Jan. 6 Capitol Riot*, Associated Press (Jan. 5, 2024), https://apnews.com/article/capitol-riot-jan-6-criminal-cases-anniversary-bf436efe760751b1356f937e55bedaa5.

[12] For early arguments raising this possibility, see, e.g., Gerard Magliocca, *The 14th Amendment's Disqualification Provision and the Events of Jan. 6*, Lawfare (Jan. 19, 2021), https://www.lawfaremedia.org/article/14th-amendments-disqualification-provision-and-events-jan-6, and Mark Graber, *Treason, Insurrection, and Disqualification: From the Fugitive Slave Act of 1850 to Jan. 6, 2021*, Lawfare (Sept. 26, 2022), https://www.lawfaremedia.org/article/treason-insurrection-and-disqualification-fugitive-slave-act-1850-jan-6-2021.

[13] *See, e.g.*, New Mexico *ex rel*. White v. Griffin, No. D-101-CV-2022-00473, 2022 WL 4295619 at *24 (NM. Dist. Ct., Sept. 6, 2022) (quo warranto action against New Mexico state officeholder who participated in the January 6 attack), *cert. denied*, 144 S. Ct. 1056 (2024).

[14] William Baude & Michael Stokes Paulsen, *The Sweep and Force of Section Three*, 172 U. Pa. L. Rev. 605 (2024).

[15] *See id.*

With the impetus and inspiration provided by the Baude-Paulsen article, a number of lawsuits were filed seeking Trump's disqualification from the upcoming 2024 presidential election, many of them initiated by the activist organization Citizens for Responsibility and Ethics in Washington (CREW).[16]

Many of these cases were dismissed on various procedural grounds.[17] The lawsuit filed by CREW on behalf of a group of

[16] For an overview of these cases, see Hyemin Han & Caleb Benjamin et al., *The Trump Disqualification Tracker, Section 3 Challenges as of March 4, 2024*, Lawfare (Mar. 4, 2024), https://www.lawfaremedia.org/current-projects/the-trump-trials/section-3-litigation-tracker. As of March 4, 2024, the date of the *Trump v. Anderson* decision, Lawfare "stopped tracking state-by-state Section 3 challenges in light of the Court's ruling." *Id.*

[17] *See* Castro v. Dahlstrom, No. 1:23-cv-00011-JMK (D. Alaska Jan. 26, 2024), https://s3.documentcloud.org/documents/24427447/castro-v-dahlstrom-et-al_dismissal.pdf (dismissed for lack of jurisdiction); Castro v. Fontes, No. CV-23-01865-PHX-DLR, 2023 U.S. Dist. LEXIS 215802, at *17 (D. Ariz. Dec. 4, 2023) (dismissed for lack of subject matter jurisdiction), *aff'd* Castro v. Fontes, No. 23-3960, 2024 U.S. App. LEXIS 13639 (9th Cir. Mar. 29, 2024) (affirming dismissal following the decision in *Trump v. Anderson*); Castro v. Weber, No. 2:23-cv-02172 DAD AC (PS), 2023 WL 6931322, at *2 (E.D. Cal. Oct. 19, 2023) (dismissed with prejudice for lack of subject matter jurisdiction); Castro v. Trump, No. 23-80015-CIV, 2023 WL 7093129, at *1 (S.D. Fla. June 26, 2023) (dismissed for lack of Article III standing and ripeness), *cert. denied*, 144 S. Ct. 265 (2023); Chafee v. Trump, Nos. 24-01, 24-02 (Mass State Ballot Law Comm'n Jan. 22, 2024), https://s3.documentcloud.org/documents/24372010/dismissal-without-prejudice.pdf (dismissed for lack of jurisdiction); LaBrant v. Benson, No. 23-000137-MZ, 2023 WL 8786168 (Mich. Ct. Cl. Nov. 14, 2023) (denied), *aff'd sub nom.* Davis v. Wayne Cnty. Election Comm'n, No. 368615, 2023 WL 8656163 (Mich. Ct. App. Dec. 14, 2023), *appeal denied sub nom*, LaBrant v. Sec. of State, 998 N.W.2d 216 (Mich. 2023); Growe v. Simon, 2 N.W.3d 490 (Minn. 2024) (per curiam) (dismissed with prejudice as to primary ballot; dismissed without prejudice as to general election ballot); Castro v. Aguilar, No. 2:23-cv-01387-GMN-BNW, 2024 WL 81388, at *2 (D. Nev. Jan. 8, 2024) (dismissed for lack of standing); Castro v. N.H. Sec'y of State, No. 23-CV-416-JL, 2023 WL 7110390, at *9 (D.N.H. Oct. 27, 2023) (dismissed for lack of standing), *aff'd sub nom.* Castro v. Scanlan, 86 F.4th 947 (1st Cir. 2023); Castro v. Toulouse Oliver, No. 1:23-CV-00766-MLG-GJF, 2024 U.S. Dist. LEXIS 7165, at *16 (D.N.M. Jan. 12, 2024) (dismissed for lack of subject matter jurisdiction); Martin v. N.C. State Bd. of Elections, No. 23CV037438-910 (N.C. Super. Ct. Dec. 20, 2023) (dismissed for lack of jurisdiction, pending appeal); State *ex rel.* Nelson v. Griffin-Valade, No. S070658, 2024 Ore. LEXIS 2 (Or. Jan. 12, 2024) (denying relief without prejudice), *petition for reconsideration denied*, State *ex rel.* Nelson v. Griffin-Valade, No. S070658, 2024 Ore. LEXIS 56 (Sup. Ct. Or. Feb. 1, 2024); Castro v. Amore, No. CV 23-405 JJM, 2023 WL 8191835, at *1 (D.R.I. Nov. 27, 2023) (dismissed in light of the First Circuit's opinion in *Castro*, 86 F.4th 947); Castro v. Trump, No. CV 3:23-4501-MGL-SVH, 2023 WL 8767192, at *12 (D.S.C. Nov. 7, 2023)) (recommendation that relief be denied), *adopted in part sub nom.* Castro v. SC Elections Comm'n, No. 3:23-4501-MGL, 2024 WL 340779 (D.S.C. Jan. 30, 2024), *appeal dismissed*, Castro v. Trump, No. 3:23-4501-MGL, 2024 U.S. App. LEXIS 5300 (4th Cir. Mar. 5, 2024) Castro v.

Colorado voters opposed to Trump was the first to proceed to a decision on the merits. The state trial court ruled for Trump on the ground that Section 3 does not apply to the President, even though—significantly—the court also found that he had engaged in insurrection.[18] The Colorado Supreme Court ruled against Trump,[19] overturning the trial court decision on the issue of the application of Section 3 to the President, and also holding for the plaintiffs on the other issues at stake in the case.

Later, an Illinois state court and the Secretary of State of Maine also ruled against Trump in their states' respective Section 3 cases.[20] They relied on reasoning similar to that of the Colorado Supreme Court.

Trump, No. 4:23-CV-556-Y (N.D. Tex. Feb. 7, 2024), https://s3.documentcloud.org/documents/24427301/177116604801.pdf (dismissed for insufficient service of process); Castro v. Doe, 2024 U.S. Dist. LEXIS 54759 (N.D. Tex., Jan. 10, 2024), *adopted*, Castro v. Doe, No. 4:23-cv-00613-P, 2024 U.S. Dist. LEXIS 52231 (N.D. Tex. Mar. 25, 2024) (dismissed for want of personal jurisdiction and failure to timely serve); Castro v. Copeland-Hanzas, No. 2:23-CV-453 (D. Vt. Feb. 12, 2024), https://s3.documentcloud.org/documents/24429114/dismissal-without-prejudice_copeland.pdf (dismissed following Castro's failure to serve the defendants); Ithaka et al. v. Trump, No. 24-2-00119 (Wash. Super. Ct. Jan. 19, 2024) (dismissed); Castro v. Warner, No. 2:23-CV-00598, 2023 WL 8853726, at *6 (S.D. W. Va. Dec. 21, 2023) (dismissed for lack of standing), *appeal dismissed sub nom.* Castro v. Sec'y of W. Va., No. 24-1040, 2024 WL 3339290 (4th Cir. Mar. 5, 2024); Castro v. Wis. Elections Comm'n, No. 2023CV002288 (Wis. Cir. Ct. Mar. 4, 2023) (dismissed); Bangstad v. Trump, No. 2024CV000053 (Wis. Cir. Ct. Mar. 4, 2024) (dismissed); Newcomb v. Gray, No. 2023-CV-003610, (Wyo. Dist. Ct. Jan. 4, 2024), https://s3.documentcloud.org/documents/24357996/order-granting-defendant-s-motion-to-dismiss.pdf (dismissed for lack of ripeness; on appeal).

[18] Anderson v. Griswold, 2023 WL 8006216 (Colo. Dist. Ct., Nov. 17, 2023), *rev'd*, 543 P.3d 283 (Colo. 2023), *aff'd on other grounds sub nom.* Trump v. Anderson, 601 U.S. 100 (2024).

[19] *See* Anderson v. Griswold, 543 P.3d 283, *rev'd sub nom.* Trump v. Anderson, 601 U.S. 100 (2024).

[20] *See* Anderson v. Trump, No. 2024COEL000013, slip op. at 36–37 (Ill. Cir. Ct. Feb. 28, 2024), https://s3.documentcloud.org/documents/24449331/2024_illinois.pdf (Trump disqualified;decision stayed pending appeal); In re Challenges of Rosen, et al., Ruling of the Secretary of State (Me. Sec'y of State, Dec. 28, 2023), https://www.maine.gov/sos/news/2023/Decision%20in%20Challenge%20to%20Trump%20Presidential%20Primary%20Petitions.pdf, *aff'd sub nom.* Trump v. Bellows, No. AP-24-01, 2024 WL 989060, at *9 (Me. Super. Ct. Jan. 17, 2024) (Trump disqualified; case remanded to Secretary of State Bellows pending the outcome of *Trump v. Anderson*), *appeal dismissed sub nom.* Trump v. Sec'y of State, 307 A.3d 1089 (Me. 2024).

The federal Supreme Court quickly decided to hear the Colorado case, which it did on an accelerated schedule, in order to resolve it before the Colorado state Republican primary scheduled for March 5, 2024. The Supreme Court's decision in *Trump v. Anderson* overturned the Colorado Supreme Court ruling disqualifying Donald Trump from the presidency under Section 3 of the 14th Amendment.[21] It did so on the grounds that Section 3 is not "self-executing."

II. What the Court Got Wrong on Self-Enforcement

In a per curiam opinion jointly authored by five Justices, including Chief Justice John Roberts, the Court ruled that only Congress, acting through legislation, has the power to determine who is disqualified and under what procedures. This outcome was predictable based on the oral argument,[22] which focused on this issue to the exclusion of virtually all the other questions at stake in the case. But the Court nonetheless got the issue badly wrong.

The Court's unanimity in reversing the Colorado Supreme Court undermines claims that the result was dictated by the conservative Justices' partisan or ideological sympathy for Trump. Nonetheless, unanimity is no guarantee of correctness. And the seeming unanimity was belied by four Justices' rejection of much of the majority's reasoning. Section 3 states that "No person" can hold any state or federal office if they had previously been "a member of Congress, . . . an officer of the United States," or a state official and then "engaged in insurrection or rebellion against the same, or given aid or comfort to the enemies thereof."[23]

By focusing exclusively on the self-execution issue, the Court left for another day all the other arguments at stake in *Trump v. Anderson*, such as whether the January 6, 2021, attack on the Capitol qualifies as an "insurrection," whether Trump "engaged" in it, whether his actions were protected by the First Amendment, whether Trump received adequate due process, and whether the President is an "officer

---

[21] 601 U.S. 100 (2024).

[22] For my analysis of the oral argument, see Ilya Somin, *Thoughts on the Supreme Court Oral Argument in the Trump Section 3 Case*, REASON (Feb. 8, 2024), https://reason.com/volokh/2024/02/08/thoughts-on-the-supreme-court-oral-argument-in-the-trump-section-3-case/.

[23] U.S. CONST. amend. XIV, § 3.

of the United States" covered by Section 3.[24] The Justices may have hoped they could avoid ever having to decide these questions. As William Baude, one of the main architects of the Section 3 argument against Trump, suggested, perhaps "[t]he ruling's real function was to let the court reverse the Colorado Supreme Court and avoid the political firestorm that might have ensued, without requiring the court to take sides on what happened on Jan. 6."[25]

The Court's resolution of the self-enforcement issue is based on badly flawed reasoning and relies heavily on dubious policy arguments invoking the overblown danger of a "patchwork" of conflicting state resolutions of Section 3 issues. The Court's venture into policy was also indefensibly one-sided, failing to consider the practical dangers of effectively neutering Section 3 with respect to candidates for federal office and holders of such positions.

A. Text and Original Meaning

Under the Court's approach, only Congress has the power to determine which people are to be disqualified and under what procedures—at least when it comes to candidates for federal office and officials holding those offices. The majority claimed that Congress's Section 5 power to enact "appropriate" legislation enforcing the 14th Amendment is the exclusive mode of enforcing Section 3.[26] It held that "[t]he Constitution empowers Congress to prescribe how . . . determinations [on Section 3 disqualification] should be made" and that "[t]he relevant provision is Section 5, which enables Congress, subject of course to judicial review, to pass 'appropriate legislation' to 'enforce' the Fourteenth Amendment."[27]

This language appears to exclude any other mode of enforcing Section 3, at least against federal officeholders and candidates for federal office.[28] To be sure, the majority also referred to the fact that "[i]n the years following ratification, the House and Senate exercised their unique powers under Article I to adjudicate challenges

---

[24] All of these issues were addressed at length in the Colorado Supreme Court ruling. *See* Anderson v. Griswold, 543 P.3d at 306–42.

[25] Will Baude, *A Principled Supreme Court, Unnerved by Trump*, N.Y. Times (July 5, 2024), https://www.nytimes.com/2024/07/05/opinion/supreme-court-trump.html.

[26] Trump v. Anderson, 601 U.S. at 109–16.

[27] *Id.* at 109–10.

[28] *See* Part V, *infra*, for discussion of implications for state and local offices.

contending that certain prospective or sitting Members could not take or retain their seats due to Section 3."[29] But it did not indicate that these deliberations were constitutionally permissible, and it did not reject or modify its earlier statement that Section 5 is "the relevant provision" for enforcing Section 3.[30]

There are several flaws in the Court's analysis. The most basic is that there is no good reason to believe that Section 5 is the *exclusive* mode of enforcing Section 3. Nothing in the text suggests otherwise. To repeat, Section 3 states that "No person shall be a Senator or Representative in Congress, or elector of President and Vice-President, or hold any office, civil or military, under the United States, or under any State, who, having previously taken an oath, as a member of Congress, or as an officer of the United States, or as a member of any State legislature, or as an executive or judicial officer of any State, to support the Constitution of the United States, shall have engaged in insurrection or rebellion against the same, or given aid or comfort to the enemies thereof."[31] This reads like a categorical prohibition. It is not limited only to those people covered by enforcement legislation. Nor are there any other exceptions, other than for those who have been specifically exempted by a two-thirds vote in both houses of Congress. In the absence of such a legislative exemption, the text presumes that covered persons are to be disqualified, regardless of anything else that might happen. As Baude and Paulsen put it, "Section Three requires no implementing legislation by Congress. Its commands are enacted into law by the enactment of the Fourteenth Amendment."[32] Section 3, they note, "does not grant a power to Congress (or any other body) to enact or effectuate a rule of disqualification. It enacts the rule itself," much like other presidential qualifications laid out in the Constitution, such as the requirement that the president be at least 35 years old.[33]

Section 5 in no way changes that textual presumption. As the Colorado Supreme Court emphasized in its ruling,[34] Section 5 em-

---

[29] Trump v. Anderson, 601 U.S. at 114.

[30] *Id.* at 109.

[31] U.S. CONST. amend. XIV, § 3.

[32] Baude & Paulsen, supra note 14, at 622.

[33] *Id.* at 622–23.

[34] *See* Anderson v. Griswold, 543 P.3d at 312–13.

powers Congress to enforce not just Section 3 but also every other part of the Fourteenth Amendment, including its protections against racial and ethnic discrimination, the Due Process Clause, and more. These other provisions are all considered to be self-executing, under longstanding federal Supreme Court precedent.[35] Section 5 legislation is not the exclusive mode of enforcement for these other parts of the amendment.

Thus, state governments and federal courts can enforce these provisions even in the absence of congressional Section 5 enforcement legislation. Otherwise, as the Colorado Supreme Court noted, "Congress could nullify them by simply not passing enacting legislation."[36] Why should Section 3 be any different? The Supreme Court decision does not give us any good answer to that question.

Allowing such nullification would be inconsistent with the primary goal of Section 3, preventing the return to power of former Confederate insurrectionists.[37] If Congress could prevent that merely by failing to enact enforcement legislation or by repealing previously enacted law, that objective would be gravely compromised.

As the Supreme Court ruling notes,[38] Congress's Section 5 power is "remedial" in nature. Under the Court's landmark precedent in *City of Boerne v. Flores*, an exercise of Section 5 power must be "congruent and proportional" to the violations of the amendment it is intended to remedy.[39] If Section 5 legislation is remedial in nature, including when it comes to enforcing Section 3, that implies other entities—state governments and federal courts—have the initial responsibility for ensuring compliance with Section 3. The role of Section 5 is to remedy violations of that duty, not to be the exclusive enforcement mechanism.

Under the text such purported congressional exclusivity is even more problematic for Section 3 than for other parts of the

---

[35] *See, e.g.,* The Civil Rights Cases, 109 U.S. 3, 20 (1883) (the Fourteenth Amendment "is undoubtedly self-executing without any ancillary legislation, so far as its terms are applicable to any existing state of circumstances.").

[36] Anderson v. Griswold, 543 P.3d at 314.

[37] On the centrality of this objective for the framers of the Fourteenth Amendment, see Mark A. Graber, Punish Treason, Reward Loyalty: The Forgotten Goals of Constitutional Reform After the Civil War 92–94 (2023). [from Mark to War in large and small caps]

[38] Trump v. Anderson, 601 U.S. at 115 (noting that "Section 5 is strictly remedial") (quotation marks omitted).

[39] *See generally* City of Boerne v. Flores, 521 U.S. 507 (1997).

Fourteenth Amendment. Section 3 explicitly indicates that Congress may lift disqualifications "by a vote of two-thirds of each House." There would be little need for that provision if Congress could prevent disqualification simply by not passing implementing legislation or by affirmatively exempting those it wished to protect from any enforcement legislation it chooses to enact. As the three liberal justices—Ketanji Brown Jackson, Elena Kagan, and Sonia Sotomayor—noted in their concurring opinion, "[i]t is hard to understand why the Constitution would require a congressional supermajority to remove a disqualification if a simple majority could nullify Section 3's operation by repealing or declining to pass implementing legislation."[40]

The per curiam opinion argues that the "remedial" nature of Section 5 indicates that states are barred from enforcing Section 3 because, "such state enforcement might be argued to sweep more broadly than congressional enforcement could under our precedents," thereby leading to the "implausible" conclusion that "the Constitution grants the States freer rein than Congress to decide how Section 3 should be enforced with respect to federal offices."[41]

But there is no reason to think such state enforcement authority would be significantly broader than that of Congress. After all, both congressional and state enforcement authority would only extend to disqualifying persons who previously held relevant offices and "shall have engaged in insurrection or rebellion against the [the United States], or given aid or comfort to the enemies thereof."[42]

If the scope of Congress's "remedial" authority is narrowly construed to include only situations where a violation of Section 3 has already occurred, then perhaps state power would be broader, since the latter could make provision for enforcement in advance of violations. But such a divergence is entirely plausible in a situation where one entity has "remedial" authority, while another must ensure that violations that require remedies do not arise in the first place. And, as a practical matter, any enforcement

---

[40] Trump v. Anderson, 601 U.S. at 121 (Sotomayor, Kagan, & Jackson, JJ., concurring in the judgment).

[41] Id. at 115 (per curiam opinion).

[42] U.S. CONST. amend. XIV, § 3.

measures taken in advance of possible violations could only disqualify officials and candidates who have engaged in activities that trigger disqualification. They could not, for example, be disqualified merely on suspicion that they might start an insurrection or rebellion in the future.

The per curiam opinion also complains that state enforcement is impermissible because it would "burden" Congress's power to remove Section 3 disabilities by a two-thirds vote in each house.[43] The majority feared that "if States were free to enforce Section 3 by barring candidates from running in the first place, Congress would be forced to exercise its disability removal power before voting begins if it wished for its decision to have any effect on the current election cycle."[44] But it is inherent in the nature of a power to lift a disqualification that it only takes effect after it is exercised. Until then, the disqualification remains in force. The "burden" on Congress arises from this inherent attribute of the combination of disqualifications and the power to remove them. If Congress wants the removal to have effect at Time X, it must enact it before X occurs. Because of the majority's neglect of relevant text and original meaning, prominent right-of-center originalist legal scholar Michael Rappaport labelled the Court's ruling an "originalist disaster," even though he ultimately believes that Trump should not have been disqualified because the January 6 attack was a "riot," not an "insurrection."[45] As Rappaport noted, the per curiam "opinion relies upon spurious, non-textual reasoning," because, while the constitutional text bars states from violating the Fourteenth Amendment, it does not prevent them from enforcing it.[46]

---

[43] Trump v. Anderson, 601 U.S. at 113.

[44] Rappaport, *supra* note 45.

[45] Michael Rappaport, *The Originalist Disaster in* Trump v. Anderson, THE ORIGINALISM BLOG (Mar. 5, 2024), https://originalismblog.typepad.com/the-originalism-blog/2024/03/the-originalist-disaster-of-trump-v-andersonmike-rappaport.html; see also Aziz Z. Huq, *Structural Logics of Presidential Disqualification: An Essay on* Trump v. Anderson, HARV. L. REV. (forthcoming), available at https://papers.ssrn.com/sol3/papers.cfm?abstract_id=4900090 at 7–8 (emphasizing the majority's deviation from originalist methodology). Huq also offers additional criticisms of the majority's reliance *on City of Boerne* and the "remedial" nature of Section 5. *Id.* at 20–22.

[46] *Id.*

The per curiam opinion emphasizes the need for uniformity in determining eligibility for federal office and argues that states lack the power to make such determinations:

> Because federal officers "'owe their existence and functions to the united voice of the whole, not of a portion, of the people,'" powers over their election and qualifications must be specifically "delegated to, rather than reserved by, the States." *U. S. Term Limits, Inc. v. Thornton*, 514 U. S. 779, 803–804 (1995) . . . . But nothing in the Constitution delegates to the States any power to enforce Section 3 against federal officeholders and candidates.[47]

This argument ignores the long-standing role of states in enforcing and adjudicating other constitutional qualifications for candidates for federal office, such as the requirements that the President must be 35 years old and a "natural born" citizen of the United States.[48] In 2016, there was litigation over claims brought by Trump supporters to the effect that Texas Republican Senator Ted Cruz, then Trump's chief rival for the GOP presidential nomination, was not a natural born citizen. State courts in Pennsylvania and New Jersey ruled that Cruz was eligible, rejecting the arguments against him.[49] But no one doubted that these state courts had the authority to adjudicate the issue.

In a 2012 decision written when he was a lower-court judge on the U.S. Court of Appeals for the Tenth Circuit, Supreme Court Justice Neil Gorsuch upheld a decision by Colorado state officials to bar from the ballot a would-be presidential candidate who was clearly not a natural born citizen. Then-Judge Gorsuch wrote that "a state's legitimate interest in protecting the integrity and practical functioning of the political process permits it to exclude from the ballot candidates who are constitutionally prohibited from assuming office."[50] This reasoning applies to Section 3 just as readily as to the Natural Born Citizen Clause. As Aziz Huq puts it, "[w]hy should one read

---

[47] Trump v. Anderson, 601 U.S. at 111 (citation omitted).

[48] U.S. CONST. art. II, § 5, Cl. 1; *cf.* Huq, *supra* note 45, at 25–26 (noting this inconsistency).

[49] *See* Elliott v. Cruz, 137 A.3d 646 (Pa. Cmwlth. Ct. 2016); Williams v. Cruz, OAL Dkt. No. STE 5016-16 (N.J. Off. of Admin. Law, Apr. 12, 2016), https://media.philly.com/documents/Judge's+ruling+Ted+Cruz+to+remain+on+NJ+ballot.pdf.

[50] Hassan v. Colorado, 495 F. App'x 947, 948 (10th Cir. 2012) (Gorsuch, J.).

the Constitution to allow States to enforce all other disqualification provisions in the Constitution except one hinging on past participation in insurrection or rebellion?"[51]

U.S. Term Limits v Thornton, a 1995 precedent heavily relied on by the Court, holds that states cannot impose term limits on members of Congress, reasoning that states lack the power to impose additional qualifications for holding federal office beyond those specified in the Constitution.[52] But that is not what Colorado did here. The state was merely trying to enforce a qualification already in the Constitution (that spelled out in Section 3), not impose a new one.

U.S. Term Limits was a close 5–4 decision, featuring a strong dissent by Justice Clarence Thomas, in which he argued that states can in fact add additional qualifications for candidates for federal office on their ballots, so long as doing so isn't specifically forbidden by the Constitution. As Thomas put it, "Nothing in the Constitution deprives the people of each State of the power to prescribe eligibility requirements for the candidates who seek to represent them in Congress."[53] If so, the same reasoning would empower states to prescribe requirements presidential candidates must meet to secure their electoral votes.

Thomas nonetheless joined the per curiam opinion in *Trump v. Anderson*. Perhaps he did so based on respect for precedent. But the per curiam opinion actually goes further in constraining states than *U.S. Term Limits* did. The former blocks states from enforcing an existing qualification for office mandated by the Constitution, not just imposing new ones.

The per curiam opinion relies heavily on a distinction between Section 3 disqualifications from state office and disqualifications from holding federal office.[54] It holds that states may potentially apply Section 3 to the former but cannot reach the latter without specific authorization from congressional legislation.[55]

This distinction between state and federal offices is nowhere to be found in the text and original meaning of Section 3. Indeed, as the Court indicated in a footnote, at least one candidate for federal

---

[51] Huq, *supra* note 45, at 26.

[52] *See generally* U.S. Term Limits v. Thornton, 514 U.S. 779 (1995).

[53] *Id.* at 845 (Thomas, J., dissenting).

[54] *See* Trump v. Anderson, 601 U.S. at 111–13.

[55] *See id.*

office—John Christy, a former Confederate who had won an election for a Georgia seat in the House of Representatives—was disqualified prior to any congressional enforcement legislation.[56] More such cases could easily have occurred, if not for the fact that in 1872—just four years after the ratification of the Fourteenth Amendment—Congress passed a sweeping amnesty act lifting Section 3 disqualifications for all but a few of those covered by Section 3.[57]

The per curiam *Trump v. Anderson* opinion also relies on *Griffin's Case*,[58] an 1869 ruling written by Supreme Court Chief Justice Salmon P. Chase, indicating that congressional legislation is required to enforce Section 3.[59] But, as the three liberal Justices noted in their concurring opinion, *Griffin's Case* was a "nonprecedential, lower court opinion by a single Justice in his capacity as a circuit judge."[60] In the nineteenth century, Supreme Court Justices routinely heard lower court cases in this way.[61] Rulings that Justices issued in that capacity did not speak for the Supreme Court as a whole. Even if the decision had some precedential weight for lower courts in the region where it was decided (Virginia),[62] it was not binding on the federal Supreme Court, or on state and federal courts elsewhere, including in Colorado.

In addition, Chief Justice Chase contradicted his own conclusion from *Griffin's Case* in *In re Davis*,[63] an 1868 circuit court case involving the treason prosecution of former Confederate President

[56] *See id.* at 113 & n.3.

[57] *See* An Act to Remove Political Disabilities Imposed by the Fourteenth Article of the Amendments to the Constitution of the United States, ch. 193, 17 Stat. 142 (1872). The act has come to be known as the General Amnesty Act of 1872. *See Presidential Pardons and Congressional Amnesty to Former Confederate Citizens, 1865–1877*, NATIONAL ARCHIVES (Nov. 2014), https://www.archives.gov/files/research/naturalization/411-confederate-amnesty-records.pdf.

[58] *See* Trump v. Anderson, 601 U.S. at 109 (citing Griffin's Case, 11 F. Cas. 7, 26 (No. 5,815) (C.C. Va. 1869) (Chase, Circuit Justice)).

[59] For a detailed critique of *Griffin's Case*, see Baude & Paulsen, *supra* note 14, at 644–59. For a defense, see Blackman & Tillman, *supra* note 5, at 404–483.

[60] *Id.* at 122 (Sotomayor, Kagan, & Jackson, JJ., concurring in the judgment).

[61] Supreme Court justices routinely "rode circuit" until 1911. *See* David R. Stras, *Why Supreme Court Justices Should Ride Circuit Again*, 91 MINN. L. REV. 1710, 1711–12 (2007).

[62] *See* Blackman & Tillman, *supra* note 5, at 498 (suggesting *Griffin's Case* might be a binding precedent in the Fourth Circuit, which includes Virginia). *But see* Cawthorn v. Amalfi, 35 F.4th 245, 278 n.16 (4th Cir. 2022) (Richardson, J., concurring) (arguing that *Griffin's Case* is not binding).

[63] In re Davis, 7 F. Cas. 63, 90, 92–94, (C.C.D. Va. 1871) (Chase, Circuit Justice).

Jefferson Davis. There, Chase held that Section 3 is in fact self-executing.[64] *In re Davis* is no more a binding precedent than *Griffin's Case*. But the contradiction between the two suggests that Chase is far from a consistent and reliable source on the issue of self-execution.

From the standpoint of original meaning, it is also notable that Congress enacted multiple bills granting Section 3 amnesties to ex-Confederates by the required two-thirds majority, between 1868 and 1870, before it had enacted any enforcement legislation.[65] Such acts would make little sense if Section 3 was understood to create disqualifications only for people covered by additional enforcement legislation.

Academic critiques of the Section 3 case against Trump fail to plug these holes in the Supreme Court's reasoning on self-enforcement.[66] The most extensive such defense, that by Josh Blackman and Seth Barrett Tillman,[67] fails to account for the fact that the text gives no indication that additional legislation is required. Nor does it account for the numerous ex-Confederates who were disqualified or presumed to be disqualified even before any enforcement legislation was enacted.

Blackman and Tillman try to reconcile Chief Justice Chase's positions in *Griffin's Case* with that in *In re Davis*, on the ground that the former involved "offensive" use of Section 3 as a "sword" (an attempt to disqualify an official from office), while the latter was a "defensive" use of Section 3 as a "shield" (an attempt by Davis to use Section 3 to forestall a prosecution for treason).[68] However, they admit they have no clear evidence of what Chase's reason for distinguishing the two cases was, and no such distinction is recorded in the cases themselves.[69]

---

[64] *See id.*

[65] For an overview, see RON FEIN & GERARD MAGLIOCCA ET AL., STATES CAN ENFORCE SECTION 3 OF THE 14TH AMENDMENT WITHOUT ANY NEW FEDERAL LEGISLATION, FREE SPEECH FOR PEOPLE, ISSUE REPORT NO. 2023-01 6–7 (2023), https://www.justsecurity.org/wp-content/uploads/2023/04/backgrounder-free-speech-for-people.pdf.

[66] For leading academic defenses of Trump's position in the litigation, see Blackman & Tillman, *supra* note 5, and Kurt Lash, *The Meaning and Ambiguity of Section Three of the Fourteenth Amendment*, 47 HARV. J. L. & PUB. POL'Y 310 (2024).

[67] *See generally* Blackman & Tillman, *supra* note 5.

[68] *Id.* at 484–502.

[69] *See id.* at 487 (discussing Chase's ruling in *Davis*, and noting "If you're looking for a clear statement of how Chase viewed the question, you're out of luck").

More generally, the "sword-shield" theory runs afoul of the lack of any such distinction in the text of the amendment, and of the many cases where ex-Confederates were presumed to be disqualified even before enforcement legislation was enacted.[70] In the recent case of *DeVillier v. Texas*,[71] decided a few weeks after Trump v. Anderson, the Supreme Court did note that "[c]onstitutional rights do not typically come with a built-in cause of action to allow for private enforcement in courts."[72] Josh Blackman has cited this ruling as additional support for his and Tillman's position.[73] But the Court in *DeVillier* chose not to resolve the issue of whether the Takings Clause of the Fifth Amendment is self-enforcing, because the Justices concluded there is a remedy available in state court.[74] So the scope of this pronouncement on self-execution is unclear, and is in any event a dictum unnecessary to the resolution of the case.

Perhaps more important, Section 3 is not a "constitutional right," but a structural limitation on government power, preventing some types of dangerous individuals from holding office. Even if constitutional rights are not self-enforcing in some situations, it doesn't follow that such structural constraints must be. The "sword-shield" distinction makes little sense in a structural context, because the point of structural constraints is not to protect individuals against violations of specified rights, but to protect society as a whole against excessive assertions of government power or (as in the case of Section 3) allowing that power to fall into the wrong hands.

When dealing with individual rights, it is at least plausible to argue that the holder needs judicial protection more when threatened with criminal or civil sanctions by the state, then when he or she seeks to use the right "offensively." Arguably, the danger to

---

[70] *See supra* note 66 and accompanying text.

[71] 601 U.S. 285 (2024).

[72] *Id.* at 291.

[73] Josh Blackman, *Unanimous Supreme Court Adopts the Sword-Shield Dichotomy to Explain How Constitutional Rights Can Be Litigated*, Reason (Apr. 17, 2024), https://reason.com/volokh/2024/04/17/unanimous-supreme-court-adopts-the-sword-shield-dichotomy-to-explain-how-constitutional-rights-can-be-litigated/.

[74] *DeVillier*, 601 U.S. at 292 (holding that "this case does not require us to resolve that question").

the individual is greater in the former case than the latter. By contrast, the offense-defense distinction makes little difference when it comes to Section 3. Regardless of who started the legal proceedings in question, the purpose of Section 3 is not to protect specific individuals, but all of society. The value of that protection depends on the nature of the office that the insurrectionist holds or aspires to, and how egregiously he or she might abuse its powers if given the chance.

Professor Kurt Lash has highlighted evidence that leading Republican federal Representative Thaddeus Stevens and Pennsylvania state Representative Thomas Chalfant both believed that enforcement legislation was necessary.[75] In the case of Stevens, it is not clear whether he thought that enforcement legislation was legally essential or merely necessary for pragmatic reasons, because enforcement would not be effective without it. For example, Stevens opined that Section 3 "will not execute itself, but as soon as it becomes a law, Congress at the next session will legislate to carry it out both in reference to the presidential and all other elections as we have the right to do."[76]

But Stevens could simply have been referring here to the possibility that enforcement legislation would be needed to overcome possible resistance by recalcitrant southern state authorities. In the very same speech quoted by Lash, Stevens referred to the danger that, if Section 3 were enacted, "there will be if not a Herod, then a worse than Herod elsewhere to obstruct our actions."[77] Herod, of course, was the notoriously tyrannical King of Israel at the time of the birth of Christ. This clearly refers to obstructionism by former Confederate states. Enforcement legislation, Stevens suggested, was needed to overcome that resistance.[78]

The same goes for Stevens's June 13, 1866, reference to the need for "proper enabling acts," also cited by Lash.[79] This statement occurs in the context of Stevens's fears that the removal of provisions

---

[75] *See* Lash, *supra* note 5, at 374–79.

[76] *See id.* at 375 (quoting CONG. GLOBE, 39th Cong., 1st Sess. 2544 (1866)).

[77] CONG. GLOBE, 39th Cong., 1st Sess. 2544 (1866).

[78] *See id.*

[79] Lash, *supra* note 59, at 375 (quoting CONG. GLOBE, 39th Cong., 1st Sess. 3148 (1866)).

that would have disenfranchised "all rebels" was a mistake that "endanger[ed] the Government of the country, both state and national," by creating the possibility that the "next president and Congress" would be under the control of "reconstructed rebels."[80] The purpose of the "proper enabling acts" that Stevens had in mind was to forestall this possibility by enacting legislation which "shall do justice to the freedmen and enjoin [their] enfranchisement as a condition precedent" to admitting members of Congress from the southern states.[81] This is rather clearly *not* a statement that additional legislation was required merely to ensure disqualification of those covered by Section 3. But even if Stevens's statements referred to legal rather than practical necessity, the statements of one member of the House of Representatives are not sufficient to outweigh both the clear meaning of the text and the general understanding that many ex-Confederates were presumptively disqualified even prior to the enactment of any enforcement legislation.[82]

Chalfant's statements are even less compelling evidence than those of Stevens. Chalfant was a Democrat and an opponent of the Fourteenth Amendment, and his views are not good evidence of the views of the amendment's supporters.[83] Moreover, Chalfant did not argue that enforcement legislation was legally necessary, but merely that disqualification required that "guilt must be established" by a "tribunal."[84] Chalfant did not explain why state courts or federal courts could not qualify as such tribunals. Finally, Chalfant's implicit assumption that disqualification is analogous to a criminal penalty[85] goes against the reality that disqualifica-

---

[80] CONG. GLOBE, 39th Cong., 1st Sess. 3148 (1866).

[81] *Id.*

[82] *See supra* note 58 and accompanying text.

[83] *See* Lash, *supra* note 5 at 375 (noting Chalfant's opposition).

[84] *Id.* at 375–76 (quoting Hon. Thomas Chalfant, member from Columbia County, in the House, January 30, 1867, on Senate Bill No. 3 (the proposed amendment), THE APPENDIX TO THE DAILY LEGISLATIVE RECORD CONTAINING THE DEBATES ON THE SEVERAL IMPORTANT BILLS BEFORE THE LEGISLATURE OF 1867, at LXXX (George Bergner ed., 1867)).

[85] For example, he argued that disqualification was a "question of guilt or innocence." *Id.* at 377. He also suggested that refusals to seat members of Congress disqualified under Section 3 would require transforming Congress "into a criminal court, for the trial of its members on criminal charges, for crimes committed years before the election?" *Id.*

tion is merely a civil disability, comparable to failure to meet other qualifications for officeholding.[86]

B. The Overblown Specter of a "Patchwork" of Conflicting State Decisions

The main motive for the Court's decision seems to have been not purely legal considerations, but rather practical concerns that letting states adjudicate Section 3 disqualifications will lead to a "patchwork" of conflicting procedures and determinations.[87] The per curiam majority opines that "state-by-state resolution of the question whether Section 3 bars a particular candidate for President from serving would be quite unlikely to yield a uniform answer."[88] Similarly, the concurring opinion by the three liberal Justices invokes the danger of "a chaotic state-by-state patchwork, at odds with our Nation's federalism principles."[89] On top of that, some critics of the Section 3 case against Trump warned that partisan state officials will seek to disqualify opposing-party candidates for specious reasons.[90]

These are at least somewhat legitimate concerns. But they are overblown. If state officials or state courts reach unsound or contradictory legal conclusions about the meaning of Section 3 (for example, by adopting overbroad definitions of what qualifies as an "insurrection" or what qualifies as "engaging" in it), their determinations could be reviewed in federal court, and the Supreme Court could impose a uniform definition of the terms in question. Indeed, the Court could have done so in this very case. Non-uniform interpretations of provisions of the federal Constitution by state and lower federal courts can and do occur in many contexts. Settling such issues is one of the reasons we have a Supreme Court in the first place. A large part of its docket routinely consists of cases where state supreme courts and federal appellate courts have reached divergent interpretations of one or another federal law or constitutional provision. Section 3 challenges need not be any different.

---

[86] *See* discussion in § II.D, *infra*.

[87] Trump v. Anderson, 601 U.S. at 116.

[88] *Id.*

[89] *Id.* at 118–19 (Sotomayor, Kagan, & Jackson, JJ., concurring in the judgment).

[90] *See, e.g.*, Michael McConnell, *Responding About the Fourteenth Amendment, "Insurrection," and Trump*, REASON (Aug. 12, 2023), https://reason.com/volokh/2023/08/12/prof-michael-mcconnell-responding-about-the-fourteenth-amendment-insurrection-and-trump/.

Perhaps Section 3 cases are special because they are more likely to turn on contested factual claims than litigation over a candidate's age or "natural born" citizen status. But conflicting factual determinations about candidate eligibility for office can also arise with respect to other constitutional qualifications for the presidency. For example, there might be disputes over the accuracy or validity of a candidate's birth certificate (recall "birther" claims that Barack Obama wasn't really born in the United States and that his birth certificate was fake). The same goes for the requirement that the President must have been a resident of the United States for 14 years prior to taking office. There could potentially be factual disputes about where the President lived at any given time.

The possibility of divergent conclusions on such issues is an unavoidable aspect of a system in which control over elections for federal offices is largely left to individual states rather than reserved to a federal government agency. As leading conservative legal scholar Christopher Green notes, "Federalism itself is a state-by-state patchwork" and "lack of uniformity in the Electoral College is a feature, not a bug."[91] He points out that the Constitution's "conferral of power to 'each state' to decide how electors are to be selected requires that we tolerate disuniformity . . . [because] it was designed for the very purpose of creating disuniformity: independent decisions by those in each state about what qualities were most important in a President."[92] Perhaps the Framers of the Constitution made a mistake in structuring the system that way. Maybe it would be better if we had a national agency administering all elections for federal office, like Elections Canada, which fulfills that function in our neighbor to the north.[93]

---

[91] Christoper Green, Trump v. Anderson *and Federalist 68*, THE ORIGINALISM BLOG (Mar. 4, 2024), https://originalismblog.typepad.com/the-originalism-blog/2024/03/trump-v-anderson-and-federalist-68.html. *See also* Vikram D. Amar & Jason Mazzone, *The Supreme Court's Misplaced Emphasis on Uniformity in* Trump v. Anderson *(and* Bush v. Gore*)*, JUSTIA, VERDICT (Mar. 25, 2024), https://verdict.justia.com/2024/03/25/the-supreme-courts-misplaced-emphasis-on-uniformity-in-trump-v-anderson-and-bush-v-gore (making a similar point).

[92] Green, *supra* note 80 (quoting U.S. CONST. art. II, § 1, cl. 2).

[93] For an overview of the powers of Elections Canada, see *The Role and Structure of Elections Canada*, ELECTIONS CAN. (Nov. 7, 2023), https://www.elections.ca/content.aspx?section=abo&dir=role&document=index&lang=e.

But the Founders chose otherwise. As the per curiam opinion recognizes, "the Elections and Electors Clauses . . . authorize States to conduct and regulate congressional and Presidential elections, respectively."[94] That gives state governments initial authority (subject to federal judicial review) to enforce other constitutionally required qualifications for federal office. Section 3 is no different. Even if the Fourteenth Amendment does not delegate states any specific authority to enforce Section 3, such power is inherent in the general grant of authority to conduct and regulate presidential and congressional elections that is already present in Articles I and II.

Concerns about a potential "patchwork" of conflicting state rulings are ultimately policy objections to the Constitution's decentralized state-by-state scheme of election administration. As the conservative Justices (rightly) love to remind us in other contexts, courts are not permitted to second-guess policy determinations that are under the authority of other branches of government, nor are they permitted to second-guess—as in this case—the Framers and ratifiers of the Constitution.

Professor Neil Siegel offers a somewhat different rationale for the Court's reliance on concerns about inconsistent state decisions, at least when it comes to enforcing Section 3 against presidential candidates.[95] He argues that states lack the power to disqualify presidential candidates with broad support, because doing so could create a spillover effect where one or a few states can prevent the election of a presidential candidate with broad support in the nation as a whole, one that would otherwise have the support of an electoral college majority.[96] The validity of Siegel's argument turns in part on the broader validity of his "collective action federalism" theory of constitutional interpretation, which argues that the federal government has broad power to forestall "collective action" problems between the states, which arise when states have poor incentives to produce public goods they all value, or when states create spillover effects

---

[94] Trump v. Anderson, 601 U.S. at 112 (citing U.S. Const.art. I, § 4, cl. 1; art. II, § 1, cl. 2).

[95] Neil Siegel, *Narrow But Deep: The* McCulloch *Principle, Collective-Action Theory, and Section Three Enforcement,* Duke Public Law & Legal Theory Series No. 2024-48 (2024), https://papers.ssrn.com/sol3/papers.cfm?abstract_id=4909114.

[96] *Id.* at 13–16.

harming other states.[97] Elsewhere, I have outlined significant reservations about the theory.[98]

Even aside from more general concerns about collective action federalism, it is important to recognize that any such collective action problem created by allowing state disqualification should be weighed against the danger to the Constitution and our democratic system of allowing an insurrectionist to hold the most powerful office in the land.[99] If such a scenario occurs, it could cause grave harm, far outweighing that of preventing a potentially legitimate political leader from holding office. Moreover, the latter problem is in large part mitigated by the availability of federal court (including Supreme Court) review of state disqualification decisions.[100]

If a combination of partisan bias and voter ignorance leads to the election of a dangerous insurrectionist to high office,[101] that too is a collective action problem, arising from the fact that most individual voters have little incentive to seek out relevant information and use it wisely.[102] Moreover, individual states may have little or no incentive to address the problem of voter ignorance by means other than Section 3 disqualification, since much of the harm caused by ignorance within one state will be borne by people in other states, Thus, widespread availability of state-level Section 3 remedies is itself way to alleviate interstate collective action problems.

If the Court was going to base its ultimate decision in the *Trump v. Anderson* Section 3 case on policy considerations, it should have at least weighed the practical concerns on the other side: the danger of letting insurrectionists return to power and subvert liberal democracy again. That danger is especially acute in a case where the insurrectionist is a candidate for the most powerful office in the land. Moreover, some

---

[97] For elaboration of that theory, see Neil Siegel, The Collective Action Constitution (2024); and Robert Cooter & Neil Siegel, *Collective Action Federalism: A General Theory of Article I, Section 8*, 63 Stanford L. Rev. 115 (2010).

[98] Ilya Somin, *Federalism and Collective Action*, Jotwell, June 20, 2011, available at https://conlaw.jotwell.com/federalism-and-collective-action/.

[99] *See* Part IV, *infra*, (discussing this danger).

[100] *See id.* (discussing this point in more detail).

[101] *See id.* (discussing this possibility).

[102] On voter ignorance and bias as a collective action problem, see Ilya Somin, Democracy and Political Ignorance: Why Smaller Government is Smarter ch. 3 (2nd ed. 2016).

degree of "patchwork" divergence may be preferable to a uniform-but-wrong resolution of a Section 3 issue by the federal government, or to congressional nullification of Section 3 by inaction.

C. *The Concurring Opinions*

While the Supreme Court ruling was unanimous, it is notable that both Justice Amy Coney Barrett (writing for herself alone) and the three liberal Justices (in a joint opinion) wrote concurrences that seem to reject, or at least call into question, much of the majority's reasoning. Barrett agreed that "States lack the power to enforce Section 3 against Presidential candidates," and suggested that the Court should have limited its holding to that point, without ruling that "federal legislation is the exclusive vehicle through which Section 3 can be enforced."[103] But she failed to explain how the Court could have found a rationale for holding that Section 3 enforcement requires congressional legislation when it comes to presidential candidates that would not apply with equal force to other federal officeholders. Similarly, she did not explain what other mechanism, besides federal legislation, there might be for Section 3 enforcement, if states lack the power to do it, especially in a system where states generally control the mechanics of the electoral process.

The three liberal Justices also argued that the Court's reasoning went too far. They correctly emphasized that the majority had "next to no support for its requirement that a Section 3 disqualification can occur only pursuant to legislation enacted for that purpose."[104] But if that is their view, they should have dissented rather than concurred in judgment. The supposed need for legislation the primary basis for the Court's holding that states cannot enforce Section 3. Indeed, metadata in the electronic version of the decision publicized by the Supreme Court reveal that the concurring opinion by the three liberals was originally drafted as a dissent written by Justice Sonia Sotomayor alone (it is not clear whether the other two liberal Justices planned to join it).[105]

---

[103] Trump v. Anderson, 601 U.S. at 118 (Barrett, J., concurring in part and in the judgment).

[104] *Id.* at 122 (Sotomayor, Kagan, & Jackson, JJ., concurring in the judgment).

[105] *See* Mark Joseph Stern, *Supreme Court Inadvertently Reveals Confounding Late Change in Trump Ballot Ruling*, SLATE (Mar. 4, 2024), https://slate.com/news-and-politics/2024/03/supreme-court-metadata-sotomayor-trump-dissent.html.

Instead, Sotomayor and the other two liberals decided to concur in the result, relying on *U.S. Term Limits* and other similar precedents and emphasizing the fear that divergent state decisions might cause practical problems.[106] But, as we have seen, these issues are overblown, and can arise with state adjudications of cases involving other constitutional qualifications for the presidency.

D. Why A Criminal Conviction is Not Required for Disqualification Under Section 3

In the public debate over the Section 3 cases, much was made of the idea that Trump could not be disqualified unless he were first convicted on criminal charges of insurrection. As conservative *Washington Post* columnist Jim Geraghty, put it, "[i]f you're going to throw a presidential candidate off the ballot for engaging in an insurrection through his personal actions, shouldn't he first be convicted of engaging in an insurrection?"[107] Similar arguments were advanced in a number of amicus briefs filed in support of Trump, including one by several former Republican Attorneys General.[108]

The argument that a criminal conviction is necessary for disqualification is a variant of the idea that Section 3 is not self-enforcing. It holds that enforcement legislation is not only needed, but also must take the form of a statute imposing criminal liability for insurrection.

Neither the text nor the original meaning of Section 3 requires a preexisting criminal conviction.[109] Nothing in Section 3's text

---

[106] *See* Trump v. Anderson, 601 U.S. at 119–20 (Sotomayor, Kagan, & Jackson, JJ., concurring in the judgment).

[107] James Geraghty, *The Colorado Supreme Court Just Proved Trump's Point*, WASH. POST (Dec. 20, 2023), https://www.washingtonpost.com/opinions/2023/12/20/colorado-supreme-court-ballot-decision-helped-trump/.

[108] *See* Brief of Former Attorneys' General Edwin Meese III, et al., in Support of Petitioner, Trump v. Anderson, 601 U.S. 100 (No. 23-719), at 24–25 ("This statute looks exactly like what one would expect for legislation implementing Section 3. It defines the elements of the pertinent crimes, sets forth the range of punishments, and commands that any person convicted under it be disqualified from holding an office 'under the United States.' The big problem for those advocating for the Colorado decision is that President Trump has not been convicted of violating Section 2383. For that matter, he has never even been *charged* with violating Section 2383."); *see also* Brief of U.S. Senator Ted Cruz, et. al., in Support of Petitioner, Trump v. Anderson, 601 U.S. 100 (No. 23-719), at 7–9.

[109] Some points in this section are adapted from my amicus brief in *Trump v. Anderson. See generally* Somin, Amicus Brief, *supra* note 4.

mentions a conviction—or even a criminal charge—much less makes it a precondition for disqualification.[110] If Section 3's drafters had wanted to disqualify only individuals who had previously been convicted of insurrection or some other criminal offense, they easily could have said so in the text. Instead, Section 3 simply states that it applies to a person who has "engaged in insurrection"—not a person "convicted for engaging in insurrection."[111]

When interpreting Section 3, courts should prioritize ordinary meaning over "secret or technical meanings that would not have been known to ordinary citizens in the founding generation."[112] Nothing in the text would lead an ordinary citizen in 1868 to assume that Section 3 requires a prior criminal conviction before disqualification can be imposed. To the contrary, the text suggests that anyone who "engaged in insurrection" is automatically disqualified, regardless of whether they have been convicted of a crime or not. And disqualification from office is not itself a criminal punishment any more than it is a punishment to be barred from the presidency by virtue of lacking one of the other constitutionally required qualifications, such as being a "natural born citizen" or being at least 35 years old.

Members of the drafting Thirty-Ninth Congress who supported the Fourteenth Amendment maintained that Section 3 amended the constitutional qualifications for office rather than imposed punishment. For example, Senator Lot Morrill of Maine highlighted the "obvious distinction between the penalty which the State affixes to a crime and that disability which the State imposes and has the right to impose against persons whom it does not choose to entrust with official station."[113] Senator Waitman Willey agreed that Section 3 is "not . . . penal in its character, it is precautionary. It looks not to the past, but it has reference, as I understand it, wholly to the future. It is a measure of self-defense."[114]

---

[110] *See* Worthy v. Barrett, 63 N.C. 199 (N.C. 1869); State *ex rel.* Sandlin v. Watkins, 21 La. Ann. 631 (La. 1869); In re Tate, 63 N.C. 308 (N.C. 1869); Jennifer K. Elsea, Cong. Rsch. Serv., LSB10569, The Insurrection Bar to Office: Section 3 of the Fourteenth Amendment 2 (2022), https://crsreports.congress.gov/product/pdf/LSB/LSB10569 ("Section 3 of the Fourteenth Amendment does not expressly require a criminal conviction, and historically, one was not necessary.").

[111] U.S. Const. amend. XIV, § 3.

[112] District of Columbia v. Heller, 554 U.S. 570, 577 (2008).

[113] Cong. Globe, 39th Cong., 1st Sess. 2916 (1866).

[114] *Id.* at 2918.

Moreover, in its implementation, Section 3 in the vast majority of cases would have been either unnecessary or utterly ineffective if interpreted to disqualify only persons previously convicted of criminal offenses. No one at the time of drafting and ratification in 1866-68 suggested that persons serving long prison terms were a threat to hold office. The possibility of prior criminal conviction was rendered nearly impossible after President Johnson issued his two broad pardons for former Confederates.[115]

Near the end of the war, General Ulysses S. Grant allowed Robert E. Lee and the Army of Northern Virginia to surrender under terms that allowed "each officer and man . . . to return to their homes, *not to be disturbed by United States authority* so long as they observe their paroles and the laws in force where they may reside."[116] Lee's army—and other Confederate forces who surrendered on similar terms—included many men who could have been disqualified under Section 3, because they had previously held public office. This included Lee himself, subject to disqualification by virtue of his previous service as a high-ranking U.S. Army officer (Section 3 disqualifies any insurrectionist who had previously taken an oath as an "officer of the United States," a category that included commissioned military officers).[117] Certainly, neither the framers nor ratifiers of Section 3 thought that Lee and others like him were exempt from disqualification merely because they were

---

[115] *See* President Andrew Johnson, *Proclamation of Amnesty and Reconstruction* (May 29, 1865), https://www.loc.gov/resource/rbpe.23502500/?st=pdf&pdfPage=2; President Andrew Johnson, *Granting Full Pardon and Amnesty for the Offense of Treason Against the United States During the Late Civil War*, Proclamation No. 179 (Dec. 25, 1868), https://www.presidency.ucsb.edu/documents/proclamation-179-granting-full-pardon-and-amnesty-for-the-offense-treason-against-the. For further discussion, see Gerard N. Magliocca, *Amnesty and Section Three of the Fourteenth Amendment*, 36 CONST. COMMENT. 87, 94–95 (2021).

[116] General Ulysses S. Grant to Gen. Robert E. Lee, Apr. 9, 1865, https://www.battlefields.org/learn/primary-sources/lt-gen-ulysses-s-grants-terms-agreement-entered-gen-robert-e-lee-appomattox (emphasis added).

[117] *See* JOHN REEVES, THE LOST INDICTMENT OF ROBERT E. LEE: THE FORGOTTEN CASE AGAINST AN AMERICAN ICON 131 (2018). There was debate over whether the terms of Lee's parole precluded future prosecution, but many believed it would. *Compare id.* at 54 ("[R]eporters seemed to believe that . . . the agreement with Grant protected Lee and his officers from prosecution by federal authorities. . . ."), *with id.* at 64 ("[President] Johnson . . . believed [the United States] could still prosecute Lee once the end of the war was declared.").

not prosecuted for insurrection—and likely could not have been prosecuted, given the terms of their surrender.

Instead, when implemented during Reconstruction, it was clear that disqualification under Section 3 could not and did not hinge on a prior criminal conviction. Even though Jefferson Davis was not convicted, there was broad agreement that he was disqualified from office even after his treason prosecution was abandoned.[118] Hundreds of individuals submitted amnesty requests believing that Section 3 applied to them even though none of them were ever convicted of crimes related to their roles in the Civil War.[119] More recently, a 2022 decision by the Georgia Office of Administrative Hearings, drawing upon Reconstruction-era history, also rejected a requirement of a prior criminal conviction.[120]

At least eight public officials, ranging from a U.S. Senator to a local postmaster, have been formally adjudicated to be disqualified from public office under the Disqualification Clause since its ratification in 1868, including six disqualified during Reconstruction.[121] Yet, during Reconstruction no person disqualified from public office after the Fourteenth Amendment was ratified, no person whom the government attempted to disqualify, no person who sought amnesty under Section 3, and no person amnestied under Section 3 was first convicted of a relevant offence stemming from disloyal behavior.[122]

---

[118] *See* Brief of *Amici Curiae* American Historians in Support of Respondents, Trump v. Anderson, 601 U.S. 100 (No. 23-719), at 27–30.

[119] FEIN & MAGLIOCCA, *supra* note 66, at 8, 12.

[120] Rowan v. Greene, Docket No. 2222582 2222582-OSAH-SECSTATE-CE-57-Beaudrot, at 13 (Ga. Off. State Admin. Hearings May 6, 2022), https://s3.documentcloud.org/documents/21902607/marjorie-taylor-greene-ruling.pdf ("Nor does 'engagement' require previous conviction of a criminal offense."); *see also* New Mexico *ex rel.* White v. Griffin, 2022 WL 4295619, at *24 ("[N]either the courts nor Congress have ever required a criminal conviction for a person to be disqualified under Section Three.").

[121] For a detailed listing of officials disqualified under Section 3, see CREW, PUBLIC OFFICIALS ADJUDICATED TO BE DISQUALIFIED UNDER SECTION 3 OF THE FOURTEENTH AMENDMENT (2023), https://www.citizensforethics.org/reports-investigations/crew-reports/past-14th-amendment-disqualifications/. For further discussion of these cases, see Gerard N. Magliocca, *Amnesty and Section 3 of the Fourteenth Amendment*, 36 CONST. COMMENT. 87 (2021), and ELSEA, *supra* note 111.

[122] *See* Myles S. Lynch, *Disloyalty & Disqualification: Reconstructing Section 3 of the Fourteenth Amendment*, 30 WM. & MARY BILL RTS. J. 153, 196–214 (2021); FEIN & MAGLIOCCA, *supra* note 66, at 9–10.

A standard element of our legal system is that the same events often give rise to both civil and criminal liability. For example, a person who commits rape, murder, or assault is subject to criminal penalties and also to civil suits by his or her victims. In such cases, a criminal conviction is *not* a prerequisite to civil liability. Indeed, even an actual *acquittal* on criminal charges does not necessarily preclude civil lawsuits against the perpetrator. Consider the case of O.J. Simpson, who was famously acquitted of criminal charges in the murders of his ex-wife Nicole Brown Simpson and Ron Goldman, but later lost a civil case filed by the victims' families.[123] The criminal acquittal did not stop Simpson from incurring $33.5 million in civil liability.[124] The criminal and civil cases were distinct, and the result of one did not determine that of the other. The same reasoning applies here.

If there is no general requirement of a criminal conviction, there can also be no specific requirement that disqualification requires a conviction under 18 U.S.C. § 2383, the federal insurrection statute (despite claims to the contrary by some amicus briefs).[125] In his dissenting opinion before the Colorado Supreme Court, Justice Carlos Samour stated that "[i]f any federal legislation arguably enables the enforcement of Section Three, it's Section 2383" and cited the failure to prosecute and convict Trump under that provision as one of the reasons for his opposition to the majority decision.[126]

But nothing in that law indicates that it is the exclusive mode of enforcing Section 3. Indeed, Section 2383 has its origins in the Confiscation Act of 1862, enacted six years before the Fourteenth Amendment, and many aspects of Section 2383 indicate that it has a distinct purpose that only partially overlaps with Section 3.[127] The Colorado Supreme Court majority rightly concluded that Section 2383 "cannot be read to mean that *only* those charged and convicted of violating that law are constitutionally disqualified from holding future office without assuming a great deal of meaning not present in the text of the law."[128]

---

[123] *See* Rufo v. Simpson, 103 Cal. Rptr. 2d 492 (Cal. Ct. App. 2001) (upholding civil judgment against Simpson).

[124] *See id.* at 493–94.

[125] *See* Meese et al., Amicus Brief, *supra* note 109; Cruz et al., Amicus Brief, *supra* note 109.

[126] Anderson v. Griswold, 543 P.3d at 348, 355 (Samour, J., dissenting).

[127] I have covered this issue in detail in my amicus brief in the case. *See* Somin, Amicus Brief, *supra* note 4, at 12–16.

[128] Anderson v. Griswold, 543 P.3d. at 316.

To be sure, Section 2383 does state that anyone who "engages in any rebellion or insurrection against the authority of the United States or the laws thereof, or gives aid or comfort thereto, shall be fined under this title or imprisoned not more than ten years, or both; and shall be incapable of holding any office under the United States."[129] But, unlike Section 3, it applies to anyone who engages in "rebellion or insurrection," and not just to current and former officeholders. In addition, it only bars future officeholding in the federal government—unlike Section 3, it does not also apply to state offices.

For these and other reasons,[130] it seems clear that Section 2383 is distinct from Section 3, in some respects imposing a more sweeping disqualification than Section 3 does, while in other respects not going as far. At the very least, it cannot be regarded as the exclusive mode of enforcing Section 3.

III. Why the January 6 Attack on the Capitol Was an Insurrection

One of the points at issue in the Supreme Court case considering whether Trump should be disqualified under Section 3 of the Fourteenth Amendment is whether the events of that day qualify as an "insurrection." It should be an easy call. The January 6 attack was an insurrection under any plausible definition of that term.[131] This may be why Donald Trump's lawyer before the Supreme Court, Jonathan Mitchell, did not even attempt to contest this issue in his brief before the Court.[132]

As legal scholar Mark Graber has shown, contemporary definitions of "insurrection" prevalent at the time the Fourteenth Amendment was enacted were quite broad—possibly broad enough to encompass any violent resistance to the enforcement of a federal statute, when that resistance was motivated by a "public purpose."[133]

---

[129] 18 U.S.C. § 2383.

[130] *See* Somin, Amicus Brief, *supra* note 4, at 12–16.

[131] Some material in this Part is adapted, in revised form, from Ilya Somin, *The January 6 Attack was an Insurrection*, REASON (Jan. 6, 2024), https://reason.com/volokh/2024/01/06/the-january-6-attack-was-an-insurrection/.

[132] *See* Brief for the Petitioner, Trump v. Anderson, 601 U.S. 100 (No. 23-719), at 33–38 (arguing that President Trump did not *personally* engage in insurrection but not contesting that the events of January 6 themselves constituted an insurrection).

[133] Graber, *supra* note 12, at 4; *see also* Mark Graber, *Section Three of the Fourteenth Amendment: Insurrection*, WM. & MARY BILL RTS. J. (forthcoming), https://papers.ssrn.com/sol3/papers.cfm?abstract_id=4733059; Baude & Paulsen, *supra* note 5, at 674–716 (reaching a similar conclusion).

That definition surely includes the January 6 attack, mounted by people who believed Trump was entitled to remain President for another term and were willing to use force to ensure he could do so.

I am not convinced that courts should actually adopt such a broad definition. It could set a dangerous precedent. As Graber notes, on that theory people who violently resisted enforcement of the Fugitive Slave Act would qualify as insurrectionists, too.[134]

But January 6 was an insurrection even under a narrow definition that covers only violent attempts to illegally seize control of the powers of government. After all, the attackers were using force to try to keep the loser of the 2020 election in power, blocking the transfer of authority to the rightful winner. If that isn't a violent attempt to seize government power, it's hard to know what is.

It is true that many, of those who participated genuinely thought that they were acting to support the rightful winner of the election and thus believed they weren't doing anything illegal.[135] But much the same could be said of the ex-Confederates who were the original targets of Section 3.[136] Most of them believed their states had a constitutional right to secede, and they had much better grounds for that belief than Trumpists ever had for the utterly indefensible claim that the election was stolen from him (a belief uniformly rejected in numerous court decisions, including by judges appointed by Trump himself).[137]

It is sometimes claimed that the mob attacking the Capitol was unarmed or not violent enough to qualify as an insurrection. That would be news to the five people who were killed, and the over 140 police officers injured.[138] There could easily have been many more fatalities had the attackers been more successful in carrying out their plans to

---

[134] Graber, *supra* note 12.

[135] For the argument that this proves January 6 was not an insurrection, see Lawrence Lessig, *A Terrible Plan to Neutralize Trump Has Entranced the Legal World*, SLATE (Sept. 19, 2023), https://slate.com/news-and-politics/2023/09/trump-disqualification-colorado-ballot-hail-mary.html.

[136] I discuss this point in detail in Ilya Somin, *Insurrectionists Who Think they are Upholding the Constitution are Still Insurrectionists—and Still Subject to Disqualification Under Section 3 the Fourteenth Amendment*, REASON (Sept. 22, 2023), https://reason.com/volokh/2023/09/22/insurrectionists-who-think-they-are-upholding-the-constitution-are-still-insurrectionists-and-still-subject-to-disqualification-under-section-3-the-fourteenth-amendment/.

[137] *See id.*

[138] *See* Richer & Kunzelman, *supra* note 11.

"hang Mike Pence" and kill members of Congress. Donald Trump apparently expressed support for this goal at the time;[139] Pence and the members managed to escape. And it just isn't true that the mob was unarmed. After extensive consideration of evidence, Colorado courts found otherwise:

> [C]ontrary to President Trump's assertion that no evidence in the record showed that the mob was armed with deadly weapons or that it attacked law enforcement officers in a manner consistent with a violent insurrection, the district court found—and millions of people saw on live television, recordings of which were introduced into evidence in this case—that the mob was armed with a wide array of weapons . . . . The court also found that many in the mob stole objects from the Capitol's premises or from law enforcement officers to use as weapons, including metal bars from the police barricades and officers' batons and riot shields and that throughout the day, the mob repeatedly and violently assaulted police officers who were trying to defend the Capitol . . . . The fact that actual and threatened force was used that day cannot reasonably be denied.[140]

A New Mexico trial court ruling holding that a New Mexico state official who participated in the attack on the Capitol is disqualified under Section 3, similarly concluded that the attack was an "insurrection":

> The mob that arrived at the Capitol on January 6 was an assemblage of persons who engaged in violence, force, and intimidation by numbers. The mob numbered at minimum in the thousands. Many came prepared for violence in full tactical gear. They used a variety of weapons, brutally attacked and injured more than one hundred police officers, sought to intimidate the Vice President and Congress, and called for the murder of elected officials, including the Vice President.[141]

---

[139] *See* Betsy Woodruff Swan & Kyle Cheney, *Trump Expressed Support for Hanging Pence during Capitol Riot, Jan. 6 Panel Told*, Poltico (May 25, 2022), https://www. politico.com/news/2022/05/25/trump-expressed-support-hanging-pence-capitol-riot-jan-6-00035117.

[140] Anderson v. Griswold, 543 P.3d at 330–31.

[141] New Mexico *ex rel*. White v. Griffin, 2022 WL 4295619, at *18.

Prominent conservative legal scholar Steven Calabresi nonetheless argues that January 6 was not an insurrection.[142] He relied on a definition of "insurrection" from the 1828 edition of Webster's Dictionary:

> A rising against civil or political authority; the open and active opposition of a number of persons to the execution of a law in a city or state. It is equivalent to sedition, except that sedition expresses a less extensive rising of citizens. It differs from rebellion, for the latter expresses a revolt, or an attempt to overthrow the government, to establish a different one or to place the country under another jurisdiction. It differs from mutiny, as it respects the civil or political government; whereas a mutiny is an open opposition to law in the army or navy. [I]nsurrection is however used with such latitude as to comprehend either sedition or rebellion.[143]

The events of January 6 fit this definition to a T! The attack on the Capitol was obviously a "rising against civil or political authority" and even more clearly "the open and active opposition of a number of persons to the execution of a law in a city or state."[144] The mob incited by Trump sought to prevent the "execution" of the laws requiring transfer of power to the winner of the election.

Calabresi suggests that the January 6 attack was actually a "riot,"[145] a position also embraced by Michael Rappaport.[146] Perhaps so. But "riot" and "insurrection" are not mutually exclusive concepts. An event can be both at the same time; people can simultaneously engage in mass civil disorder (a riot), while doing so for the purpose of seeking to seize control of government power or some other "public purpose." Indeed, that is a common occurrence in history. The French Revolution, for example, began as a riot attacking the Bastille.[147]

---

[142] *See* Steven G. Calabresi, *Donald Trump and Section 3 of the 14th Amendment*, REASON (Dec. 31, 2023), https://reason.com/volokh/2023/12/31/donald-trump-and-section-3-of-the-14th-amendment/.

[143] *Insurrection*, WEBSTER'S DICTIONARY (1828), https://webstersdictionary1828.com/Dictionary/insurrection.

[144] *Id.*

[145] Calabresi, *supra* note 143.

[146] *See* Rappaport, *supra* note 45.

[147] *See* SIMON SCHAMA, CITIZENS: A CHRONICLE OF THE FRENCH REVOLUTION 399–406 (1989).

Calabresi also argues that the attack was not large enough to qualify as an insurrection because it "occurred for three-and-one-half hours in one city only in the United States, Washington D.C., and not as an overall insurgency in multiple cities across the United States."[148] But the definition he himself cites indicates that an insurrection is "the open and active opposition of a number of persons to the execution of a law in *a* city or state."[149] That suggests one city is enough.

And there is no historical or modern evidence indicating that an insurrection must last some minimum length of time. A revolt that is quickly put down can still be an insurrection. The same goes for a revolt that is poorly planned and easily defeated.

If actions in multiple cities are required, a great many attempted coups and armed revolts would not count as "insurrections." It is common for attempts to seize power to focus on the capital city where the government is located. If the revolt is put down, it may not spread elsewhere. But that doesn't mean it was not an insurrection.

The Bolshevik seizure of power in Russia in 1917 initially involved just the capital city of St. Petersburg.[150] If the Provisional Government had managed to swiftly crush it, thereby preventing it from spreading to other cities, would that have meant it wasn't an insurrection?

Similarly, it seems obvious that Adolf Hitler's 1923 Beer Hall Putsch was as an insurrection. Yet, like the January 6 attack, it lasted only about one day (the evening of November 8, 1923 to the evening of the following day) and was limited to a single city (Munich, the capital of the German state of Bavaria).[151] The number of participants (several thousand) and the number of people injured was also similar to that of January 6; 1,265 people have been charged with offenses related to the attack on January 6, and many other participants likely got away without being identified or charged.[152]

---

[148] Calabresi, *supra* note 143.

[149] WEBSTER'S, *supra* note 144 (emphasis added); *see also* Calabresi, *supra* note 143.

[150] For a detailed account, see RICHARD A. PIPES, THE RUSSIAN REVOLUTION Ch. 11 (1991).

[151] For details, see HAROLD J. GORDON, HITLER AND THE BEER HALL PUTSCH (1972) and IAN J. KERSHAW, HITLER, 1889–1936: HUBRIS 129–219 (1998).

[152] For the number of participants in the Beer Hall Putsch, see works cited *supra* note 152. On the number charged in the January 6 attack, see U.S. District Attorney's Office, District of Columbia, Three Years Since the Jan. 6 Attack on the Capitol, Jan. 6, 2024, https://www.justice.gov/usao-dc/36-months-jan-6-attack-capitol-0.

There were somewhat more fatalities (21) in the Beer Hall Putsch.[153] But 16 of them were participants in the coup (the others were four police officers and a civilian bystander).[154] The Bavarian police and troops who put down the revolt were less restrained in their use of force than U.S. law enforcement officers on January 6 (who only killed one of the attackers). That surely isn't a decisive difference between the two cases. More aggressive law enforcement action cannot by itself transform a mere "riot" into an insurrection, assuming the two are distinct categories to begin with.

It seems obvious that both the Beer Hall Putsch and the January 6 attack were insurrections, for the simple reason that both involved the use of force to illegally seize control of government power. It matters not how long they lasted, or that they were poorly planned and quickly put down. And it certainly does not matter that they both occurred in just one city.

Finally, it is worth noting that Section 3 imposes disqualification for participation in "rebellion" as well as "insurrection."[155] The two most famous pre–Civil War events in American history generally labeled rebellions were Shays's Rebellion (1786–87), and the Whiskey Rebellion of 1793.[156] Both were on a scale similar to the January 6 attack. Each involved no more than a few thousand rebels (only about 600 in the case of the Whiskey Rebellion; many fewer than January 6). Each occurred in one part of just one state (western Massachusetts and western Pennsylvania, respectively). The number of combat fatalities (nine for Shays's Rebellion, three or four for the Whiskey Rebellion, five on January 6) is also similar.[157]

The best argument for Trump on the "insurrection" issue is not that there was no insurrection at all, but that Trump himself did not

---

[153] *See Beer Hall Putsch*, HISTORY.COM (Nov. 9, 2009), https://www.history.com/topics/european-history/beer-hall-putsch#section_2.

[154] *See id.*

[155] U.S. CONST. amend. XIV, § 3.

[156] I develop this point in more detail in Ilya Somin, *Insurrection, Rebellion, and January 6: Rejoinder to Steve Calabresi*, REASON (Jan. 6, 2024), https://reason.com/volokh/2024/01/06/insurrection-rebellion-and-january-6-rejoinder-to-steve-calabresi/. This piece was a rejoinder to Steven G. Calabresi, *January 6, 2021 Was Not an Insurrection*, REASON (Jan. 6, 2024), https://reason.com/volokh/2024/01/06/january-6-2021-was-not-an-insurrection/.

[157] *See Somin, supra* note 157.

"engage" in it. After all, he did not participate in the attack himself, and he did not give specific orders to those who did.

On this issue, I have little to add to the detailed and thorough analyses by the trial judge in the Colorado case and by the Colorado Supreme Court. They, rightly in my view, both concluded that Trump "engaged" in insurrection because he knowingly and deliberately incited violence calculated to keep himself in power after losing an election. And he began doing so long before his now-famous speech to the crowd that later stormed the Capitol, on January 6, where he urged them to "fight like hell"—a statement that in other contexts might be interpreted to be just metaphorical.[158] As Judge Sarah Wallace wrote in the trial court decision, "Trump acted with the specific intent to incite political violence and direct it at the Capitol with the purpose of disrupting the electoral certification."[159]

One point, however, has not gotten enough attention in other analyses of the case: As the Colorado Supreme Court noted, while the attack on the Capitol was ongoing and the mob sought to kill or injure members of Congress, "President Trump ignored pleas to intervene and instead called on Senators, urging them to help delay the electoral count, which is what the mob, upon President Trump's exhortations, was also trying to achieve."[160] This was likely an attempt to use the violence as leverage to intimidate lawmakers to keep him in power. A political leader who uses violence by his supporters as leverage to try to seize power that does not belong to him is "engaged in insurrection" even if he does not otherwise participate in the violence. At the very least, that is true when those directly involved in the violence are pursuing the exact same goal as he is.

Leaders of terrorist groups who use hostage-taking as leverage to secure concessions desired by their organization are surely engaged in terrorism, even if they did not directly participate in the hostage-taking, and even if they may not have known about it in advance. This

---

[158] *See* Anderson v. Griswold, 543 P.3d. at 331–36 (recounting the relevant evidence and concluding that Trump "engaged in" insurrection); Anderson v. Griswold, 2023 WL 8006216, at *41–43 (same); *cf.* Baude & Paulsen, *supra* note 5, at 734–40 (presenting additional arguments that Trump "engaged in" insurrection).

[159] Anderson v. Griswold, 2023 WL 8006216 at *41.

[160] Anderson v. Griswold, 543 P.3d. at 335.

may have been true of Hamas terrorist leaders in Qatar who did not directly participate in the October 7, 2023, terrorist attack on Israel, but then tried to use the resulting seizure of hostages as leverage to force Israeli concessions, which was also the goal of the terrorists who did directly participate in the attack.[161] The Qatar-based Hamas leaders surely "engaged in" terrorism. By the same logic, Trump was "engaged in" insurrection when he sought to use the attack on the Capitol as leverage to achieve the exact same end sought by the attackers.

IV. Disqualification and Democracy

An important non-originalist criticism of efforts to disqualify Trump is the idea that doing so would undermine democracy.[162] The logic here seems obvious: removing a candidate from consideration necessarily limits the power of voters by narrowing the range of choices available to them. In that sense, it is anti-democratic. But constraints on voter choice can nonetheless sometimes help protect democracy and other liberal values. Section 3 is one such democracy-enhancing constraint on voter choice.

A striking flaw in the Supreme Court's majority and concurring opinions in *Trump v. Anderson* is the total failure of the Justices to consider the potential democracy-protecting benefits of disqualification. This might have been understandable if the Court had chosen to focus solely on originalist and textualist arguments, without reference to consequences. But once the Justices chose to rely heavily on practical consequentialist considerations about a "patchwork" of state decisions,[163] they should have considered consequentialist considerations on the other side, as well.

---

[161] Ismail Haniyeh and other Hamas leaders based in Qatar may not have known about the October 7 attack in advance, but later sought to use it as leverage. *See, e.g.,* Samia Nakhoul & Stephen Farrell, *Who Was Ismail Haniyeh and Why Is His Assassination a Blow to Hamas?*, Reuters (July 31, 2024), https://www.reuters.com/world/middle-east/obituary-tough-talking-haniyeh-was-seen-more-moderate-face-hamas-2024-07-31/.

[162] For this kind of argument, see, for example, Ross Douthat, *The Anti-Democratic Quest to Save Democracy From Trump*, N.Y. Times (Dec. 23, 2023), https://www.nytimes.com/2023/12/23/opinion/colorado-ruling-trump.html (arguing that disqualification would be "a remarkably undemocratic act"); Samuel Moyn, *Trump Should Not Be Disqualified by an Ambiguous Clause*, N.Y. Times (Dec. 29, 2023), https://www.nytimes.com/2023/12/29/opinion/trump-section-3-14th-amendment.html (arguing disqualification is not "democratically appropriate").

[163] *See* § II.B, *supra*.

Democracy-preservation looms large among them. The potential consequences of an insurrectionist returning to power—especially to the most powerful office in the nation—are sufficiently grave that they could well easily outweigh any potential harm caused by "patchwork" determinations. This is especially true since judicial review can constrain the latter.[164]

Both the U.S. Constitution and the laws of many other democracies include various provisions disqualifying people from office-holding. These restrictions serve a variety of purposes, including ensuring that officeholders are at least minimally qualified, barring candidates who are likely to undermine democracy by promoting authoritarianism, and excluding those who threaten basic civil liberties and other liberal values.

Under the Constitution, the President must be at least 35 years old, be a "natural born citizen" of the United States, and have resided in the United States for at least 14 years.[165] The Twenty-Second Amendment bars from the presidency anyone who has already served two terms as President.[166] There are also age and residency restrictions for members of Congress.[167]

The natural-born-citizen requirement has been the object of much criticism, and I myself have argued that it is based on little more than xenophobic prejudice against immigrants and that it should be abolished.[168] But few would contend the other restrictions are so problematic as to be unacceptable in a democratic society, even though all of them significantly constrain voters' options. The age and residency restrictions are presumably intended to ensure that the President has the requisite maturity and knowledge of the country.

The Twenty-Second Amendment is particularly notable because it is intended to prevent the undermining of democracy through

---

[164] *See* discussion, § II.B, *supra*.

[165] U.S. CONST. art. II, § 5, cl. 1.

[166] U.S. CONST. amend. XXII.

[167] *See* U.S. Const. art. I, § 3, cl. 3 (qualification requirements for senators); U.S. CONST. art. I, §, cl. 2 (qualification requirements for members of the House of Representatives).

[168] *See* Randall Kennedy & Ilya Somin, *Remove the Natural Born Citizen Clause from the Constitution. Let Immigrants be President*, USA TODAY (Sept. 18, 2020), https://www.usatoday.com/story/opinion/2020/09/18/immigrants-president-repeal-natural-born-citizen-clause-column/5805710002/.

consolidation of authority in the hands of one person, using the power of prolonged incumbency. Presidents who have already served two terms may be popular with voters, and their experience may make them unusually well-qualified for the job.

Indeed, the amendment was inspired by Franklin D. Roosevelt's serving four terms.[169] Many believe that FDR was one of the greatest Presidents. But the danger of creeping authoritarianism was enough to justify barring such individuals from further time in office. A former President who tried to use force and fraud to stay in power after losing an election is surely at least as great a menace to the future of liberal democratic institutions as one who consolidates power by serving more than two terms. Indeed, the former is most likely more reprehensible and dangerous than the latter.

Other democracies have sometimes taken broader measures to bar from office those who pose a threat to liberal democratic values. In the aftermath of World War II, West Germany banned both the Nazi and Communist parties from contesting elections.[170]

More recently, several post-communist Eastern European democracies have enacted "lustration" laws barring from office some categories of former officials under the Communist dictatorships overthrown between 1989 and 1991—particularly former agents of the secret police.[171]

It is possible that more countries should have adopted lustration laws. Had Russia followed the example of nations barring former Communist secret police officers from office, for instance, the world might have been spared the horrific reign of ex-KGB Lieutenant Colonel Vladimir Putin, with all its repression and unjust wars.

Disqualification laws might be unnecessary if voters could be relied on to reject dangerously illiberal, anti-democratic, incompetent

---

[169] For a brief overview of the Amendment's origins, see Scott Bomboy, *How the 22nd Amendment Came into Existence*, NAT'L CONST. CTR. (Dec. 5, 2019), https://constitution center.org/blog/how-the-22nd-amendment-came-into-existence.

[170] *See* Ilya Somin, *Section 3 Disqualifications for Democracy Preservation*, LAWFARE (Sept. 6, 2023), https://www.lawfaremedia.org/article/section-3-disqualifications-for-democracy-preservation. For a more generally overview of disqualification provisions in democratic constitutions, see Tom Ginsburg et. al., *Democracy's Other Boundary Problem: The Law of Disqualification*, 111 Cal. L. Rev. 1633 (2023).

[171] *See id.*

candidates at the polls. But widespread voter ignorance and bias makes exclusive reliance on electoral safeguards problematic.[172] That is especially true in eras of severe polarization like the current one when fear and hatred of the opposing party makes voters reluctant to penalize wrongdoing by their own party's leaders, or even leads them to embrace it.[173] We are currently in an era of "negative partisanship" when many voters hate and fear the opposing party, and therefore are reluctant to ever support it,[174] even if the alternative is a menace to democratic institutions. Ironically, but logically, democracy-preserving limitations on democracy are most necessary in situations where candidates who menace democratic values enjoy substantial popular support.

Liberal democratic institutions are less vulnerable to erosion in long-established democracies like the U.S. than in post-communist Russia or post-Nazi Germany. But social scientists warn it would be a mistake to discount the dangers of "deconsolidation" entirely.[175]

It is sometimes argued that voters have an inherent right to choose whatever leaders they want, even if their judgment is dangerously flawed. John Stuart Mill effectively rebutted this argument in his classic work *Considerations on Representative Government*, where he pointed out that "the exercise of any political function, either as an elector or as a representative, is power over others."[176] Mill thus contends that choosing leaders cannot be a purely individual right that voters can exercise as they please.

---

[172] For an overview of the dangers of political ignorance, see generally ILYA SOMIN, DEMOCRACY AND POLITICAL IGNORANCE: WHY SMALLER GOVERNMENT IS SMARTER (2nd ed. 2016).

[173] For an overview of ways in which voter ignorance and bias are more dangerous in periods of severe polarization, see Ilya Somin, *Perils of Partisan Bias*, VOLOKH CONSPIRACY, WASH. POST (Dec. 16, 2016), https://www.washingtonpost.com/news/volokh-conspiracy/wp/2016/12/16/the-perils-of-partisan-bias/.

[174] For an overview, see Alan I. Abramowitz & Steven W. Webster, *Negative Partisanship: Why Americans Dislike Parties but Behave Like Rabid Partisans*, 39 ADVANCES IN POL. PSYCH. 119 (2018).

[175] For an overview of the potential for "deconsolidation," see Roberto Stefan Foa and Yascha Mounk, *The Danger of Deconsolidation; The Democratic Disconnect*, 27 J. DEMOCRACY 5 (2016). *See also* STEVEN LEVITSKY & DANIEL ZIBLATT, HOW DEMOCRACIES DIE (2017).

[176] JOHN STUART MILL, CONSIDERATIONS ON REPRESENTATIVE GOVERNMENT 206 (Henry Holt & Co. ed. 1873).

As Mill pointed out, a free society can justifiably restrict access to political office far more than individual liberties, which generally affect mostly the rights-holders themselves and those who voluntarily interact with them. It would be unjust and unconstitutional to severely restrict the personal liberty of people under the age of 35, or to bar Nazis and communists from expressing their views. But banning the former from seeking the presidency, and the latter from running for public office in post-World War II Germany, is far more defensible.

The right to wield the coercive power of government should often be more narrowly restricted than the right of individuals to control their own lives. Indeed, sometimes it may be necessary to limit the former in order to protect the latter.

If voters are prone to systematic errors that could undermine the institutions of liberal democracy, it makes sense to have structural constitutional safeguards against them. And if some categories of people—whether they be insurrectionists or former functionaries of authoritarian regimes—are likely to prove a menace to democracy or to liberal values if given the power to do so, it makes sense to bar them from holding public office.

Reliance on electoral checks alone is particularly problematic in situations where the would-be officeholder has a record of trying to undermine electoral democracy itself, and could well do so again if allowed access to power. Putin and other former communist secret police officers tasked with suppressing dissent are obvious examples. And so too are Trump and others complicit in his attempt to use force and fraud to stay in power after losing an election. One of the most compelling reasons to deny such people access to political power is that they are likely to use it to destroy the very institutions of electoral accountability that usually serve to constrain politicians.

To put it a different way: Sometimes, limits on voter choice are necessary to protect democracy from itself. One such democracy-protective limitation on democracy is excluding from power people whose track record indicates they are likely to undermine democratic institutions.

Exclusion serves the obvious function of preventing these people from getting another chance to destroy democratic institutions. Those who have tried to do so once are disproportionately likely to do so again, if given the opportunity. In addition, disqualification can serve as a deterrent. If ambitious officeholders know that involvement in insurrection leads to a lifetime bar from further access to public office, they may be less likely to take the risk of engaging in such activities.

Perhaps things are different in situations where these people have atoned for their past actions and credibly committed to changing their ways. But, even then, it's not clear whether such promises can be trusted. And Trump has shown no remorse and continues to claim his actions were entirely justified.[177]

It is, obviously, by no means certain that Trump or other insurrectionists would again try to subvert the democratic process if they return to positions of power, or even that they will be able to return to power at all. As I write these words in the late summer of 2024, Trump is again the GOP nominee for the presidency, but he might well lose the general election, which looks to be a close call. But even a relatively small risk of such recidivism is a grave danger. Even if the chance of such action is "only," say 10 or 20 percent, that is a severe risk, especially if we remember that even an unsuccessful attempt to seize power illegally can result in substantial loss of life and injuries, as the January 6 attack did. The danger is, of course, magnified when the office the insurrectionist holds is the most powerful in the land: the presidency. Such a grave danger clearly outweighs the risks of a "patchwork" of state decisions, especially since the latter can be mitigated by judicial review.[178]

In addition to protecting democracy from itself, disqualification can also serve other valuable purposes. Some limitations on democracy are necessary to protect other liberal values. This is the traditional justification for constitutional limits on democratic majorities' power, for purposes of protecting civil liberties and property rights, and preventing invidious state-sponsored discrimination on the basis of race, sex, and religion. In many cases, these dangers can be mitigated by enforcing constitutional rules after the fact, through

---

[177] *See, e.g.*, Karen Yourish & Charlie Smart, *Trump's Pattern of Sowing Election Doubt Intensifies in 2024*, N.Y. Times, (May 24, 2024), https://www.nytimes.com/interactive/2024/05/24/us/politics/trump-election-results-doubt.html (documenting numerous instances where Trump has continued to claim the 2020 election was rigged, and defended his efforts to overturn it).

[178] *See* discussion in § II.B, *supra*.

judicial review, and other institutions. But we cannot categorically exclude the possibility that sometimes liberal rights can be protected only by barring those who intend to violate them from coming to power in the first place.

The democracy and liberalism-protecting functions of Section 3 are not without risk. Some "insurrections" are morally justified, as when people resist enforcement of deeply unjust laws such as the Fugitive Slave Acts of the nineteenth century.[179] In addition, there could be "slippery slope" risks from partisan election officials seeking to use Section 3 to disqualify their political opponents. For example, Professor Michael McConnell warned that disqualifying Trump could "empower . . . partisan politicians such as state Secretaries of State to disqualify their political opponents from the ballot."[180]

Both problems are worth taking seriously. But the former danger is mitigated by the fact that, in a well-established democracy, insurrectionists are far more likely to be illiberal authoritarians than those seeking to defend liberal values. Thus, the risk of disqualifying a few "good" insurrectionists is outweighed by the benefit of disqualifying a larger number of evil ones. The slippery slope danger is constrained by requirements of due process and judicial review. If biased officials adopt overly broad definitions of "insurrection" or otherwise abuse the process, disqualified candidates can challenge such determinations and get them reversed in state or federal courts.[181] Indeed, the Trump disqualification litigation itself illustrates how this process could work. In each state where it was attempted, Trump was able to present evidence and arguments in court explaining why he should not be disqualified (with the exception of those where efforts to disqualify him were dismissed on procedural grounds).[182]

And such disqualifications can ultimately be reviewed by the federal Supreme Court, which can override rogue disqualifications by possibly biased state courts. If the Supreme Court had not

---

[179] See Somin, *Democracy Preservation, supra* note 150. *C.f.* Graber, *supra* note 12.

[180] Michael McConnell, *Responding About the Fourteenth Amendment, "Insurrection," and Trump*, REASON (Aug. 12, 2023), https://reason.com/volokh/2023/08/12/prof-michael-mcconnell-responding-about-the-fourteenth-amendment-insurrection-and-trump/.

[181] For more detailed discussion, see *id.*

[182] *See* cases cited in note 17, *supra.*

dismissed *Trump v. Anderson* on dubious self-execution grounds, it could have exercised that review function in this very case, and in the process it could have established a useful precedent for future disqualification cases.

V. The Impact of the Court's Decision

The most significant impact of the Court's decision is that it largely neuters Section 3, at least with respect to candidates seeking federal office. The sweeping nature of the Court's reasoning goes far beyond the specific case of Trump, or even presidential candidates more generally. It covers nearly all potential disqualifications of insurrectionists seeking federal office. Even if Trump himself never again holds public office, the Court's decision creates a risk that other dangerous former insurrectionists might. In principle, Congress could enact new Section 5 enforcement legislation. But in this era of severe polarization, that is unlikely to happen at any time in the near future, if ever.

Perhaps the one good aspect of the Court's ruling is that it eliminates most, if not all, remaining uncertainty about whether Trump can assume the presidency if he wins the 2024 election. By holding that Section 5 enforcement legislation is the sole mechanism by which federal officeholders can be disqualified, the decision likely forestalls such potential scenarios as a Democratic-controlled Congress refusing to certify Trump's election. In theory, Congress could enact new enforcement legislation between now and January 20, 2025 (when Trump would take office, should he win). But that is incredibly unlikely. After the new administration takes power on January 20, 2025, any new enforcement legislation that might threaten Trump (should he be elected) would be subject to his veto, and it is almost impossible that Congress would muster the two-thirds majorities in both houses needed to override it.

Some observers have suggested that the Court's ruling does not clearly bar Congress from refusing to certify Trump's electoral votes in the event he wins the 2024 general election.[183] But I believe such a conclusion is implicit in the Court's repeated emphasis on the idea

---

[183] *See* Scott Anderson et al., *Section 3 Disqualification Answers—and Many More Questions*, LAWFARE (Mar. 4, 2024), https://www.lawfaremedia.org/article/section-3-disqualification-answers-and-many-more-questions (suggesting this possibility).

that Section 5 legislation is the exclusive enforcement mechanism.[184] Refusal to certify electoral votes is not Section 5 legislation, or indeed legislation at all.[185] The Court did suggest that Congress might have authority to consider the Section 3 eligibility of its own members.[186] But the President, of course, is not a member of Congress. Still, there may be some residual uncertainty on the certification issue, because the Court did not directly address it.

The price of relative certainty is that Section 3 is largely neutered with respect to federal officeholders. Unless and until Congress enacts new Section 5 enforcement legislation, former officeholders who engaged in insurrection will be mostly free to return to power and try their hand at subverting democracy again, at least if their goal is to seek federal offices as opposed to state ones.

The Court suggested that state governments could still disqualify insurrectionists from holding state office, though it stopped short of definitively indicating even that much.[187] That question may need to be further litigated in the future. On March 18, 2024, just two weeks after it decided *Trump v. Anderson*, the Supreme Court refused to hear the case of a New Mexico January 6 participant who had been disqualified from a state office by a state court.[188] Potentially, people who engaged in insurrection while holding federal office (or after

---

[184] *See* discussion in §II.A, *supra*.

[185] *See* INS v. Chadha, 462 U.S. 919, 952 (1983) (explaining that Article I requires "bicameralism and presentment" in order to enact legislation); *but cf.* Derek T. Muller, *Administering Presidential Elections and Counting Electoral Votes After* Trump v. Anderson, SSRN (Aug. 5, 2024), https://papers.ssrn.com/sol3/papers.cfm?abstract_id=4916797 (arguing Congress could still refuse to certify electoral votes for candidates it deems ineligible under Section 3, though also urging that it not do so in the absence of prior legislation enacting standards for determining eligibility); Gerard N. Magliocca, *The Potential for Chaos in the Wake of the Supreme Court's Colorado Ballot Decision*, WASH. MONTHLY (Mar. 13, 2024), https://washingtonmonthly.com/2024/03/13/the-potential-for-chaos-in-the-wake-of-the-supreme-courts-colorado-ballot-decision/ (arguing that there could be additional litigation in the event of such a scenario); Huq, *supra* note 45, at 38–41 (arguing there could be post-election conflict over Trump's eligibility).

[186] *See* Trump v. Anderson, 601 U.S. at 114.

[187] Trump v. Anderson, 601 U.S. at 109–14 (emphasizing the distinction between federal and state offices).

[188] *See* Griffin v. New Mexico *ex rel.* White, 144 S. Ct. 1056 (2024) (denying petition for certiorari); *see also* Mariana Alfaro, *Supreme Court Rejects Appeal by New Mexico Official Ousted from Office over Jan. 6*, WASH. POST (Mar. 18, 2024), at https://www.washingtonpost.com/politics/2024/03/18/griffin-supreme-court-insurrection-clause/ (describing the case).

doing so) might still be disqualified from holding or seeking state office by state courts or state election officials. The Court's reasoning focuses on the office that insurrectionists currently hold or seek at the time disqualification is sought, rather than the one they held while engaged in insurrection.

Some insurrectionist federal officeholders or candidates for federal office might be potentially convicted under 18 U.S.C. § 2383, the federal insurrection statute, which the Court's opinion describes as enforcement legislation under Section 5.[189] But such convictions may be difficult to obtain, especially in the case of those who promoted and aided insurrection indirectly, as Trump did.

Perhaps political norms will prevent insurrectionists from being elected to powerful offices in the future. But if norms were that effective, Trump probably would never have been elected to office in the first place, and he certainly would not once more be a major-party nominee for the presidency, despite his attempt to use force and fraud to stay in power after losing the 2020 election. As in the period after the Civil War, which gave rise to the enactment of Section 3, norms today are far from a fool-proof protection against former insurrectionists returning to power.

Conclusion

Section 3 is intended to protect liberal democracy against allowing insurrectionists to return to power in situations where norms fail. It is one of a number of constitutional safeguards intended to protect democracy and liberal values against catastrophically bad choices by voters. In *Trump v. Anderson*, the Supreme Court largely gutted that protection on the basis of highly dubious reasoning at odds with text and original meaning. The Court's reasoning is also defective on consequentialist grounds; the Justices overvalued the dangers of a "patchwork" of state decisions, and underestimated the danger of letting authoritarian insurrectionists return to power. We can only hope the Court's error does not turn out to have grave costs for American democracy.

---

[189] *See* Trump v. Anderson, 601 U.S. at 115.

Looking Ahead: October Term 2024

Jeremy J. Broggi*

Introduction

"Is everything sad going to come untrue? What's happened to the world?"[1] So asked the hobbit Sam Gamgee of the wizard Gandalf in J.R.R. Tolkien's *The Lord of the Rings*, upon awakening in Ithilien to find that his quest had not been a dream and that the One Ring was destroyed.

Those attuned to what Chief Justice John Roberts has called "the danger posed by the growing power of the administrative state"[2] may now be asking similar questions. Following a dramatic Term in which the Supreme Court "unmade" *Chevron* deference and several other administrative law doctrines along with it, some may hope (or fear) that the world is changing.

The upcoming Term may provide clarity. Already, the Court has granted several cases that involve federal administrative agency interpretations across a wide array of federal statutory schemes covering topics including guns, health care, and the environment. These and other grants still to come could elaborate on passages in *Loper Bright Enterprises v. Raimondo*,[3] where the Court appeared to temper *Chevron*'s end with nods toward statute-by-statute grants of discretion and "respect" for administrative interpretations.

The Court will of course also take up many other issues. In the two grants that so far appear most likely to generate headlines, the Court

* Mr. Broggi is a partner at Wiley Rein LLP. He clerked for Judge Gregory G. Katsas of the U.S. Court of Appeals for the D.C. Circuit and Judge Richard J. Leon of the U.S. District Court for the District of Columbia and served as a policy aide in the Bush-Cheney White House. The views in this essay are his, not those of Wiley Rein LLP or its clients.

[1] J.R.R. Tolkien, The Lord of the Rings 692 (Reset ed., HarperCollins 2021) (1954).

[2] City of Arlington v. FCC, 569 U.S. 290, 315 (2013) (Roberts, C.J., dissenting).

[3] 144 S. Ct. 2244, 2262 (2024).

will consider an equal protection challenge to a Tennessee statute that limits sex-transition treatments for minors and a First Amendment challenge to a Texas statute that restricts minors' access to commercial pornographic websites by requiring these websites to verify the age of their visitors.

Throughout these and other cases, the Court will confront several persistent issues. The Texas and Tennessee cases, for example, each implicate the Court's often stated, but seemingly seldom followed, preference for as-applied constitutional challenges. And in its agency cases, the Court may again confront issues about the scope of available remedies that have troubled lower courts and spurred separate writings from several Justices.

Suits against State Officials

The Court kicks off its Term with a pair of cases involving 42 U.S.C. §§ 1983 and 1988. Sections 1983 and 1988 are the most important statutes authorizing suits against state officials for violations of the federal Constitution and other laws of the United States. Enacted in 1871 to combat the influence of the Ku Klux Klan in state governments across the South, Section 1983 provides a remedy against any person who, acting under color of state law, subjects any other person "to the deprivation of any rights, privileges, or immunities secured by the Constitution and laws."[4] Section 1988, enacted later, allows federal courts to award attorney's fees to the "prevailing party" in these and certain other cases.[5]

In *Williams v. Washington*, the Supreme Court will decide whether exhaustion of state administrative remedies is required to bring claims under Section 1983 in state court. All agree that Section 1983 lacks a textual exhaustion requirement. And 40 years ago, in *Patsy v. Board of Regents*, the Supreme Court rejected a lower federal court's attempt to imply one.[6] Nevertheless, the Alabama Supreme Court held last year that it could not compel the Alabama Department of Labor to adjudicate applications for unemployment benefits within the time frame mandated by a federal statute because the plaintiffs in that case had not exhausted mandatory administrative remedies.

---

[4] 42 U.S.C. § 1983.

[5] 42 U.S.C. § 1988(b).

[6] Patsy v. Bd. of Regents, 457 U.S. 496 (1982).

The Alabama Supreme Court said that although *Patsy* had held that Section 1983 lacked an exhaustion requirement, that did not prevent state law from adding one. The court added that "even if" independent exhaustion requirements found in state law were preempted by Section 1983, "that preemption would at most allow the plaintiffs to bring their unexhausted claims in *federal* court."[7]

It seems unlikely that the Supreme Court will allow the Alabama decision to stand. The Alabama court did not discuss (and as the state's brief in opposition complains, the plaintiffs' state-court briefing did not cite) the Supreme Court's decision in *Felder v. Casey*. That decision, contrary to what the state court said, applied *Patsy* to find that Wisconsin's exhaustion requirement was preempted as to a suit in that state's courts.[8] To be sure, *Felder*'s reasoning could be characterized as purposivist: It said that because "Congress enacted § 1983 in response to the widespread deprivations of civil rights in the Southern States and the inability or unwillingness of authorities in those States to protect those rights or punish wrongdoers," Congress could not also have "contemplated that those who sought to vindicate their federal rights in state courts could be required to seek redress in the first instance from the very state officials whose hostility to those rights precipitated their injuries."[9] But that reasoning also accords with the absence of any exhaustion requirement in the text of Section 1983. And as the Court stated recently, "[t]he fact that multiple grounds support a result is usually regarded as a strength, not a weakness."[10]

Turning from the ability to bring a Section 1983 case to the incentive to do so, the Court in *Lackey v. Stinnie* will decide whether a plaintiff who obtains a preliminary injunction is a "prevailing party" entitled to attorney's fees under Section 1988 when there is no final ruling on the merits. In that case, the Virginia General Assembly repealed a state statute after a federal district judge held that it was likely unconstitutional. Virginia then tried to avoid paying attorney's fees by arguing that the preliminary injunction was not a final decision.

---

[7] Johnson v. Washington, No. SC-2022-0897, 2023 WL 4281620, at *4 (Ala. June 30, 2023), *cert. granted sub. nom* Williams v. Washington, 144 S. Ct. 679 (2024).

[8] Felder v. Casey, 487 U.S. 131, 147 (1988).

[9] *Id.* at 147.

[10] Biden v. Nebraska, 143 S. Ct. 2355, 2375 n.9 (2023).

The en banc Fourth Circuit rejected Virginia's position. In a decision that joined "[e]very other circuit to consider the issue," the Fourth Circuit overturned its own prior precedent to hold that "a preliminary injunction may confer prevailing party status in appropriate circumstances."[11] "Although many preliminary injunctions represent only 'a transient victory at the threshold of an action,'" the court said that "some provide enduring, merits-based relief" that entitles a plaintiff to status as a "prevailing party" under Section 1988.[12]

Virginia, obviously, has a different view. So does the United States. (Although the federal government cannot be sued under Section 1983, it is subject to fee shifting under the Equal Access to Justice Act and other statutes that employ the "prevailing party" language.[13]) In an amicus brief supporting Virginia, the Solicitor General argued that the lower threshold required to obtain preliminary relief and the potential for later reversal both indicate that a party who has obtained preliminary relief has not "prevailed" in the sense of the statute.[14]

Both sides cite a 2007 decision by the Supreme Court. In *Sole v. Wyner*, the Court held that a "plaintiff who secures a preliminary injunction, then loses on the merits as the case plays out and judgment is entered against her" is not a "prevailing party" because she "has won a battle but lost the war."[15] However, the *Sole* Court was careful to "express no view on" the issue that is now presented in *Lackey*: "[W]hether, in the absence of a final decision on the merits of a claim for permanent injunctive relief, success in gaining a preliminary injunction may sometimes warrant an award of counsel fees."[16]

Both views have something to recommend them. After all, a plaintiff who succeeds in obtaining a merits-based preliminary injunction seems to be a "prevailing party" as a practical matter. To be sure, where such relief is later reversed—as in *Sole*, where the district

---

[11] Stinnie v. Holcomb, 77 F.4th 200, 203 (4th Cir. 2023) (en banc); *see id.* at 209 (collecting cases); *id.* at 209 n.6 (explaining that among the courts of appeals, only "[t]he First Circuit has not yet opined on the issue"), *cert. granted sub nom.* Lackey v. Stinnie, 144 S. Ct. 1390 (2024).

[12] *Id.* at 203.

[13] *See* 28 U.S.C. § 2412(d); 5 U.S.C. § 504 *et seq.*

[14] 42 U.S.C. § 1988(b). *See also* Brief of the United States as *Amicus Curiae* Supporting Petitioner at 8–10, Lackey v. Stinnie, No. 23-621 (U.S. June 27, 2024).

[15] Sole v. Wyner, 551 U.S. 74, 86 (2007) (cleaned up).

[16] *Id.*

court eventually ruled against the plaintiffs after initially granting them preliminary relief—the plaintiff has not prevailed. But where such relief is not reversed and a further ruling can never happen because the case was mooted after the plaintiff obtained initial relief, the plaintiff appears to have accomplished what it intended. That is the situation in *Lackey*, where a district court held Virginia's law likely unconstitutional and Virginia mooted the case by removing the statute from the books.[17]

Against this interpretation, the Fourth Circuit dissenters argued that "prevailing party" is a term of art with a more limited meaning.[18] The case will likely turn on how well that argument is developed in the merits briefs—the fact that states or the federal government would prefer not to pay attorney's fees after losing is certainly no reason to supplant the statutory text.

Suits against Federal Agencies

For its first post-*Chevron* Term, the Supreme Court has granted several cases that involve an agency's interpretation of a statute that it administers. In addition to providing an initial look at the course correction that the Court signaled in *Loper Bright*,[19] each case is important for the regulated community it affects. Also lurking behind some of these cases are cross-cutting issues affecting the scope of permissible remedies under the Administrative Procedure Act (APA) and other agency review statutes.

Start with *Garland v. VanDerStok*,[20] which joins *Lackey* on the second day of argument and is otherwise known as the "ghost guns" case.[21] Fresh off the Supreme Court's rejection of its bump stock

---

[17] Lest one conclude that this is a one-off situation, Georgia, the only other sovereign to file an amicus brief, similarly repealed a state law and tried to resist paying attorney's fees after a plaintiff obtained a preliminary injunction on constitutional grounds. *See* Common Cause/Georgia v. Billups, 554 F.3d 1340, 1355 (11th Cir. 2009).

[18] *See Stinnie*, 77 F.4th at 220 (Quattlebaum, J., dissenting).

[19] 144 S. Ct. at 2262. *Loper Bright*, as the readers of this article surely know, overturned Chevron U.S.A., Inc. v. Nat. Res. Def. Council, 467 U.S. 837 (1984).

[20] 144 S. Ct. 1390 (2024) (order granting petition for certiorari).

[21] *See, e.g.*, Mark Sherman, *Supreme Court Will Take Up Legal Fight over Ghost Guns, Firearms without Serial Numbers*, ASSOCIATED PRESS (Apr. 22, 2024), https://apnews.com/article/supreme-court-ghost-guns-regulation-1a29729cf1bee46590d82ac46ab7b8f4.

rule,[22] the Bureau of Alcohol, Tobacco, Firearms and Explosives (ATF) is defending a regulation that would require homemade guns to bear serial numbers. In the Fifth Circuit's estimation, the new regulation "flouts clear statutory text and exceeds the legislatively-imposed limits on agency authority" in service of the agency's "public policy" goal.[23]

The statutory dispute appears straightforward. The Gun Control Act of 1968 imposes restrictions on a "firearm," a term it defines to include the "frame or receiver" of a weapon.[24] ATF was concerned that some hobbyists were not subject to the Act's restrictions because they had purchased unfinished weapons parts kits and later made a frame or receiver themselves from the materials included in these kits. So ATF issued what it called "an updated, more comprehensive definition" of the terms "firearm" and "frame or receiver" that includes within those definition "unfinished" frames or receivers.[25] The problem, as the Fifth Circuit saw it, was that the revised definition "states that the phrase 'frame or receiver' includes things that are admittedly not yet frames or receivers."[26] "This confusion highlights ATF's attempt to stretch the [Gun Control Act's] language to fit modern understandings of firearms without the support of statutory text."[27]

The case has already been before the Supreme Court once via the emergency docket. Last August, the Court voted 5–4 to stay the district court's vacatur pending appellate review.[28] In addition to defending its statutory interpretation, the government argued that the APA's instruction to "set aside" unlawful rules does not authorize what it (somewhat redundantly) called "nationwide vacatur."[29]

---

[22] *See* Garland v. Cargill, 602 U.S. 406 (2024).

[23] VanDerStok v. Garland, 86 F.4th 179, 182 (5th Cir. 2023).

[24] 18 U.S.C. § 921(a)(3)(C).

[25] *VanDerStok*, 86 F.4th at 182–83 (quoting Definition of "Frame or Receiver" and Identification of Firearms, 87 Fed. Reg. 24652 (Apr. 26, 2022) (to be codified at 27 C.F.R. pts. 447, 478–79)).

[26] *Id.* at 189–90.

[27] *Id.* at 190.

[28] Garland v. VanDerStok, 144 S. Ct. 44 (2023) (staying district court order).

[29] Application for a Stay of the Judgment Entered by the United States District Court for the Northern District of Texas at 31–32, Garland v. VanDerStok, 144 S. Ct. 44 (2023) (No. 23A83) (July 5, 2023).

Justice Neil Gorsuch made a similar point in a different case,[30] sparking a thoughtful response from Justice Brett Kavanaugh at the end of last Term that persuasively defended the practice.[31] Now more muted, the anti-vacatur argument is still present in ATF's merits brief.[32] *VanDerStok* may thus become a catalyst for more thinking from the Justices on the subject.

Next consider *City and County of San Francisco v. EPA*,[33] also scheduled for the October sitting. There, the Court will decide whether the Clean Water Act authorizes the EPA to impose narrative limitations in National Pollutant Discharge Elimination System permits that subject permit holders to enforcement for violating water quality standards without identifying specific numeric limits to which their discharges must conform.[34]

The Ninth Circuit upheld the EPA's practice as consistent with the statute, pointing specifically to a 1994 agency policy that interprets the Clean Water Act not only to authorize but in fact to "*require* . . . narrative limitations when necessary to satisfy applicable" water quality standards.[35] San Francisco, which holds a federal permit to discharge wastewater into the Pacific Ocean, argues that the EPA's narrative limitations are in conflict with the statute because they are indeterminate and because they premise liability

---

[30] *See* United States v. Texas, 599 U.S. 670, 695 (2023) (Gorsuch, J., concurring) ("[The APA] does not say anything about 'vacating' agency action[.]").

[31] *See* Corner Post, Inc. v. Bd. of Governors of Fed. Rsrv. Sys., 144 S. Ct. 2440, 2462 (2024) (Kavanaugh, J., concurring) ("[T]he text and history of the APA, the longstanding and settled precedent adhering to that text and history, and the radical consequences for administrative law and individual liberty that would ensue if vacatur were suddenly no longer available" each show that "the APA authorizes vacatur of unlawful agency actions, including agency rules[.]"); *see also* United States v. Texas, 599 U.S. at 721 (Alito, J., dissenting) ("[T]he . . . argument . . . that the APA's 'set aside' language may not permit vacatur . . . would be a sea change in administrative law[.]").

[32] *Cf.* Brief for the Petitioners at 27, Garland v. VanDerStok, No. 23-825 (U.S. June 25, 2024) ("If ATF ever sought to apply the Rule to a parts kit that could not readily be converted into a functional firearm, the affected parties would be free to challenge that action as beyond ATF's statutory authority. But the hypothetical possibility of such invalid applications does not justify relief in this facial, pre-enforcement challenge.").

[33] No. 23-753 (U.S. May 28, 2024), 2024 U.S. LEXIS 2342 (granting petition for certiorari).

[34] *See* Petition for Writ of Certiorari at i, City & Cnty. of San Franciso v. EPA (U.S. Jan. 8, 2024) (No. 23-753).

[35] City & Cnty. of San Francisco v. EPA, 75 F.4th 1074, 1090 (9th Cir. 2023).

on receiving water quality rather than on the nature or content of its own point source discharges.[36]

That the EPA has a prior administrative interpretation on the books may afford the Court an opportunity to elaborate an issue left open after *Loper Bright*.[37] There, the Court appeared to leave *Skidmore* respect intact even as it overturned *Chevron* deference, emphasizing that "courts may—as they have from the start—seek aid from the interpretations of those responsible for implementing particular statutes."[38] Indeed, that is something that the Court itself did in another recent Clean Water Act case, where it cited favorably the EPA's "longstanding regulatory practice" while pointedly stating that it "d[id] not defer . . . to EPA's interpretation of the statute embodied in this practice."[39]

Despite *Loper Bright* having left this path open, early reports indicate that most courts are not taking it.[40] And it is not clear that the Supreme Court should here either. After all, the 1994 EPA policy cited by the Ninth Circuit was issued decades after the Clean Water

[36] *See* Brief for Petitioner at 21, City & Cnty. of San Francisco v. EPA, No. 23-753 (U.S. July 19, 2024) (describing permit obligations as "hopelessly indeterminate") (quoting Sackett v. EPA, 598 U.S. 651, 681 (2023)); *id.* at 24–37 (arguing that "[t]he CWA does not authorize EPA to impose permit conditions that hold permitholders directly liable for the quality of receiving waters").

[37] For a focused discussion of the EPA's prior interpretation, see Brief of *Amici Curiae* Public Wastewater and Stormwater Agencies and Municipalities Supporting Petitioner at 16–20, City & Cnty. of San Francisco v. EPA, No. 23-753 (U.S. July 26, 2024) (citing, inter alia, 40 C.F.R. § 122.44(d)(1) *et seq.*; U.S. Env't Prot. Agency, *NPDES Permit Writers' Manual*, §§ 6.2 & 6.3 (Sept. 2010), https://www.epa.gov/sites/default/files/2015-09/documents/pwm_chapt_06.pdf).

[38] Loper Bright Enters. v. Raimondo, 144 S. Ct. 2244, 2262 (2024); *see also* Skidmore v. Swift & Co., 323 U.S. 134, 140 (1944) ("[R]ulings, interpretations and opinions" of agencies, "while not controlling," "do constitute a body of experience and informed judgment to which courts and litigants may properly resort for guidance," "depend[ing] upon the thoroughness evident in its consideration, the validity of its reasoning, its consistency with earlier and later pronouncements, and all those factors which give it power to persuade. . . .").

[39] Cnty. of Maui v. Haw. Wildlife Fund, 590 U.S. 165, 178 (2020); *see also* Jeremy J. Broggi, *With* En Banc *Review, Tenth Circuit Foreshadows Potential Split with D.C. Circuit on* Chevron *Waiver*, WASH. LEGAL FOUND., 35 LEGAL BACKGROUNDER 19 (Sept. 25, 2020), https://www.wlf.org/wp-content/uploads/2020/09/9252020Broggi_LB.pdf. (discussing *Hawaii Wildlife*'s approach in more detail).

[40] *See* Robert Iafolla, *Courts Show Little Interest in* Skidmore *as a* Chevron *Alternative*, BLOOMBERG LAW (July 29, 2024), https://news.bloomberglaw.com/daily-labor-report/courts-show-little-interest-in-skidmore-as-a-chevron-alternative ("[F]ederal courts didn't refer to 1944's *Skidmore v. Swift & Co.* in 19 of 20 rulings on agency actions that cited *Loper Bright*, according to a Bloomberg Law review[.]").

Act,[41] and it may not be a reliable indicator of the statute's meaning at the time of its enactment. Regardless, the Court's ultimate treatment of the 1994 EPA policy in the context of deciding the statutory question presented may provide a signal to how the Court is thinking about administrative interpretations in a post-*Chevron* world.

Two more statutory cases involving agencies could have cross-cutting effects. The first is *Advocate Christ Medical Center v. Becerra*,[42] concerning the calculation of Medicare payments to hospitals. The petition asks whether the phrase "entitled . . . to benefits" means the same thing for supplementary security income that it does for Medicare Part A, with the hospitals arguing that the agency erred by giving identical phrases different meanings.[43] But the D.C. Circuit, in a careful opinion by Judge Gregory Katsas, explained that "the phrase 'entitled to supplementary security income benefits . . . under subchapter XVI'" is materially different from "the phrase 'entitled to benefits under part A'" because the two schemes referenced by the two phrases in fact operate in two different ways.[44] The case is thus at least superficially similar to *Yates v. United States*[45] and *Fischer v. United States*,[46] insofar as it appears to again pit a woodenly literal reading of isolated terms against a more contextual interpretation.

---

[41] The statute today called the Clean Water Act results from the 1972 amendments to the Federal Water Pollution Control Act of 1948. *See History of the Clean Water Act*, U.S. Env't Prot. Agency (June 12, 2024), https://www.epa.gov/laws-regulations/history-clean-water-act.

[42] No. 23-715 (U.S. June 10, 2024), 2024 U.S. LEXIS 2572 (granting petition for certiorari).

[43] Petition for a Writ of Certiorari at i, 2–3, Advocate Christ Med. Ctr. v. Becerra, No. 23-715 (U.S. June 10, 2024), 2024 U.S. LEXIS 2572.

[44] Advoc. Christ Med. Ctr. v. Becerra, 80 F.4th 346, 352–53 (D.C. Cir. 2023).

[45] 574 U.S. 528 (2015). The question in *Yates* was whether a fish was a "tangible object" within the meaning of a provision in the Sarbanes-Oxley Act, a federal statute addressing corporate and accounting deception and coverups. *See* 18 U.S.C. § 1519. While acknowledging that "[a] fish is no doubt an object that is tangible," the Court held the provision's placement within the overall statutory scheme showed that a tangible object captured by it "must be one used to record or preserve information." *Yates*, 574 U.S. at 532.

[46] 144 S. Ct. 2176 (2024). *Fischer*, like *Yates*, involved the construction of a broadly worded provision in Sarbanes-Oxley. The Court held that a subsection imposing criminal liability on anyone who "otherwise obstructs, influences, or impedes any official proceeding, or attempts to do so" was limited by the immediately preceding subsection that established liability for anyone who corruptly "alters, destroys, mutilates, or conceals a record, document, or other object, or attempts to do so, with the intent to impair the object's integrity or availability for use in an official proceeding." *Id.* at 2181 (quoting 18 U.S.C. § 1512(c)(1) and § 1512(c)(2)).

Next is *Seven County Infrastructure Coalition v. Eagle County*,[47] where the Court will decide whether the National Environmental Policy Act (NEPA) requires an agency to study environmental impacts beyond the proximate effects of the action over which the agency has regulatory authority. In the decision below,[48] the D.C. Circuit rejected as inadequate an environmental review conducted by the Surface Transportation Board. The court held that an agency "cannot avoid" environmental review "on the ground that it lacks authority to prevent, control, or mitigate" environmental effects that are "reasonably foreseeable."[49] "As a result," the petition explains, the D.C. Circuit "ordered the Board to study the local effects of oil wells and refineries that lie outside the Board's regulatory authority."[50]

Seven County defies the typical posture in an agency case because the reviewing court demanded that the agency exercise *more* authority than the agency had claimed for itself. Because NEPA is not administered by a single agency, the Board's decision would not have been a candidate for *Chevron* deference even prior to *Loper Bright*. But the D.C. Circuit was apparently concerned that no other regulator could step in if the Board declined to study the potential environmental effects of the increased number of oil wells and refineries that would result from a new rail line,[51] underscoring that deference to unaccountable agencies may not be the only "danger" that enables "the growing power of the administrative state."[52]

The only nonstatutory agency case that has been granted as of this writing is *FDA v. Wages & White Lion Investments*.[53] There, the Biden administration asks the Court to reverse a decision of the en banc Fifth Circuit setting aside the Food and Drug Administration's denial of certain applications for authorization to market new

---

[47] Seven Cnty. Coal. v. Eagle Cnty., No. 23-975 (U.S. June 24, 2024) (granting petition for certiorari).

[48] Eagle Cnty. v. Surface Transp. Bd., 82 F.4th 1152 (D.C. Cir. 2023).

[49] *Id.* at 1180 (cleaned up), *cert. granted sub nom.* Seven Cnty. Coal. v. Eagle Cnty., No. 23-975 (U.S. June 24, 2024).

[50] Petition for a Writ of Certiorari at i, Seven Cnty. Coal. v. Eagle Cnty., No. 23-975 (U.S. June 24, 2024).

[51] *See Eagle Cnty.*, 82 F.4th at 1180.

[52] City of Arlington v. FCC, 569 U.S. 290, 315 (2013) (Roberts, C.J., dissenting).

[53] No. 23-1038 (U.S. July 2, 2024), 2024 U.S. LEXIS 2902 (granting petition for certiorari).

e-cigarette products.[54] Although the government has yet to file its merits brief, this is another case to watch for whether the government attempts to revive arguments that it made below about the scope and nature of relief authorized by the APA.[55] The case may also offer insight into how the Court is currently thinking about the arbitrary and capricious standard, which it often describes as "deferential" but which sometimes appears to involve a hard look at agency action.[56]

False Claims Act

The False Claims Act authorizes private parties to bring actions on behalf of the United States against other private parties who submit false and fraudulent claims for money or property to the federal government.[57] In *Wisconsin Bell, Inc. v. United States, ex rel. Heath,*[58] the Court will decide whether reimbursement requests submitted to the Federal Communications Commission's (FCC's) E-rate program are "claims" under the Act.

---

[54] For the opinion of the Fifth Circuit, see Wages & White Lion Invs., LLC v. FDA, 90 F.4th 357 (5th Cir. 2024) (en banc). For the government's petition seeking certiorari, see Petition for a Writ of Certiorari, Wages & White Lion Invs., LLC v. FDA, No. 23-1038 (U.S. July 2, 2024), 2024 U.S. LEXIS 2902.

[55] *Cf.* Application for a Stay of the Judgment Entered by the United States District Court for the Northern District of Texas at 31–32, Garland v. VanDerStok, 144 S. Ct. 44 (2023) (No. 23A83); Brief for the Petitioners at 27, Garland v. VanDerStok, No. 23-825 (U.S. June 25, 2024).

[56] For an article discussing the Court's apparent "oscillation" between deference and scrutiny in application of the arbitrary-and-capricious standard of review, see Eli Nachmany, *Arbitrary and Capricious Review at the Court after FCC v. Prometheus Radio Project: From the Return of "Hard Look" to the "Zone of Reasonableness,"* FED. SOC. BLOG (July 27, 2021), https://fedsoc.org/commentary/fedsoc-blog/arbitrary-and-capricious-review-at-the-court-after-fcc-v-prometheus-radio-project-from-the-return-of-hard-look-to-the-zone-of-reasonableness; *compare* Baltimore Gas & Elec. Co. v. NRDC, 462 U.S. 87, 103 (1983) (describing standard of review as "most deferential"), *and* FCC v. Prometheus Radio Project, 592 U.S. 414, 423 (2021) (explaining that the standard of review "simply ensures that the agency has acted within a zone of reasonableness"), *with* Dep't of Com. v. New York, 588 U.S. 752, 785 (2019) (cautioning that courts are "not required to exhibit a naiveté from which ordinary citizens are free") (quoting United States v. Stanchich, 550 F. 2d 1294, 1300 (2d Cir. 1977) (Friendly, J.)).

[57] *See* 18 U.S.C. §§ 286, 287; 31 U.S.C. § 3729.

[58] No. 23-1127 (U.S. June 17, 2024), 2024 U.S. LEXIS 2699 (granting petition for certiorari).

The FCC's E-rate program provides discounted telecommunications and internet service to eligible schools and libraries.[59] The program is administered by the Universal Service Administrative Company, a private, nonprofit corporation funded by statutorily required contributions from telecommunications carriers.[60] In this case, a private individual sued Wisconsin Bell alleging that it had overcharged schools and libraries under the E-rate program. The theory of the case is that such overcharging would render reimbursement requests submitted to the Universal Service Administrative Company false claims.[61]

The principal legal issue concerns the provenance of the funds disbursed by the Universal Service Administrative Company. The False Claims Act defines a "claim" to include a request to a "contractor, grantee, or other recipient" if the federal government "provided any portion of the money" requested.[62] The en banc Seventh Circuit found that the E-rate program satisfied that statutory definition because Congress ordered telecommunications carriers to contribute to the program and the FCC ultimately oversees its administration.[63] But Wisconsin Bell argues that under the term's ordinary meaning, the government "provides" money only if the government is itself the source of that money.[64] And here, the funds contributed to the private administrator undisputedly come from private telecommunications carriers who are assessed a fee for that purpose, not from the U.S. Treasury out of general tax revenues.[65]

Lurking in the background are also questions about the constitutionality of the Universal Service Administrative Company. About a month after the Supreme Court granted cert in *Wisconsin Bell*,[66] the en banc Fifth Circuit held that the FCC violated the private

---

[59] *See generally E-Rate: Universal Service Program for Schools and Libraries*, Fed. Comms. Comm'n (Feb. 27, 2024), https://www.fcc.gov/consumers/guides/universal-service-program-schools-and-libraries-e-rate.

[60] *See generally About USAC: Universal Service*, Univ. Serv. Admin. Co., https://www.usac.org/about/universal-service/ (last visited Aug. 19, 2024).

[61] *See* United States ex rel. Heath v. Wis. Bell, Inc., 92 F.4th 654, 659 (7th Cir. 2023).

[62] 31 U.S.C. § 3729(b)(2)(A)(ii)(I); *see id.* § 3729(c).

[63] *See Wisconsin Bell*, 92 F.4th at 668–71.

[64] Brief for Petitioner at 13–14, Wis. Bell, Inc. v. United States ex rel. Heath, No. 23-1127 (U.S. Aug. 13, 2024) (summarizing argument).

[65] *See id.* at 14–15.

[66] No. 23-1127 (U.S. June 17, 2024), 2024 U.S. LEXIS 2699.

nondelegation doctrine by authorizing a private corporation to collect funds from the telecommunications carriers in the first place.[67] Although that question is not presented here, Wisconsin Bell has argued that the Universal Service Administrative Company is not an "agent of the United States" within the meaning of the False Claims Act.[68] That argument seems to touch on similar themes. Expect merits briefing and questions at oral argument to look more closely than did the Seventh Circuit at the nature of the Universal Service Administrative Company and its relationship to the FCC.

Securities Fraud

During a wave of securities fraud litigation that accompanied the internet technology boom in the 1990s, Congress passed the Private Securities Litigation Reform Act.[69] The Act makes such cases more difficult to bring by imposing heightened pleading standards on the complainant. In this way, Congress sought to protect the emerging technology companies that were then fueling the national economy from what Congress viewed as largely frivolous lawsuits.[70]

The Court will weigh in on the Private Securities Litigation Reform Act pleading standard in *NVIDIA Corp. v. E. Ohman J:or Fonder AB*.[71] The case involves a shareholder lawsuit against NVIDIA, one of the world's largest producers of graphics processing units. The lawsuit alleges that NVIDIA and its chief executive misrepresented how much of the company's revenue was attributable to cryptocurrency mining.[72] The Court will decide whether plaintiffs must plead with particularity the contents of internal company documents, and whether

---

[67] Consumers' Rsch. v. FCC, No. 22-60008, 2024 WL 3517592, at *1 (5th Cir. July 24, 2024) (en banc).

[68] *See* 31 U.S.C. § 3729(b)(2)(A)(i); Brief for Petitioner at 15–17, Wisconsin Bell, Inc. v. United States ex rel. Heath, No. 23-1127 (U.S. Aug. 13, 2024) (summarizing argument).

[69] 109 Stat. 737 (Dec. 22, 1995) (codified at 15 U.S.C. §§ 77(k), 77(l), 77(z)(1)–(2), 78(a), 78(j)(1), 78(u)(4)–(5)).

[70] *See* S. REP. No. 104-98, at 9 (1995) (describing an "in terrorem effect on Corporate America" from class action lawsuits brought by "professional plaintiffs" burdening "high-technology companies," especially "[s]maller start-up[s]").

[71] No. 23-970 (U.S. June 17, 2024), 2024 U.S. LEXIS 2688 (granting petition for certiorari).

[72] *See* E. Ohman J:Or Fonder AB v. NVIDIA Corp., 81 F.4th 918, 923 (9th Cir. 2023). Cryptocurrency mining, the Ninth Circuit explained, is the act of using a computer's "processing power to solve 'a difficult mathematical puzzle through laborious trial-and-error work'" that is then "rewarded with new issues of cryptocurrency." *Id.* at 924.

expert opinion can substitute for factual allegations.[73] The case will be watched closely by both plaintiff and defense bars because the Private Securities Litigation Reform Act pleading standard affects not only cryptocurrency but most securities fraud claims across the country.

Online Speech

The Supreme Court decided five cases last Term involving the application of the First Amendment to social media and the internet.[74] In *Free Speech Coalition, Inc. v. Paxton*,[75] the Court will decide the standard for assessing the constitutionality of a Texas statute that restricts minors' access to commercial pornographic websites by requiring these websites to verify the age of their visitors.

The Fifth Circuit upheld Texas's age verification requirement.[76] Beginning with the undisputed premise that under binding Supreme Court precedent the "regulation of the distribution *to minors* of speech obscene *for minors* is subject only to rational-basis review,"[77] the court found that this standard was easily satisfied because "the age-verification requirement is rationally related to the government's legitimate interest in preventing minors' access to pornography."[78] As for adults, the Fifth Circuit found that their rights were not implicated because the Texas law "allows adults to access as much pornography as they want whenever they want" and "whatever 'burden'" arises from the age-verification requirement is

---

[73] *See* Petition for a Writ of Certiorari at i, NVIDIA Corp. v. E. Ohman J:Or Fonder AB, No. 23-970 (U.S. June 17, 2024), 2024 U.S. LEXIS 2688.

[74] *See* Lindke v. Freed, 601 U.S. 187 (2024) (holding that a public official's social media activity constitutes state action if the official had actual authority to speak on behalf of the government and purported to exercise that authority); O'Connor-Ratcliff v. Garnier, 601 U.S. 205 (per curiam) (remanding a similar case for reconsideration in light of *Lindke*); Moody v. NetChoice, LLC, 144 S. Ct. 2383 (2024) (consolidated opinion remanding two cases for the lower courts to perform the necessary inquiry in reviewing facial challenges to state laws that regulate social media); Murthy v. Missouri, 144 S. Ct. 1972 (2024) (rejecting challenge to asserted censorship by government coercion of social media companies for lack of Article III standing).

[75] No. 23-1122 (U.S. July 2, 2024), 2024 U.S. LEXIS 2897 (granting petition for certiorari).

[76] *See* Free Speech Coal., Inc. v. Paxton, 95 F.4th 263 (5th Cir. 2024).

[77] *Id.* at 270; *see also* Ginsberg v. New York, 390 U.S. 629, 639 (1968) ("[I]t was rational for the legislature to find that the minors' exposure to such material might be harmful[.]").

[78] *Free Speech Coal.*, 95 F.4th at 267.

of "the same type" as that "required to enter a strip club, drink a beer, or buy cigarettes."[79]

The petitioning adult industry trade associations argue that the Fifth Circuit underestimated the burden the law places on adults.[80] In their view, the age-verification requirement is a content-based speech restriction that "subjects adults to significant and chilling burdens" that must be reviewed under "strict scrutiny."[81] Although the associations acknowledge that the Supreme Court in *Ginsberg v. New York* upheld a state law that prohibited the sale of "girlie picture magazines" to minors,[82] their petition says that the internet "poses unique security and privacy concerns" that require a different analysis.[83]

Free Speech Coalition represents the Supreme Court's first foray in an area of increasing activity by state legislatures. In addition to age restrictions for accessing online pornography (the petition says there are eight such laws already in existence, including the one pending the Court's review, and 12 more under consideration),[84] the National Conference of State Legislatures reports that at least 30 states and Puerto Rico have enacted or are considering bills that purport to protect children's online privacy in some way.[85] Many regulate more broadly than Texas. For example, California has enacted an Age-Appropriate Design Code Act, which was preliminarily enjoined by a federal district court[86] and which

---

[79] *Id.* at 275–76.

[80] *See* Petition for Writ of Certiorari at 1–2, Free Speech Coal., Inc. v. Paxton, No. 23-1122 (U.S. July 2, 2024), 2024 U.S. LEXIS 2897 ("[T]he Act imposes significant burdens on adults' access to constitutionally protected expression. Of central relevance here, it requires every user, including adults, to submit personally identifying information to access sensitive, intimate content over a medium—the Internet—that poses unique security and privacy concerns.").

[81] *Id.* at 22.

[82] *Ginsberg*, 390 U.S. at 634; *see also* Petition for Writ of Certiorari, *Free Speech Coal.*, *supra* note 80, at 6.

[83] Petition for Writ of Certiorari, *Free Speech Coal.*, *supra* note 80, at 1–2.

[84] *See id.* at 34.

[85] *See Social Media and Children 2024 Legislation*, Nat'l Conference of State Legislatures (June 14, 2024), https://www.ncsl.org/technology-and-communication/social-media-and-children-2024-legislation.

[86] *See* NetChoice, LLC v. Bonta, 2023 U.S. Dist. LEXIS 165500, at *5 (N.D. Cal. Sept. 18, 2023) (stating that the Act "likely violates the First Amendment" and issuing a preliminary injunction), *aff'd in part and rev'd in part*, 2024 U.S. App. LEXIS 20755 (9th Cir. Aug. 16, 2024).

has been copied by proposed or enacted bills in Connecticut and Maryland.[87] California's law requires many different kinds of businesses to assess and report whether their online content is "harmful, or potentially harmful" if accessed by children and to develop a mitigation plan.[88] Unlike California's law and those modeled on it, the Texas statute purports to regulate only speech that the Supreme Court considers outside the First Amendment's protection as to minors. For that reason, the Supreme Court could resolve this case narrowly. But whatever action the Court takes, *Free Speech Coalition* will be closely watched for any insight into how the Justices are thinking about state regulation of children's online activities.

Free Speech Coalition may also provide insight into issues that the Supreme Court identified in *Moody v. NetChoice, LLC* and *NetChoice, LLC v. Paxton*,[89] two social media cases decided last Term. There, the Court reiterated its preference for resolving constitutional challenges to statutes on an as-applied basis, observing that its precedents "made facial challenges hard to win" "even when a facial suit is based on the First Amendment."[90]

Free Speech Coalition may give the Court an opportunity to elaborate on what it meant in the *NetChoice* cases. The Texas age verification statute appears more circumscribed than the social media statutes at issue in those cases, which would make potential factual development much easier. But the petitioning adult industry trade associations do not assert that particular adults have had their use of pornography chilled by the age verification statute. Nor do they explain why the statute's alternatives for age verification (which, according to the Fifth Circuit, include means similar to in-person age verification) are too burdensome in practice. Presumably, the associations believe such details are unnecessary. But these are exactly the types of unknowns that have given some of the Justices pause

---

[87] *See* Md. Code. Ann., Com. Law, §§ 14-4601–4613 (2024); H.B. No. 6253, Jan. Sess., 2023 (Conn. 2023).

[88] Cal. Civ. Code § 1798.99.31; *see also* NetChoice, LLC v. Bonta, 692 F. Supp. 3d at 944 (issuing preliminary injunction).

[89] The two cases were joined and adjudicated by the same decision. *See* Moody v. NetChoice, LLC, 144 S. Ct. 2383 (2024).

[90] *Id.* at 2397–98.

in other facial challenges.[91] *Free Speech Coalition* may thus spur additional clarification about what is needed when plaintiffs seek broad-based relief.

Equal Protection

Perhaps the most controversial case granted so far also concerns state regulation of children. In *United States v. Skrmetti*,[92] the Biden administration seeks facial invalidation of a Tennessee statute that limits sex-transition treatments for minors experiencing gender dysphoria.[93]

As with *Free Speech Coalition*, the key legal issue is the standard of review. The Sixth Circuit applied rational basis review, which all parties agree is the correct equal protection standard for challenges to laws that make distinctions based on "age" and "medical condition."[94] The Tennessee statute distinguishes based on at least those factors, but the Biden administration contends that it also contains sex-based distinctions that should subject it to heightened scrutiny.

The challenged provisions prohibit health care providers from administering puberty blockers and hormone therapy to minors for sex-transition treatment.[95] Although the prohibitions are facially neutral in that they apply whether patients are boys or girls, the petition's lead argument is that they are "sex-based" in operation because they restrict only minors "who seek to induce physiological effects inconsistent with their sex assigned at birth": "An adolescent assigned female at birth cannot receive puberty blockers or testosterone to live as a male, but an adolescent assigned male at birth can. And vice versa, an adolescent assigned male at birth cannot receive puberty blockers or estrogen to live as a female, but an adolescent assigned female at birth can."[96]

---

[91] *See, e.g., id.* at 2397–99 (rejecting facial challenge and remanding to lower courts given uncertainty regarding "the laws' full range of applications").

[92] No. 23-477 (U.S. June 24, 2024), 2024 U.S. LEXIS 2780 (granting petition for certiorari).

[93] *See* Petition for a Writ of Certiorari at 18–19, 29, United States v. Skrmetti, 2024 U.S. 2780 (U.S. June 24, 2024) (No. 23-477).

[94] *See* L.W. v. Skrmetti, 83 F.4th 460, 479–80 (6th Cir. 2024).

[95] *See* Tenn. Ann. Code § 68-33-103.

[96] Cert. Petition, *Skrmetti, supra* note 93, at 18–19 (cleaned up).

The Sixth Circuit acknowledged the law's different effects with respect to specific hormones but attributed these to "biological sex," "a lasting feature of the human condition."[97] Because "only females can use testosterone as a transition treatment" and "only males can use estrogen as a transition treatment," the Sixth Circuit found that the law restricts sex-transition treatments "evenhandedly" "for all minors, regardless of sex."[98] The court thus agreed with Tennessee that the law "treat[s] boys and girls exactly the same for constitutional purposes."[99]

Interestingly, although the initial challengers argued they could win even under rational basis review,[100] the Biden administration dropped that argument in its petition.[101] As an alternative path to heightened review, the petition asks the Supreme Court to designate transgender individuals as a new constitutionally protected class.[102] But the Court has not taken that route in over a half century. Unless the Court is inclined to do so now, the oral argument will need to explore each side's underlying assumptions about the nature of biological sex. Although at least one Justice is famously "not a biologist,"[103] *Skrmetti* is the second case in as many Terms that could turn on the Court's understanding of biological functions.[104]

---

[97] *Skrmetti*, 83 F.4th at 481.

[98] *Id.* at 480–81. *Cf.* Dobbs v. Jackson Women's Health Org., 597 U.S. 215, 236–37 (2022) ("The regulation of a medical procedure that only one sex can undergo does not trigger heightened constitutional scrutiny unless the regulation is a 'mere pretex[t] designed to effect an invidious discrimination against members of one sex or the other.'") (quoting Geduldig v. Aiello, 417 U.S. 484, 496 n.20 (1974)).

[99] *Skrmetti*, 83 F.4th at 482.

[100] *See* Plaintiffs' Motion for Preliminary Injunctive Relief at 21–22, Doe v. Thornbury, 679 F. Supp. 3d 576 (W.D. Ky. 2023) (No. 3:23-cv-00230-DJH) ("[T]here is no logical or rational connection between the Treatment Ban and any justifications that may be proffered by Defendants[.]") (citing Romer v. Evans, 517 U.S. 620 (1996)).

[101] *See* Cert. Petition, *Skrmetti*, *supra* note 93, at 17 (arguing that intermediate scrutiny should apply).

[102] *See id.* at 24–25.

[103] Myah Ward, *Blackburn to Jackson: Can you define 'the word woman'?* Politico (Mar. 22, 2022), https://www.politico.com/news/2022/03/22/blackburn-jackson-define-the-word-woman-00019543.

[104] *Compare* City of Grants Pass v. Johnson, 144 S. Ct. 2202, 2228 (2024) (Sotomayor, J., dissenting) ("Sleep is a biological necessity, not a crime."), *with id.* at 2225 (majority opinion) ("[W]hat are people entitled to do . . . to . . . fulfill . . . 'biological necessities'?").

Skrmetti may also present questions about the scope of relief. The district court issued broad preliminary injunctive relief that blocked all enforcement of the Tennessee statute.[105] But the Sixth Circuit, in addition to overruling that decision on the merits, cited the Supreme Court's *Salerno* standard under which a plaintiff seeking facial relief "must establish that no set of circumstances exists under which the statute would be valid," and specifically faulted the district court for failing to consider "every potentially valid application, say with respect to individuals too young to consent to a regimen of hormone treatments."[106] Although the Court need not reach this issue, *Skrmetti* could spur writings from the Justices about facial and as-applied relief.

Mandatory Minimums

The First Step Act was signed into law by President Donald Trump in 2018.[107] The statute reduces the mandatory minimum sentences for some federal drug and gun crimes (among other things) and is often cited by the former President as part of his plan to help "forgotten Americans."[108]

The First Step Act provides that its sentencing reductions "shall apply to any offense that was committed before the date of enactment of this Act, if a sentence for the offense has not been imposed as of such date of enactment."[109] The question before the court in both *Hewitt v. United States*[110] and *Duffey v. United States*[111] is whether

---

[105] *See* Doe v. Thornbury, 679 F. Supp. 3d 576 (W.D. Ky. 2023).

[106] *Skrmetti*, 83 F.4th at 489–90 (cleaned up); *see* United States v. Salerno, 481 U.S. 739 (1987).

[107] For an overview of the legislation, see *An Overview of the First Step Act*, FED. BUREAU OF PRISONS, https://www.bop.gov/inmates/fsa/overview.jsp (last visited Aug. 19, 2024).

[108] *President Donald J. Trump Has Championed Reforms That Are Providing Hope to Forgotten Americans*, THE WHITE HOUSE (Feb. 20, 2020), https://trumpwhitehouse.archives.gov/briefings-statements/president-donald-j-trump-championed-reforms-providing-hope-forgotten-americans/.

[109] First Step Act, §§401(c), 403(b), Pub. L. No. 115-391, 132 Stat. 5194, 5221–22 (2018).

[110] No. 23-1002 (U.S. July 2, 2024), 2024 LEXIS 2900 (granting petition for certiorari and consolidating cases).

[111] No. 23-1150 (U.S July 2, 2024), 2024 LEXIS 2905 (granting petition for certiorari and consolidating cases).

that includes a defendant who was originally sentenced before the law was enacted but was then resentenced after the law's enactment.

The answer to that question is of obvious importance to the criminal defendants in these and other cases. For example, petitioner Tony Hewitt says that application of the First Step Act would have reduced his mandatory minimum sentence by 80 years, from 105 years to just 25.[112] At the certiorari stage, the government agreed with Hewitt (and Corey Duffey) that the First Step Act should apply at resentencing. But the government urged the Court to allow further percolation among the lower courts.[113] Given the parties' apparent agreement on the underlying legal issue, the cases necessitated the appointment of counsel to defend the interpretation taken by the court of appeals.[114]

Still to Come

As of this writing more than half the Court's docket remains to be filled. For some perspective, at this time last year, the Court had not yet granted *Corner Post*,[115] a case that together with *Loper Bright*[116] and *SEC v. Jarkesy*[117] helped define the October Term 2023 as a milestone in administrative law.

Three pending petitions are highlighted here. The first involves political speech, a topic in which the Court is often interested. In *No on E, San Franciscans Opposing the Affordable Housing Production Act v. Chiu*,[118] petitioners ask the Court to decide whether the First Amendment allows San Francisco to require groups that run political advertisements to identify in those advertisements their top three

---

[112] *See* Petition for a Writ of Certiorari at 4, Hewitt v. United States, No. 23-1002 (U.S. July 2, 2024), 2024 LEXIS 2900.

[113] *See* Brief for the United States in Opposition at 9, Hewitt v. United States, No. 23-1002 (U.S. July 2, 2024), 2024 LEXIS 2900; Duffey v. United States, No. 23-1150 (U.S. July 2, 2024), 2024 LEXIS 2905.

[114] *See* Hewitt v. United States, No. 23-1002 (U.S. July 26, 2024), 2024 U.S. LEXIS 2978; Duffey v. United States, No. 23-1150 (U.S. July 26, 2024), 2024 U.S. LEXIS 2977 (inviting Michael H. McGinley to brief and argue the case as amicus curiae in support of the judgments below).

[115] Corner Post, Inc. v. Bd. of Governors of Fed. Rsrv. Sys., 144 S. Ct. 2440 (2024).

[116] Loper Bright Enterprises v. Raimondo, 144 S. Ct. 2244, 2262 (2024).

[117] SEC v. Jarkesy, 144 S. Ct. 2117 (2024).

[118] 85 F.4th 493, 506–7 (9th Cir. 2023), *petition docketed*, No. 23-926 (U.S. Feb. 27, 2024).

political donors (and, in some circumstances, each of those donors' top two political donors for a grand total of nine donors in all).[119] The district court record showed that for some 15-second and 30-second video ads, San Francisco's required disclosures occupied the entire ad, leaving no room for the speaker's own message.[120] And even for longer video ads of 60 seconds, San Francisco was still the primary speaker, occupying more than half of the ad time.[121] These stark facts make the case a potentially attractive vehicle for elaborating "exacting scrutiny," the minimum amount of First Amendment scrutiny applicable to compelled donor disclosures under *Americans for Prosperity Foundation v. Bonta*.[122]

Two more petitions involve state efforts to regulate global climate change by suing oil companies for common-law torts including nuisance, trespass, and negligence. In *Shell PLC v. City and County of Honolulu*[123] and *Sunoco LP v. City and County of Honolulu*,[124] Hawaii's highest court allowed these claims to go forward, stating that the "case concerns torts committed in Hawai'i that caused alleged injuries in Hawai'i" and that the claims were not preempted by the Clean Air Act or federal common law.[125] The petitions, for their part, argue that climate change is, by its nature, a global issue, and that any injury necessarily results from emissions all over the world.[126]

---

[119] *See* Petition for a Writ of Certiorari at i–ii, No on E, San Franciscans Opposing the Affordable Housing Prod. Act v. Chiu, No. 23-926 (U.S. Feb. 23, 2024).

[120] *See* No on E v. Chiu, 85 F.4th 493, 506–07 (9th Cir. 2023).

[121] *See id.* at 507.

[122] 594 U.S. 595 (2021); *see id.* at 606–08 (plurality opinion) ("exacting scrutiny" applies to "compelled disclosure" requirements); *id.* at 619 (Thomas, J., concurring in part and concurring in the judgment) ("[S]trict scrutiny [applies] to laws that compel disclosure of protected First Amendment association[.]'"); *id.* at 623 (Alito, J., joined by Gorsuch, J., concurring in part and concurring in the judgment) ("I see no need to decide which standard should be applied here.").

[123] 537 P.3d 1173 (Haw. 2023), *petition docketed*, No. 23-952 (U.S. Mar. 1, 2024).

[124] 537 P.3d 1173 (Haw. 2023), *petition docketed*, No. 23-947 (U.S. Mar. 1, 2024).

[125] City & Cnty. of Honolulu v. Sunoco LP, 537 P.3d 1173, 1181 (Haw. 2023).

[126] *See* Petition for a Writ of Certiorari at 2–3, Shell PLC v. City & Cnty. of Honolulu, No. 23-952 (U.S. Feb. 28, 2024) (introducing argument); Petition for a Writ of Certiorari at 3, Sunoco LP v. City & Cnty. of Honolulu, No. 23-947 (U.S. Feb. 28, 2024) (asking the Court to consider "whether federal law precludes state-law claims seeking redress for injuries allegedly caused by the effects of interstate and international greenhouse-gas emissions on the global climate").

In the oil companies' views, the Constitution delegates authority to regulate cross-border emissions solely to the federal government, displacing the states.[127] The Court has signaled some interest in the cases, calling for the views of the Solicitor General.[128]

Conclusion

With *Chevron* ended, will everything sad come untrue in administrative law as Sam expected for Middle Earth? Some may be hoping that "all that was made or begun with that power will crumble" and that an administrative state shorn of its weapon will, like Sauron, "be maimed for ever, becoming a mere spirit of malice that gnaws itself in the shadows,"[129] but that result seems unlikely. Regardless, the October Term 2024 should provide an early glimpse at the Court's revised approach to the proper interpretation of statutes that are administered by federal agencies. And the remaining cases the Court has granted already will shed light on the meaning of other federal statutes, as well as apply the Constitution to new forms of state regulation, with more cases still to come.

---

[127] *See* Cert. Petition, *Shell, supra* note 125, at 20–21; Cert. Petition, *Sunoco, supra* note 125, at 5.

[128] *See* Shell PLC v. City & Cnty. of Honolulu, No. 23-952, 2024 U.S. LEXIS 2515 (U.S. June 10, 2024).

[129] J.R.R. Tolkien, The Lord of the Rings 640 (Reset ed., HarperCollins 2021) (1954).

Contributors

Derek Bambauer is the Irving Cypen Professor of Law at the University of Florida Levin College of Law, where he teaches internet law, cybersecurity, and intellectual property. A National Science Foundation-funded investigator, Bambauer's research areas include artificial intelligence, cybersecurity, internet censorship, and intellectual property. A former principal systems engineer at Lotus Development Corp. (part of IBM), he spent two years as a research fellow at the Berkman Center for Internet & Society at Harvard Law School. While at the Berkman Center, he was a member of the OpenNet Initiative, an academic consortium that tested and studied internet censorship in countries such as China, Iran, and Vietnam. Bambauer maintains an active pro bono practice representing innovators, entrepreneurs, and security research. He holds an A.B. from Harvard College and a J.D. from Harvard Law School.

Jack Beermann is the Philip S. Beck Professor of Law at Boston University School of Law. His scholarship focuses on civil rights litigation and administrative law. He is an authority on the circumstances under which state and local officials, and local governments, should be held liable for their constitutional violations. Beermann has authored or co-authored four books on administrative law, including a widely used casebook and the *Emanuel Law Outline* on the subject. He has also written extensively on the degree to which federal courts should defer to the legal determinations of federal agencies, on the problem of midnight rulemaking, in which outgoing administrations promulgate dozens of regulations at the end of their administrations and on the legal aspects of the funding crisis facing public employee pension funds in the United States. His articles have appeared in prominent American journals such as the *Stanford Law Review, UCLA Law Review, Duke Law Journal,* and *Boston University Law Review,* and in foreign law journals including Germany's

Rechtstheorie and China's *Administrative Law Review*. Recent articles include "The Public Pension Crisis" in the *Washington & Lee Law Review*, "Congressional Administration" in the *San Diego Law Review* and the "Constitutional Law of Presidential Transition" in the *North Carolina Law Review*. In 1998, he co-authored an article that examined civil rights violations in the popular television drama NYPD Blue, and in 1993 he wrote "The Supreme Court's Narrow View on Civil Rights" for the prestigious *Supreme Court Review*. Before joining the Boston University faculty in 1984, Professor Beermann clerked for Judge Richard Cudahy of the United States Court of Appeals for the Seventh Circuit. In 2017, he was appointed as a public member of the Administrative Conference of the United States. In 2008, 2011 and 2014 he was visiting professor at Harvard Law School and in 1997, he was distinguished visiting professor at DePaul Law School. In 2004, 2005 and 2007, he taught at the Interdisciplinary Center in Herzliya, Israel, and in 2002, he taught at the China University of Political Science and Law in Beijing. He has lectured in Israel, Germany, Australia, Morocco, Portugal, and Canada.

Thomas Berry is a legal fellow in the Cato Institute's Robert A. Levy Center for Constitutional Studies and editor-in-chief of the *Cato Supreme Court Review*. Before joining Cato, he was an attorney at Pacific Legal Foundation and clerked for Judge E. Grady Jolly of the U.S. Court of Appeals for the Fifth Circuit. Berry's areas of interest include the separation of powers, executive branch appointments, and First Amendment freedom of speech. Berry's academic work has appeared in the *NYU Journal of Law and Liberty*, the *Washington and Lee Law Review Online*, and the *Federalist Society Review*, with shorter pieces in the *Yale Journal on Regulation's Notice & Comment blog*, *Lawfare*, and *Law & Liberty*. His popular writing has appeared in many outlets including the *Wall Street Journal*, *USA Today*, *CNN.com*, the *National Law Journal*, the *National Review Online*, *Reason.com*, and *The Hill*. Berry has testified before a subcommittee of the U.S. Senate on the Appointments Clause, and his work on the Vacancies Act has been cited by the U.S. District Court for the District of Columbia. Berry holds a J.D. from Stanford Law School, where he was a senior editor on the *Stanford Law and Policy Review* and a Bradley Student Fellow in the Stanford Constitutional Law Center.

Anya Bidwell is a senior attorney at the Institute for Justice, where she leads IJ's Project on Immunity and Accountability. Through this project, Anya works to promote judicial engagement and ensure that government officials are held to account when they violate individuals' constitutional rights. Anya also serves as an adviser on the American Law Institute's Restatement of the Law, Constitutional Torts project. Her most recent focus has been on First Amendment retaliation. She argued *Gonzalez v. Trevino* before the United States Supreme Court and second-chaired arguments for *Brownback v. King* and *Tennessee Wine & Spirits Retailers Association v. Thomas*. Before joining IJ, Bidwell worked for a top national law firm, handling cases in trial and appellate courts. She earned her J.D. with honors from the University of Texas. Two years prior to entering law school, Anya received a master's degree in Global Policy Studies, also from the University of Texas, and wrote a thesis on asymmetric warfare. Her work has been featured in numerous publications, including the *Washington Post*, the *Wall Street Journal*, the *New York Times*, *USA Today*, and the *Guardian*. She is also the host of live recordings for IJ's *Short Circuit* podcast and a co-producer of IJ's documentary-style podcast *Bound by Oath*.

Jeremy Broggi is a partner at Wiley Rein where he litigates constitutional, statutory, and regulatory issues before federal and state courts and administrative agencies. He has developed successful legal arguments that have been adopted in decisions at all levels of the federal judicial system, including the U.S. Supreme Court. His amicus work has also been cited favorably in appellate court decisions and in media coverage of cases. In addition to private practice, Jeremy has worked in all three branches of the federal government. He is adept at leveraging his government experience to achieve favorable outcomes in matters involving federal administrative agencies, including rulemakings, enforcement matters, and challenges to agency action.

Michael G. Collins is a professor of law at the University of Virginia School of Law. He teaches Civil Procedure, Federal Courts, Conflict of Laws, and Evidence. Before coming to UVA, where he is currently the Joseph M. Hartfield Professor of Law, Collins taught at Tulane Law School, where he was the Robert A. Ainsworth Professor of Law. After law school, he practiced commercial and employment law in Los Angeles, practiced civil rights law in New Orleans, and was a Bigelow Fellow at the University of Chicago Law School. He has also been a visiting professor at Boston University, George Washington, Ohio State and Richmond. While at Tulane, he was a three-time recipient of the law school's distinguished teaching award. And in 2013, he was a recipient of the University of Virginia's All-University Teaching Award. Collins's research interests lie in the areas of federal courts, procedure, and legal history. His recently published works include the casebook *Transnational Civil Litigation* (with Joachim Zekoll and George Rutherglen), an article on the obligation of state courts to entertain sister-state claims (with Ann Woolhandler) and an article titled "Reconstructing *Murdock v. Memphis*." His writings have appeared in the *California Law Review, Columbia Law Review, Emory Law Review, Georgetown Law Journal,* and *Virginia Law Review.* He has also co-authored casebooks on federal jurisdiction and on first-year civil procedure, and he has published a handbook on constitutional tort litigation.

Eric Goldman is a professor of law at Santa Clara University School of Law and co-director of the High Tech Law Institute. His research and teaching focuses on Internet, IP, and advertising law topics, and he blogs on these topics at the *Technology & Marketing Law Blog. Managing IP* magazine has twice named him to a shortlist of North American "IP Thought Leaders," and he has been named an "IP Vanguard" by the California State Bar's Intellectual Property Section. Before joining the Santa Clara Law faculty, he was an assistant professor at Marquette University Law School in Milwaukee, Wisconsin. Before that, he practiced law for eight years in the Silicon Valley as general counsel of Epinions.com and an internet and technology transactions attorney at Cooley Godward LLP. Eric received his B.A., *summa cum laude* and Phi Beta Kappa, in Economics/ Business from UCLA in 1988. He received his J.D. from UCLA in 1994, where he was a member of the UCLA Law Review, and concurrently received his MBA from the Anderson School at UCLA.

Patrick Jaicomo is a senior attorney with the Institute for Justice and one of the leaders of IJ's Project on Immunity and Accountability.

Through the project, Jaicomo works to promote judicial engagement and ensure that government officials are held to account when they violate individuals' constitutional rights. In November 2020, he argued the police brutality case *Brownback v. King* before the U.S. Supreme Court. In March 2024, he returned to the high court for the First Amendment retaliation case *Gonzalez v. Trevino*, which his colleague Anya Bidwell argued. Jaicomo has litigated accountability issues—including qualified immunity, judicial immunity, and the restriction of constitutional claims against federal workers—across the country and at every level of the court system. Before joining IJ, Jaicomo was a litigator at a private firm, where he cultivated a civil rights practice and handled all manner of cases in state and federal court. He earned his law degree from the University of Chicago and a degree in economics and political science from the University of Notre Dame. Patrick's work has been featured in numerous publications, including the *New York Times*, *Wall Street Journal*, *Washington Post*, and *USA Today*. He has also appeared on numerous podcasts and television programs, authored academic articles, and frequently gives presentations on his areas of expertise.

Julia D. Mahoney is a professor of law at the University of Virginia School of Law. She teaches courses in property, government finance, constitutional law, and nonprofit organizations. A graduate of Yale Law School, she joined the University of Virigina faculty as an associate professor in 1999 and is now John S. Battle Professor of Law. She has also taught at the University of Southern California Law School and the University of Chicago Law School, and before entering the legal academy, practiced law at the New York firm Wachtell, Lipton, Prosen & Katz. Her scholarly articles include works on land preservation, eminent domain, health care reform and property rights in human biological materials.

Hon. Bridget Mary McCormack is an adjunct clinical assistant professor of law at Michigan Law. She was chief justice of the Michigan Supreme Court from 2019 to 2022, following six years of service as a justice. While on the Court, she championed innovation and the use of technology to improve access to justice. She is now president and CEO of the American Arbitration Association–International Centre for Dispute Resolution. Before joining the Law School faculty, she was a Cover Fellow at Yale Law School and taught in Yale's clinical programs. She previously worked as a staff attorney with the Office of the Appellate Defender and was a senior trial attorney with the Criminal Defense Division of the Legal Aid Society, both in New York City. McCormack was elected to The American Law Institute in 2013. The attorney general of the United States appointed her to the National Commission on Forensic Science in 2014. In 2019, the governor of Michigan named her co-chair of the Michigan Joint Task Force on Jail and Pretrial Incarceration. In 2020, she joined the American Bar Association's Council on Legal Education and Admission to the Bar and currently serves as vice chair. In 2021, the governor of Michigan asked her to co-chair the Michigan Task Force on Forensic Science and to chair the Michigan Jail Reform Advisory Council. She also chaired the Michigan Judicial Council, the strategic planning body for the judicial branch. In 2021, McCormack was also appointed to serve nationally on The Council of State Governments Healthy States National Task Force and the ABA Center for Innovation's Governing Council. She was also named chair of the ABA Board of Elections. McCormack is an editor of the ABA's preeminent publication, *Litigation Journal*. She speaks and writes frequently about access to justice, innovation in the legal profession, and legal education. She has been published in the *University of Pennsylvania Law Review*, the *Georgetown Journal of Legal Ethics*, the *Tennessee Law Review*, and the *Windsor Access to Justice Journal*. She received the Justice for All Award (with Innocence Clinic co-director Professor David Moran) from the Criminal Defense Attorneys of Michigan in 2010, as well as Cooley Law School's Distinguished Brief Award and the Washtenaw County Bar Association's Patriot Award.

Sean McElroy is a Lecturer in Law at Stanford Law School and an associate at Fenwick & West LLP, where he advises clients on tax matters related to blockchain and cryptocurrency ecosystems, including on issues relating to token generation events, private token sales, NFTs, mining, staking, decentralized autonomous organizations (DAOs), and centralized and decentralized cryptocurrency structures. His clients in this space include protocol development teams, founders, investment platforms, cryptocurrency exchanges, and individual investors. Sean has also represented taxpayers in controversies relating to the taxation of cryptocurrency, including in *Jarrett v. United States*, a leading case on the taxation of staking. He has spoken at numerous conferences and events on issues relating to the taxation of cryptocurrency. McElroy has advised several Fortune 100 companies on international and domestic tax planning matters, including transfer pricing, foreign tax credit utilization, GILTI, Subpart F, and international M&A and restructurings. He has also been counsel on various tax controversy matters. After graduating from Stanford Law School, he clerked for the Honorable Dale S. Fischer on the U.S. District Court for the Central District of California.

George Mocsary is a professor of law at the University of Wyoming College of Law. Prior to his appointment at Wyoming, he served as an assistant professor of law at the Southern Illinois University School of Law and spent two years as a visiting assistant professor at the University of Connecticut School of Law. He entered academia after practicing corporate and bankruptcy law at Cravath, Swaine and Moore in New York. Before that, he clerked for the Honorable Harris L. Hartz of the U.S. Court of Appeals for the Tenth Circuit. Mocsary holds a J.D. from Fordham Law School where he graduated first in his class and *summa cum laude*. He also served as Notes and Articles Editor of *the Fordham Law Review* and was the recipient of the Benjamin Finkel Prize for Excellence in Bankruptcy and the Fordham Law Alumni Association Medal in Constitutional Law. He earned his MBA from the University of Rochester Simon School of Business and ran a successful management consulting practice. Mocsary is a co-author of *Firearms Law and the Second Amendment: Regulation, Rights, and Policy* (3rd ed. 2021), the first casebook on its topic. He has also published in the *George Washington Law Review*, *George Mason Law Review*, *Fordham Law Review*, and other journals. His work has been cited by United States Supreme Court.

Clark Neily is senior vice president for legal studies at the Cato Institute. His areas of interest include constitutional law, overcriminalization, coercive plea bargaining, police accountability, and gun rights. Before joining Cato in 2017, Neily was a senior attorney and constitutional litigator at the Institute for Justice and director of the Institute's Center for Judicial Engagement. Neily is an adjunct professor at George Mason's Antonin Scalia School of Law, where he teaches constitutional litigation and public-interest law. He served as co-counsel in *District of Columbia v. Heller,* in which the Supreme Court held that the Second Amendment protects an individual's right to own a gun. Neily is the author of *Terms of Engagement: How Our Courts Should Enforce the Constitution's Promise of Limited Government.* He also contributed a chapter to Libertarianism.org's *Visions of Liberty.* Neily received a BA in Plan II (with concentrations in philosophy and Russian) from the University of Texas at Austin, and he received his law degree from the University of Texas, where he was chief articles editor of the *Texas Law Review.*

Ilya Somin is a professor of law at George Mason University Antonin Scalia School of Law and the B. Kenneth Simon Chair in Constitutional Studies at the Cato Institute. His research focuses on constitutional law, property law, democratic theory, federalism, and migration rights. He is the author of *Free to Move: Foot Voting, Migration, and Political Freedom* (Oxford University Press, revised and expanded edition, 2022), *Democracy and Political Ignorance: Why Smaller Government is Smarter* (Stanford University Press, revised and expanded second edition, 2016), and *The Grasping Hand:* Kelo v. City of New London *and the Limits of Eminent Domain* (University of Chicago Press, 2015, rev. paperback ed., 2016), coauthor of *A Conspiracy Against Obamacare: The Volokh Conspiracy and the Health Care Case* (Palgrave Macmillan, 2013), and co-editor of *Eminent Domain: A Comparative Perspective* (Cambridge University Press, 2017). *Democracy and Political Ignorance* has been translated into Italian and Japanese. Somin's work has appeared in numerous scholarly journals, including the *Yale Law Journal, Stanford Law Review, Northwestern University Law Review, Georgetown Law Journal, Critical Review,* and others. Somin has also published articles in a variety of popular press outlets, including the *New York Times, Washington Post, Wall Street Journal, Los Angeles Times, CNN, NBC, The Atlantic, USA Today, Boston Globe, US News and World Report, South China Morning Post, National Law Journal* and *Reason.* Somin's writings have been cited in decisions by the United States Supreme Court, multiple state supreme courts and lower federal courts, and the Supreme Court of Israel. He has testified before the U.S. Senate Judiciary Subcommittee on the Constitution, Civil Rights, and Human Rights. In 2009, he testified on property rights issues at the United States Senate Judiciary Committee confirmation hearings for Supreme Court Justice Sonia Sotomayor. Somin writes regularly for the popular *Volokh Conspiracy* law and politics blog, now affiliated with *Reason* magazine (previously affiliated with the *Washington Post* from 2014 to 2017). From 2006 to 2013, he served as Co-Editor of the *Supreme Court Economic Review*. Before joining the faculty at George Mason, Somin was the John M. Olin Fellow in Law at Northwestern University Law School. In 2001–2002, he clerked for the Honorable Judge Jerry E. Smith of the U.S. Court of Appeals for the Fifth Circuit.

Chad Squitieri is an assistant professor of law at The Catholic University of America Columbus School of Law. Squitieri joined the Catholic Law faculty in 2022 after having practiced law at Gibson, Dunn & Crutcher LLP as a member of the Appellate and Constitutional Law and Administrative Law and Regulatory practice groups. He previously served as a Special Assistant to former United States Secretary of Labor Eugene Scalia, and as a law clerk to then-Chief Judge D. Brooks Smith of the United States Court of Appeals for the Third Circuit. Squitieri's scholarship addresses administrative law and constitutional law topics. He also serves as a Fellow within the Project for Constitutional Originalism and the Catholic Intellectual Tradition (CIT).

John Stinneford is a professor of law at the University of Florida Levin College of Law. He researches, teaches, and consults about legal ethics, criminal law, criminal procedure, and constitutional law. His work has been cited by the United States Supreme Court, several state supreme courts, federal courts of appeals, and numerous scholars. His work has been published in numerous scholarly journals, including the *Georgetown Law Journal*, the *Northwestern University Law Review*, the *Virginia Law Review*, the *Notre Dame Law Review*, and the *William & Mary Law Review*. The Stanford-Yale Junior faculty forum selected one of his articles as the best paper in the category of Constitutional History, and the AALS Criminal Justice Section named another article as the best paper in its Junior Scholars Paper Competition. In the fall of 2015, he was a Visiting Scholar at the Georgetown Law Center, Center for the Constitution. Stinneford was the inaugural Director and serves as a Senior Fellow of the Hamilton Center for Classical and Civic Education at the University of Florida, whose mission is to promote civic education and civic discourse and to foster intellectual diversity. Before joining the Florida faculty in 2009, Stinneford clerked for the Honorable James Moran of the U.S. District Court for the Northern District of Illinois, served as an Assistant United States Attorney, and practiced law with Winston & Strawn in Chicago.

Keith Whittington is the David Boies Professor of Law at Yale Law School. He is the author of *Repugnant Laws: Judicial Review of Acts of Congress from the Founding to the Present* (which won the Thomas M. Cooley Book Prize) and *Speak Freely: Why Universities Must Defend Free Speech* (which won the PROSE Award for best book in education and the Heterodox Academy Award for Exceptional Scholarship), as well as *Constitutional Construction: Divided Powers and Constitutional Meaning, and Constitutional Interpretation: Textual Meaning, Original Intent, and Judicial Review,* and *Political Foundations of Judicial Supremacy: The Presidency, the Supreme Court, and Constitutional Leadership in U.S. History* (which won the C. Herman Pritchett Award for best book in law and courts and the J. David Greenstone Award for best book in politics and history), and *Judicial Review and Constitutional Politics,* and *American Political Thought: Readings and Materials.* He is the editor (with Neal Devins) of *Congress and the Constitution* and editor (with R. Daniel Kelemen and Gregory A. Caldeira) of *The Oxford Handbook of Law and Politics* and editor of *Law and Politics: Critical Concepts in Political Science.* He is also the author (with Howard Gillman and Mark A. Graber) of *American Constitutionalism, vol. 1: Structures of Government* and *American Constitutionalism, vol. 2: Rights and Liberties* (which together won the Teaching and Mentoring Award for innovative instructional materials in law and courts), and *American Constitutionalism: Powers, Rights and Liberties* (a one-volume abridgement). He has published widely on American constitutional theory, American political and constitutional history, the law and politics of impeachment, judicial politics, the presidency, and free speech. He is currently the chair of the Academic Committee of the Academic Freedom Alliance and a Hoover Institution Visiting Fellow. He is editor (with Gerald Leonard) of the *New Essays on American Constitutional History* and editor (with Maeva Marcus, Melvin Urofsky, and Mark Tushnet) of the *Cambridge Studies on the American Constitution.* He is currently completing book projects on the impeachment power, constitutional crises in the United States, and the intellectual history of democracy in the United States. His work for a general audience has appeared in the *Washington Post, Wall Street Journal, New York Times, The Atlantic, Reason,* and *Lawfare.* He blogs at the *Volokh Conspiracy,* and he is the host of *The Academic Freedom Podcast.*

Ann Woolhandler is a professor of law at the University of Virginia School of Law. She is an expert on the federal court system and civil procedure. She was previously a professor of law at Tulane University, and she has been a visiting professor at Harvard and Boston University, and on the faculty of the University of Cincinnati.

Will Yeatman is a senior legal fellow on Pacific Legal Foundation's Constitutional Scholarship team and specializes in administrative law. He has testified many times before Congress and state legislatures, and he is a frequent contributor to major media outlets. His scholarly work has appeared in such academic journals as *Georgetown Law Journal, Cato Supreme Court Review,* and *Appalachian Natural Resources Law Journal.* His popular writing has appeared in the *Wall Street Journal, Foreign Policy,* and *Bloomberg.* Prior to joining PLF, he worked at the Competitive Enterprise Institute (CEI), where he specialized in environmental policy. While at CEI, Yeatman pursued a law degree at Georgetown University Law Center. After graduating, he moved to the Cato Institute's Center for Constitutional Studies, where he wrote amicus briefs and scholarly articles on controversies involving administrative law doctrine and regulatory reform.